Authors & Artists for Young Adults

ISSN 1040-5682

Authors & Artists for Young Adults

VOLUME 16

E. A. Des Chenes
Editor

Gale Research

An ITP Information/Reference Group Company

I⟨T⟩P
_____
Changing the Way the World Learns

NEW YORK • LONDON • BONN • BOSTON • DETROIT
MADRID • MELBOURNE • MEXICO CITY • PARIS
SINGAPORE • TOKYO • TORONTO • WASHINGTON
ALBANY NY • BELMONT CA • CINCINNATI OH

E. A. Des Chenes, *Editor*

Linda R. Andres, Shelly Andrews, Julie Karmazin, Thomas F. McMahon,
and Diane Telgen, *Associate Editors*

Mindi Dickstein, David P. Johnson, Ronie-Richele Garcia-Johnson,
Marian C. Gonsior, Janet L. Hile, Laurie Collier Hillstrom, Michael Scott Joseph,
Nancy E. Rampson, Megan Ratner, Susan M. Reicha, Kenneth R. Sheperd,
Tracy J. Sukraw, Sarah Verney, Barbara A. Withers, Laura M. Zaidman,
Sketch Contributors

Victoria B. Cariappa, *Research Manager*
Donna Melnychenko, *Project Coordinator*

Maria E. Bryson, Norma Sawaya, and Amy T. Steel, *Research Associates*
Alicia Noel Biggers, *Research Assistant*

Marlene S. Hurst, Permissions Manager
Margaret A. Chamberlain, *Picture Permissions Specialist*
Margaret McAvoy-Amoto, *Permissions Associate*

Mary Beth Trimper, *Production Director*
Shanna Heilveil, *Production Associate*

Barbara J. Yarrow, *Graphic Services Manager*
Randy Bassette, *Image Database Supervisor*
Robert Duncan, *Scanner Operator*
Pamela A. Hayes, *Photography Coordinator*

♾™ The paper used in this publication meets the minimum requirements of
American National Standard for Information Sciences—Permanence Paper
for Printed Library Materials, ANSI Z39.48-1984.

Library of Congress Catalog Card Number 89-641100
ISBN 0-8103-9368-9
ISSN 1040-5682

10 9 8 7 6 5 4 3 2 1

Printed in the United States of America

I(T)P™ Gale Research Inc., an International Thomson Publishing Company.
ITP logo is a trademark under license.

Contents

Introduction

Authors and Artists for Young Adults is a reference series designed to serve the needs of middle school, junior high, and high school students interested in creative artists. Originally inspired by the need to bridge the gap between Gale's *Something about the Author,* created for children, and *Contemporary Authors,* intended for older students and adults, *Authors and Artists for Young Adults* has been expanded to cover not only an international scope of authors, but also a wide variety of other artists.

Although the emphasis of the series remains on the writer for young adults, we recognize that these readers have diverse interests covering a wide range of reading levels. The series therefore contains not only those creative artists who are of high interest to young adults, including cartoonists, photographers, music composers, bestselling authors of adult novels, media directors, producers, and performers, but also literary and artistic figures studied in academic curricula, such as influential novelists, playwrights, poets, and painters. The goal of *Authors and Artists for Young Adults* is to present this great diversity of creative artists in a format that is entertaining, informative, and understandable to the young adult reader.

Entry Format

Each volume of *Authors and Artists for Young Adults* will furnish in-depth coverage of twenty to twenty-five authors and artists. The typical entry consists of:

—A detailed biographical section that includes date of birth, marriage, children, education, and addresses.

—A comprehensive bibliography or filmography including publishers, producers, and years.

—Adaptations into other media forms.

—Works in progress.

—A distinctive essay featuring comments on an artist's life, career, artistic intentions, world views, and controversies.

—References for further reading.

—Extensive illustrations, photographs, movie stills, cartoons, book covers, and other relevant visual material.

A cumulative index to featured authors and artists appears in each volume.

Compilation Methods

The editors of *Authors and Artists for Young Adults* make every effort to secure information directly from the authors and artists through personal correspondence and interviews. Sketches on living authors and artists are sent to the biographee for review prior to publication. Any sketches not personally reviewed by biographees or their representatives are marked with an asterisk (*).

Highlights of Forthcoming Volumes

Among the authors and artists planned for future volumes are:

W. H. Auden	Carole Nelson Douglas	Belinda Hurmence
Charlotte Bronte	David Eddings	Stephen King (revision)
Emily Bronte	Clyde Edgerton	Lael J. Littke
James L. Brooks	Esther Forbes	Madonna
Terry Brooks	James Douglas Forman	Julian May
Octavia Butler	Athol Fugard	Robert McCammon
Jim Carroll	Ernest Gaines	Jay McInerney
Alden Carter	Michael Hague	Walter Mosley
Gary Crew	Robert Heinlein	Gary Paulsen (revision)
Clive Cussler	Ernest Hemingway	Arnold Schwarzenegger
Ossie Davis	David Hockney	Cindy Sherman
Thomas Disch	Gale Ann Hurd	Gus Van Sant

The editors of *Authors and Artists for Young Adults* welcome any suggestions for additional biographees to be included in this series. Please write and give us your opinions and suggestions for making our series more helpful to you. Direct your comments to: Editors, *Authors and Artists for Young Adults,* Gale Research, Inc., 645 Griswold St., Suite 835, Penobscot Building, Detroit, MI 48226-4094.

Authors & Artists for Young Adults

Richard Adams

Florida, Gainesville, 1975, and Hollins College, 1976. *Military service:* British Army, 1940–45; served on the Philistine Plain near Gaza, with the British Airborne Forces in Europe, and in Singapore. *Member:* Royal Society of Literature (honorary fellow), Royal Society of Arts (fellow), Royal Society for the Prevention of Cruelty to Animals (former president).

■ Personal

Full name, Richard George Adams; born May 9, 1920, in Newbury, Berkshire, England; son of Evelyn George Beadon (a surgeon) and Lilian Rosa (Button) Adams; married Barbara Elizabeth Acland (an author and lecturer on chinaware), September 26, 1949; children: Juliet Vera Lucy, Rosamond Beatrice Elizabeth. *Education:* Attended Bradfield College, Berkshire; Worcester College, Oxford, B.A., M.A., 1948. *Religion:* Church of England.

■ Addresses

Home—26 Church St., Whitchurch, Hampshire RG28 7AR, England. *Agent*—David Highman Associates Ltd., 5–8 Lower John St., London W1R 4HA, England.

■ Career

British Home Higher Civil Service, London, England, worked in Ministry of Housing and Local Government, 1948–68, assistant secretary in the Department of the Environment, 1968–74; full-time writer, 1974—. Writer in residence, University of

■ Awards, Honors

Carnegie Medal, 1972, and Guardian Award for children's literature, 1973, both for *Watership Down;* California Young Readers' Association Award, 1977.

■ Writings

NOVELS

Watership Down, Rex Collings, 1972, Macmillan, 1974.

Shardik, Allen Lane-Rex Collings, 1974, Simon & Schuster, 1975.

The Plague Dogs, illustrated by A. Wainwright, Allen Lane-Rex Collings, 1977, Knopf, 1978.

The Girl in a Swing, Knopf, 1980.

Maia, Viking, 1984, Knopf, 1985.

The Bureaucrats, illustrated by Robin Jacques, Viking Kestrel, 1985.

Traveller, Knopf, 1988.

POETRY

The Tyger Voyage, illustrated by Nicola Bayley, Knopf, 1976.

The Adventures and Brave Deeds of the Ship's Cat on the Spanish Maine: Together with the Most Lamentable Losse of the Alcestis and Triumphant Firing of the Port of Chagres, illustrated by Alan Aldridge and Harry Willock, Knopf, 1977.

The Legend of Te Tuna (narrative poem), Sylvester and Orphanos, 1982.

EDITOR

Grimm's Fairy Tales, illustrated by Pauline Ellison, Routledge, 1981.

Richard Adams's Favorite Animal Stories, illustrated by Beverly Butcher, Octopus, 1981.

The Best of Ernest Thompson Seton, Fontana, 1982.

(Editor and contributor) *Occasional Poets: An Anthology,* Viking, 1986.

OTHER

(With Max Hooper) *Nature through the Seasons,* illustrated by David Goddard and Adrian Williams, Simon & Schuster, 1975.

(With Hooper) *Nature Day and Night,* illustrated by Goddard and Stephen Lee, Viking, 1978.

The Watership Down Film Picture Book, Macmillan, 1978.

The Unbroken Web: Stories and Fables (collection of nineteen folktales), illustrated by Yvonne Gilbert and Jennifer Campbell, Crown, 1980, published in England as *The Iron Wolf and Other Stories,* Allen Lane, 1980.

(With Ronald Lockley) *Voyage through the Antarctic,* Allen Lane, 1982, Viking, 1986.

A Nature Diary, Viking, 1985.

The Day Gone By: An Autobiography, Century Hutchinson, 1990, Knopf, 1991.

Also author of introduction to *Faithful Ruslan* by Georgi Vladimov, translated by Michael Glenn, Simon & Schuster, 1979. *Watership Down* has been translated into thirteen languages.

■ Adaptations

Watership Down was adapted as an animated feature film by Avco-Embassy, 1978; *The Girl in a Swing* was produced as a motion picture in 1989; *The Plague Dogs* was also adapted to film by Nepenthe Productions.

■ Sidelights

In 1972 a middle-aged British civil servant, who had never written a book before in his life, published an epic novel of heroism, murder, friendship, and breathtaking, death-defying escapes that captured the hearts of millions of readers in both England and the United States, as well as in translated versions around the world. The success of the book as a work of literature, however, has ever since been the subject of serious debate among critics, who have variously called it original, unoriginal, allegorical, straightforward, an instant classic, and an overrated mediocrity. It has been compared to such classics as J. R. R. Tolkien's *The Lord of the Rings* trilogy, Kenneth Grahame's *The Wind in the Willows,* and George Orwell's *Animal Farm,* but the basic premise of the book had Adams's publishers so confused that it has been marketed as both a children's book and as an adult novel. Who would ever have guessed a story about rabbits called *Watership Down* could raise such a furor? Certainly not its author, who, in a *Pittsburgh Press* article by Sylvia Sachs, declared that his book "is a story about rabbits, that is all." Adams has written and edited many books since the publication of *Watership Down,* but although he has received praise for such novels as *Shardik* and *The Plague Dogs,* his name is still most often associated with his first literary work.

Adams's Early Life

Born in the Berkshire countryside that would later become the setting for his first novel, Adams was the youngest of three children born to a surgeon and his wife. The setting was idyllic: the family lived in a large house on three acres of land. Adams's father quickly instilled a love of literature in his son by reading him stories about Doctor Dolittle. That education was continued in boarding school and Horris Hill prep school at Bradfield College, where he discovered that he had a talent for telling stories to his classmates, one of whom was Christopher Robin Milne, the son of *Winnie the Pooh* author A. A. Milne. Adams's education was interrupted, however, with the onset of World War II, in which he served in both the European and Asian theaters. When he returned, he completed his education at Oxford University, receiving a master's degree in modern history.

With a happy childhood and quality education behind him, Adams seemed destined for a secure life. He found a good job in the British civil service and soon married and settled down in a cottage near Watership Down. Years went by before the Adamses had children: two daughters they named Juliet and Rosamond. The birth of his children was to be an important turning point in Adams's life. Resolving to be the best father possible, he decided he would do what his father had done for him: teach Juliet and Rosamond to love and appreciate good music and literature. So it was that Adams began to expose them to the likes of Mozart and Shakespeare, and part of this educational process was to take his daughters on trips to Stratford to watch live performances of the Bard's plays.

It was while on these trips—or just before his daughters' bedtime—that Adams began making up stories from his own imagination. "First there were Richard Richard and Thelma Kitten, a kind of feline Laurel and Hardy," related Al Burt in a *Miami Herald* article, "and one day a pair of rabbits, Hazel and Fiver, came along. They wandered the English countryside near Watership Down where the Adamses had their cottage."

Adams viewed these tales as mere amusements for the pleasure of his daughters, but Julie and Rosamond saw something more in them than that. "They said the stories were too good to be wasted, but I resisted . . . ," Adams told Burt. "I was too busy. But Julie, the older, insisted. She's a pertinacious kid and she stuck to it." So Adams began to write down the adventures of Hazel, Fiver, and their friends. During this same period, Adams was going through a difficult time at the Department of the Environment where he worked. After being a civil servant for more than twenty years, he had begun to realize that he was "temperamentally unsuited" for the job. "I'm too emotional, too mercurial. I was due for a service (high level) post and I could not see myself in that. I thought, well, I'll write the rabbit story for relaxation."

But working on the story on an on-again, off-again basis, during which Adams would sometimes set his writing aside untouched for days, wasn't the way to go about writing a novel, the author discovered. "Soon I found that if you don't hang in there with the characters they won't tell you what's going to happen next," Adams told Burt. "You've got to get inside of their world so that it's more real than the other. After that I began to write four or five nights a week. The second half of the book is better because of that."

After two years of writing, Adams was ready to begin submitting his manuscript to publishers. The publishers and literary agents were initially less enthusiastic than Adams's daughters, however, and the author was rejected several times. For the sake of simply having the book printed so that he would have something to give to his daughters, Adams was considering publishing the story at his own expense, but then he found a publisher, Rex Collings, who was willing to give the book a chance. With a modest first printing of two thousand copies, *Watership Down* was placed on the children's shelves in British book stores, where it was quickly discovered by delighted readers. Word of mouth soon spread into critical acclaim in England—and later in the United States—culminating in Adams's winning of the 1972 Carnegie Medal. He also had a financial triumph on his hands: selling seven hundred thousand hardcover

Adams's most popular work tells the tale of an adventurous group of rabbits in search of a new home.

copies in the United States, *Watership Down* was on the *New York Times* best-seller list for thirty-three weeks, and Adams received a record-breaking advance—$800,000—for paperback rights to his story, as well as money for the rights to the animated movie adaptation that appeared in theaters in 1978.

Watership Down

Watership Down begins when Fiver, a young rabbit who was the runt of his litter, has a horrible vision that his home, Sandleford Warren, is going to be destroyed and all the rabbits killed. Fiver convinces his brother, Hazel, that something needs to be done. The brothers then ask Bigwig, a member of the "Owsla," a lapin version of the police, to take them to see "the Threarah," the warren's respected but aging leader, to try to convince him to evacuate the warren. The Threarah, however, isn't about to believe Fiver's incredible premonition, so Hazel and Fiver are left to try to persuade the others that they must leave. A few, including Bigwig, do go just before Fiver's prediction comes true: humans come and gas the warren with poison to clear the way for a housing development.

Though they have escaped with their lives, Hazel and company face new and just as threatening dilemmas. They have to fight against their natural fear of being above ground with no holes in which to hide from predators; they have to find a new home; and, because the only ones who escaped were males, they have to find does (female rabbits) so that any new warren they establish will have descendants to live in it. The story thus focuses on the rabbits' efforts to find a new home. On their travels they run into other warrens. At first, it seems they have found the ideal place when they chance upon a warren where the rabbits live in peace without fear of predators and have all the lettuce and carrots they can eat. But soon Hazel and the others discover that it is no paradise at all, but rather a place where a man protects the rabbits for the purpose of catching them in snares and eating them.

Realizing that life at this warren is no life at all, the Sandleford rabbits leave to continue their quest. The next warren they come across is called Efrafa and led by General Woundwort, a tyrant who has organized his warren into a totalitarian state. Under Woundwort's rule, the Efrafans have lost all personal liberties and live in constant fear of the "Owslafa," the warren's secret police. Driven by their need to find does, Hazel sends Bigwig to infiltrate Efrafa's ranks and free as many of the rabbits as possible. Against all odds, a daring escape is made culminating in a fight between Bigwig and General Woundwort and then Woundwort's lethal confrontation with a fierce dog.

Finally reaching the peaceful Watership Down, and with their numbers increased by the Efrafan rabbits and other does that Hazel and the Sandleford rabbits have freed from the hutches at Nuthanger Farm, the rabbits make their new home. Though it is not a paradise, it is free of oppression and governed by the love and respect the rabbits have for each other. Hazel has risen to leadership position, Bigwig has become a war hero whose tales of fighting the General thrill the warren's kittens (baby rabbits), and Fiver finds a mate and starts a family.

Of course, Adams put more into his story than a few rabbits searching for a new warren. In *Watership Down* he has created an entire lapin culture, including a unique rabbit language, a religion (centered upon the sun god Frith and the Black Rabbit of Inle, who represents death), and an oral tradition (which largely concerns the rabbits' folk hero, El-ahrairah). Much of the detail in the story is also scientifically accurate. Adams spent considerable time researching the biology and habits of rabbits, relying mostly on R. M. Lockley's *The Private Life of the Rabbit* for his facts. Adams's appreciation for nature, which, like his love of literature, was learned from his father and long walks in the Berkshire countryside, also enriches his story; his broad knowledge of literature is made evident in the epigraphs that begin each chapter and draw from such sources as Malory, Aeschylus, Xenophon, Yeats, Tennyson, Shakespeare, Homer, and the Bible.

Despite Adams's insistence that *Watership Down* should be read as a straightforward adventure story, because he has put so many other elements into his story it has consequently become the subject of much critical analysis and speculation. Because of its length (over four hundred pages) and its literary and philosophical depth, critics have debated whether or not it is indeed a children's book. As Graham Hammond observed in *Children's*

Watership Down came to the screen as a full-length animated film in 1978.

Literature in Education, "Richard Adams's book is interesting, apart from its merit and its enthusiastic reception, because it raises in a particularly striking way the familiar question, how are we to judge children's books? At one level, immediately accessible to children, we have the story about the rabbits and their adventures. At another level, intelligible to some children at some stage, is the significance of the anthropomorphic rabbits and the comment the author is making through them about human nature and the human predicament."

Looking Deeper into *Watership Down*

It is this second level that has caused some critics to deem the work unsuitable for children. Richard Gilman, writing in the *New York Times Book Review,* remarked, "I doubt that Richard Adams's *Watership Down* is really aimed at young children, despite his having said that it arose from impromptu stories he used to tell his small children. I can't imagine many readers under 13 or 14 . . . having the patience and grasp of extended allegorical strategies to persevere to

the end of a 426-page epic." *Spectator* contributor Leon Garfield, however, noted that the allegorical elements are only a part of *Watership Down* and aren't necessary for readers to understand and appreciate it. As Garfield wrote, the book "has many parallels—political, social, philosophic—with our own society . . . , these parallels are only parallels; they are not the heart of the book." In a chapter published in *The Thorny Paradise: Writers on Writing for Children,* Adams said that he was encouraged by the writings of Rudyard Kipling not to "be afraid to let your writing be difficult, or to make big demands on your readers. Say what you have to say and don't be deterred by wondering whether they're going to be able to follow you."

Given that Adams has put these extra, challenging elements into his tale, Hammond was confused by what the author was actually trying to say. The critic noted that Adams handles the story's complexities "with impressive skill and the book is on the whole a remarkable feat of organization and integration of many strands. But ultimately one is left with two questions: whether the rabbits' system of values and beliefs corresponds with the author's own and as such is being commended to the child reader; and whether these values and beliefs constitute profound insights or conventional wisdom." Hammond breaks down the beliefs conveyed in the book into three parts: the rabbits sense of fatalism, "a belief in Elahrairah's power to protect and guide . . . , and a morality based on enlightened self-interest. . . . One may ask where the author stands in all this and in what relation to his child reader."

One of the central themes of *Watership Down,* observed Ann Swinfen in her book, *In Defense of Fantasy: A Study of the Genre in English and American Literature since 1945,* is political, the thrust of the story concerning a group of characters searching for "a more perfect community" in which to live. "*Watership Down* is not a straightforward political allegory like *Animal Farm,*" Swinfen admitted, "but like Orwell's animal society it shows the influence of particular aspects of twentieth-century history on the author." Swinfen suggested, as other critics have, that Efrafa represents the totalitarian state and was influenced by the "political atmosphere of the 1930s and 1940s." This is not surprising, since Adams lived and fought through World War II, and he noted in Sachs's article that Hazel was inspired by the leader of his parachute group, John Gifford.

Swinfen went on to discuss how the Sandleford rabbits' journey is the quest for a utopia and how each society Hazel and company come across represent some kind of dystopia or other imperfect society. The unnamed first warren they come to after they flee Sandleford—where the rabbits are being fattened for a man's dinner plate—is a superficial utopia, where the rabbits are provided with all their needs but at the cost of their culture, their "rabbitness." Unwilling to admit to themselves that they are doomed to die in the man's snares, they become "obsessed with the illusory surface of their lives, and will not confront reality."

Efrafa is on the opposite extreme, where the danger to the rabbits' lives and happiness is, unlike the hidden snares, out in the open. Although General Woundwort's original intention for Efrafa was simply to establish a warren safe from enemies, "his insatiable longing for power has developed into the determination to conquer and enslave all

surrounding warrens," wrote Swinfen, "and to reduce his subjects to mere cyphers in his power game." Finally, the Sandleford warren is "a third type of society which Adams implicitly criticizes." An old, crowded, and established warren, Sandleford represents "a community where there is no room for mental growth or the appreciation of fresh ideas [such as Fiver's unconventional warning against the arrival of the humans, and so] . . . social stagnation sets in, political development atrophies, and the community becomes a natural victim to outside forces. . . . Complacency culminates in disaster."

Swinfen suggested that Sandleford represents modern Britain, and, indeed, Adams has revealed some

Snitter and Rowf—escapees from animal research facility—find themselves facing new and terrifying foes as they seek a new life in the wilderness.

personal dissatisfaction with developments in his native country. "Adams has the feeling that England has lost its grip on its own society," Burt wrote in his *Miami Herald* article. Comparing England to the United States, Adams told Burt, "I am worried and depressed about the way things are going in England. . . . You in the United States have a standard of pride in work and country that you don't find in England. . . . We sit around and do nothing. You act." Although Adams had not been to the United States before he wrote *Watership Down,* the society Hazel and the others establish at the new warren resembles America in some ways. Composed of rabbits from more than one warren, it is like an American melting pot with the democratic goal that, as Swinfen observed, "all the rabbits should be free and happy, and that the weaker members of the community should not be tyrannized by the stronger."

The claim that *Watership Down* will become a classic work of children's literature is still a debatable matter, according to some critics who see flaws in the novel. Adams's writing style has been one target of these attacks. For example, while Hammond observed that the author's love of nature "enables him to give this novel an unusually strong and vivid sense of place," he also "indulges himself in passages of considerable artistry but sometimes questionable literary taste." Occasional forays into lavishly descriptive passages seem to Hammond to be a "self-conscious attempt at fine writing [that] borders on the absurd and defeats the author's laudable desire to share with the young reader his delight in nature." Hammond further complained of Adams's "determination to miss not a single opportunity for elaboration, [which] is the cause of a number of weaknesses in the book, leading not only to its excessive length but more seriously to the unsatisfactory denouement. . . . [The] author shows a tendency to indulge himself at the expense of the book."

Other critics have complained that Adams's characterization is weak. As Peter Hunt wrote in a chapter of *The Signal Approach to Children's Books: A Collection,* "some critics have pointed out [that] plot and character are not greatly different from a hundred B-picture war stories." *National Review* contributor D. Keith Mano also bore exception to some reviewers claims that *Watership Down* is a "true original." Mano maintained that it is no more original than a John Wayne movie: "*Watership Down* is pleasant enough," he wrote, "but it has about the same intellectual firepower as *Dumbo.* . . . [If] Hazel and Bigwig and Dandelion were men, they'd make very commonplace characters. What seems a moral, an insight, is just a novelty."

That critics such as Hammond and Mano have missed the essence of the story is another side to the argument. While admitting that *Watership Down* is "not a comfortable nor even a lovely book," Aidan Chambers said in his *Horn Book* review that it "is deeply moving and vividly memorable in the way that all 'good' books, all works of true art, are: They implant themselves . . . into the living tissues of your being, to remain there, illuminating your view of life ever after." Hunt observed that *Watership Down* has suffered from the same phenomenon that followed the publication of *The Lord of the Rings:* "extravagant praise followed by round condemnation." Hunt praised Adams's integration of a compelling narrative with a factual—with the exception of some necessary anthropomorphism—presentation of lapin behavior. "[He] was more successful than he is sometimes given credit for," Hunt concluded.

When considered as the straightforward story it was intended to be, critics have found much to admire in *Watership Down.* Asserting that the allegorical elements, while definitely present, are "not pressed or made too heavy," *New York* reviewer Eliot Fremont-Smith admired the narrative control Adams maintained in writing about a subject that could easily have become too maudlin or cute. He concluded that the story is "a wise and sunny book, a suspenseful epic that readers twelve and up are going to enjoy for a long time to come."

Much of the value in *Watership Down* can be found in Adams's descriptions of and respect for nature. "In as much as Mr. Adams has a message for his readers," remarked Janet Adam Smith in the *New York Review of Books,* "I'd say it is to make them more sensitive to the complex balance of nature, more aware of the needs and ways of other species." Margery Fisher, writing about the book in her *Margery Fisher Recommends Classics for Children & Young People,* commended it above all other reasons for the author's "fine picture of Hampshire downland." She also remarked that, all literary, political, and social parallels aside, one had to admit that *Watership* is "a rattling good adventure story."

The Beklan Empire: *Shardik* and *Maia*

Despite the unexpected success of *Watership Down*, Adams decided not to leave his civil service job right away. He did have plans to become a full-time writer, but he wanted to see whether he had the ability to be more than a "one-book author." So Adams sat down to the task of writing a second novel, which became *Shardik* and was published in England in 1975. *Shardik*, which Adams also intended for children, is, at over five hundred pages, even longer than *Watership Down*. As with *Watership Down*, Adams created an entire fictional society: the Beklan Empire, which the author devised complete with its own unique religion, art, and customs. Unlike the first book, however, the geography has no basis in reality. It is a completely imaginary place that supposedly existed in ancient Asia Minor.

The title character is an immense bear who is the object of a religion in this fictional world. Unlike Adams's rabbits, however, Shardik is not anthropomorphized in any way. Shardik acts as a real bear would, and any human or godlike qualities attributed to the bear are purely the result of the other characters' imaginations and beliefs. The central character in *Shardik* is a young hunter named Kelderek, whom Shardik saves one day from a leopard's attack. Kelderek's people take this as a sign that he has been selected by the god for a great task. By reigniting his people's faith in the godhead Shardik, Kelderek leads his people in a great military struggle that restores the Beklan Empire's might and establishes Kelderek as the kingdom's leader.

But Kelderek misuses his power, which is granted to him through the symbol of Shardik. "To finance the final conquests," a *Choice* reviewer summarized, "he permits the reintroduction of a legalized slave trade and sets in motion the forces that bring about the kingdom's downfall." Because Kelderek has blindly followed Shardik without trying to understand its nature, he has brought his people to ruin by unwittingly reintroducing evil into the empire in the form of the slave trade and poignantly represented by the character Genshed, the amoral slave trader who enjoys

murdering and torturing children. The rest of the novel involves the personal trials Kelderek must endure to heal the physical, moral, and psychological wounds he has suffered. The great bear Shardik dies at the end of the tale, but Kelderek finally experiences a true revelation, and, in so doing, finds happiness at last.

Like *Watership Down* there is the theme of a struggle—as seen through Kelderek's efforts—to establish a utopia, but a more important theme in *Shardik* deals with how people's perceptions of God affect their values and, consequently, their lives. As Peter Wolfe put it in his *New Republic* review, "Shardik embodies the hopes and fears of the people touched by his divinity." Allison Lurie also elaborated upon this theme in her *New York Review of Books* article: "In *Shardik*," she wrote, "belief causes men to act cruelly and destructively as well as nobly; the bear is a kind of test which brings out hidden strengths and weaknesses, even in those who do not believe in him."

In explaining why Adams chose an imaginary world in which to set his story, *New York Times Book Review* critic Paul Zweig commented that for the author "epic events require a world created to their measure . . . , a morally coherent fiction: a world constructed of mythic elements." Yet Zweig doesn't believe that Adams succeeded in this endeavor because his human characters, unlike Hazel, Fiver, and the other rabbits, are not as realistic. "One concludes that Adams's animals are more human than his humans—to the misfortune of his moral and his book," wrote Zweig. Kenneth Graham, writing in the *Listener*, similarly noted that *Shardik* "almost works as intended," but that the "book is too long, and too uneven. There is no real grasp of the inward reaches of character, only of the grand simplicities of archetype." And *Time* contributor John Skow, remarked that Adams "spins out his romance entertainingly, but without dealing seriously with the questions he raises: of belief and its perversion, of authority and its corruption."

Other reviewers, however, received *Shardik* in a more positive light. Some, like *Newsweek* reviewer Arthur Cooper, even considered it a stronger effort than *Watership Down*, calling the book a "more ambitious, deeper, darker and more richly textured" novel. Bruce Allen, furthermore, declared in his *Saturday Review* article that *Shardik* "has the satisfying wholeness of the great [epics] it dares

NATIONWIDE BESTSELLER!

"BEAUTIFUL, HAUNTING EROTIC LOVE AND AN ABSOLUTELY TERRIFYING GHOST STORY."
—THE NEW YORK TIMES BOOK REVIEW

THE GIRL IN A SWING

RICHARD ADAMS

AUTHOR OF MAIA

NOW A MAJOR MOTION PICTURE FROM MIRAMAX FILMS

A young man's love for a mysterious woman unleashes terrible secrets in this 1980 work.

to rival: it should be told, and retold, for many generations."

Ten years later, Adams wrote another novel set in the Beklan Empire. *Maia* is set in another part of that world and is about a young woman who is sold into slavery. She becomes the concubine of the emperor's high counselor, who is later murdered in a political upheaval. Caught up in events much grander than her humble peasant beginnings, Maia discovers great inner strength within herself and, with the benefit of her remarkable swimming ability, manages to save the kingdom and become a hero to her people. Critics have not given *Maia* as much attention as *Shardik*, noting its value as more of a pure adventure story.

Chicago Tribune Bookworld reviewer Robert Hughes, for example, wrote: "One might long for more multidimensional characters in a work of this weight. . . . What we have instead is mainly an adventure story, and a good one."

More Animal Stories

After the successful publication of *Shardik* (although reviews were mixed, the novel sold well), Adams quit his regular job for good to become a full-time author. He left England for the United States in 1975 to become a writer in residence at the University of Florida and Hollins College in Virginia. It was while at Hollins that Adams wrote his third novel, *The Plague Dogs*. Returning to the device of anthropomorphized animals, Adams developed two canine characters, Rowf and Snitter, who have been subjected to pointless and cruel scientific experiments at the Animal Research, Surgical and Experimental center (with the comically appropriate acronym, A.R.S.E.) in England's Lake District.

Rowf, a large, black dog, has been subjected to stress tests in which he is nearly drowned repeatedly, while Snitter, a fox terrier, was part of a brain surgery experiment, the result of which causes him to suffer hallucinations. Luckily, the two canines manage to escape from the research center and into the countryside, where they befriend a fox who teaches them how to survive in the wild. When word goes out that the dogs might have been infected with bubonic plague at the center, the chase is on. Adams brings his heroes close to capture again and again, but Snitter and Rowf manage to escape in the end, though their friend the fox is less lucky. *The Plague Dogs* is an obvious condemnation of senseless and cruel animal experimentation. "If you are put off by tracts," Adams told *Globe and Mail* writer Jan Rodger, "you are probably not going to like *The Plague Dogs*. But I do feel very indignant about animal experimentation and perhaps my indignation got the better of me."

A *Publishers Weekly* reviewer called *The Plague Dogs* "Adams's most impressive novel to date and . . . his most salable." A big reason for this is the appeal of his sympathetic animal characters, from the traumatized Rowf and trusting Snitter to their roguish fox friend. "The novel is so haunting . . . that no one with any love of animals can fail to be deeply moved by it" the critic concluded. Although *Time* contributor Paul Gray found that Adams is sometimes "a windy sentimentalist" who "overwrites almost every scene," he admitted that, for the most part, it "is hard to say anything critical about such a heartwarming story." *School Library Journal* reviewer Linda Serafini concluded that "*The Plague Dogs* ranks with the best that Adams has written," and observed that, despite its length, it has definite appeal for young adults.

Adams's next novel featuring an animal protagonist is *Traveller,* which is a unique narrative of the American Civil War as told by General Robert E. Lee's faithful horse, Traveller. The story begins after the end of the war, and Traveller is reminiscing to Lee's cat, Tom Nipper. There is some irony involved in telling Lee's story through Traveller's eyes in that, for one thing, the horse doesn't realize that the South lost the war, nor does he even have the vaguest idea what all the fighting was about. In fact, when he recalls the rejoicing of the humans when it is announced they are all going to war, Traveller is excited at the prospect of going to "War," which he assumes to be a fabulous place judging by everyone's attitude. But, unexpectedly, Union soldiers, whom Traveller calls "the Blue Men," attack them again and again, and when the fighting at last ends three years later, Traveller is disappointed that he never did get to go to War.

"The charm of the book comes from the developing personality of Traveller," according to *Los Angeles Times Book Review* critic Dee Brown, who also enjoyed Traveller's battlefield narrations in which he becomes like "an equine Huckleberry Finn." A *Publishers Weekly* contributor felt that, while Adams's human characters are not entirely convincing, he demonstrates a "gift for conveying both the physical life and the interior essence of an animal." One *Library Journal* reviewer was also disappointed that *Traveller* lacks the "mythic clarity and enchantment of *Watership Down* and *Shardik.*" However, Rita Mae Brown, writing in the *New York Times Book Review,* observed that Adams is making a point about human nature by telling his story through Traveller's unique perspective: "Seeing war through the horse's eyes is ironic, because the animal has no human motivation to kill. Somehow that makes the carnage more horrible. Just who is the dumb animal?"

Not all of Adams's novels have featured animals. Notable among these is his 1980 book, *The Girl in a Swing,* a haunting tale about an Englishman named Alan Desland and the mysterious German woman he marries, Kaethe. A combination of passionate romance novel and horrifying ghost story, *The Girl in a Swing* was widely praised by critics. Robert Kiely, for one, wrote in his *New York Times Book Review:* "Richard Adams turns his commonplace man into the hero-victim of a tale of fatal passion. . . . He remains completely believable throughout. The love scenes between him and Kaethe are presented with lyrical beauty, a touch of humor and increasing obsessiveness. Kaethe's ability to enchant is never in doubt. Finally, the ghost story is absolutely terrifying, as gripping and psychologically penetrating as anything in [Henry] James or [Edgar Allan] Poe. Richard Adams has written, with marvelous tact and narrative power, a strange, beautiful, haunting book."

Despite the success of *The Girl in a Swing,* it is Adams's novels featuring animal characters—especially his first, *Watership Down*—that have earned him his reputation as one of the most unconventional English authors writing today. Adams's work, which appeals to readers of all ages, differs from mainstream modern novels that feature, as Allison Lurie put it, protagonists who are "sad, bumbling failures; hysterical combatants in the sex war; or self-deceptive men and women of ill-will. What a relief to read of characters who have honor and courage and dignity." Bruce Allen also noted this, writing in his review of *Shardik* that one of "this book's greatest strengths is its rejection of the modern novel's emphasis on subjective uncertainty. It urges that truth is knowable." But Adams admitted that expressing these truths in a realistic, contemporary setting is a challenge for him. He told Dick Adler in the *Los Angeles Times* that is why he resorts to "the anthropomorphic distance of using animals."

Adams gladly admits that his books are not the norm one finds in children's literature. In a *Milwaukee Journal* article by Leslie Cross, Adams proudly stated that he has nevertheless received numerous fan letters from young readers: "He prizes his many letters from children who have thrilled to the adventures of Hazel, Fiver, and his other gallant rabbits. . . . A good story, he thinks, is exactly that, without any age lines." "I would say," Adams concluded in *The Thorny Paradise,* "beware principles and rules about children—the value of an established moral order and all that. One can easily get so blinkered by the rules that one can no longer judge a book by the light of the heart. That light, of course, is what is used by the children themselves."

■ Works Cited

Adams, Richard, "Some Ingredients of Watership Down," in *The Thorny Paradise: Writers on Writing for Children*, edited by Edward Blishen, Kestrel Books, 1975, pp. 163–73.

Adler, Dick, interview with Richard Adams, *Los Angeles Times*, July 20, 1975.

Allen, Bruce, "Epic in Wonderland," *Saturday Review*, May 31, 1975, pp. 26–27.

Brown, Dee, "The Civil War from a Horse's Mouth," *Los Angeles Times Book Review*, June 26, 1988, pp. 1, 13.

Brown, Rita Mae, "Tales of a War Horse," *New York Times Book Review*, June 5, 1988, p. 13.

Burt, Al, "Adams in Wonderland . . . Watership Down to U.S.A.?," *Miami Herald*, April 20, 1975.

Chambers, Aidan, "Letter from England: Great Leaping Lapins!," *Horn Book*, June, 1973, pp. 253–55.

Cooper, Arthur, "Bear Market," *Newsweek*, April 28, 1975, pp. 77–78.

Cross, Leslie, "In Publishing, This Is the Year of the Rabbit," *Milwaukee Journal*, September 1, 1974.

Fisher, Margery, *Margery Fisher Recommends Classics for Children & Young People*, Thimble Press, 1986.

Fremont-Smith, Eliot, review of *Watership Down*, *New York*, March 4, 1974, p. 60.

Garfield, Leon, "Burrow in Berkshire," *Spectator*, February 3, 1973, p. 141.

Gilman, Richard, "The Rabbits' Iliad and Odyssey," *New York Times Book Review*, March 24, 1974, pp. 3–4.

Graham, Kenneth, "Bear Garden," *Listener*, January 1, 1975, p. 30.

Gray, Paul, "Puppy Love," *Time*, March 13, 1978, pp. 95–96.

Hammond, Graham, "Trouble with Rabbits," *Children's Literature in Education*, fall, 1973, pp. 48–63.

Hughes, Robert, "Adams' 'Maia' Ventures into Realm of Living Fantasy," *Chicago Tribune Bookworld*, February 17, 1985, p. 23.

Hunt, Peter, "The Good, the Bad and the Indifferent: Quality and Value in Three Contemporary Children's Books," in *The Signal Approach to Children's Books: A Collection*, edited by Nancy Chambers, Scarecrow Press, 1980, pp. 225–46.

Kiely, Robert, review of *The Girl in a Swing*, *New York Times Book Review*, April 27, 1980.

Lurie, Allison, "The Power of Smokey," *New York Review of Books*, June 12, 1975, pp. 34–35.

Mano, D. Keith, "Banal Bunnies," *National Review*, April 26, 1974, pp. 484–85.

Review of *The Plague Dogs*, *Publishers Weekly*, January 16, 1978, pp. 92, 94.

Rodger, Jan, interview with Richard Adams, *Globe and Mail* (Toronto), November 16, 1977.

Sachs, Sylvia, "'Rabbit' Writer Hops into Limelight," *Pittsburgh Press*, March 20, 1974.

Serafini, Linda, review of *The Plague Dogs*, *School Library Journal*, September, 1978, p. 168.

Review of *Shardik*, *Choice*, July/August, 1975, p. 678.

Skow, John, "Ursus Saves?," *Time*, April 28, 1975, p. 93.

Smith, Janet Adam, "Exodus," *New York Review of Books*, April 18, 1974, pp. 8–9.

Swinfen, Ann, *In Defense of Fantasy: A Study of the Genre in English and American Literature since 1945*, Routledge & Kegan Paul, 1984, pp. 190–229.

Review of *Traveller*, *Library Journal*, June 15, 1988, p. 67.

Review of *Traveller*, *Publishers Weekly*, April 22, 1988, p. 63.

Wolfe, Peter, review of *Shardik*, *New Republic*, May 3, 1975.

Zweig, Paul, review of *Shardik*, *New York Times Book Review*, May 4, 1975.

■ For More Information See

BOOKS

Adams, Richard, *The Day Gone By: An Autobiography*, Knopf, 1991.

Egoff, Sheila, *Thursday's Child: Trends and Patterns in Contemporary Children's Literature*, American Library Association, 1981, pp. 80–129.

Harrison, Barbara, and Gregory Maguire, editors, *Innocence & Experience: Essays & Conversations on Children's Literature*, Lothrop, Lee & Shepard Books, 1987, pp. 99–101.

Inglis, Fred, *The Promise of Happiness: Value and Meaning in Children's Literature*, Cambridge University Press, 1981, pp. 182–210.

Waggoner, Diana, *The Hills Faraway: A Guide to Fantasy*, Atheneum, 1978, pp. 36–64.

PERIODICALS

Booklist, May 1, 1975, p. 892; February 15, 1978, p. 975; April 15, 1988, p. 1369.

Children's Book Review, April, 1973, pp. 43–44.

Commonweal, September, 27, 1974.

Economist, December 23, 1972, p. 47.

English Journal, March, 1987, pp. 56–59.

Harper's, May, 1975, pp. 53–54.

Horn Book, August, 1974, pp. 405–8; February, 1975, pp. 3–4; April, 1975, p. 99.

Library Journal, April 1, 1978, p. 773; March 1, 1991, p. 97.

National Review, April 26, 1974, pp. 484–85.

New Republic, March 23, 1974, pp. 28–29.

Newsweek, March 18, 1974, p. 114.

New York, March 4, 1974, p. 60.

New York Times Book Review, June 30, 1974, p. 39; June 2, 1991, p. 20.

Publishers Weekly, January 3, 1986, p. 51; February 22, 1991, p. 203.

Time, March 18, 1974, pp. 92–93.

Times Literary Supplement, December 8, 1972, p. 1489; September 11–17, 1990, p. 488.

Village Voice, March 21, 1974, p. 25.

Virginia Quarterly Review, summer, 1974, p. lxxxii.

Washington Post Book World, May 25, 1975, p. 3; April 27, 1986, p. 12.

Wilson Library Bulletin, October, 1974, pp. 152–56.

—Sketch by Janet L. Hile

Jeffrey Archer

Greater London Council for Havering, 1966-70; executive, British Theatre Museum. *Member:* Royal Society of the Arts (fellow), Oxford University Athletics Club (president, 1965), Somerset Amateur Athletics Association (president), Carlton Cricket Club, Marylebone Cricket Club.

■ Personal

Born April 15, 1940, in Mark, near Weston-super-Mare, Somerset, England; son of William (a professional soldier) and Lola (a journalist; maiden name, Cook) Archer; married Mary Weeden (a chemist), 1966; children: two sons. *Education:* Attended Brasenose College, Oxford, 1963-66; received diploma in sports education from Oxford Institute. *Politics:* Conservative. *Hobbies and other interests:* Theatre, squash, watching Somerset play cricket.

■ Addresses

Home—93 Albert Embankment, London SE1, England; and The Old Vicarage, Grantchester, England.

■ Career

Writer. Arrow Enterprises Ltd., London, England, chairman of the board, beginning 1968; Conservative member of the British Parliament, 1969-74; deputy chairman, British Conservative Party, 1985-86. Chairman, Nigeria Consultants, Inc.; member,

■ Writings

NOVELS

Not a Penny More, Not a Penny Less, Doubleday, 1976.
Shall We Tell the President?, Viking, 1977.
Kane & Abel (Literary Guild alternate selection), Simon & Schuster, 1980.
The Prodigal Daughter, Linden Press, 1982.
First among Equals, Linden Press, 1984.
A Matter of Honor, Linden Press, 1986.
As the Crow Flies, HarperCollins, 1991.
Honor among Thieves, HarperCollins, 1993.

STORIES

A Quiver Full of Arrows, Linden Press, 1982.
A Twist in the Tale, HarperCollins, 1989.
Twelve Red Herrings, HarperCollins, 1994.

JUVENILE

By Royal Appointment, Octopus, 1980.
Willy Visits the Square World, Octopus, 1980.

Willy and the Killer Kipper, Hodder & Stoughton Children's Books, 1981.
The First Miracle, HarperCollins Children's Books, 1994.

PLAYS

Beyond Reasonable Doubt (first produced on West End, London, 1987), Samuel French, 1989.
Exclusive, first produced on West End, London, 1989.

OTHER

(With others) *Gemma Levine's Faces of the 80s,* Collins, 1987.
(Editor with Simon Bainbridge) *Fools, Knaves, and Heroes: Great Political Short Stories,* W. W. Norton, 1991.

■ Adaptations

Not a Penny More, Not a Penny Less was adapted for British television and serialized on British radio; *Kane & Abel* was made into a mini-series for Columbia Broadcasting System (CBS-TV), 1985; Stephen Spielberg has purchased the film rights to *A Matter of Honor.*

■ Sidelights

It has often been said that Jeffrey Archer's career is reflected in his fiction—or, in some cases, that his fiction is reflected in his career. Both have attracted a lot of public attention and have become the center of much controversy. A man of boundless energy, Archer has walked the corridors of power with England's politicians and has earned a reputation as one of the most popular authors in both England and America. "The great contradiction of Jeffrey Archer's life," declares Bill Bryson in the *New York Times Magazine,* "is that the one thing he has tried hardest to do—become a successful politician—is the one thing he has most signally failed to accomplish."

Turns Energy into Success

Jeffrey Archer was born in England's West Country—Somerset—in Mark, a small village slightly south of the resort town of Weston-super-Mare. His father, William, had been a soldier and had worked as a printer in London, but was also

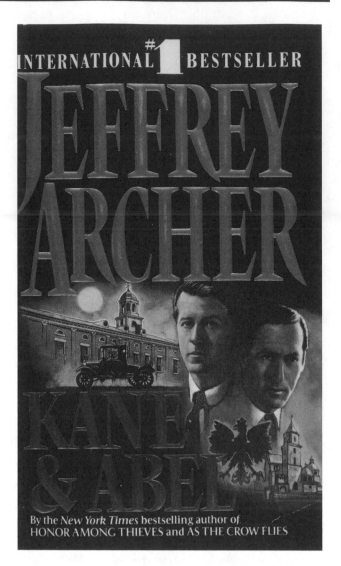

In this story covering three generations, two young men—one born into poverty, the other to a life of riches—battle for love and power.

chronically ill and died when his son was only fifteen years old. As a young man, Archer demonstrated his energy by working summer odd jobs, such as selling ice cream and renting beach chairs to vacationers. He later attended boarding school in Somerset and developed a talent for track. "He was a fine runner," declares Michele Field in *Publishers Weekly,* "and, overall, was far better at sports than at his academic studies." As Archer explains to Jean Ross in a *Contemporary Authors* interview, his sports activities taught him valuable lessons in self-discipline. "That demanded hours of hard training to be international standard. You can only do that on your own; you can't get anyone else to do it for you."

Although Archer's lack of academic achievement kept him out of the universities, "he impressed everyone with his enthusiasm for anything he tried," Field asserts. He earned a position teaching physical education at Dover College, a high school, then went on to acquire a degree in phys ed at the Oxford Institute. While working on his degree, Archer also participated in track and field at Oxford University (an institution not connected with the Oxford Institute). "His record of 9.6 seconds in the 100-yard dash," declares Bryson, "stood as a school record for many years." He also met and married Mary Weeden, a leading science student, who has since become a celebrity in her own right: she served as the first female director for the insurance company Lloyd's of London, as chair of the National Energy Foundation, and as a teacher at Cambridge University.

Archer founded his own company, Arrow Enterprises, after receiving his degree. Drawing on his experiences in fundraising and public relations for the university as well as his own tremendous energy, he quickly earned a fortune. "I think energy is a God-given gift," he tells Ross, "in the way the ability to play a violin, the ability to sing, the ability to paint is a gift. People underestimate energy. If you have one gift plus energy, you'll go to the very top. I've always said the formula is: one gift plus energy, you'll be a king; energy and no gift, you're a prince; a gift and no energy, you're a pauper. I think energy is much underestimated. You will see it in the truly successful. It's the one thing Maria Callas, Pablo Picasso, and Margaret Thatcher have in common."

In 1969, Archer put his money to work by running for, and winning by a landslide, a seat in Parliament. Only 29 years old, he took his place in the House of Commons as its youngest member. For five years he served as a Conservative politician, enjoying political power and personal wealth—including a house in a posh London district, expensive sports cars, and a heavy investment in a famous art gallery. In 1974, however, Archer's dream of a political career exploded in his face. He had borrowed over £250,000 and invested it in a Canadian industrial cleaning company called Aquablast. The directors of the company embezzled the funds and Aquablast collapsed with over $8 million in debts. "I lost every penny," Archer tells Bryson. "The shares were £3.20 on one day and 7 pence the next day. I never had a chance." Although Archer was a vic-

tim of the fraud, he felt obliged to not seek re-election and to devote himself to repaying his debts of $620,000. He left Parliament, borrowed a room in Oxford, and went to work writing a book loosely based on his own experiences.

Bad Fortune Leads to First Novel

Not a Penny More, Not a Penny Less tells about four men—a doctor, a college professor, an art dealer, and a member of the aristocracy—who invest one million dollars in a company to exploit oil in the North Sea. The businessman who runs the company proves to be dishonest, however, and the quartet determine to get their money back by cheating him in return. *Not a Penny More, Not a*

After being swindled by a smooth-talking con man, four disparate people band together to seek revenge.

Penny Less went on to become an instant best-seller in the United States (where it was first published) after having been turned down by a dozen British publishers. Its success surprised Archer, among others, who revealed to Ross that he had "absolutely" no previous experience as a writer, and no previous ambitions to become an author. "I'd been to university and was certainly educated, but I'd never done any writing at all, which makes me think that probably there are a lot of storytellers out there, or, more important, people who could do a second career and haven't thought about it. . . . I am by nature a person who enjoys other people's company. But I didn't mind being on my own during that time, because I needed to readjust, and I needed to put some work in to make up for my own stupidity."

Although *Not a Penny More, Not a Penny Less* did not earn enough to pay all of Archer's debts, its great success encouraged him to write more. *Shall We Tell the President?*, Archer's second novel, did not make the best-seller lists in the United States, but it did generate a great deal of controversy. Set in the early 1980s, it tells of a plan to assassinate President Edward Kennedy. American reviewers were outraged by what they perceived as Archer's callousness. Jacqueline Kennedy Onassis, President John F. Kennedy's widow, resigned her position as an editor with Viking, although she had no direct connection with the book. "The new editions in the bookshops," Archer reveals to Ross, "have Florentyna Kane"—the heroine of his novel *The Prodigal Daughter*—"as the president, not Edward Kennedy." Skillful marketing of the book and its paperback and movie rights netted Archer around $750,000—enough to pay off all his debts.

Archer's next novel, *Kane & Abel,* was also partially based on real people. It tells the story of William Kane, a Boston banker, and Abel Rosnovski, a Polish immigrant and hotelier, and their ferocious hatred for each other. Kane earns Rosnovski's hostility when his bank withholds crucial help from the Pole's American benefactor after the stock market crash of 1929. The benefactor then commits suicide, and Rosnovski launches a vendetta against Kane that lasts for decades. "I met two such men in New York," Archer explains to Ross. "They were very close friends, unlike Kane and Abel, who were enemies. But they came from totally different backgrounds. One was a Polish aristocrat, and the other was one of

America's most successful multimillionaires. They both told me their [stories]. I was quite interested in that, but I thought it would be much more interesting if they were deadly enemies. So I wrote the book with them as background material, but my own story." *Kane and Abel* sold more than a quarter million copies in hardcover and eight times that in paperback.

The Prodigal Daughter, a sequel about Rosnovski's daughter, followed *Kane and Abel* in 1982. It tells how Florentyna Rosnovski—now married to Kane's son Richard—becomes the first female president of the United States. "I wanted to write the story of the first woman president of the United States," Archer confides to Ross. "I wanted

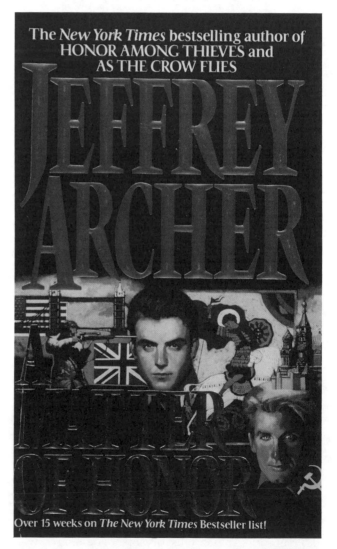

The *New York Times* bestselling author of HONOR AMONG THIEVES and AS THE CROW FLIES

JEFFREY ARCHER

Over 15 weeks on *The New York Times* Bestseller list!

Adam Scott's life is turned upside-down after he receives a strange legacy from his disgraced father.

an Englishman to write it, so that the Americans would realize that we're still awake over here. And you must remember that it was written some time before Geraldine Ferraro was chosen to be a vice-presidential candidate [in the 1988 election]. People laughed at me to begin with. They said it could never happen." Like *Kane and Abel, The Prodigal Daughter* topped best-seller lists in Great Britain and the United States.

Archer established a precedent in *The Prodigal Daughter* by creating two versions of the story: one for his British audience and another for his American fans. For instance, he made changes in the novel to simplify the American political system. "The British, of course," Archer explains to Ross, "find reading *The Prodigal Daughter* a fairly simple way of learning about the American system." More sweeping changes are apparent in the two versions of Archer's *First among Equals,* which tells about the competition between four British candidates for the office of Prime Minister. One of the main characters in the British version of the book is almost totally absent in the American counterpart, and each version of the book has a different prologue and a different ending. "The Americans do seem interested," Archer confides to Ross. "They have a desire to learn about other countries. *First among Equals* is a very simple way of understanding our strange parliamentary system."

Archer's rewriting pays off, however, because his books sell in record numbers, and even reviewers who fault his style admit to becoming absorbed in what they are reading. *Not a Penny More, Not a Penny Less* "is fascinating," declares Charles J. Keffer, writing for the periodical *Best Sellers.* "The story contains some interesting plot development, a clear and plausible story line, and its share of suspense." A. J. Anderson, reviewing the same book for *Library Journal,* declares that it "has about as much substance as a soap bubble, but it is quite entertaining." *Shall We Tell the President?* received some harsh criticism for its lack of sensitivity toward the Kennedy family—*Times Literary Supplement* contributor Charles Wheeler called it "a sick idea"—but Betty Lukas, writing in the *Los Angeles Times Book Review,* labels *The Prodigal Daughter* "pure romance," and adds, "Don't knock it. . . . Archer creates so much suspense in the dialogue that the usual chase scene seems like a turtle race." "Settle into the blankets" and enjoy it, she advises. "It's that kind of novel."

A treasured United States document is the bait as two agents race against time to expose a terrorist plot.

Critical opinion has been similarly divided over Archer's more recent novels. *As the Crow Flies* tells the story of how Charlie Trumper, a man of working-class origins, serves in World War I and then rises to become the founder and head of a chain of department stores. Ken Gross, reviewing the book for *People,* praises Archer's choice of theme and his execution of it. The author "doesn't possess the prose skills of a Fitzgerald or the thundering moral outrage of Dostoevsky. But he tells a nice story." The reviewer concludes that the novel "is like a long, languid, comforting soak in a warm tub." Maggie Scarf, writing in the *New York Times Book Review* about the same book, makes a similar comment: "If [Archer's] writing does appear somewhat naive at times . . . it nevertheless conveys the message that what is right will be rewarded and what is evil will inevitably be punished." "Jeffrey Archer may not be portraying the world as it is," she concludes, "but he is giving us an uncomplicated view of life that was deeply comfortable and gratifying. Archer's simpler world is, in many ways, far preferable to the one we inhabit."

In *Honor among Thieves* Archer tries his hand at the international spy-novel genre. The book has a long, complicated plot about Iraqi president Saddam Hussein's plan to steal the original Declaration of Independence and burn it live on television. Sent to foil Hussein's plot are a Yale University law professor named Scott Bradley and a model-turned-Mossad-agent named Hannah Kopec. Simon Louvish, in a review for the *New Statesman*, asserts that the book "appears to have been written by a committee of ten year olds as an assignment," and accuses Archer of maintaining some pulp magazine prejudices. "But who needs the muse," he concludes, "if the cash tills sing so well unaided?" On the other hand, Gene Lyons states in *Entertainment Weekly* that Archer "has an undeniable flair for . . . ingeniously plotted, grandiose tales of derring-do." However, he also complains that the story is too formulaic. Archer himself has few pretensions about his fiction. "I'm a storyteller," the author tells Ross. "I never know what's going to be in the next line, the next paragraph, or the next page. And if I did, you would. If I don't know what's on the next page, how can you know?"

Rides the Political Roller-coaster Again

Archer's success in writing helped bring him back into politics. In 1985, Margaret Thatcher, Prime Minister of Great Britain and a reputed Archer fan (as well as a main character in *First among Equals*), appointed the author to the post of deputy chairman of the Conservative party. A purely honorary job, the position nonetheless recognized Archer's devotion to the Conservatives and exploited his huge popularity and his fundraising prowess. However, Archer also attracted media attention for his incautious, politically dangerous comments. According to Bryson, at one point he suggested that the Reverend Ian Paisley—a fervent Protestant preacher—would make a suitable leader after Northern Ireland united with the rest of the island.

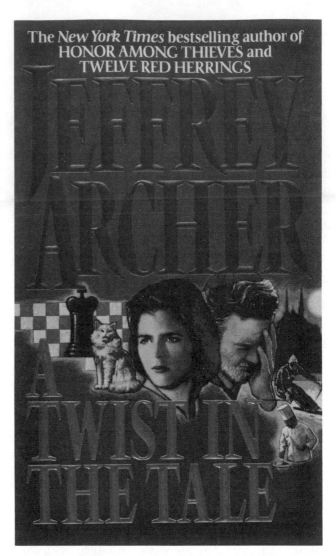

Archer's ability to blend intriguing plots with interesting characters is displayed in this collection of twelve short stories.

Late in 1986, however, a scandal resembling an episode from one of his novels made international headlines. A prostitute, backed by two English tabloid newspapers—the *Star* and the *News of the World*—claimed that she had sex with Archer and that he paid her to leave the country. Archer denied any personal contact with the woman, but admitted that he had given her money in order to avoid bad publicity. He resigned his position and sued both papers. In 1987 he was awarded $800,000 in damages from the *Star,* plus legal costs and a public apology. Most of the money, Archer reveals to Bryson, "went into the new roof of Ely Cathedral." "Politically, it was terrible," he confesses. "Things were just beginning to turn for me. We were near a general election. I was actually doing some good. So, of course, it was a tremendous disappointment to have to step down."

Archer currently divides his time between his writing and the Playhouse, a West End theater he owns. Archer remains a firm supporter of Conservative politicians; after Margaret Thatcher left the Prime Minister's office, another of his friends, John Major, took her place. Most analysts believed that Archer had no future in politics, but in 1993, he was elevated to the House of Lords. "The things that have happened to him," newspaper editor John Bryant tells Bryson, "would have buried the political career of anyone else. But you can never count Jeffrey Archer out."

■ Works Cited

Anderson, A. J., review of *Not a Penny More, Not a Penny Less, Library Journal,* May 1, 1976, p. 1141.

Archer, Jeffrey, interview with Jean W. Ross, *Contemporary Authors New Revision Series,* Volume 22, Gale, 1987, pp. 25-29.

Bryson, Bill, "Tory Storyteller," *New York Times Magazine,* November 25, 1990, pp. 35, 75, 77, 79.

Field, Michele, "PW Interviews: Jeffrey Archer," *Publishers Weekly,* April 26, 1991, pp. 42-43.

Gross, Ken, review of *As the Crow Flies, People,* August 5, 1991, pp. 25 26.

Keffer, Charles J., review of *Not a Penny More, Not a Penny Less, Best Sellers,* July, 1976, p. 106.

Louvish, Simon, "Dubbed into Lebanese," *New Statesman,* July 2, 1993, p. 38.

Lukas, Betty, "A Probe of Power, Pride, Politics," *Los Angeles Times Book Review,* October 24, 1982, p. 10.

Lyons, Gene, "Businessman's Special," *Entertainment Weekly,* July 30, 1993, p. 51.

Scarf, Maggie, "Barrow Boy Makes Good," *New York Times Book Review,* June 9, 1991, p. 52.

Wheeler, Charles, "Gunning for Office," *Times Literary Supplement,* October 28, 1977, p. 1258.

■ For More Information See

BOOKS

Contemporary Literary Criticism, Volume 28, Gale, 1986.

PERIODICALS

Chicago Tribune, August 8, 1982; September 10, 1985.

Chicago Tribune Book World, April 27, 1980.

Detroit Free Press, September 5, 1985.

Los Angeles Times, August 19, 1982; October 24, 1982; March 11, 1983; July 21, 1984.

Los Angeles Times Book Review, April 27, 1980.

New York Times, August 30, 1984; November 10, 1984; October 10, 1985.

New York Times Book Review, October 23, 1977; May 4, 1980; July 6, 1980; July 11, 1982; November 28, 1982; June 19, 1983.

Time, July 28, 1986; November 10, 1986.

Times (London), October 27, 1986.

Times Literary Supplement, September 10, 1976; October 8, 1977; November 1, 1980; December 5, 1986.

Globe and Mail (Toronto), September 13, 1986.

Washington Post, March 7, 1980; April 16, 1986; July 27, 1986.

Washington Post Book World, July 23, 1982; August 5, 1984.

—*Sketch by Kenneth R. Shepherd*

Patricia Beatty

■ Personal

Full name, Patricia Robbins Beatty; also wrote under pseudonym Jean Bartholomew; born August 26, 1922, in Portland, OR; died July 9, 1991, in Riverside, CA; daughter of Walter M. and Jessie (Miller) Robbins; married John Louis Beatty (a professor of history and humanities), September 14, 1950 (died, 1975); married Carl G. Uhr (a professor of economics), July 31, 1977; children: (first marriage) Ann Alexandra. *Education:* Reed College, B.A., 1944; graduate study at University of Idaho, 1947-50, and University of Washington, Seattle, 1951. *Politics:* Democrat. *Religion:* Protestant. *Hobbies and other interests:* Gardening, English history, the American West, learning languages, extra-sensory perception studies, archaeology, philosophical studies.

■ Career

Writer. High school English and history teacher, Coeur d'Alene, ID, 1947-50; Dupont Company, Wilmington, DE, technical library worker, 1952-53; business and science librarian, Riverside, CA, 1953-56; University of California, Los Angeles, Exten-

sion Division, teacher of fiction writing for children, 1967-69. Established the John and Patricia Beatty Award, California Library Association, 1988.

■ Awards, Honors

Commonwealth Club of California Medal for best juvenile California author, 1965, for *Campion Towers; Horn Book* honor list citation, 1966, for *A Donkey for the King;* Southern California Council on Children's and Young People's Literature Medal notable book, 1967, for *The Royal Dirk;* Golden Kite Award honor book, Society of Children's Book Writers, 1973, for *Red Rock over the River;* California Council medal, 1974, for "distinguished body of work," and 1976, for "comprehensive contribution of lasting value to the field of children's literature"; Junior Library Guild selections, 1976, for *By Crumbs, It's Mine!,* 1977, for *I Want My Sunday, Stranger!,* and 1979, for *Lacy Makes a Match;* Western Writers of America honor book, 1978, for *Wait for Me, Watch for Me, Eula Bee;* Jane Addams Children's Book Award honor book, 1982, for *Lupita Manana;* Southern California Council on Children's and Young People's Literature Medal for distinguished work of fiction, 1983, for *Jonathan Down Under;* Western Writers of America Awards, 1984 and 1987; Scott O'Dell Award for Historical Fiction, 1987, for *Charley Skedaddle.*

■ Writings

JUVENILE FICTION

Indian Canoemaker, illustrated by Barbara Beaudreau, Caxton, 1960.

Bonanza Girl, illustrated by Liz Dauber, Morrow, 1962.

(With husband, John Louis Beatty) *At the Seven Stars,* illustrated by Douglas Gorsline, Macmillan, 1963.

The Nickel-Plated Beauty, illustrated by Dauber, Morrow, 1964.

(With J. L. Beatty) *Campion Towers,* Macmillan, 1965.

Squaw Dog, illustrated by Franz Altschuler, Morrow, 1965.

(With J. L. Beatty) *The Royal Dirk,* illustrated by Altschuler, Morrow, 1966.

The Queen's Own Grove, illustrated by Dauber, Morrow, 1966.

(With J. L. Beatty) *A Donkey for the King,* illustrated by Ann Siberell, Macmillan, 1966.

The Lady from Black Hawk, illustrated by Robert Frankenberg, McGraw, 1967.

(With J. L. Beatty) *The Queen's Wizard,* Macmillan, 1967.

(With J. L. Beatty) *Witch Dog,* illustrated by Altschuler, Macmillan, 1968.

Me, California Perkins, illustrated by Dauber, Morrow, 1968.

Blue Stars Watching, Morrow, 1969.

(With J. L. Beatty) *Pirate Royal,* Macmillan, 1969.

Hail Columbia, illustrated by Dauber, Morrow, 1970.

The Sea Pair, illustrated by Altschuler, Morrow, 1971.

A Long Way to Whiskey Creek, Morrow, 1971.

(With J. L. Beatty) *King's Knight's Pawn,* Morrow, 1971.

O the Red Rose Tree, illustrated by Dauber, Morrow, 1972.

(With J. L. Beatty) *Holdfast,* Morrow, 1972.

The Bad Bell of San Salvador, Morrow, 1973.

Red Rock over the River, Morrow, 1973.

How Many Miles to Sundown, Morrow, 1974.

(With J. L. Beatty) *Master Rosalind,* Morrow, 1974.

Rufus, Red Rufus, illustrated by Ted Lewin, Morrow, 1975.

(With J. L. Beatty) *Who Comes to King's Mountain?,* Morrow, 1975.

By Crumbs, It's Mine!, Morrow, 1976.

Something to Shout About, Morrow, 1976.

Billy Bedamned, Long Gone By, Morrow, 1977.

I Want My Sunday, Stranger!, Morrow, 1977.

Just Some Weeds from the Wilderness, Morrow, 1978.

Wait for Me, Watch for Me, Eula Bee, Morrow, 1978.

Lacy Makes a Match, Morrow, 1979.

The Staffordshire Terror, Morrow, 1979.

That's One Ornery Orphan, Morrow, 1980.

Lupita Manana, Morrow, 1981.

Eight Mules from Monterey, Morrow, 1982.

Jonathan Down Under, Morrow, 1982.

Melinda Takes a Hand, Morrow, 1983.

Turn Homeward, Hannalee, Morrow, 1984.

The Coach That Never Came, Morrow, 1985.

Behave Yourself, Bethany Brant, Morrow, 1986.

Charley Skedaddle, Morrow, 1987.

Be Ever Hopeful, Hannalee, Morrow, 1988.

Sarah and Me and the Lady from the Sea, Morrow, 1989.

(With Phillip Robbins) *Eben Tyne, Powdermonkey,* Morrow, 1990.

Jayhawker, Morrow, 1991.

Who Comes with Cannons?, Morrow, 1992.

OTHER

Station Four (novella), Science Research Associates, 1969.

(Under pseudonym Jean Bartholomew) *The Englishman's Mistress* (adult gothic novel), Dell, 1974.

Also author of materials on English history for Science Research Associates.

■ Sidelights

The shelves of historical children's fiction created by Patricia Beatty invite her readers to share in her fascination with the past. Reflecting her interest in meticulous research, which she likened to detective work, the stories include lively details that transport the reader to another time. Critics pointed to her strong sense of humor as a particular asset in her work, as well as a sharp sense of place. A committed feminist, Beatty featured both heroines and heroes who engage in dramatic, absorbing and credible conflicts that involve questions of morality and courage. Again and again, her books were cited for awards and honors, and she received countless fan letters from readers of various ages and backgrounds.

The eldest of two children, Beatty was born and raised in the Pacific Northwest, where her father,

Walter Robbins, was a U.S. Coast Guard commander. In the 1920s, the Coast Guard stations were often located on Indian reservations, and Beatty moved to quite a few with her family. Living among Native Americans taught Beatty much about their culture and customs, material she later drew on for many of her books, including her very first, *Indian Canoemaker*. The Quillayute tribe, into which Beatty was adopted because her birthday coincided with one of their holidays, is the main focus of this early work.

Both Beatty's father and her mother, Jessie, were enthusiastic readers and their daughter soon picked up the habit. Writing in *Something about the Author Autobiography Series* (*SAAS*) she remembered her first reader with delight, "I loved every word of it. . . . One sentence in particular thrilled me. . . . All others went, 'He said, "This is my dog,"' or 'She said, "This is my ball."' The sentence I loved so was inverted to read '"This is my house," said she.' *Said she!* . . . It was poetry to my six-year-old mind." It was this love of reading that helped carry Beatty through a five-month long bout with severe illness when she was ten, an infection so serious that she had to be hospitalized. In her *SAAS* essay, Beatty pointed to this episode as especially important in her eventual decision to write. "I read somewhere that many authors who write especially for young people are individuals who have had suffering in their own childhoods . . . or known intense loneliness. I believe such suffering while young makes for a deeper, more sensitive person, who can feel the pain and problems of others and put himself or herself into the other person's difficult place. Putting yourself into another person's place, putting on his skin, zipping it up, and trying to think and act as he or she would is what an author does in every book he or she writes."

From Horsewoman to Scholar and Writer

Beatty's family life made a huge shift shortly after this period when, in 1935, she moved from the small coastal towns and outposts into Portland, Oregon. Although initially overwhelmed by a real city and disdainful of her junior high school, Beatty had more luck with high school, where she befriended an English teacher who inspired her to join this profession. She also discovered what she described in her *SAAS* essay as a "treasure house": the Vernon Branch Library.

Beatty at age sixteen in Portland, Oregon

Beatty continued to read at the blistering pace she'd established earlier, working her way through the children's collection and then right on into the adult section.

Horses were another major preoccupation for the teenage Beatty. Saturdays were usually spent at a riding academy near the Columbia River where she mastered both English and Western saddle styles, unknowingly gathering information that she would later feature in her books. Her descriptions in these novels were based on pure memory: she gave up riding at the end of high school because it would have interfered with academic work.

By the time she entered Reed College in 1941, Beatty was set on becoming a high school teacher. Inspired by her childhood beachcombing and a favorite biology professor, Beatty also considered marine biology. But the departure of this professor prompted the writer to focus on her other interests, literature and history. Though her days as a horsewoman were behind her, Beatty distinguished herself on the soccer field and in fencing, an activity that would feature prominently in her books on English history. It was during this time that Beatty met fellow student John Beatty, who would become her husband and coauthor; they were married in 1950, following his tour of military duty.

After college, Beatty began teaching English and history in Idaho. Living in this harsh area, she learned how to fish and how to live through cruelly cold winters, but never how to hunt, an activity she deplored. Later, while her husband worked toward his doctorate in history at the University of Washington, she worked as an index compiler and secretary. The couple moved around the country, going wherever John was hired to teach, while Beatty worked as a librarian. By 1953 they had settled in Riverside, California.

Her undemanding job as a librarian at the Riverside Public Library gave Beatty plenty of time to read, but she found herself eager to make something as well. Though she'd done commercial art and drawn all her life, she was anxious not to appear unprofessional. Finally, she decided to write her first book for young people, *Indian Canoemaker,* which describes the Quillayutes' way of life before the changes made by the arrival of the American missionaries. Caxton Printers, Ltd. bought the book and the contract reached Beatty the same day in 1957 that she gave birth to her daughter, Ann Alexandra.

She wrote her second novel, *Bonanza Girl,* during Ann's nap times. Although the story, which is set in the mining region of northern Idaho in the 1880s, got rave reviews, Beatty encountered a very different reaction from women she knew in Riverside. Questioning the propriety of her writing books when she had a husband and child to look after, the women acted "as if writing were a disease I'd contracted," she described in *SAAS.* The effect was to turn her "into a feminist, a person devoted to the interest and welfare of other women, when it could have made me hate all women as catty individuals." This feminism carried over into Beatty's writings as well, through the self-reliant and courageous heroines she created.

The Beatty "System": Two Books a Year

When the family moved to England in 1960, Beatty and her husband wrote the first of many collaborative efforts, *At the Seven Stars,* a spy novel featuring three famous figures from the eighteenth century. Following this first co-authored work, Beatty devised a system whereby she produced two books a year: one in conjunction with her husband whose topic was English history, the other based on American history and written only by her. One of these, *Hail Columbia,* which Beatty wrote in 1969, was a direct response to her feminist beliefs. The story concerns 13-year-old Louisa who recounts how the visit from her suffragette aunt changed the lives of her family and the entire town in 1890s Oregon. Written before the women's movement had really taken hold, it was one of the first feminist books specially written for girls.

The annual production of two books continued through ten more books, until John Beatty's early death in 1975; Beatty did not write for several of the following years. Remarking on the swift change in her life, she recalled in *SAAS* that "I was totally alone except for my feminist women friends. They kept me busy. . . . Widowhood was lonely and sad for me and I wondered if I would ever write again." Then, in 1977, she married economics professor Carl Uhr, himself recently widowed. And not long after, Beatty set to work on a new writing project.

Throughout her writing career, Beatty usually alternated between third- and first-person narration in her work. What critics have termed her "lighter" novels often deal with plucky heroines coping with the struggles of frontier life in the West. For example, a tomboy, her younger brother, and her pet longhorn accompany a 15-year-old boy searching for his father through Texas and the New Mexico and Arizona territories in *How Many Miles to Sundown;* in *By Crumbs, It's Mine* a 13-year-old girl finds herself alone in the Arizona territory in the 1880s and eventually becomes the owner of a traveling hotel; and in *Melinda Takes a Hand* another 13-year-old girl is stranded in Goldendale, Colorado, finding herself involved in the problems of the townspeople.

The American Civil War remained almost an obsession for Beatty throughout her life and her more serious novels center on this period. In *Turn*

Homeward, Hannalee, a young girl and her little brother are caught in the midst of the Sherman's march to the sea, a tale Elizabeth Reardon, writing in *School Library Journal,* termed "fast-moving . . . with a spunky heroine and fine historical detail." The parallels to *Gone with the Wind* were noted by Beatty herself and reviewers Beth and Ben Helms remarked in *English Journal* that "Hannalee is only twelve, but her adventures will appeal to older readers and inform them of the effects of the war on a social class far removed from that of Scarlett O'Hara."

In *Behave Yourself, Bethany Brant,* Beatty returned to the West for a story about a preacher's daughter who has an event-filled 18 months after a fortune-teller's predictions come true for her in 1898 Texas. A *Publishers Weekly* reviewer called this one a "rouser," and Ann A. Flowers, writing in *Horn Book,* was impressed with the "valuable information about the customs of the times—monetary, educational and societal" that Beatty appended in an author's note. Many of Beatty's novels include a preface or afterward that makes reference to the historical period and issues at stake at the time the story is set.

The Goal: Educating While Entertaining

Charley Skedaddle is also set during the Civil War and tells the story of 12-year-old Charles Quinn who joins Union army enlistees to escape his sister's fiancé's plan to send him to an orphanage. Terrified by his first brush with combat, Charley runs away and is promptly caught by a mountain woman. Aware of the risk he runs from both Union and Confederate soldiers, he stays on as her mute "Boy." *School Library Journal* contributor Barbara Chatton praised the award-winning book for its "unusual characters and events, and fascinating historical detail," adding that readers would appreciate "Charley's quiet acceptance that there is no one 'right' side to the war." A *Publishers Weekly* reviewer deemed *Charley Skedaddle* "well-crafted," and went on to conclude that the keenly observed settings and emotional life of Charley "give this novel depth and make it one of Beatty's best."

Hannalee reappears in *Be Ever Hopeful, Hannalee,* which picks up the story in post-Civil War Atlanta, where Hannalee and all the members of her family have to work hard to make ends meet.

Hannalee must learn to abandon her negative views of Yankees, to see that there are good and bad people in every group. *Voice of Youth Advocates* contributor Eleanor Klopp missed the humor she'd seen in other Beatty books and felt that *Be Ever Hopeful, Hannalee* "suffers as a sequel," but that together with *Turn Homeward, Hannalee* it presents "an accurate and interesting picture of a rarely described aspect of the Civil War and its effects on the lives of ordinary people." A *New York Times Book Review* contributor singled the book out for being "unusually ambitious and well researched," and a reviewer in *Horn Book* praised Hannalee's "plain-spoken and often colorful idiom."

Despite her fascination with the Civil War, Beatty did not shield her readers from the horrors of battle and the devastation it brings to the land. In *Jayhawker,* her protagonist Lije Tulley is an

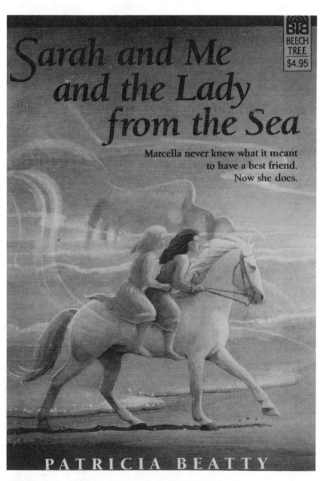

Marcella's initial distaste at moving from the city to the country begins to change after she meets some very special—perhaps even magical—new friends.

abolitionist raider (the jayhawker of the title) from Kansas who gets caught in the raids and skirmishes between the pro-slavery bushwhackers and the jayhawkers in Missouri just before and during the Civil War. A *Publishers Weekly* reviewer lauded the novel for being neither pro-North nor pro-South but rather "a dramatic and compelling antiwar narrative." Bruce Anne Shook noted in *School Library Journal* that the book's strength lies in telling a "fast-paced suspenseful story while presenting a clear picture of a crucial period in U.S. history." And in *Booklist* Deborah Abbott picked up on the antiwar theme, writing that Beatty "admits that violence is an inevitable part of history. It is how people respond to conflict that determines the moral fiber of an individual as well as of a nation."

After her father's death, Truth Hopkins moves in with her aunt and uncle and becomes involved in the underground railroad.

In *Who Comes with Cannons?* Beatty returned to a female protagonist, 12-year-old Truth Hopkins, a Quaker. As pacifists, the Quakers were scorned by both sides in the Civil War. When the orphaned girl goes to live with her uncle's family in North Carolina, she discovers that their house is a station on the Underground Railroad and is eager to help. A *Horn Book* reviewer found the novel "believable, nicely paced and rich in historical detail. A good choice for a women's studies curriculum as well as civil war history." And *Booklist*'s Carolyn Phelan complimented Beatty for acknowledging "the moral and physical courage of those who refused to take sides."

Careful research into the customs, language, and dress of historical characters is a hallmark of all Beatty's work, which encompasses not only the Civil War, but English and Australian history, too; she didn't disregard historical accuracy just because her writing was aimed at a young audience. She once explained: "I want to share my excited sense of the past with children and I try by every means at my command . . . to make them aware of how life was lived at some particular period. I have tried to convey a sense of the past to young readers and at the same time not overwhelm them with detail. I love to insinuate bits of historical information and educate at the same time I entertain. I think this is one of the best ways of all to teach history."

Several of Beatty's books have been translated into Danish, Spanish, German and Norwegian. She received many awards, and in 1988 Beatty founded the John and Patricia Beatty Award through the California Library Association, whose purpose is to encourage the writing of children's books about the heritage of California. She was anxious to convey not only her sharp sense of history's crucial role in everyone's life, but also the need for a well-developed sense of humor. As Beatty summed it up in *SAAS,* "I am told my books make readers laugh. I like to think my gift to all my readers is not only some easily-gotten historical knowledge but laughter. . . . Writing is what makes me who I am! It makes me feel I have done something with my life!"

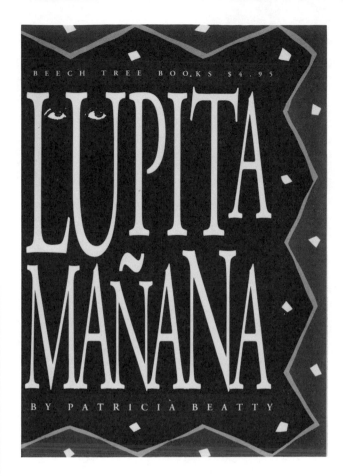

After their father dies in a fishing accident, Mexican-born Lupita and her brother Salvador must illegally cross the United States border in order to find work to support their family.

■ Works Cited

Abbott, Deborah, review of *Jayhawker, Booklist,* September 1, 1991, p. 41.

Review of *Be Ever Hopeful, Hannalee, Horn Book,* January/February, 1989, pp. 65-66.

Review of *Be Ever Hopeful, Hannalee, New York Times Book Review,* March 12, 1989, p. 35.

Beatty, Patricia, essay in *Something about the Author Autobiography Series,* Volume 4, Gale, 1987, pp. 35-52.

Review of *Behave Yourself, Bethany Brant, Publishers Weekly,* December 26, 1986, p. 57.

Review of *Charley Skedaddle, Publishers Weekly,* October 9, 1987, p. 88.

Chatton, Barbara, review of *Charley Skedaddle, School Library Journal,* November, 1987, p. 103.

Flowers, Ann A., review of *Behave Yourself, Bethany Brant, Horn Book,* January/February, 1987, pp. 54-55.

Helms, Beth and Ben, review of *Turn Homeward, Hannalee, English Journal,* March, 1986, p. 106.

Review of *Jayhawker, Publishers Weekly,* September 6, 1991.

Klopp, Eleanor, review of *Be Ever Hopeful, Hannalee, Voice of Youth Advocates,* December, 1988.

Phelan, Carolyn, review of *Who Comes with Cannons?, Booklist,* January 1, 1993, p. 804.

Reardon, Elizabeth, review of *Turn Homeward, Hannalee, School Library Journal,* January, 1985, pp. 80-81.

Shook, Bruce Anne, review of *Jayhawker, School Library Journal,* September, 1991, p. 250.

Review of *Who Comes with Cannons?, Horn Book,* January/February, 1993, pp. 83-84.

■ Obituaries

PERIODICALS

Chicago Tribune, July 14, 1991, section 2, p. 6.

Detroit Free Press, July 12, 1991, p. 2B.

Los Angeles Times, July 13, 1991, p. Λ28.

New York Times, July 11, 1991, p. B6.

Publishers Weekly, August 9, 1991.

—Sketch by Megan Ratner

Malcolm Bosse

■ Personal

Full name, Malcolm Joseph Bosse; born May 6, 1933, in Detroit, MI; son of Malcolm Clifford (a stockbroker) and Thelma (Malone) Bosse; married Marie-Claude Aullas (a translator), July 4, 1969; children: Malcolm-Scott. *Education:* Yale University, B.A., 1950; University of Michigan, M.A., 1956; New York University, Ph.D., 1969. *Hobbies and other interests:* Tai-Chi Chuan, yoga, Oriental mythology, archaeology, myrmecology (the study of ants), Asian history, art (especially sculpture), music, (especially jazz), watching football on television, classical ballet, Chinese cooking, jogging, swimming.

■ Addresses

Office—Department of English, City College of the City University of New York, New York, NY 10031.

■ Career

Author and professor of English. *Barron's Financial Weekly,* New York City, editorial writer, 1950– 52; freelance writer, 1957–66; novelist, 1959—; City College of the City University of New York, New York City, professor of English, 1969—. Lecturer in Bangladesh, Burma, China, Fiji Islands, Hong Kong, India, Japan, Malaysia, Singapore, Taiwan, Thailand. *Military Service:* U.S. Navy, 1950–54; received two Bronze Stars. Also served in U.S. Army and U.S. Merchant Marines. *Member:* PEN, Authors Guild, Society of Eighteenth Century Studies and Scholars (England), Modern Language Association of America, Yale Club, Andiron Club, Fulbright-Hays Alumni Association, Henry James Associates, Phi Gamma Delta, Phi Beta Kappa.

■ Awards, Honors·

Masefield Award, Yale University, 1949, for poetry and fiction; Jule and Avery Hopwood Awards, University of Michigan, 1956, for poetry and fiction; best novels of the year citation, *Saturday Review of Literature,* 1960, for *The Journey of Tao Kim Nam;* University Scholar Award, New York University, 1969; Newberry Library Fellowship, 1970; Edgar Allan Poe nominations, for best first mystery, 1974, for *The Incident at Naha,* and for best mystery of the year, 1975, for *The Man Who Loved Zoos;* certificate of merit, Society of the Dictionary of International Biography, 1976, for distinguished service to the community; National Endowment for the Arts creative writing fellowship, 1977–78; Fulbright-Hays lectureship grants for India, 1978 and 1979, and for Indonesia, 1987;

Notable Book citation, 1979, American Library Association (ALA), best books of the year citation, Library of Congress, 1980, Dorothy Canfield Fisher Award nomination, 1981, Preis der Leseratten for best children's book of the year, German Television ZDF Schulerexpress, 1984, Dutch Children's Book Prize, 1984, Prix du livre pour la jeunesse de la fondation de France, 1986, and Prix Lecture-Jeunesse, 1987, all for *The Seventy-nine Squares;* special commendation from International Communication Agency, 1980, for work in India; Notable Book citation, ALA, 1981, notable book in the field of social studies citation, National Council of Social Studies Teachers, 1981, and Deutscher Jugendliteraturpreis nomination, 1984, all for *Cave beyond Time;* Notable Book citation, ALA, 1982, Honor List of Book Awards, Austrian Ministry of Education and Arts, 1982, Deutscher Jugendliteraturpreis, 1983, American Book Award nomination, Parent's Choice Award, Omar Award, and notable children's trade book in the field of social studies citation, all for *Ganesh;* Parent's Choice Award, 1994, for *The Examination.*

■ Writings

JUVENILE NOVELS

The Seventy-nine Squares, Crowell, 1979.

Cave beyond Time, Crowell, 1980.

Ganesh, Crowell, 1981, published as *Ordinary Magic,* Farrar, Straus, 1993.

The Barracuda Gang, Dutton, 1982.

Captives of Time, Delacorte, 1987.

Deep Dream of the Rain Forest, Farrar, Straus, 1993.

The Examination, Farrar, Straus, 1994.

ADULT NOVELS

Journey of Tao Kim Nam, Doubleday, 1959.

The Incident at Naha (mystery), Simon & Schuster, 1972.

The Man Who Loved Zoos (mystery), Putnam, 1974.

The Warlord, Simon & Schuster, 1983.

Fire in Heaven (sequel to *The Warlord*), Simon & Schuster, 1986.

Stranger at the Gate, Simon & Schuster, 1989.

Mister Touch, Ticknor & Fields, 1991.

The Vast Memory of Love, Ticknor & Fields, 1992.

COEDITOR

Foundations of the Novel, Garland, 1974.

The Flowering of the Novel, Garland, 1975.

The Novel in England: 1700–1775 (contains *Foundations of the Novel* and *The Flowering of the Novel*), Garland, 1977.

Also coeditor, "Representative English Mid-Eighteenth Century Fiction, 1740–1775" series, Garland, 1975.

OTHER

Contributor of major critical essay to *Charles Johnstone's Chrysal: 1760–1765.* Garland Publishing. Member of advisory board, *Pequod* magazine. Also contributor of articles, short stories, and poems to periodicals, including *Literary Criterion, Remington Review, Voyages, California Quarterly, North American Review, Michigan Quarterly, Artesian, Massachusetts Review,* and *New York Times.* Work included in *Mississippi Valley Writers Collection.*

■ Adaptations

The Man Who Loved Zoos was made into a French film titled *Agent Trouble* in 1987.

■ Sidelights

"Everything I have written has had an excellent critical reception, but not a wide audience. I thought I was relegated to write books that were liked, but not read," Martin Bosse told Robert Dahlin in a *Publishers Weekly* interview. Bosse's love for writing emerged in adolescence, in spite of a "nonliterary" family background, and he published his first poetry at age fifteen. He received the Yale University Masefield Award for poetry and fiction in 1949; he won the Jule and Avery Hopwood Awards for fiction and poetry in 1956 while in graduate school at the University of Michigan.

Bosse described his family to Dahlin in the *Publishers Weekly* interview: "My father was a stockbroker, and my mother was a housewife. They wanted me to become a doctor, but in a rebellious frame of mind, I dropped premed and went into American studies—sociology, economics, history." Bosse went on to develop his skills as a writer and lecturer, publishing his first novel, *The Journey of Tao Kim Nam* in 1959 while completing his master's degree at the University of Michigan. Over the next twenty years Bosse published only two books, both widely acclaimed mysteries. He focused on his academic career, completing his

Ph.D. at New York University in 1969. He has been a professor of English at City University of New York since that time, specializing in eighteenth-century English literature.

Bosse's first novel drew upon his experiences traveling throughout Asia while serving in the military, including the army, the navy, and the merchant marine. Bosse recalls the influence of this period of his life in the *Publishers Weekly* interview: "That was my introduction to the Far East, and I loved it. It seemed so comfortable to me in a way that Europe is not. In the Far East I feel at home, for some reason. The Hindus would say that in other lives I was an Oriental." This early experience, along with two years spent in India as a Fulbright Scholar, greatly influenced his work. Two of his young adult novels—*Ganesh* and *The Seventy-nine Squares*—are set in the United States, but use techniques of Eastern meditation as a major story element. His young adult novel *The Examination* is set in China of the Middle Ages. Other works of fiction that have Asian settings or themes drawn from Eastern mysticism include *The Incident at Naha* and *The Warlord*.

Across Age and Cultural Barriers

Bosse has written as many novels for young adults as for adults, but does not set his two audiences apart. He once noted: "I consider any reader above 10 or 12 years old (depending upon the rate of maturation) to be an adult. I write for a young person as I would for someone my own age, leaving out perhaps the worst of my philosophical reflections or distortions, which, of course, is all for the best." *Cave Beyond Time* and *The Barracuda Gang* are examples of Bosse's adventure stories and historical fiction. *Cave Beyond Time*, for instance, is the story of a young man named Ben, who falls unconscious after a rattlesnake bite while working on an archaeological site in Arizona. In his delirium, Ben dreams that he is a member of an ancient nomadic tribe, and gains wisdom from his struggle with wild animals and from a variety of father-figures.

However, Bosse is more widely known for his coming-of-age novels featuring adolescents who have to struggle hard while making their own way toward maturity. In *The Seventy-nine Squares*, his first novel for young adults, the author "presents a moving, very private story of one boy's

DEEP DREAM OF THE RAIN FOREST

MALCOLM BOSSE

While on trip into the rainforest with his uncle, Harry is kidnapped by a young tribesman who thinks the teen holds the key to a strange prophecy.

friendship with an elderly man. . . . [Y]oung readers . . . will feel, as Eric does, that they have been in on something very special," states Jack Forman in the *New York Times Book Review*. Eric, who is fourteen and on probation for vandalism at school, meets Mr. Beck, an eighty-two-year-old man recently released from prison because he is dying of cancer. To the bafflement of his parents, gang, and probation officer, Eric develops an important relationship with this grumpy old man who murdered his wife years before in a fit of jealous passion. "The book offers some good insights into old age, friendship, prejudices, nature, and family relationships," says Kathy Piehl writing in the *School Library Journal*. Beck introduces Eric "to the natural beauty and life of the garden in which he now spends most of his time. He instructs Eric to divide the garden into seventy-nine squares, asking that the boy spend one hour a day in each square and watch life unfold—from ant to the squirrel," writes Forman, who calls the novel, "a very moving, very private story." A *Publishers Weekly* critic concludes that the book "is vivid, carefully plotted and a strong lesson in values."

Ganesh, another of Bosse's young adult novels, is not "light entertainment" but "a shining little jewel to be savored and treasured by those who already know the merits of fine literature," declares Bryna J. Fireside in the *New York Times Book Review.* "Ganesh," the name of a Hindu god of strength and wisdom, is the nickname of fourteen-year-old Jeffery Moore, who is uprooted from his home in India after his parents' deaths. He was born and reared in India; his American parents came to India on business. After his mother's death, Jeffrey's father sought solace in Hinduism. Jeffrey was cared for by the villagers while his father accompanied a revered religious leader on spiritual pilgrimages for weeks at a time.

Once his father dies, Jeffrey goes to live with his Aunt Betty in the Midwest where his experiences with Hinduism, yoga, and mantras are considered alien. Despite his alienation from his American heritage, Jeffrey finds a way to apply his own values in his new home. *Ganesh,* declares Fireside. is at bottom "a deeply moving novel of a young boy's search for roots in two countries worlds apart." Ellen D. Warwick, writing in the *School Library Journal,* states that "the book's strong points include a loving evocation of Indian village life and some fine insights on cultural differences," but decries the "poorly motivated characters and implausible plot." This book, states Dominic Hibberd, reviewing the story for the *Times Literary Supplement,* "neither condemns nor urges alternatives [to modern culture] but brings the ancient message that strength comes from within."

Adventures in Time

Bosse incorporates similar messages in some of his other stories, including fiction that has a historical theme. Betsy Hearne, writing in the *Bulletin of the Center for Children's Books,* describes *Deep Dream of the Rain Forest* as "an ambitious adventure story . . . set in a Borneo jungle during the 1920s, when East and West come face to face in the form of two strong men and a lame young woman with

spiritual vision." The two worlds come face to face when Harry Windsor, a British orphan who comes from a long tradition of exploration and imperialism, meets Bayang, a young Iban warrior following a dream that will bring him power to lead his people. Assisting Bayang in his search is Tambong, or Duck Foot, an Iban woman who helps him interpret and realize his dreams. Harry is kidnapped by Bayang and Duck Foot and has to travel with them through the Borneo rain forest to help realize Bayang's dream-quest.

Through their shared experiences, Bayang, Tambong, and Harry come to respect each other. Sue Krumbein felt the story to be interesting, but the excitement was in the setting. She writes in the *Voice of Youth Advocates:* "Here I was, finally, in a

Fourteen-year-old Jeffrey Moore—born and raised in India—must adapt to a very different lifestyle in the Midwest after his father dies.

rain forest and able to make some sense of what it would be like to live/be there. . . . The place comes alive, and it is interesting the way the author has developed both the setting and the plot to create a very satisfying story." Ellen Fader reviewing the book for the *School Library Journal,* declares, "One of the book's strengths is its insight into the way of life of English colonials and of the Iban [tribe]. This is a multilayered story that has many rewards for patient readers who enjoy learning about the natural history of a very different country and the people who inhabit it." A reviewer for *Parents' Choice* magazines writes that "[the author's] descriptions of the rain forest leave the reader feeling a bit breathless, and amazed." "This smoothly paced story offers strong characters, thoughtful insights, and a glimpse of global connections," states Mary Romano Marks in *Booklist.* "Students will simply enjoy a good read."

Captives of Time is set in the late Middle Ages; the story centers around Ann Valens, sixteen years old, who travels with her younger brother across Europe to find their uncle after their parents are murdered. She and her uncle develop plans for the construction of tower clocks, a revolutionary invention. Maureen Quilligan in the *New York Times Book Review* writes: "Ann lives in a world of complete strangers, a lonely if independent young woman; human tenderness centers on her love for her mute (and rather idiosyncratically) struck-by-lightning younger brother and his pet rabbit." After her uncle's death, Ann finds that she must build the new clock. However, given her unusual ability to read and calculate, some people believe her to be a witch and react hostilely. Quilligan finds that these qualities in Ann make the book "so wildly anachronistic as to negate history." In a contrary view, Ruth M. McConnell of the *School Library Journal* believes "readers will be grateful" for the historical detail because "the crafting is so good and the writing so vivid."

In *The Examination* Bosse presents a story of two Chinese brothers traveling from Sichuan Province to the Forbidden City. A young Confucian scholar, Chen, age nineteen, is to take the final examination for a top-level civil service position. His fifteen-year-old brother Hong is determined to go with his brother to Beijing. Bosse provides much historical and social detail to highlight his story, including "fighting crickets, Taoist kite-flying and Mandarin Duck infantry formations, and even in-

cludes an occasional adage from Confucius," declares Diane Manuel in the *New York Times Book Review.* She credits Bosse with bringing "a sharp eye and a penchant for research to his work." But the reviewer concludes that "once the final pages are turned, young readers who devour historical fiction may find themselves wishing there were more substance to this book." However, "Bosse renders a graphic picture of sixteenth-century China—its violence, ceremony, scholarship, and strict class order—in this stimulating and timeless story," states a *Kirkus Reviews* critic, and John Philbrook, writing in the *School Library Journal,* calls it "a unique and absorbing novel."

Writing is an intense activity for Malcolm Bosse. *The Warlord,* for instance, took two years to complete, working seven days a week. "Bosse's workstation is a typewriter positioned on a sculptor's table, at which he works standing up. 'It helps keep me awake, and I see writing as a physical activity. My body is involved in the act of writing.' When he tires, Bosse lies on the floor and takes a nap, two or three of them a day," wrote Dahlin in *Publishers Weekly.* Bosse's work continues to interest both adult and juvenile readers. "I figured that to write a good book for teenagers, you were required to write with clarity and honesty and economy," he tells Dahlin. "I thought I'd learn a lot with those books, and I did."

■ Works Cited

Dahlin, Robert, "Publishers Weekly Interviews: Malcolm Bosse," *Publishers Weekly,* May 20, 1983, pp. 238–39.

Review of *Deep Dream of the Rain Forest, Parents' Choice,* Volume 18, number 4, 1994, p. 28.

Review of *The Examination, Kirkus Reviews,* August 15, 1994, p. 1121.

Fader, Ellen, review of *Deep Dream of the Rain Forest, School Library Journal,* October, 1993, p. 148.

Fireside, Bryna J., review of *Ganesh, New York Times Book Review,* August 9, 1981, p. 24.

Forman, Jack, review of *The Seventy-nine Squares, New York Times Book Review,* December 9, 1979, p. 35.

Hearne, Betsy, review of *Deep Dream of the Rain Forest, Bulletin of the Center for Children's Books,* October 1993, p. 39.

Hibberd, Dominic, "Cultures on Other Terms," *Times Literary Supplement,* July 23, 1982, p. 790.

Krumbein, Sue, review of *Deep Dream of the Rain Forest, Voice of Youth Advocates,* December, 1993, p. 288.

Manuel, Diane, review of *The Examination, New York Times Book Review,* November 13, 1994, p. 28.

Marks, Mary Romano, review of *Deep Dream of the Rain Forest, Booklist,* October 1, 1993, p. 329.

McConnell, Ruth M., review of *Captives of Time, School Library Journal,* November, 1987, pp. 112–13.

Philbrook, John, review of *The Examination, School Library Journal,* November, 1994, p. 118.

Piehl, Kathy, review of *The Seventy-nine Squares, School Library Journal,* September, 1979, pp. 152–53.

Quilligan, Maureen, review of *Captives of Time, New York Times Book Review,* January 31, 1988, p. 36.

Review of *The Seventy-nine Squares, Publishers Weekly,* July 2, 1979, p. 106.

Warwick, Ellen D., review of *Ganesh, School Library Journal,* May, 1981, p. 70.

—*Sketch by Barbara A. Withers*

Ben Bova

■ Personal

Full name, Benjamin William Bova; born November 8, 1932, in Philadelphia, PA; son of Benjamin Pasquale (a tailor) and Giove (Caporiccio) Bova; married Posa Cucinotta, November 28, 1953 (divorced, 1974); married Barbara Berson Pose, June 28, 1974; children: (first marriage) Michael Francis, Regina Marie. *Education:* Temple University, B. S., 1954; State University of New York at Albany, M.A., 1987. *Religion:* None. *Hobbies and other interests:* History, anthropology, fencing, music, astronomy.

■ Addresses

Home and office—Naples, FL. *Agent*—Barbara Bova Literary Agency, 40 Seagate Dr. #1201, Naples, FL 33940.

■ Career

Writer, editor and marketer. *Upper Darby News,* Upper Darby, PA, editor, 1953–56; Martin Aircraft Co., Baltimore, MD, technical editor on Vanguard Project, 1956–58; Massachusetts Institute of Technology, Cambridge, MA, screenwriter for Physical Science Study Committee, 1958–59; Avco-Everett Research Laboratory, Everett, MA, marketing manager, 1960–71; *Analog,* New York City, editor, 1971–78; *Omni,* New York City, 1979–82, fiction editor, 1978–80, editorial director, 1980–81, vice-president, 1981–82; special science and technology consultant, *CBS Morning News* Columbia Broadcasting System, Inc., 1982–84. Member of editorial board, World Future Society, 1982—, and Tor Books, 1982—. Lecturer at universities and businesses; science consult to motion picture studios. *Member:* PEN, British Interplanetary Society (fellow), National Space Society (president, 1984–89, chairman, board of directors, 1989—), Science Fiction Writers of America (president, 1990–1992), American Association for the Advancement of Science, American Institute of Aeronautics and Astronauts, Free Space Society (honorary chair), National Space Club, Planetary Society, Nature Conservancy, New York Academy of Science, Explorers Club, Amateur Fencer's League of America.

■ Awards, Honors

The Milk Way Galaxy, The Fourth State of Matter, and *Welcome to Moonbase* were named best science books of the year, American Library Association; Hugo Award (best editor), World Science Fiction Society, 1973–77, and 1979; E. E. Smith Memorial Award, New England Science Fiction Society, 1974; named distinguished alumnus, Temple University, 1981; Balrog Award, 1983; Inkpot Award, 1985.

■ Writings

SCIENCE FICTION

The Star Conquerors, Winston, 1959.

Star Watchman, Holt, 1964.
The Weathermakers, Holt 1967.
Out of the Sun, Holt, 1968.
The Dueling Machine, Holt, 1969.
THX 1138 (adapted from the screenplay by George Lucas and Walter Murch), Paperback Library, 1971.
As on a Darkling Plain, Walker, 1972.
When the Sky Burned, Walker, 1972.
The Winds of Altair, Dutton, 1973.
Forward in Time (short stories), Walker, 1973.
(With Gordon R. Dickson) *Gremlins, Go Home!*, St. Martin's, 1974.
The Starcrossed, Chilton, 1975.
City of Darkness, Scribner, 1976.
Escape!, Holt, 1976.
Millennium, Random House, 1976.
The Multiple Man, Bobbs-Merrill, 1976.
Colony, Pocket Books, 1978.
Kinsman, Dial, 1979.
Test of Fire, Tor Books, 1982.
Privateers, Tor Books, 1985.
The Kinsman Saga, Tor Books, 1987.
Peacekeepers, Tor Books, 1988.
Cyberbooks, Tor Books, 1989.
Future Crime, Tor Books, 1990.
Mars, Bantam, 1992.
Triumph, Tor Books, 1992.
To Save the Sun, Tor Books, 1993.
Sam Gunn, Bantam, 1993.
Empire Builders, Tor Books, 1993.
Challenges, Tor Books, 1993.
The Watchmen, Baen Books, 1994.
To Fear the Light, Tor Books, 1994.
Death Dream, Bantam, 1994.

Author, with Bill Pogue, of *Trikon Deception*, 1992.

"EXILE" SERIES

Exiled from Earth, Dutton, 1971.
Flight of Exiles, Dutton, 1972.
End of Exile, Dutton, 1975.
The Exiles Trilogy (contains *Exiles From Earth*, *Flight of Exiles*, and *End of Exile*), Berkley, 1980.

"ORION" SERIES

Orion, Simon & Schuster, 1984.

Vengeance of Orion, Tor Books, 1988.
Orion in the Dying Time, Tor Books, 1990.
Orion and the Conqueror, Tor Books, 1994.
Orion Among the Stars, Tor Books, 1995.

"VOYAGERS" SERIES

Voyagers, Doubleday, 1981.

The Alien Within, Tor Books, 1986.
Star Brothers, Tor Books, 1990.

NONFICTION

The Milky Way Galaxy: Man's Exploration of the Stars, Holt, 1961.

Giants of the Animal World, Whitman Publishing, 1962.
Reptiles since the World Began, Whitman Publishing, 1962.
The Uses of Space, Holt, 1965.
In Quest of Quasars: An Introduction to the Stars and Starlike Objects, Crowell, 1970.
Planets, Life and LGM, Addison-Wesley, 1970.
The Fourth State of Matter: Plasma Dynamics and Tomorrow's Technology, St. Martin's, 1971.
The Amazing Laser, Westminster Press, 1972.
The New Astronomies, St. Martin's, 1972.
Starflight and Other Improbabilities (Junior Library Guild selection), Westminster Press, 1972.
Man Changes the Weather, Addison-Wesley, 1973.
(With Barbara Berson) *Survival Guide for the Suddenly Single*, St. Martin's, 1974.
The Weather Changes Man, Addison-Wesley, 1974.
Workshops in Space, Dutton, 1974.
Through Eyes of Wonder, Addison-Wesley, 1975.
Science: Who Needs It, Westminster Press, 1975.
Notes to a Science Fiction Writer, Scribner, 1975.
Viewpoint, NESFA Press, 1977.
The Seeds of Tomorrow, McKay, 1977.
The High Road, Houghton, 1981.
Vision of the Future: The Art of Robert McCall, Abrams, 1982.
Assured Survival: Putting the Star Wars Defense in Perspective, Houghton, 1984, revised paperback edition published as *Star Peace: Assured Survival*, Tor Books, 1986.
Welcome to Moonbase!, Ballantine, 1987.
The Beauty of Light, Wiley, 1988.
(With Sheldon L. Glashow) *Interactions: A Journey through the Mind of a Particle Physicist and the Matter of this World*, Warner, 1988.
First Contact: The Search for Extraterrestrial Intelligence, Dutton, 1991.

The Craft of Writing Science Fiction That Sells, Writer's Digest Books, 1994.

SHORT STORY COLLECTIONS

Maxwell's Demons, Baronet, 1978.

Escape Plus, Books, 1984.
The Astral Mirror, Tor Books, 1985.
Prometheans, Tor Books, 1986.
Battle Station, Tor Books, 1987.

EDITOR

The Many Worlds of SF, Dutton, 1971.

SFWA Hall of Fame, Volume II, Doubleday, 1973.
Analog 9, Doubleday, 1973.
The Analog Science Fact Reader, St. Martin's, 1974.
Analog Annual, Pyramid Publications, 1976.
Aliens, Futura, 1977.
The Best of Astounding, Baronet, 1977.
(With Trudy E. Bell) *Closeup: New Worlds,* St. Martin's, 1977.
Analog Yearbook, Baronet, 1978.
The Best of Analog, Baronet, 1978.
(With Don Myrus) *The Best of Omni Science Fiction,* four volumes, Omni Publications International, 1980–82.
Best of the Nebulas, St. Martin's, 1989.
(With Byron Preiss) *First Contact: The Search for Extraterrestrial Intelligence,* NAL Books, 1990.

OTHER

Contributor of numerous articles and short stories to periodicals, including *American Film, Astronomy, Science Digest, Smithsonian,* and *Writer.* Contributor to books, including *Blueprint for Space: Science Fiction to Science Fact,* edited by Frederick I. Ordway and Randy Liebermann, Smithsonian Institution Press, 1992, and *Future Quartet: Earth in the Year 2042: A Four-part Invention,* Morrow, 1994. Author of introduction, *The New Race for Space: The U.S. and Russia Leap to the Challenge for Unlimited Rewards,* by James E. Orberg, Stackpole, 1984.

Bova's manuscripts are housed in the David C. Paskow Collection, Temple University Libraries, Philadelphia, PA.

■ Sidelights

In large part, Ben Bova writes books to satisfy his internal curiosity. "That is what my novels do for me," the author noted in an essay for *Contemporary Authors Autobiography Series (CAAS).* "I begin with a few characters with a basic conflict, and then I turn them loose. The characters create the story. They show me what is happening. They resolve the original conflict." Bova's science and fantasy fiction—which includes novels such as *Exiled from Earth* and *Mars*—has been praised by critics for reflecting both a basic belief in human virtue and faith that scientific advances can create a positive future. When not creating new literary worlds, Bova has enjoyed great success as an editor, serving long terms with both *Analog* and *Omni* magazines. In summing up his work for *CAAS,* Bova remarked that he regards his novels as "explorations of the near future . . . tales of real human beings at the frontiers of knowledge. . . . I look forward to . . . a host of new possibilities. They are the grist for my mill. They are the raw

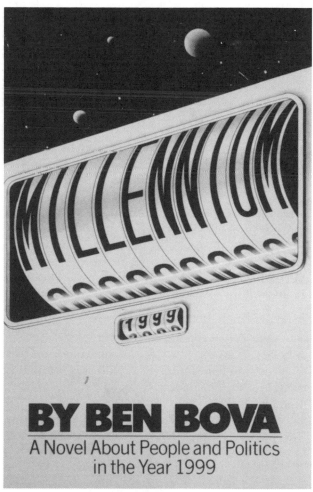

BY BEN BOVA
A Novel About People and Politics
in the Year 1999

Bova's interest in the future of society is highlighted in this novel from 1976.

material for exciting fiction, and the foundation of the world that we will live in tomorrow. I want to show that world to my readers."

Bova was born during the Great Depression. His family was deeply effected by the economic upheaval, especially after Bova's father lost his job. "The family fortune consisted of an unheated one-room apartment on which rent was owed, a seven week-old-baby (me), one dime, and a can of Campbell's pork and beans," Bova related in his essay.

Bova first became enamored with science during a field trip in junior high school, when what promised to be a boring day at a "museum" turned into a moment of personal discovery. The outing was spent at the Franklin Institute (a science museum) and the Fels Planetarium. While at the planetarium, Bova and his fellow students were treated to an astronomy show. "That moment changed my life entirely, " Bova recalled. "In that one instant I became hooked on astronomy." Young Bova enjoyed the planetarium so much that it became one of his favorite haunts for many years.

Bova wrote for his high school newspaper, *The Southron,* as well as the school yearbook. His favorite academic topic was science, which he hoped to study at the university level. When Bova applied to colleges, however, his entrance exams revealed a weakness in chemistry. He then turned to his second plan—applying to Temple University's journalism program. Bova was accepted and began a difficult schedule of work and studying. During his senior year at Temple, Bova started working as a reporter for the *Upper Darby News,* a weekly publication. The experience was, in the author's words, "great."

Early Career

In 1956, Bova realized a unique opportunity to mix his interest in science with his journalism background. He answered an engineering advertisement for the Glen L. Martin Company (later to become the giant Martin Marietta Corporation). After some quick talking, Bova was hired as a technical writer, later rising to technical director of the Vanguard satellite project. The writing assignment was the first position that allowed Bova to be directly involved in scientific work. (His task was to write about the process of placing the first

In this 1992 work, the author explores a subject that had fascinated him since childhood—the possible exploration and colonization of Mars.

American satellite into orbit, specifically to make complex scientific information accessible to the general public).

Screenwriting for the Massachusetts Institute of Technology was the second science-related position Bova held. In 1959, he also started making films for the Physical Science Study Committee. These educational films were made for high school students to encourage interest in and knowledge about physics. When this project ended, Bova moved to the Avco-Everett Research Laboratory. At Avco-Everett, Bova had access to groundbreaking research in such diverse areas as lasers and artificial hearts. Taking the job as a science writer in 1960, the author remained with Avco-Everertt until 1971. During this tenure, Bova also became marketing manager (all the while writing about science fact and fiction in his off-hours).

Bova's early works reflect his ongoing interest in various areas of the scientific spectrum. While his chief interest was still the exploration of space, Bova found time to write a number of science-based titles for young people, including *Giants of the Animal World* and *Reptiles since the World Began.*

Bova also wrote novels during these years, many of which concern how people use—and sometimes abuse—scientific developments. *The Weathermakers* and *The Dueling Machine,* for example, both reflect the author's long-standing concern about the misuse of scientific knowledge. *The Weathermakers* explores the societal problems that result when controlling the weather becomes a reality. *The Dueling Machine* focuses on the difficulties of maintaining equilibrium when one group of people learns to control a "peace machine." Elizabeth Haynes

of *School Library Journal* called *The Dueling Machine* a "fast-moving, thoughtful SF novel" that is "entertaining, above-average science fiction."

Bova also wrote short stories for a variety of publications—including *Analog*—during this time. Yet, even though he produced a fair amount of material during the years at Martin Aircraft, the Massachusetts Institute of Technology, and Avco-Everett, Bova wished for more writing time. Two changes helped make this possible, one personal and the other professional. During the late 1960s, Bova's first marriage became strained, eventually to the point of divorce. Then, in 1971, Bova became editor of *Analog* after the death of the periodical's long-standing manager, Joseph Campbell. "I was asked to take over [Campbell's] position. . . . In the world of science fiction, this was akin to being tapped to be Pope or drafted to run for President," he remembered in his essay. "You are afraid that the job is beyond your capabilities, but you dare not refuse it."

Editing *Analog* and *Omni*

Assuming the editorship of *Analog* was an enormous step for Bova. His worries about being capable were unfounded, however, and *Analog* continued to be a highly-regarded science fiction/fantasy publication. In fact, Bova was so successful at his new job that he eventually won a number of Hugo awards for his work. According to J. D. Brown in the *Dictionary of Literary Biography,* Bova "left his own distinctive stamp on *Analog.* . . . He granted more license to his writers on sexual topics; more significantly, he broadened the range of speculative fiction appearing in the magazine and heightened its quality. Bova's principle of selection was his belief that imaginative fiction had a special mission: to put a human face on the skeleton of scientifically plausible future."

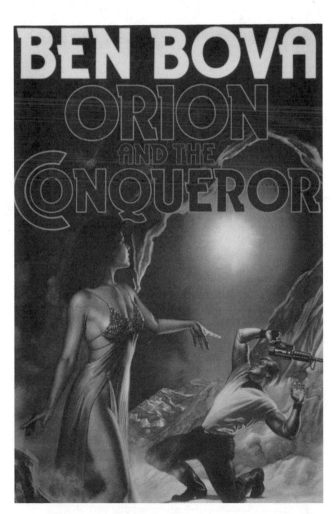

The "Orion" books—including this 1994 entry—feature strange new worlds and unique characterizations.

Bova's own writing during this time was balanced between fiction and factual books, as well as editing collections of shorter pieces. One of Bova's more popular fictional works of the period was *The Exiles Trilogy,* which was written over a four year period. The trilogy begins with *Exiled from Earth,* continues in *Flight of Exiles,* and wraps up with *End of Exile.* All three books tell how and why the world's genetic scientists are forcefully removed from Earth, and sent on a journey to another planet. The struggles which face each generation as the exile ship progresses to possible new planets form the basis for the books' action. In a typical response to the series, Beryl Robinson of *Horn Book* called *Exiled from Earth* a "rapidly-paced, tightly plotted story."

Other works Bova created while editing *Analog* focused on the political problems of power, and the social consequences of political decisions. *City of Darkness* presents New York City as a huge enclosed area inhabited by gangs where oblivious, wealthy people come to vacation. *The Multiple Man* offers a scenario in which there is more than one "president," while both *Millennium* and *Colony* highlight the relationship between the residents of bases on the Moon and the remainder of Earth's population. Edward Wood commented on the two latter novels in a review for *Analog:* "I'm sure I was not alone in being displeased when Ben Bova's *Millennium* failed to make it to the Hugo nominations for best novel of 1976. However, in *Colony* . . . Bova has written an even better novel which means it is his best to date."

Not all of Bova's writing embraces serious themes. Some of the author's satirical humor is found in *The Starcrossed,* which reveals the inner workings of a television show under three-dimensional production. Bova's experience as science advisor for an ill-fated science fiction series called *The Starlost* helped the author formulate the novel. Bova's *Starlost* job was to spot inaccuracies in the series' scripts and find inexpensive ways to correct them; unfortunately, all the author's suggestions were ignored. Bova noted in his essay that "I still cringe to think that my name is attached to [the show]."

The factual material Bova wrote while acting as editor of *Analog* shows his continued interest in the various sciences. Several works have special appeal for young readers, including *Workshops in Space,* which describes four different stations/ships: Skylab, Earth Resources Satellite, Apollo-Soyuz Mission, and the Space Shuttle. Other Bova nonfiction works concern writing science fiction. In *Through the Eyes of Wonder,* the author discusses the similarities that exist between science and science fiction. *Notes to a Science Fiction Writer* examines what a writer needs to do in order to successfully create science fiction works. In *Notes,* Bova writes that "there is no older, more honored, more demanding, more frustrating, more rewarding profession in the universe [than writing]. If the only thing that separates us from the beasts is our intelligence and our ability to speak, then

story-telling is the most uniquely human activity there can be."

Bova's editorship of *Analog* continued until 1978, when he once again decided to write full-time. He commented: "The truth is that although I enjoyed running *Analog* I really wanted to write full-time. That had been my ambition since I had been working on newspapers. And by this time my income from writing exceeded my salary as an editor. If I could write full-time, I reasoned, I would be completely happy and financially better off." Shortly after deciding to leave the periodical, Bova was asked to edit a new magazine called *Omni.* He refused, and was *then* asked to

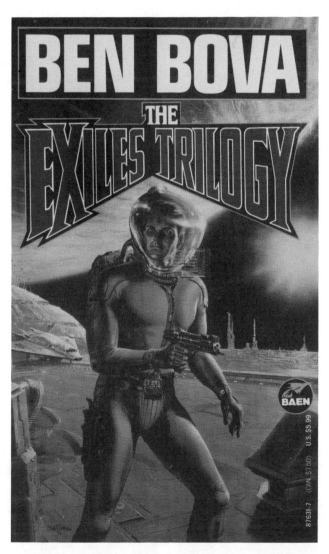

After the world is united under one governing body, a group of disenfranchised scientists and their familes are forced to make a new home for themselves among the stars.

be the fiction editor. Bova refused this also, but through a strange twist of fate, he eventually agreed to "sit in as fiction editor until they could find someone else. I found myself enjoying the job immensely." Two years later, Bova became head editor of *Omni*.

Writing Full Time

Bova's self-described focus since 1982 has been concentrating on "writing novels set in the near future, thematic novels that explore the interactions where big science meets big government or big corporate power." While fiction may be the author's primary focus, several of his nonfiction titles have received special critical attention for their timeliness. *Assured Survival: Putting the Star Wars Defense in Perspective* was the first book to seriously discuss the defense system proposed by President Reagan in 1993. A *Publishers Weekly* contributor stated that Bova's arguments in *Assured Survival* "command serious attention, and [Bova's] concept offers hope from the source that undid us in the first place: technology." *The Beauty of Light* was described by Rosemary Herbert of *Publishers Weekly* as demonstrating the author's "commitment to arousing in the general reader a sense of wonder about science." One of the special observations critics made about *Light* referred to Bova's ability to talk about science in a fashion the average reader understands. "What I'm particularly fascinated by is how the products of our minds, our science, our knowledge, our technology have become the leading force for change," Bova told Herbert.

Bova returned to fiction with works like *Triumph*, a novel which presents an alternative ending to World War II in which Josef Stalin is killed by radiation poisoning administered by Winston Churchill. A critic for *Library Journal* said that *Triumph* reveals Bova's "talent for revealing those lucky or unlucky" acts that make up history. In 1992, Bova published *Mars,* a book the author had wanted to write since childhood. Writing in *Voice of Youth Advocates*, Fred Lerner calls *Mars* a "convincing glimpse of the future."

Although he has covered many topics over the course of his writing career, Bova has always remained focused on an early literary aim: to explore the humanity's use of science and technology. Brown summed up Bova's continued literary success with this topic by noting that the author

has "consistently pushed beyond formal restrictions and sought new forms to render in human terms the potential meaning and experience of science in the future, a bright, humane future, as opposed to the dark collapse of civilization."

■ Works Cited

Review of *Assured Survival, Publishers Weekly,* September 21, 1984.

Bova, Ben, *Notes to a Science Fiction Writer,* Scribner's, 1977, p. 173.

Bova, Ben, essay in *Contemporary Authors Autobiography Series,* Volume 18, Gale, 1994, pp. 47–62.

Brown, J. D., "Ben Bova," *Dictionary of Literary Biography Yearbook: 1981,* Gale, 1982, pp. 164–168.

Haynes, Elizabeth, review of *The Dueling Machine, School Library Journal,* November, 1969, p. 126.

Herbert, Rosemary, "Ben Bova," *Publishers Weekly,* November 4, 1988, pp. 63–64.

Lerner, Fred, "Stand by for Mars," *Voice of Youth Advocates,* April, 1993, pp. 22–23.

Robinson, Beryl, review of *Exiled from Earth, Horn Book,* October, 1971.

Review of *Triumph, Library Journal,* December, 1992, p. 191.

Wood, Edward, Review of *Colony, Analog,* March, 1979, pp. 166–67.

■ For More Information See

BOOKS

Children's Literature Review, Volume 3, Gale, 1978, pp. 29–36.

Contemporary Literary Criticism, Volume 45, Gale, 1987, pp. 65–76.

Twentieth-Century Science-Fiction Writers, 2nd edition, St. James Press, 1986, pp. 68–69.

PERIODICALS

Booklist, April 1, 1993.

Choice, January, 1972.

Los Angeles Times, November 1, 1981.

Los Angeles Times Book Review, November 1, 1988.

Magazine of Fantasy and Science Fiction, January, 1972; November, 1976; July, 1977.

National Review, May 14, 1982.

New York Times Book Review, November 10, 1974; March 7, 1976; April 11, 1976; September 11, 1988.

School Library Journal, February, 1982.
Science Books and Films, March/April, 1982.
Science Fiction Review, September/October, 1978.
Times Literary Supplement, January 27, 1976.
Washington Post Book World, September 27, 1981.*

—Sketch by Hollis Helmeci

Patricia D. Cornwell

■ Personal

Full name, Patricia Daniels Cornwell; born June 9, 1956, in Miami, FL.; daughter of Sam (an attorney) and Marilyn (a secretary; maiden name, Zenner) Daniels; married Charles Cornwell, June 14, 1980 (divorced, 1990). *Education:* Attended King College; Davidson College, B.A., 1979. *Religion:* Presbyterian. *Avocational interests:* Tennis.

■ Addresses

Home—Richmond, VA. *Agent*—International Creative Management, 40 West 57th St., New York, NY 10019.

■ Career

Writer; founder and president, Bell Vision Productions, Los Angeles, CA. *Charlotte Observer,* Charlotte, NC, police reporter, 1979-81; Office of the Chief Medical Examiner, Richmond, VA, computer analyst, 1985-91. Volunteer police officer. *Member:* International Crime Writers Association, International Association of Chiefs of Police, International Association of Identification, Authors Guild, National Association of Medical Examiners.

■ Awards, Honors

Investigative reporting award, North Carolina Press Association, 1980, for a series on prostitution; Gold Medallion Book Award for biography, Evangelical Christian Publishers Association, 1985, for *A Time for Remembering;* John Creasey Award for best first crime novel, British Crime Writers' Association, Edgar Award for best first crime novel, Mystery Writers of America, Anthony Award, Boucheron—The World Mystery Convention, Macavity Award, Mystery Readers International, and French Prix du Roman d'Aventure, all 1990, all for *Postmortem;* Gold Dagger Award, British Crime Writers Association, 1994, for *Cruel and Unusual.*

■ Writings

CRIME NOVELS

Postmortem, Scribner, 1990.

Body of Evidence, Scribner, 1991.
All That Remains, Scribner, 1992.
Cruel and Unusual, Scribner, 1993.
The Body Farm, Scribner, 1994.
From Potter's Field, Scribner, 1995.

OTHER

A Time for Remembering: The Story of Ruth Bell Graham (biography), Harper, 1983.

■ Adaptations

Brilliance Corp. released a sound recording of *Body of Evidence* in 1992; sound recordings are also available for *Postmortem, All That Remains, Cruel and Unusual, The Body Farm,* and *From Potter's Field.* Negotiations are in progress for the film rights to *From Potter's Field.*

■ Sidelights

"I'm not sure I could have read my last book if I hadn't written it," Patricia Cornwell told Sandra McElwaine in *Harper's Bazaar.* "The violence is so real, I think it would have scared me to death." Since 1990, Cornwell has made a career of scar-

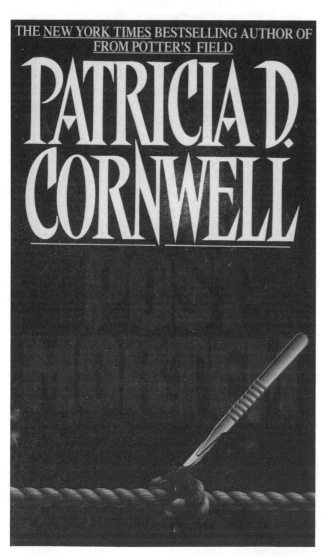

Cornwell received much critical praise for this novel which introduced intrepid investigator—and Chief Medical Examiner—Kay Scarpetta.

ing people to death with her popular novels about medical examiner Dr. Kay Scarpetta. Cornwell weaves technologically dazzling forensic sleuthing with villains that chill readers to the bone. Her details are believable because Cornwell did research in the Virginia medical examiner's office and witnessed scores of autopsies, in addition to going out on police homicide runs.

Cornwell was born in Miami, Florida. When she was only five years old, she had an experience that was to shape her for the rest of her life. A security guard whom she knew molested her near her parent's home. Her brother scared him away, but she was left with a fear of random violence and being victimized that would later show in her personal and professional life.

When she was still young, her parents divorced and she moved with her mother and brother to North Carolina. The divorce was devastating for Cornwell, for she missed her family in Miami terribly. Her mother later suffered a nervous breakdown, leaving Cornwell to be cared for by neighbors and strangers, which further fed her feelings of isolation. Tennis became her solace. She was a young tennis star in her town, and continued when she went to King College in Tennessee. She soon dropped out of school, however, when she felt her skills were lacking and she was losing matches.

Moving back home to Montreat, North Carolina, she leaned on friend Ruth Graham, the wife of evangelist Billy Graham, for support. It was Graham who encouraged her to pursue writing. "I felt she had real ability," Graham told Joe Treen in *People.* "I've kept every note I ever got from her." With Graham's encouragement, Cornwell went back to school at Davidson College in North Carolina, majoring in English. Right after graduation she married Charles Cornwell, one of her former professors, and won a job as a crime reporter at the *Charlotte Observer.*

She dove into crime writing with vigor. "I had a compulsion to get close to every story. I really wanted to solve crimes," she told McElwaine. Because of her fearless work, she was honored with an award for a series she did on prostitution. Unfortunately, just when she felt her career was getting underway, her husband decided that he wanted to become a minister, and the couple moved to Richmond, Virginia, where he attended

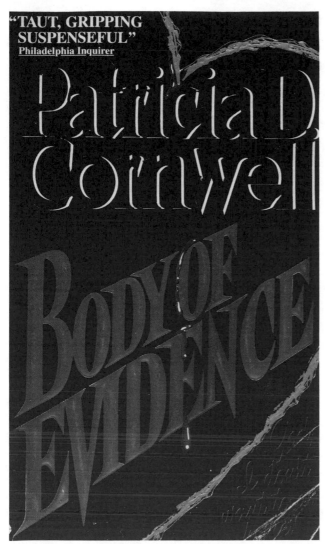

"TAUT, GRIPPING
SUSPENSEFUL"
Philadelphia Inquirer

Patricia D. Cornwell

BODY OF EVIDENCE

In Cornwell's 1991 novel, Scarpetta must match wits with a killer whose obsession with a novelist turns deadly.

Union Theological Seminary. She didn't cherish this move. "I did not want to give up the *Observer*," she told Treen. "It was a very bad time for me." She was left to virtually fend on her own in a new town, with no job.

Cornwell decided it would be a good time to write a biography of her good friend, Graham, and that kept her busy for a few years until it was published in 1983. She had always pictured herself as a novelist, so she decided to try writing crime novels with the information she had gathered as a reporter. She realized that she would need to do more in-depth research to make her murder plots seem more believable. A friend recommended that she might try talking to the

deputy medical examiner at the Virginia Morgue. Cornwell took the advice and made an appointment with pathologist Dr. Marcella Fierro.

Appointment with Murder

Her first appointment with Fierro was fascinating to Cornwell. There was a whole world of high-tech forensic procedures that she knew nothing about. "I was shocked by two things," Cornwell told Joanne Tangorra in *Publishers Weekly*. "One, by how fascinating it was, and two, by how absolutely little I knew about it. I realized I had no idea what a medical examiner would do—Did they put on gloves, wear lab coats and surgical greens? They do none of the above." She told Fierro about her ideas for a murder novel and discussed some of the gory details.

Cornwell and Fierro hit it off so well that she asked for another interview, and soon became a regular visitor at the forensic center. Fierro was so impressed with Cornwell that she offered the former reporter some technical writing projects for the morgue. She took the assignments, knowing that this was the perfect chance for her to absorb more of the forensic knowledge she found so fascinating.

She also became a volunteer police officer. "Though a lot of it was mundane," she related to Tangorra, "I got a taste of what it's like to be out there in the rank and file." She earned the right to tag along with homicide detectives on their late-night "graveyard shifts," gaining first-hand knowledge of violence and murder by surveying the crime scenes. Cornwell watched everything the detectives did, and later used that knowledge when writing about police in her novels.

Because she was proving to be an excellent and dedicated employee for the morgue, they eventually gave her a full-time job as a computer analyst. It was at that time that she began writing her crime novels, with a main character who was a male detective and a minor character named Dr. Kay Scarpetta, a female medical examiner. She had bad luck marketing these novels—they were rejected by every publisher to whom they were sent, and she had a hard time getting anyone to even look at the third one. It was also proving impossible for her to find an agent who might help her sell her work.

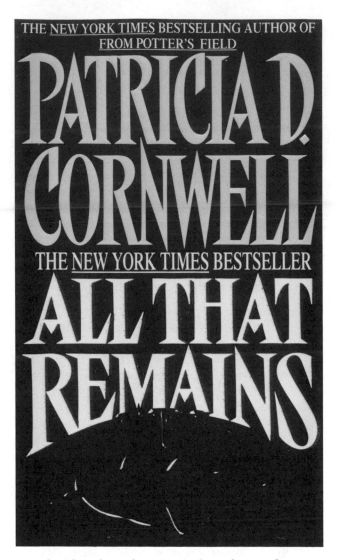

THE <u>NEW YORK TIMES</u> BESTSELLING AUTHOR OF
FROM POTTER'S FIELD

PATRICIA D. CORNWELL

THE <u>NEW YORK TIMES</u> BESTSELLER

ALL THAT REMAINS

An abandoned car becomes a key clue as Scarpetta tries to decipher the mystery behind four couples' disappearances.

At her wits' end, Cornwell decided to send the first few chapters of one of her novels to the celebrated mystery writer P. D. James. James wrote back quickly, saying that she did not critique the manuscripts of others, but also enclosed a very encouraging note. It was enough to keep Cornwell from quitting. With equal aplomb, Cornwell asked Sara Ann Fried, an editor at Mysterious Press—a publisher who had already rejected her manuscripts—if she could offer any ideas. "I needed to know if it was worth it to keep trying, and she was very encouraging," she told Tangorra. "And she gave me some very sage advice. She said that I should write about what I knew, instead of esoteric poisonings set in river mansions somewhere. And she advised me to make Scarpetta the main

character. The male detective just wasn't believable."

In Richmond, Virginia, in the summer of 1987, a series of horrible rape-murders had been taking place. One of the victims was a young female physician, who was known by many in the morgue. Cornwell was very moved by the murders and how they affected the victim's colleagues. "I wondered, if I made [Scarpetta] the main character, what she would do," she related to Tangorra. "I wanted to approach it from a psychological perspective—Scarpetta projecting onto the life of this murdered female physician and identifying with her. That's how *Postmortem* evolved. I never studied the details of the cases because I didn't want to be influenced by them."

Morgue Mayhem

While on a family vacation in Miami, Cornwell was invited to go to the dedication of the new morgue there. Fortuitously, while there she met Edna Buchanan, the famous crime reporter and mystery writer. They talked for a while, and Buchanan ended up giving Cornwell the name of her agent. Cornwell packed off the manuscript to him, and after an anxious few months, he decided to represent her. In 1988, he sent the manuscript off to publishers. It was rejected by several houses before Scribner decided to purchase it for the modest price of $6,000.

Postmortem, published in 1990, told the story of the fictional Chief Medical Examiner of Virginia, Dr. Kay Scarpetta. Scarpetta is racing against the clock to try to track down a rapist-murderer whose victims are well-to-do Richmond women. She has an arsenal of high-tech forensic equipment to aid her, including a computer fingerprint matcher and DNA testing equipment, but she sometimes lacks the support she would like from her male colleagues, some of whom are extremely chauvinistic. Critics were impressed with Cornwell's first book, and especially with her strong main character. Charles Champlin, writing in the *Los Angeles Times,* commented that *Postmortem* "is a first-rate first thriller, and I hope to run into Dr. Scarpetta again." The book won several important awards in both the U.S. and Great Britain, becoming the first novel to win the Edgar, Creasey, Anthony, and Macavity Awards all in the same year.

Postmortem sold very well, and Cornwell, not tired of her character, quickly finished the next book of Scarpetta's adventures, *Body of Evidence.* Published in 1991, the story centers on Beryl Madison, a young woman who is writing a controversial book. She has received death threats and is being harassed. Shortly after she reports these events she is murdered—apparently after allowing the killer to enter her home. Scarpetta must once again use tiny bits of evidence to track down the brutal killer. *Los Angeles Times Book Review* critic Champlin commented that the novel "lacks the startling freshness of the debut," but adds that "the essential mystery is interesting and well-plotted, strewn with some vivid characters and suggesting again that Scarpetta is here to stay." Simi-

larly, a *Publishers Weekly* critic noted that the novel contains "plenty of complex, satisfying forensic sleuthing" that leads to "a powerful conclusion." *Body of Evidence* sold exceptionally well, and was listed on the *New York Times* best-seller list, putting Cornwell into the upper echelon of today's crime writers.

Because of the success of *Body of Evidence,* Cornwell was given an advance of nearly $1 million to produce the next two Scarpetta books, *All That Remains* and *Cruel and Unusual.* Published in 1992, *All That Remains* follows Scarpetta as she tries to find evidence for a series of teenagers being killed in gruesome "couple murders." Bodies of the victims are hidden in rural areas and often not found for a year, leaving few clues at the murder sites. When one of the victims is identified as the daughter of a important government official, Scarpetta is under the gun to find the killer. Champlin was thrilled with the author's latest venture into morgue mystery, commenting that Cornwell "seems to get better and better, surer in her delineations of characters and relationships, subtler in her plotting. . . . The Scarpetta series is one of the best." "Cornwell demonstrates that clues about character are as vital as physical evidence," a *Publishers Weekly* reviewer stated, terming *All That Remains* "her best novel to date." Carolyn E. Gecan wrote in *School Library Journal* that Cornwell's gory, yet realistic books will appeal to a wide variety of audiences, adding: "Mystery-loving YAs and fans of Cornwell's previous novels will enjoy her latest."

In 1993, Cornwell published *Cruel and Unusual,* the fourth book in her Scarpetta series. This book features another serial murderer—this time, one who is predisposed to cannibalism and mutilates his victims in a distinctive fashion. The cases Scarpetta is finding bear a strong resemblance to cases that happened a few years ago, but the man convicted of those crimes is locked up in jail on death row. The latest rash of murders makes Scarpetta question whether the right person was identified as the killer. To make matters worse, she has to defend herself against someone on her staff who seems to be deliberately fouling up her work. *New York Times Book Review* mystery critic Marilyn Stasio praised the book for the "expert engineering" of its plot, calling it "grimly fascinating." Patricia Craig similarly found the book to be of high quality, commenting in the *Times Literary Supplement* that Cornwell "achieves a high level

THE NEW YORK TIMES BESTSELLER

PATRICIA D. CORNWELL

"CORNWELL'S BEST" Washington Post Book World

Too Late

Scarpetta is stumped when a dead man's fingerprints turn up at a new crime scene in this 1993 mystery.

of entertainment and intrigue." *Cruel and Unusual* earned Cornwell Britain's most prestigious crime writer's award, the Gold Dagger, making her the first American woman thus honored.

In 1994, Cornwell released *The Body Farm,* possibly her most gruesome novel to date. This book finds Scarpetta in a difficult personal situation while she is trying to solve another tough professional puzzle. She is having an affair with a married F.B.I. agent named Benton Wesley. Meanwhile, police lieutenant Pete Marino, her frequent professional collaborator, is going through a divorce and wants to start a more personal liaison with Scarpetta. While investigating the murder of eleven-year-old Emily Steiner, Scarpetta discovers evidence that points to serial killer Temple Gault, whom she nearly captured in her last book. In order to gain more substantial evidence, Scarpetta must go to the body farm, a name given to a research facility where decomposing bodies are studied to learn more about times of death. She also has to deal with her brilliant but troublesome niece Lucy, who is working for the F.B.I. and gets herself entangled in a scandal.

Dr. Scarpetta's adventures continued to win praise from reviewers. *Library Journal* contributor Wilda Williams, for instance, noted that the novel is exceptional because of "deeper characterizations," and called the book "emotionally satisfying reading." *People* reviewer Pam Lambert remarked that the crime novel contains "all the pacing and suspense Cornwell's fans have come to expect," and despite finding the ending "unconvincing," indicated that *The Body Farm* "will cause a few sleepless nights." Bill Kent, writing in the *New York Times Book Review,* was more critical of the book. He was disappointed with the "cheaped out" cliffhanger ending of *Cruel & Unusual,* and faulted Cornwell's plots for developing "a contrived, rococo complexity." While he asserted that *The Body Farm* "may not be the best novel in the Scarpetta series," he admitted that "the book nearly redeems itself when it dwells on the irreversibly tragic effects of violence on the human spirit." He also credited the Scarpetta series, with its competent and sympathetic heroine, for bringing "new life to the moribund detective fiction genre."

Fans have also appreciated Cornwell's portrayals of Scarpetta, and the 1995 installment *From Potter's Field* earned the number one position on the *New York Times* bestseller list shortly after its publication. Temple Gault once again becomes the focus of Scarpetta's efforts after she is called onto the case of a homeless woman found murdered in New York City's Central Park. As Scarpetta searches to find the woman's identity, she becomes drawn into a battle of wits with the psychopath Gault, who has stolen her credit card number and broken into the FBI's central computer—and has his eye on Scarpetta or her niece Lucy as his next victim. "Nobody can make the details of forensic investigation as riveting [as Cornwell can]," a *Kirkus Reviews* critic observed, also praising the sustained suspense of the novel. With its "terrifying, knuckle-whitening, breathtaking climax," Emily Melton wrote in *Booklist, From Potter's Field* once again establishes Cornwell as "one of today's most talented crime fiction writers, an author who keeps her readers on the edges of their seats with magnificent plotting, masterful writing, and marvelous suspense."

The Source of Scarpetta

In her personal life, Cornwell bears a surprising resemblance to her fictitious sleuth. Treen notes that they are both "blond, from Miami, divorced, childless, drive Mercedes-Benzes, like to cook and . . . live in the same posh neighborhood." The author maintains that there is a simple reason to keep her fictional sleuth's life so similar to her own. She commented to Tangorra that "I try to use experiences from my own life to give her, and the books, greater authenticity. . . . These things don't overpower the story; they're just things I know."

Because of Cornwell's extensive research into violent and abusive crime, she has become intensely protective of her personal safety. Her home is monitored by a guard and by high-tech security devices. She has a gun on her bedstand, and frequently takes guns with her when she travels near or far. She commented to McElwaine that "Guns are a necessary evil. I have been to so many crime scenes and have images in my mind that will haunt me the rest of my life. . . . You cannot be exposed to violence and walk away unchanged." Cornwell refuses to become a victim of violence blindly. "The most important thing I have learned is that every victim of violence has one thing in common," she told McElwaine. "They all think, 'It can't happen to me.'"

Cornwell's popular writings may have given inspiration to one man in the wrong way. After discovering that he had committed a murder, police searching the suspect's house unearthed a copy of Cornwell's first book, *Postmortem.* Apparently, his crime was strikingly similar to one of the murders in her book. Cornwell took it all in stride, telling Treen that "People get inspired in very strange ways. . . . [Some] commit violence after reading the Old Testament for that matter."

Cornwell is equally balanced when discussing the success of her books. "I don't know why this has caught on the way it has," she told Treen. "It's almost if Scarpetta has a life of her own and she's out there taking over the world." Cornwell, however, refuses to glorify death in her novels, choosing instead to show the horror of violence. "Some people write horrible, sadistic scenes," she told McElwaine. "Death and pain are not sexy. They leave terrible marks that are ugly and last forever." Cornwell has no plans for abandoning her popular scientist-sleuth in the future. "I get more interested in her with each novel," she told Tangorra, "and as long as I continue to grow and change, so will she."

■ Works Cited

Review of *All That Remains, Publishers Weekly,* June 15, 1992, p. 89.

Review of *Body of Evidence, Publishers Weekly,* December 7, 1990, p. 76.

Champlin, Charles, review of *Postmortem, Los Angeles Times Book Review,* February 11, 1990, p. 5.

Champlin, Charles, review of *Body of Evidence, Los Angeles Times Book Review,* February 10, 1991, p. 9.

Champlin, Charles, review of *All That Remains, Los Angeles Times Book Review,* September 20, 1992, p. 8.

Craig, Patricia, review of *Cruel and Unusual, Times Literary Supplement,* July 16, 1993, p. 22.

Review of *From Potter's Field, Kirkus Reviews,* June 1, 1995.

Gecan, Carolyn E., review of *All That Remains, School Library Journal,* December, 1992, pp. 146-147.

Kent, Bill, "Among the Cadavers," review of *The Body Farm, New York Times Book Review,* September 16, 1994, p. 38-39.

Lambert, Pam, review of *The Body Farm, People,* October 3, 1994, pp. 37-38.

McElwaine, Sandra, "Autopsy, She Wrote," *Harper's Bazaar,* August, 1992, pp. 46, 148.

Melton, Emily, review of *From Potter's Field, Booklist,* May 1, 1995.

Stasio, Marilyn, review of *Cruel and Unusual, New York Times Book Review,* April 4, 1993, p. 19.

Tangorra, Joanne, "PW Interviews: Patricia D. Cornwell," *Publishers Weekly,* February 15, 1991, pp. 71-72.

Treen, Joe, "Murder, She Writes," *People,* August 24, 1992, pp. 71-72.

Williams, Wilda, review of *The Body Farm, Library Journal,* September 1, 1994, p. 213.

■ For More Information See

PERIODICALS

Armchair Detective, winter, 1991, p. 32.

Entertainment Weekly, June 26, 1992, p. 73.

Los Angeles Times, March 28, 1991, p. F12.

Los Angeles Times Book Review, June 13, 1993, p. 11.

Mystery Scene, January, 1990, pp. 56-57.

Newsweek, August 3, 1992, p. 55; July 5, 1993, p. 56.

New York Times Book Review, January 7, 1990, p. 29; August 23, 1992, p. 17.

Time, September 14, 1992, p. 77; October 3, 1994, p. 84.

Times Literary Supplement, July 17, 1992, p. 20.

Tribune Books (Chicago), February 3, 1991, p. 7; August 9, 1992, p. 4.

Washingtonian, June, 1993, p. 67.

Washington Post Book World, January 21, 1990, p. 6; February 17, 1991, p. 10; July 26, 1992, p. 1; June 20, 1993, p. 6.

—*Sketch by Nancy Rampson*

Brian Doyle

nadian Authors Association; Mr. Christie Book of the Year Award; three time runner-up, Governor General's Award, Canadian Authors Association.

■ Personal

Born August 12, 1935, in Ottawa, Ontario, Canada; son of Hulbert and Charlotte (Duff) Doyle; married Jacqueline Aronson, December 26, 1960; children: Megan, Ryan. *Education:* Carleton University, B.J. and B.A., 1957.

■ Addresses

Home—539 Rowanwood, Ottawa, Ontario K2A 3C9, Canada.

■ Career

Writer; Glebe Collegiate, and Ottawa Technical High School, Ottawa, Ontario, Canada, high school English teacher 1960-94. Worked variously as a journalist, waiter, taxi driver, bricklayer, and jazz singer.

■ Awards, Honors

Book of the Year awards, Canadian Library Association, 1983, for *Up to Low,* and 1989, for *Easy Avenue;* Vicky Metcalf Body of Work Award, Ca-

■ Writings

(Compiler and editor) *The Who's Who of Children's Literature,* Evelyn, 1968.

Hey, Dad!, Groundwood Books, 1978.
You Can Pick Me Up at Peggy's Cove, Groundwood Books, 1979.
Up to Low, Groundwood Books, 1982.
Angel Square, Groundwood Books, 1984.
Easy Avenue, Groundwood Books, 1988.
Covered Bridge, Groundwood Books, 1990.
Spud Sweetgrass, Groundwood Books, 1992.

Also author of children's plays.

■ Adaptations

You Can Pick Me Up at Peggy's Cove was adapted into a film directed by Don McBrearty; *Angel Square* was adapted into a film directed by Ann Wheeler.

■ Sidelights

"Hitchhiking, masturbation, menstruation, all those problems in kids' books from adultery to zits, those aren't the real concerns; those are the problems that adults see in kids," writer Brian Doyle states in an interview with Amy Vanderhoof for *Quill and Quire,* "their real concerns are the classic concerns, the ones with capital letters." He is referring to the big issues—courage, love, strength, and fear. Whether Doyle's books have a contemporary or an historical setting, the award-winning Canadian author is hailed for his insight into the inner lives of his characters, his accomplished storytelling, and his "delicious way with metaphors." His books often incorporate a physical journey as a parallel to the emotional growth of the characters, resulting in what critics cite as complex writing that doesn't patronize young people. Humor also plays a key role in Doyle's books, with scenes that are both dark and slapstick. Set largely in Ottawa, Ontario, where Doyle spent his youth and where he still lives, his stories benefit from a specific and particular atmosphere that sidesteps regionalism to become recognizable and even universal.

Doyle's family, both past and present, and his memories, play key roles in his fiction. When the writer was young, his family spent winters in an ethnically divided section of Ottawa, and summers in a town called Low, in the Gatineau Hills about forty miles north of the city. Though he was a city boy, living in Low taught Doyle much about the country, especially one childhood summer when he helped out at his godfather's nearby farm, learning the chores and carrying "a well-full of water," he recalls in his essay for *Something about the Author Autobiography Series (SAAS).* Doyle's father built the family's log cabin, its location close to where Doyle's great-grandfather Mickey Doyle settled. In an interview with Sonia Benson for *Something about the Author (SATA),* the novelist relates that Mickey "was ten years old when he got off the boat in 1847; both his parents had died on the ship of cholera so he wound up alone in a bush camp up north of Iowa." Mickey coped very well, relocating to Canada and eventually raising a family.

Though no one in Doyle's family made their living as a writer, telling stories was part of Doyle's childhood and he remembers both his father and grandfather were adept at spinning a yarn. In his *SATA* interview, Doyle admits that "neither of them were bookish. I never saw my grandfather read a book, but he was constantly reciting verse—songs and poems, ballads mostly—about this adventure and that adventure." He describes

As a young teacher, Doyle often found himself at odds with "the system," such as the time he was fired for not wearing a tie.

his father in the same interview as "the best raconteur I ever met," though he wasn't literary. Among the most highly praised aspects of Doyle's writing is his well-tuned ear, a skill he traces back to these two paternal influences. "For me listening to my father and grandfather was better than any entertainment—even going to the show on Saturdays."

Doyle's direct literary influence came largely through his mother, who, he says in his interview with Benson, "wrote well and wrote privately." Though she kept her work to herself, she showed her son her poetry; "Sea Savour," the poem that opens Doyle's second novel, *You Can Pick Me Up at Peggy's Cove,* is by his mother. His older sister Pamela, who died at 16, was also an influence— her struggles with Down's Syndrome and his strong recollection of the toll it took on Pamela and on his mother have led to the several characters with disabilities in his stories.

School was a mixed bag of success and failure for Doyle. He pole vaulted, played football, and won medals in gymnastics. In his *SAAS* essay, Doyle describes a geometry exam in high school at Christmas time in which he got only three of 100 questions right; by Easter, he scored ninety-nine out of 100. "It's as though I just suddenly woke up! The teacher is convinced I cheated." When Doyle was nominated for Head Boy, his Vice Principal removed his name from the list, telling him he was a show-off and a bum, and that he'd never amount to anything. "When he says this I realize I've been a pain for six years," continues Doyle in *SAAS*. "But what he says about never 'amounting' to anything. That hurts."

Doyle was already sending short stories out by this time, having begun to write at about the age

Megan finds herself at odds with her family when she must take a trip with them rather than stay home and be president of the "Down with Boys" club.

of ten. "The first writing I did was in the snow," he explains in his *SATA* interview. "I wrote 'Gerald is a bastard.' My father came out, and he brought me in the house, and he put a piece of paper in front of me and gave me a pencil. Then he said, 'Say some more, but don't write it in the snow because he'll see it.'" After high school, Doyle enrolled at Carleton College, and it was here that he met his future wife Jacqueline Aronson. Armed with a degree in journalism, Doyle spent four months as a reporter for the *Toronto Telegram*. But the rewards of journalism were too fleeting and he craved what he describes in *SAAS* as "a place to work where people respect the printed word."

Teaching Inspires More Writing

Doyle's next career move was to return to Ottawa and begin teaching high school English. To his surprise, he found that rather than discussions of literature and interpretation, much of his work as a teacher involved getting his students to write. Doyle's first published piece of fiction, a short story, appeared in the literary magazine *Fiddlehead* in 1960.

At the same time his writing career was beginning, Doyle and his wife became involved in local theater, an interest he carried over into his teaching. After several teaching positions, Doyle was named head of the English department at Glebe Collegiate, the school he would later incorporate into his fourth novel, *Angel Square*. His series of plays and musicals from this time period, which he describes as a great pleasure and, as he tells Agnes Nieuwenhuizen in an interview for *Magpies*, were "very big in our community," became "the flagship event of Glebe Collegiate." The school productions led to some screenwriting for television and radio as well.

Teaching and writing have always been largely separate worlds for Doyle. He credits his own children with giving him an understanding of the inner lives of children and with eventually leading him to rediscover a similar aspect of himself—and inspiring him to write his first novel, *Hey, Dad!*, which appeared in 1978. The book is the happy accident of a family road trip across Canada. Both Doyle and his daughter Megan kept journals of the vacation, showing each other their diaries at the end of the summer. And as Doyle arranged their writing into paragraphs, he began to see a story emerge. He observes in his interview with Nieuwenhuizen, "I made it funny, but included stuff she had been grappling with. Stuff about time and mortality. I read bits to the neighborhood kids and when they started asking about what was going to happen NEXT, I realized the story went beyond family interest."

Fearing that teenagers would find his work too complex and wide-ranging, the first few publishers Doyle sent the manuscript to sent it back to him. But then a friend directed Doyle to Patsy Aldana, who had just launched Groundwood publishers, and who saw that the story of a thirteen-year-old girl's attempts to come to terms with her strong love and frequent hate for her own family—and the disgust she feels at travelling with them—would strike a chord with other young people. Doyle set about making what he terms substantial changes, rewriting the piecemeal original into what he describes to Vanderhoof as "one tone, one voice." Megan, the book's narrator (who shares her name with his daughter), describes it as a chronicle of "how I hated my Dad for a while for some reason and how I loved him again for some reason and how I almost ruined a trip my family took to the Pacific Ocean and how all of a sudden I got independent for a while that summer when I was thirteen."

Reviewing the book for *In Review: Canadian Books for Children,* Irma McDonough praises the trip from Ottawa to Vancouver for its "subliminally educational" lesson in Canada's geography and the subtlety with which Doyle mirrors this in the character's internal geography. Echoing this theme, Wendy R. Katz writes in *Canadian Children's Literature* that Doyle's young characters' relationships extend outside the immediate family, allowing them to find a place for themselves "in relation to people beyond the family, friends and strangers alike, to nature, and to the universe."

Ryan, the teenage narrator of Doyle's next book, *You Can Pick Me Up at Peggy's Cove,* finds himself shunted off to his aunt's house for the summer while his father undergoes a mid-life crisis, or what Ryan calls a "C.O.L." (change of life). Unhappy to be away from his father in the tourist-ridden Nova Scotia seaside town of Peggy's Cove, Ryan (who shares his name with Doyle's son) begins a project of petty thievery with a local boy. He also spends time with one of the town fishermen and his mute partner. Ryan hopes to lure his father to Peggy's Cove by getting himself into trouble and needing to be rescued; as a means to this end he keeps a record of these dangers in a long letter to his father. By the end of the summer, when his father does in fact return, Ryan has confronted punishment, loss, and death, finally reaching a new understanding of himself and his father. Katz notes that "Doyle's emphasis is not on the adventures the children have but on their psychological states of being," an idea echoed by Adele Ashby who deems the book "sensitive, insightful, funny, sad and true," in her review for *Quill and Quire.*

This CLA "Book of the Year" winner tells the story of Tommy and Baby Bridget as they deal with life, love and death.

Into His Own Childhood

With both of his children immortalized in novels, Doyle decided to delve into his own childhood in the Gatineau Hills for *Up to Low*. Set in the middle of the twentieth century, its narrator is Young Tommy, who has just returned to the small town of Low and finds himself obsessed with eighteen-year-old Baby Bridget. She is the one-armed daughter of Mean Hughie, who is remembered for slapping his daughter when her limb was severed by a runaway binder: he told her she got in the way. His body wasted with cancer, Mean Hughie has retreated to the forest to die, and Bridget seeks him out to try to heal herself, if not physically, then psychologically. Combining mythic elements with the realism of his earlier work, Doyle shows himself to be capable of tapping into his own childhood, making use of both his memories and his imagination.

Reviewing *Up to Low* for *Maclean's*, Anne Collins points out that the plot may sound "grim," but "Doyle has a cartoon way with character that lets him get away with a plot packed with excess. It also lets him get away with his big themes of redemption, forgiveness, and love." Although critic Mary Ainslie Smith, writing in *Books in Canada*, deems Doyle's humor "often black, to say the least, and sometimes heavy, of the outhouse and open-coffin variety," Sarah Ellis of *Horn Book* lauds the novel for its "deadpan comic writing that is as strong as binder twine." The story begins with Tommy's arrival and ends with Mean Hughie's death, two events that culminate in Tommy and Bridget discovering their strengths and the power of affection for another person. In *Canadian Children's Literature,* Carol Munro maintains that "the characters are sketched with great skill, in simple strong strokes of anecdote, and much of the uniqueness of the individuals is displayed through the colorful crackerbarrel chatter of the others."

Reprising the characters of *Up to Low*, Doyle moves the action of his next book, *Angel Square,* to Ottawa, where Tommy narrates a tale of ethnic strife in the Lowertown section of the city in 1945. To reach the school he attends, which also enrolls Jewish children, Tommy must cross Angel Square, which is home to two other schools, one for French Canadians and one for the Irish. At Christmas time, the rampant anti-Semitism of the town erupts in the beating and serious injury of

Hubbo O' Driscoll's first year in high school begins badly when he must choose between his poor friends and the rich clique.

Mr. Rosenberg, father of Tommy's best friend Sammy. Driven to take action and find the perpetrators, Tommy emulates his favorite radio hero, the Shadow, and resourcefully puts the entire community of diverse neighbors to work to help him. Tommy also has to come to terms with his handicapped sister Pamela, whom he sees as "an angel who couldn't know anything," his several bad teachers and one good one, and his own perceptions of his world.

Angel Square is "a poignant message of tolerance and love," describes a reviewer in *Children's Book News.* A *Publishers Weekly* contributor, however, found this message of tolerance "heavy-handed," and Todd Morning, writing in the *School Library*

Journal, takes issue with the "forced" humor of the novel and the too-easily identified attacker of Mr. Rosenberg. Morning notes that "Doyle is best at capturing the feel of post-war Ottawa, with its wintry landscapes and ethnic strife. Tommy is an appealing hero—resourceful and courageous."

Doyle keeps his Lowertown setting but introduces the orphan Hubbo O'Driscoll as the narrator of his fifth novel, *Easy Avenue.* Poverty forces Hubbo and his distant relative, identified only as Mrs. O'Driscoll, to move from Lowertown to the Uplands Emergency Shelter. The lines between rich and poor are distinct in this part of town, a fact that becomes even more clear as Hubbo and his guardian become involved with the Glebe Collegiate Institute—he as a student, she as the cleaning woman. Hubbo finds himself pulled in two different directions as he begins to make friends at the shelter and also gets hired as a companion to a wealthy old woman. His divided loyalties are further tested when he becomes the recipient of money from a mysterious source and becomes alienated from his guardian (pretending not to know her) and his girlfriend from the shelter, Fleurette. The death of his employer and his new income reveal a deep generosity in Hubbo that helps him reconcile the two sides of his background.

With its contrasts of rich and poor, its characters either ashamed by their poverty or snobbily attached to their wealth, and its between-two-worlds protagonist, *Easy Avenue* is often compared to Charles Dickens' *Great Expectations* by reviewers. In *Canadian Children's Literature,* Lionel Adey sees this similarity but feels that "the hero's laid-back ridicule of fools in office" recalls J.D. Salinger's *The Catcher in the Rye.* Writing in *Maclean's,* Pamela Young celebrates the "delightful mix of comedy, irony and sentiment" in the story, concluding that "*Easy Avenue* offers ample cause for rejoicing."

"I'm Free! Absolutely Free!"

The idea for Doyle's next book, *Covered Bridge,* came from one of the author's very first jobs, which was to help tear down a covered bridge near Low, "my first real job doing adult work," Doyle comments in *SAAS.* In the novel, Doyle brings back Hubbo O'Driscoll, but his mission this time is to save the covered bridge slated for razing. The O'Driscolls now live on a farm in the

country, within sight of the covered bridge, whose history includes a pair of tragic local lovers, Oscar and Ophelia. Suffering from a brain tumor, Ophelia jumped to her death from the bridge and Oscar visits her grave daily. Hubbo sets himself the task of keeping the bridge intact despite the plans to destroy it, resulting in what Nieuwenhuizen calls a "hauntingly beautiful tribute to conserving and respecting old things." Sandra Martin, writing in *Quill and Quire,* takes the book to task for being "a short story tarted up as a novel," but acknowledges that Doyle "cleverly and amusingly" draws a wide-ranging cast of characters.

In 1991, Doyle retired from teaching, leaving him more time to write. As he tells Nieuwenhuizen, "you're not free as a baby or a child or in school

In this second "Hubbo" novel, the young teen helps a lonely ghost and her lover when the covered bridge where the couple meet is marked for destruction.

or at work or as a parent. But now I'm free. Absolutely free!" The discipline of daily writing continues, however, as a routine in which Doyle believes. "I don't enjoy daily writing any more than an athlete enjoys going out and doing drills," he reveals in his *SATA* interview. "You know, Shakespeare wrote his sonnets just as an exercise, although they are beautiful. He was always working on one because it kept him in shape. It's work."

Spud Sweetgrass is the title of both the seventh of Doyle's novels and its narrator. Spud, who describes himself as part Irish and part Abo (Aboriginal), works in a chipwagon (fast-food van) in Ottawa and is smitten with Connie Pan, a young Vietnamese woman. Like all Doyle's novels, this one is about the journey a young boy takes to growing up and the independence that lies at the end of the road. Along the way, Spud discovers his boss's shady business dealings, the possibly environmentally damaging arrangement he's made for dumping the old grease from his fleet of vans, and finally comes to terms with his father's death.

As Doyle moves away from his children and his own childhood into new territory, he never steers away from difficult topics, keeping his focus on issues such as forgiveness, love, hate, and loss, not only as they affect his Canadian characters, but humanity in general. Doyle observes in his *SATA* interview that there is no one solution to any one of the dilemmas these issues pose: "I don't think there are any answers. There are questions, though, that I hope my readers will ask the rest of their lives. The question is more important than the answer anyway. These things have to be asked and dealt with in some way if you're going to live a fulfilled existence."

■ **Works Cited**

Adey, Lionel, "Doyle for the Early Teens," *Canadian Children's Literature,* Number 54, 1989, pp. 71-72.

Review of *Angel Square, Children's Book News,* December, 1984, p. 3.

Review of *Angel Square, Publishers Weekly,* January 16, 1987, p. 74.

Ashby, Adele, review of *You Can Pick Me Up at Peggy's Cove, Quill and Quire,* August, 1980, p. 30.

Collins, Anne, "Tales for the Computer Generation," *Maclean's,* December 13, 1982, pp. 56-58.

Doyle, Brian, *Hey, Dad!,* Groundwood Books, 1978.

Doyle, Brian, *You Can Pick Me Up at Peggy's Cove,* Groundwood Books, 1979.

Doyle, Brian, *Angel Square,* Groundwood Books, 1984.

Doyle, Brian, in an interview with Sonia Benson for *Something about the Author,* Volume 67, Gale, 1992.

Doyle, Brian, in an essay for *Something about the Author Autobiography Series,* Volume 16, Gale, 1992.

Ellis, Sarah, "News from the North," *Horn Book,* February, 1984, pp. 99-103.

Katz, Wendy R., "'Dying and Loving Somebody,'" *Canadian Children's Literature,* Number 22, 1981, pp. 47-50.

Martin, Sandra, "YA Fiction: Old Hands, Swan Song," *Quill and Quire,* October, 1990, p. 16.

McDonough, Irma, review of *Hey, Dad!, In Review: Canadian Books for Children,* Autumn, 1978, p. 57.

Morning, Todd, review of *Angel Square, School Library Journal,* May, 1987, p. 97.

Munro, Carol, "Life and Growth and Change: Always a Journey," *Canadian Children's Literature,* Number 37, 1985, pp. 67-70.

Nicuwenhuizen, Agnes, "Looking Deeply but Not Far: An Interview with Brian Doyle," *Magpies,* November, 1994, pp. 11-13.

Smith, Mary Ainslie, review of *Up to Low, Books in Canada,* February, 1983, pp. 32-33.

Vanderhoof, Amy, "Prankster, Teacher, Writer: Brian Doyle is Up to Good," *Quill and Quire,* December, 1982, p. 27.

Young, Pamela, and others, "Tidings of Fun," *Maclean's,* December 26, 1988, pp. 60, N6.

■ **For More Information See**

BOOKS

Children's Literature Review, Volume 22, Gale, 1991.

—*Sketch by Megan Ratner*

Linda Ellerbee

■ Personal

Full name, Linda Jane Ellerbee; born August 15, 1944, in Bryan, TX; daughter of Lonnie Ray and Hallie Smith; married four times; children: Vanessa, Joshua. *Education:* Attended Vanderbilt University. *Hobbies and other interests:* Music.

■ Addresses

Office—Lucky Duck Productions, 96 Morton St., New York, NY 10014.

■ Career

Broadcast journalist. WVON, Chicago, IL, newscaster and disk jockey, 1964–67; KSJO-Radio, San Francisco, CA, program director, 1967–68; KJNO-Radio and Associated Press, Juneau, AK, reporter, 1969–72; KHOU-TV, Houston, TX, reporter, 1972–73; WCBS-TV, New York City, reporter, 1973–76; National Broadcasting Company (NBC-TV), New York City, *NBC Nightly News* correspondent in Washington, DC, 1975–78, coanchor of *NBC News Weekend,* 1978–80; coanchor and general editor of *NBC News Overnight,* 1982–83, coanchor of *Sum-*mer Sunday U.S.A., 1984; correspondent, reporter, *Today Show,* NBC-TV, 1984–85; American Broadcasting Company (ABC-TV), writer, anchor, *Our World,* 1986; Lucky Duck Productions, New York City, president, 1987––; Cable News Network, commentator, 1989; producer, writer, and host, *Nick News W/5* (news magazine program). Producer, *A Conversation with Magic: It's Only Television* (TV special), 1992; executive producer, host, *Stranger Danger,* Nick News Special Edition, 1994.

■ Awards, Honors

Peabody award, 1992, for *A Conversation with Magic: It's Only Television.*

■ Writings

"And So It Goes": Adventures in Television, Putnam, 1986.

Move On: Adventures in the Real World, Putnam, 1991.

Author of syndicated newspaper column, 1991—.

■ Sidelights

"It's easy to be smug, doing what I do," writes Linda Ellerbee in *"And So It Goes": Adventures in Television,* the first of two books about her life. "Television news is the candy store. They pay me to read. They pay me to travel around the world.

They pay me to watch things happen, to go to parades, fires, conventions, wars, circuses, coronations and police stations—all in the name of journalism—and they pay me well." One of the first women to cover Washington for television news, Ellerbee writes a "breezy story of her days as a television reporter and anchor," writes Rebecca Wondriska in a review of "And So It Goes" in Library Journal.

Ellerbee's second book, Move On: Adventures in the Real World, focuses on more than just her television career: "This is not the story of my life, but some of these are stories from my life. . . . This is about Bugs Bunny and Texas, revolutions, rock 'n' roll, finding a style, finding a job, five networks, four marriages and two children."

Linda Jane, as she was called as a child, grew up in Bryan, Texas. Among the stories she tells about her childhood in Move On, she relates getting her first ice-cream cone. "I put my tongue to the brown, cold ball, then, babbling incoherently, did my three-year-old best to become one with that ice-cream cone." She talks about getting a library card and movie money. About "The Clothes Rule" Ellerbee says, "To me, dressed is jeans, a shirt (T- for summer, sweat for winter) and shoes (sneakers for summer, boots for winter). Anything else is costume."

The roots of the future journalist's career are seen in Ellerbee's reflections in Move On. "I'm a writer because I'm a reader. The thing is, my grandmother Dovye used to say, if you don't read, you can't write, and if you can't write you must work for a living. And, she usually added, you don't know how to do anything, Linda Jane." Ellerbee also recalls an influential teacher: "Mabel Scott was special, a world-class teacher. She'd led us, pushed, bullied, encouraged and given me confidence when there'd been no reason for her to do so. Certainly she could not have seen in me much to warrant her attention, but give it she had, in abundance, five days a week." Her parents, who had not been able to attend college, were proud to send their only child, Linda Jane, to college. In 1962, she entered Vanderbilt University in Nashville, Tennessee.

After her freshman year, Ellerbee quit school and went out into the world to find out what might happen. "I was eighteen when I packed my guitar, clicked the heels of my ruby sneakers three times and left Texas the first time, and the one thing I knew for sure was that anything was possible; maybe everything was possible. If 2 + 2 = 4 today, who knew but what tomorrow we might get up and find 2 + 2 = 5? It could happen," writes Ellerbee in Move On. Ellerbee wandered from the Andes, to Memphis, to Chicago (where she worked for a FM radio station and formed a band), to Los Angeles (where she wrote for a television show). Back in Texas, she married a cowboy-poet; they moved to the Mexican border and soon had two children: Vanessa (born in 1969) and Joshua (born in 1970). The family moved to Alaska, where they lived in a farmhouse with other family groups. Soon the marriage ended and Ellerbee found herself "without a job, without a husband, without an education—but with a three-year-old daughter and a two-year-old son to raise. Then I became a journalist. . . . I needed the money. No dream. No vision. No ambition," she recalls in "And So It Goes."

In Move On, Ellerbee writes about those early years getting started. When she returned to these "roots" after twenty years, one of her former co-workers on the same radio station where she had worked said that Ellerbee "became a hotshot reporter and that started here. . . . You always wanted to know why anybody did anything." Wanting to know why and asking hard questions, Ellerbee has become a gutsy and no-nonsense newscaster, respected by her professional peers. Music has been another thread through her life. She played guitar as an adolescent, formed a band when a young adult; while working at the radio station in Juneau, Alaska, music became the source of controversy. She got permission to start a program of music during the hours from midnight Saturday until six o'clock Sunday morning. In recalling this episode, she says that "music was also politics. There were only the two radio stations in town and neither one played rock 'n' roll, not real rock 'n' roll, not the music the whole world was listening to. Not Jagger or Crosby, Stills & Nash, nor Neil Young, not the Grateful Dead, not the Who nor The Band; no Rod Steward, no John Lennon. They were, if you can believe it, considered too radical to be played on the radio in the capital city of the biggest state in the United States in the year 1971."

After being fired from radio station KJNO in Juneau—she later referred to being fired as her first cancellation—she felt it was time to return to the home of her youth. She wrote letters to radio stations and newspapers throughout the Southwest. The Dallas bureau of the Associated Press (AP) responded (she had also worked for the AP in Alaska), and she worked there for a few months before becoming a local television news reporter in Houston.

"During the next seventeen years," she writes in *Move On,* "I traveled everywhere, covered everything and if I couldn't be in two places at once, at least I could be seen trying." Ellerbee went from Houston to WCBS-TV in New York City as a "hard-news" reporter. Then she joined the National Broadcasting Company (NBC) as a news correspondent in Washington, D.C. Of this move she says in *"And So It Goes," "*. . . going to the network was considered, as a rule, a step up. Network news was more serious than local news, that was understood." She was the first woman assigned to cover the U.S. House of Representatives.

After a difficult bout with cancer, Ellerbee was able to start her own production company, Lucky Duck, which produces a wide variety of shows.

From politics, she became coanchor of a weekly television program *NBC News Weekend.*

Ellerbee gained prominence in the field of broadcast journalism as coanchor and general editor of *NBC News Overnight,* the late-night television news program that aired five times weekly from July 1982 to December 1983. Leaving network television in 1987, she formed her own television production company. Currently, she develops children's news shows for Nickelodeon, a cable television channel, writes a syndicated news column, and produces, writes, and hosts a news magazine program called *Nick News W/5.*

Learning Television

"Somebody handed me a microphone, pointed a camera at me, and said, 'You're on television, kid. Do something.' Do what? I knew nothing about television news, nothing about how it should be put together, and there is no training program for that, not at a local station and not at a network," Ellerbee writes in *"And So It Goes."* She credits the cameramen, who were also the editors of the film, for teaching her about how to put together words and pictures: " . . . trying to match words with pictures, trying not to speak of oranges when the picture is of apples, trying to choose the best pictures, regretting the picture [the reporter] forgot to make, discarding the picture not needed." Ellerbee describes the process in greater detail later in the book when she relates her experience on *NBC News Weekend.* NBC News was developing a new program and she recalls, "It was the first time I'd said to myself, 'Now there's a job I really want.' Could I write well enough for *Weekend,* with its reputation for using the right words, not too many of them, and in the right order . . . ?"

She got the job, coanchoring with Lloyd Dobyns. The set was like a classroom to her, a place where she was constantly learning. "When putting together a television news story, the usual practice is to write the words, record them, then go into the editing room and match pictures to them," she writes in *"And So It Goes."* "The pictures are supposed to fit your words. Words first, pictures second. At *Weekend* the pictures came first. That is, the film was shot, the producer arranged the pieces he chose to use in the order he chose to use them, the film editor assembled the pieces, then the reporter wrote and recorded the narration that would complete the story. It is a better way. Changing the words to fit the pictures makes

Ellerbee's work on Nickelodeon's *Nick News*—which highlights information of special interest to teens—has introduced her to a brand-new audience.

more sense, because once the film is in the house you cannot change the pictures. . . . It makes you write *to* the pictures and *with* the pictures." Radio newscasts provide all the facts verbally because sound is its medium. However, the narration for television newscasts are sparser because pictures replace the need to say some facts aloud.

Ellerbee describes Dobyns and herself as the reporters for the show, but the real news reporters are the producers, and the show had thirty producers, each of whom was a journalist. A story about a group of parents of children with Down's syndrome that aired on *Weekend* won an Emmy. The award went to Christine Huneke, the producer, instead of Ellerbee because although Ellerbee wrote the script and talked with the five-year-old boy on camera, Huneke had discovered the story, chosen the child, and decided how the story should be told.

Being Canceled

Weekend was canceled, much to Ellerbee's dismay. She missed the classroom-type environment. However, being canceled is part of life in television. A television news journalist is tough and learns to deal with change. Ellerbee's books reveal a lot of what it is like to be in the business. John M. Wilson, reviewing *"And So It Goes"* in the *Los Angeles Times Book Review*, says Ellerbee's stories are "bout a professional trying to do the best work she can and to communicate with an audience she respects." Patricia T. O'Connor comments in *New York Times Book Review* that Ellerbee is frank about television newscasting—its good side and "the absurdities it often perpetrates on the viewing public."

After two years as a reporter for *NBC Nightly News*, Ellerbee coanchored a late-night news program, *Overnight*. The show was aired live and covered stories that were interesting and unique— whether they were local stories or about areas not normally covered on other national television news shows. In this way, the anchorpersons broke the norms and did the show the way they wanted, without concern for ratings. The thirty or so people who made the show grew close and *Overnight* gained loyal viewers.

Reflecting on Life Experience

Five years after *"And So It Goes," Move On: Adventures in the Real World* was published. It was well received. A critic in *Publishers Weekly* describes the book as an "entertaining, often moving collection of essays." Chet Hagan, reviewing the book in *Library Journal,* writes that Ellerbee's use of language is "unpretentious and entertaining."

Ellerbee now focuses on television programs to educate and inform children and young adults. She recently wrote and produced a special about child abduction titled *Stranger Danger,* which was aired on the Nickelodeon cable TV channel. Rick Sherwood, in reviewing the show in *Hollywood Reporter,* makes this observation, "This is responsible television of the first order, a show that's written and produced in a forthright fashion designed to warn and educate rather than scare kids."

With a matter-of-fact approach, Ellerbee engages seven or eight kids in conversation; she brings into the discussion the director of the National Center for Missing Children to answer their questions. The show provides viewers with practical advice while exploring the right and wrong ways of dealing with the possibility of abduction. The show continually notes that kids need not be scared—just cautious—and that the high-profile cases that make the news are exceptions rather than the rule. Bob Curtright, a reviewer in the *Detroit Free Press,* quotes Ellerbee: "What the fear of nuclear war was to my generation, the fear of abduction is to today's kids. It will never, ever happen to most of them, but they have the right to know, to be safe."

"What I Have Learned"

Ellerbee has always enjoyed her work; she says in *"And So It Goes":* "I like my work. All things considered, mine is a good job to have. . . . For people like me it is never enough to watch something happen. We want to watch it, then run to tell everybody else what we saw." And she takes her work seriously. "It's up to those of us who work in the business to be honest reporters—and to learn our craft, to make sure that we know how to write, that we produce television and not radio, and that we leave a little something for the audience to do. I learned *that* on *Week-*

end." Being one of the first women in television news she has this to say: "It seems clear to me that women have proved themselves on the job, time and time again. We're still here, and resentment of us has receded *somewhat.* The pay seems to have evened out, at least for those of us on the air." Working with women has its own rewards. "The lessons I learned working for and with women on *Overnight* and *Summer Sunday* make me ashamed I used to feel complimented when someone told me I thought like a man," Ellerbee expresses in *"And So It Goes."*

In *Move On,* Ellerbee sums up learning and change: "I've learned that if you don't want to get old, don't mellow. I've learned always to set a place in life for the unexpected guest. And to be content with questions. I was right all along; questions are better. Most of all, I've learned that a good time to laugh is any time you can. . . . Change is one form of hope; to risk change is to believe in tomorrow. Hope is a gift we need later more than sooner."

■ Works Cited

Curtright, Bob, *"Stranger:* A Family Show with a Serious Message," *Detroit Free Press,* May 17, 1994, p. 5D.

Ellerbee, Linda, *"And So It Goes":* Adventures in Television, Putnam, 1986, pp. 13-14, 16-17, 23, 45, 73, 76, 112, 122-23, 243, 250.

Ellerbee, Linda, *Move On: Adventures in the Real World,* Putnam, 1991, pp. 13, 14, 16, 35, 37-8, 41, 233, 247, 266.

Hagan, Chet, *Library Journal,* April 1, 1991, p. 133.

Review of *Move On: Adventures in the Real World, Publishers Weekly,* March 22, 1991, p. 66.

O'Connor, Patricia T., *New York Times Book Review,* June 14, 1987, p. 38.

Sherwood, Rick, "Cable TV Review: 'Stranger Danger,'" *Hollywood Reporter,* May 17, 1994, pp. 11-14.

Wilson, John M., *Los Angeles Times Book Review,* May 18, 1986, p.6.

Wondriska, Rebecca, *Library Journal,* May 1, 1986, p. 118.

■ For More Information See

PERIODICALS

New York Times Book Review, May 10, 1992, p. 28.

People, May 13, 1991, pp. 117-29.

Publishers Weekly, April 11, 1986, p. 78.*

—*Sketch by Barbara A. Withers*

M.C. Escher

■ Personal

Full name, Maurits Cornelis Escher; born June 17, 1898, in Leeuwarden, in the Dutch province of Friesland; died of cancer, March 27, 1972, in Hilversum; son of George Arnold Escher (a civil engineer) and Sarah A. Gleichman; married Jetta Umiker, June 12, 1924; children: George, Arthur, Jan. *Education:* Attended secondary school in Arnhem, 1912–1918; later attended the School for Architecture and Decorative Arts in Haarlem (sometimes called the "School for Architecture and Ornamental Design in Haarlem"), 1919–1922. *Religion:* Catholic, though non–observant. *Hobbies and other interests:* Music, astronomy.

■ Addresses

Lived in Rome, 1925–1935; in 1941, relocated to Baarn, Holland, changing residences within Baarn in 1955.

■ Career

Artist, print–maker and designer. Lecturer, international conference of crystallographers, and at Massachusetts Institute of Technology (MIT), Cambridge, MA, both 1960. *Exhibitions:* First one–man exhibition, Siena, Italy, 1923. Exhibitions, The Hague, Holland, 1924, and Rome, Italy, 1926. One–man exhibitions, International Mathematical Conference, Stedelijk Museum (Amsterdam), and Whyte Gallery, Washington, DC, both 1954; Mickelson Gallery, Washington, and the Gemeentemuseum, The Hague, both 1968.

■ Awards, Honors

Escher's lithograph *Nonza* won third prize at an exhibition in Chicago, 1934; Knighted by Order of Oranje Nassau, 1955; Cultural Prize, City of Hilversum, 1965; second national decoration, 1967.

■ Writings

Regelmatige Vlakverdeling, De Roos Foundation, 1958.

Grafiek en Tekeningen M.C. Escher, Zwolle, 1959.
The Writings and Lectures of Escher, and His Collection of Clippings, The Hague, 1981.

Author of introduction, *Catalogus M.C. Escher,* Stedelijk Museum, Amsterdam, 1954. Contributor to numerous books, including *Les Timbres–poste des Pays–Bas de 1929 à 1939,* The Hague, 1939; *Catalogus Tentoonstelling S.J. de Mesquita en Mendes da Costa,* Stedelijk Museum, 1946; and *De*

Wereld van het Zwart en Wit, edited by J. Hulsker, Amsterdam, 1959. Also contributor to periodicals, including *De Delver, Phoenix,* and *Wit–grijs–zwart.*

IN ENGLISH TRANSLATION

M.C. Escher: The Graphic Work (originally published as *Grafiek en Tekeningen M.C. Escher,* Benedikt Taschen, 1992).

M.C. Escher: His Life and Complete Graphic Work: With a Fully Illustrated Catalogue, edited by J. L. Locher, Abradale Press, 1992 (originally published as *Leven en Werk van M.C. Escher*).

Also author of *The World of M.C. Escher,* 1972 (originally published as *De Werelden van M.C. Escher*).

ILLUSTRATOR

van Stolk, Aad P., *Flor de Pascua,* Baarn, 1921.

Drijfhout, E. E., *XXIV Emblemata dat zijn zinne–beelden,* Bussum, 1932.

Walch, J., *De vreeselijke avonturen van Scholastica,* Bussum, 1933.

■ Sidelights

A baby alligator crawls over a closed book, making his way cautiously up a tilted mechanical triangle to sit high atop a shiny polyhedron. He raises his head and releases two jets of smoke out of his flared nostrils, then leaps down into a small metal jar stacked with boxes of cigarettes and matches. Pausing just long enough to catch his balance, the mysteriously determined lizard then drops down onto the surface of a sketchbook, where he melds his body into a line drawing, becoming a flat lizard within a flat design of lizards.

This is just one example of the uncanny visual acts performed by Dutch artist M.C. Escher. In a career that spanned nearly fifty years, Escher used his art to show that the paradoxical was not merely possible, but could—under certain conditions—become the norm. "Sometimes it seems as though we are all obsessed with a longing for the impossible," the artist once commented. "The reality around us, the three–dimensional world surrounding us, is too ordinary, too boring, too com-

mon. We yearn for the unnatural or the supernatural . . . the impossible, the miraculous."

Although Escher built a world–wide reputation through representations of what he termed "mental imagery," the artist did not really get interested in graphics until later in life. From his teen-age years—when he first began to draw and experiment with printing techniques—until his late thirties, Escher worked primarily within the conventions of landscape art. An avid artist who displayed skillful use of color in his work, Escher never came under the spell of painting. He admitted in 1957: "I have hardly ever experienced the pleasure of the artist who uses colour for its own sake; I use colour only when the nature of my shapes makes it necessary."

Escher's first teen–age experiments with linoleum cuts, however, grew into a lifelong fascination with the graphic arts and print–making techniques, such as woodcut (which he studied under S. Jessurun de Mesquita), wood–engraving and lithography. In October, 1921, while a student at the School of Architecture and Decorative Arts in Haarlem, Escher executed a series of woodcuts for *Flor de Pascua,* a booklet containing his friend Aad van Stolk's fanciful philosophical texts. The following year, the artist broke off his studies and embarked on the first of numerous trips to Italy. Escher recorded his travel impressions in a diary (a practice he acquired from his father). He explored the cities and surrounding landscape in his journal through a series of drawings. Escher's father later noted that these pieces were "all in pen, mostly with black lines, and some with halftones obtained by scratching out."

After touching down briefly at home, Escher once again took off for the South, this time aboard a freighter. Touring through the Italian cities of Siena, Rome, Genoa, Pisa, San Gimignano, Ravello and Naples, Escher made woodcuts and drawings "so that I shall know later what I saw here, and see better what I see now." Never sure of his skill as a draftsman, Escher's continual practice led to improvement and, in August, 1923, he enjoyed his first one–man show at the Circolo Artistico in Siena, Italy. This was a time of supreme happiness for him. Escher wrote: "Rarely, if ever, have I felt calmer, more pleased, more content than in recent times. Many wonderful prints are springing from my mostly industrious hands."

A system of channels mysteriously appear to carry water uphill in Escher's 1961 lithograph, *Waterfall*.

The young artist's happiness also sprang from his having fallen in love with Jetta Umiker, the daughter of a German–Swiss manufacturer. During their extended courtship, Escher managed to arrange his first exhibition in Holland. It was held in February, 1924, at The Hague. J. Dona wrote in *Elseviers Maanblad* that the exhibition was "the work of a young fresh mind which is not intimidated and quietly goes its own way. It is cultured . . . quiet, pure and powerful, and has a strong tendency toward decoration."

During the late 1920s and early 1930s, Escher and his wife resided in Rome. While the artist's drawings and woodcuts of city views and landscapes continued to win him favorable critical attention (and patrons), some notices also disparaged the overly deliberate character of the work. Commenting in *Nieu Rotterdamsche Court*, R. W. P. de Vries noted: "Escher's pen–and–ink and brush drawings and woodcuts have a dogmatic assurance, a conscious, cool sobriety which precludes any spontaneity. [Escher] is fascinated not by the accidental or the picturesque but by the typical, the `whole,' which often has a constructional quality."

In 1935, Escher made a decision that profoundly influenced the focus of his work and his future. Faced with the spread of Italian fascism, he and Jetta left Rome to relocate in Switzerland. Although Switzerland provided safety and security, Escher bitterly grieved his loss of the "wealth and warmth of Italian landscapes" and a way of life that had nurtured his artistry and spirit for over a decade. Uninspired by his surroundings, Escher turned inward and began to explore perception itself, closely examining the principles of systematic linear perspective and the relationship of the eye and the mind. Although he was to abandon Switzerland in 1936 for Brussels, Escher remained true to his inward study. Years later, the artist recalled that, with the decision to portray the images of his own mind, the emphasis of his work shifted from excellence of craftsmanship and artistic skill to a consuming interest in the expression of ideas.

Mental Imagery

In a letter to his son, Arthur, Escher noted that his work had more in common with mathematicians than with other artists. In fact, it was not an art historian, but the mathematician Bruno

Ernst who identified seven fundamental themes in Escher's mature work. Ernst defined these themes as:

1) The penetration of worlds
2) The illusion of space
3) The regular division of the plane
4) Perspective
5) Regular solids and spirals
6) The impossible
7) The infinite

In his pieces, Escher exploited reflecting surfaces—such as polished metal spheres and pools of standing water—to combine directly perceived images and reflected images within one integrated view, or world. The best–known examples of this

The medieval costumes, eerie landscape, and fantastic architecture of the 1958 work *Belvedere* serve to heighten its powerful visual impact. (All rights reserved. Copyright 1994, M. C. Escher/Cordon Art-Baarn, Holland.)

technique are the artist's several self–portraits, created over a broad range of time: *Still Life with Spherical Mirror* (1934), *Hand with Reflecting Sphere* (1935), *Three Spheres 1* (1945) and [*Self–Portrait in Spherical Mirror*] (1950).

In his "illusion of space" designs, Escher poked fun at the mind's insistence on perceiving spatial relationships within flat, two–dimensional pictures. In *Reptiles,* for example, the reptile standing on the polyhedron really has no greater substance than the interlocking reptiles in the sketch–book drawing: all occupy two dimensions. By endowing his standing reptile with self–consciousness, a mock–heroic sense of accomplishment and greater personality than the interlocked reptiles, Escher challenges the complacency and self–importance of his viewers. In a 1951 interview for *Time,* Escher observed: "It is a very superficial picture which man creates for himself. Only in our thoughts do we try to animate the flatness of our images with depth. Suddenly it can become clear to us how silly we are, we maniacs of the flat image, with our unceasing craving for unreachable depth."

The Regular Division of The Plane

Between 1937 and 1971, Escher produced about 150 finished color drawings of repetitive, interlocking, patterns, defined by the artist as "regular divisions of the plane." This series of works was, as the artist himself once recalled, his "richest source of inspiration." Escher's patterns differed significantly from previous geometric patterns in that, where others had fitted together simple, abstract shapes—such as rectangles, triangles or diamonds—Escher manipulated recognizable, natural figures of fish, birds, reptiles and even human beings. This complex and unique artistic undertaking prompted Escher to publish an essay entitled *Regelmatige vlak Verdeling* (*The Regular Division of the Plane*), in which he wrote: "I walk around all alone in this beautiful garden, which certainly does not belong only to me, but whose gate is open to everyone. I feel a revitalizing yet oppressive sense of loneliness." A longtime devotee of the music of Bach, Escher compared his work to performing music, "when, drawing on paper or engraving in wood, the hand makes repeated rhythmic movements as in a dance."

Although Escher's preoccupation with inner visions dominated the second half of his life, early experiments and early experiences helped plant the seeds for what would come later. His special affinity for self–portraits in spherical mirrors, for example, emerged as early as *Flor de Pascua,* in which the artist inserted a woodcut called [*The Sphere*]. In this work, Escher is seated at his drawing table, captured within a luminous sphere which floats like a planet in a starry sky. An early expression of Escher's fascination with "regular solids" is also found in one of the artist's youthful diary entries. Escher recorded that on New Years' Day, 1923, while strolling around outside the Italian town of Siena, he found his "eye caught by the sparkle of quartz crystals." Gazing around, he saw "hundreds, thousands of them," and bent "down, to choose the most beautiful and take them home, as happy as if they had been diamonds."

In the late 1940s, Escher began to consider the possibilities crystals suggested for creating unusual geometric figures. While never a rival for the public favor enjoyed by his efforts on other themes Escher's crystallographic prints contain many striking and imaginative features. In *Double Planet* (1949), Escher's attraction to star–shaped solids is given form. The artist once described this work via the following: "Two regular tetrahedrons, piercing each other, float through space as a planetoid. The light–colored one is inhabited by human beings who have completely transformed their region into a complex of houses, bridges and roads. The darker tetrahedron has remained in its natural state, with rocks, on which plants and prehistoric animals live. The two bodies fit together to make a whole but they have no knowledge of each other."

Not only was *Double Planet* unprecedented in its graphic conception, it was also a masterpiece in the art of woodcut, composed as it was of four colors from four separate, intricately carved woodblocks. Nonetheless, having finished the piece, Escher was left with a sense of inadequacy. Writing to P. Kessler—an important collector of his work—in 1950, the artist revealed that he found "the whole question of the intersection of the different planes devilishly difficult." Despite his enthusiasm for the task, working out the technical execution amounted to "one constant failure," the artist lamented.

This sense of failure was no stranger to Escher, but the artist learned to turn it into a source of motivation. Philosophizing upon his experience, he remarked: "The idea you start with mentally is very fine, but as soon as you try to put it plastically, it's ruined. That's why you always begin again."

It was during the 1950s, as the artist passed through his *own* fifties, that he began to achieve international prominence (particularly in the English–speaking world). Articles about Escher appeared in influential art journals, such as *The Studio,* as well as in popular magazines, including *Life* and *Time.* Escher exhibited regularly in museums, art galleries ad universities; he also lectured widely. In 1954, Escher organized his first exhibition in the United States at the Whyte Gallery, in Washington, D.C.

The Impossible

It was during this period that Escher found a new form for his work. In such pieces as *Relativity* (1953), *Convex and Concave* (1955), *Belvedere* (1958), *Ascending and Descending* (1960) and *Waterfall* (1961), Escher demonstrated an absorption with "the impossible"—representations of architecture that defied the laws of physics. In a 1963 lecture at Amsterdam, Escher divulged his strategy for achieving success in this new enterprize. "If you want to draw attention to something impossible, you must try to deceive first yourself and then your audience, by presenting your work in such a way that the impossible element is veiled and a superficial observer would not even notice it. There should be a certain mysteriousness that does not immediately hit the eye," he commented.

In *Waterfall,* four brick channels or gutters, at right angles to each other, appear to constitute a three–dimensional watercourse. Taken by themselves, each gutter seems to be on an even level with the adjacent one, except when the water reaches the last gutter. Once there, it runs over the edge and rains straight down into a well, brushing the paddles of a water–mill which, in turn, steer it back between the brick sides of the first gutter. *Waterfall* serves up the paradox of a structure that simultaneously exists in two *and* three dimensions. The principle of *Waterfall* is explained, in part, by "Penrose's Triangle," the mystifying conceptual figure upon which the

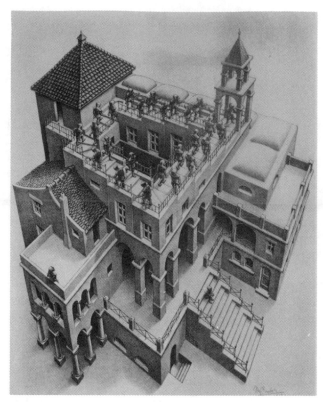

Hooded figures walk downstairs to reach higher levels and upstairs to reach lower levels in this paradoxical 1960 work, *Ascending and Descending.*

drawing is based. In "Penrose's Triangle," the lines of a figure are created so that they form an impossibility. As the viewer looks at the lines of the figure, s/he is forced to change perception and interpretation, a change also influenced by distance.

Escher's fascination with "unreal" architecture coincided with his struggle to artistically express the infinite. The turning point for him in this undertaking came with the discovery of an image in a book by the Canadian mathematician, H.S.M. Coxeter. Escher and Professor Coxeter had become friends after the latter attended one of Escher's lectures. Thereafter, the two men maintained contact, with Coxeter frequently bringing mathematical works to Escher's attention. During the late 1950s, as Escher sought without success to graphically reproduce the infinite, Coxeter's notes in *A Symposium on Symmetry* appeared to be provide the clues the artist needed. The announcement of Escher's *Circle Limit I* (1958) came in a letter to his son, Arthur. Although once again betraying concern that this new graphic adventure would run afoul of his audience's expectations, Escher also conveyed elation, declaring that "the circular limitation of infinitely small motifs [geometrically stylized fish] . . . is something I cannot take my eyes off. It approaches absolute beauty and purity." Coxeter later praised Escher's *Circle Limit III* (1959), enthusiastically reporting to the artist—in mathematical terms—just what he had accomplished. Escher noted his bewilderment to Arthur, confessing: "Three pages of explanation of what I actually did. . . . It's a pity that I understand nothing, absolutely nothing of it."

Escher's delight in the infinite continued until the close of his life. His final print, *Snakes* (1969), reveals the restlessness of the artist's mind and the liveliness of his interest. In *Snakes,* Escher employs the strategy of depicting infinitely small motifs at the center of his design. Thereby the infinite is projected within the heart of the design as its vanishing point.

Escher's interest in "the impossible"—architectural creations that defied the laws of physics—is seen in this 1953 lithograph entitled *Relativity.*

The Artist as Writer

Escher's avowed ideal as an artist was "to produce a crystal–clear reflection of himself." In his essays, lectures and correspondence, he revealed an exceptional aptitude for imparting original ideas, shades of feeling, and novel perceptions through precise language. Escher was particularly adroit at capturing the beauty of sights garnered at sea. Escher praised the excellence of sea travel in a lecture he gave in March, 1961, in Baarn. Preparing his audience by assuring them that travel by sea enabled one to experience "so–called 'reality' more intensely than [one] had dared to hope," he proceeded to describe numerous rare sights, including the legendary 'Green Flash.' In vain, he had watched for it through many years on many freighter trips through the Mediterranean, when at last, sailing along the entrance to the Gulf of California at sunset, his chance came: "When three quarters of the elliptical disc of the sun had disappeared below the horizon, I put my trusty binoculars to my eyes and (for the hundredth time) excitedly followed the fast-shrinking segment of the sun. As usual when there is little water vapour in the atmosphere, it was a blinding orange–red colour, almost up to the end. But for a fraction of a second the colour of the last visible luminous line of the sun changed to a bright green."

Even in describing the commonplace, the artist showed the clarity and deeply felt delight he experienced in the visual act. "What is there to say about the moon that everyone doesn't know already?" Escher once asked before cataloging four independent ways of looking at the moon: the way of poets, of astronomers, of people who are hurrying along, too preoccupied to give it much attention (like the indifferent laundress of *Waterfall*), and lastly, the way of "people who would like to use their intellect" sensitively. This last persona can be seen as Escher, throwing himself into the visual experience, feeling for the moon's "constructional" essence, as well as its luminous, radiant particulars, and carefully thinking about why he sees what he sees. It happens also to be the ideal attitude—alert, assertive and comfortable in the visual realm—of somebody intent on looking at a print by M. C. Escher.

■ Works Cited

de Vries, R. W. P., essay in *Nieu Rotterdamsche Court,* October 2, 1927.

Dona, J., review of one–man show, *Elseviers Maanblad,* June, 1924.

Escher, M. C., *Regelmatige vlak Verdeling* ("The Regular Division of the Plane; essay"), 1951.

Escher, M. C., interview in *Time,* April, 1951, p. 50.

■ For More Information See

BOOKS

Escher, M. C., *Escher on Escher: Exploring the Infinite,* Abrams, 1989.

Escher, M. C., *The Graphic Work: Introduced and Explained by the Artist,* Benedikt Taschen, 1992.

Hofstadter, Douglas, *Gödel, Escher, Bach: An Eternal Golden Braid,* Vintage Books, 1980.

Locher, J. L., editor, *M.C. Escher, His Life and Complete Graphic Work,* Abrams, 1992.

Schattschneider, Doris, *Visions of Symmetry: Notebooks, Periodic Drawings and Related Work of M.C. Escher,* Freeman, 1990.

PERIODICALS

Artist's Proof, Volume 3, number 2, 1963–64, p. 32.

Horizon, Volume 5, number 7, 1963, p. 10.

Life, May 7, 1951, p. 20.

New Worlds, Volume 51, number 173, 1967, p. 44.

The Studio, February, 1951, p. 50.

—*Sketch by Michael Scott Joseph*

Howard Fast

■ Personal

Full name, Howard Melvin Fast; also writes under pseudonyms E. V. Cunningham and Walter Ericson; born November 11, 1914, in New York, NY; son of Barney (an ironworker, cable car gripper, tin factory worker, and dress factory cutter) and Ida (a homemaker; maiden name, Miller) Fast; married Bette Cohen (a painter and sculptor), June 6, 1937; children: Rachel, Jonathan. *Education:* Attended National Academy of Design. *Hobbies and other interests:* "My home, my family, the theater, the film, and the proper study of ancient history. And the follies of mankind."

■ Addresses

Home—Greenwich, CT 06830. *Agent*—Sterling Lord Agency, 660 Madison Ave., New York, NY 10021.

■ Career

Writer, 1932—. United States Office of War Information, New York, NY, "American BBC" anchor writer, 1942–44; Special Signal Corps unit correspondent and war correspondent in China-India-Burma theatre, 1944–45; *Esquire* and *Coronet,* foreign correspondent in North Africa, Saudi Arabia, and India, 1945; Blue Heron Press, owner, publisher, and writer. Worked variously as a *Bronx Home News* delivery boy, cigarmaker, hat maker, butcher shop delivery man and cleaner, New York Public Library page, and dress factory shipping clerk and presser. Member of World Peace Council, 1950–55; American Labor Party candidate for U.S. Congress, 23rd New York District, 1952. Has given numerous lectures and made numerous appearances on radio and television programs.

■ Awards, Honors

Breadloaf Literary Award, 1937; Schomburg Award for Race Relations, 1944, for *Freedom Road*; Newspaper Guild Award and Jewish Book Council of America Annual Award, both 1947; Stalin International Peace Prize, Soviet Union, 1954; Screenwriters Annual Award, 1960; Secondary Education Board Annual Book Award, 1962; American Library Association "Notable Book" citation, 1972, for *The Hessian;* Emmy Award, Television Academy, 1976.

■ Writings

NOVELS

Two Valleys, Dial, 1933.
Strange Yesterday, Dodd, 1934.

Place in the City, Harcourt, 1937.

Conceived in Liberty: A Novel of Valley Forge, Simon and Schuster, 1939.

The Last Frontier, Duell, Sloan and Pearce, 1941.

The Tall Hunter, Harper, 1942.

The Unvanquished, Duell, Sloan and Pearce, 1942.

Citizen Tom Paine, Duell, Sloan and Pearce, 1943, Grove Press, 1983.

Freedom Road, Duell, Sloan and Pearce, 1944, Amsco School Publications, 1970, M. W. Sharpe, 1995.

The American: A Middle Western Legend, Duell, Sloan and Pearce, 1946.

The Children, Duell, Sloan and Pearce, 1947.

Clarkton, Duell, Sloan and Pearce, 1947, Elephant Paperbacks, 1989.

My Glorious Brothers, Little, Brown, 1948, new edition, Hebrew Publications, 1977.

The Proud and the Free, Little, Brown, 1950.

(Under pseudonym Walter Ericson) *Fallen Angel,* Little, Brown, 1951, published as *The Darkness Within,* Ace, 1953, published as *Mirage* (as Howard Fast), Fawcett, 1965.

Spartacus, Blue Heron, 1951, Citadel, 1952, Buccaneer Books, 1982.

Silas Timberman, Blue Heron, 1954.

The Story of Lola Gregg, Blue Heron, 1956.

Moses, Prince of Egypt, Crown, 1958.

The Winston Affair, Crown, 1959.

Power, Doubleday, 1962.

Agrippa's Daughter, Doubleday, 1964.

Torquemada, Doubleday, 1966.

The Hunter and the Trap, Dial, 1967.

The Crossing (based on Fast's screenplay of the same title), Morrow, 1971, New Jersey Historical Society, 1985.

The Hessian (based on Fast's screenplay of the same title), Morrow, 1972.

Max: A Novel, Houghton, 1983.

The Outsider, Houghton, 1984.

The Call of Fife and Drum: Three Novels of the Revolution (contains *The Unvanquished, Conceived in Liberty,* and *The Proud and the Free*), Citadel, 1987.

The Dinner Party, Houghton, 1987.

The Pledge, Houghton, 1988.

The Confession of Joe Cullen, Houghton, 1989, Dell, 1990.

The Novelist: A Romantic Portrait of Jane Austen, S. French, 1992.

The Trial of Abigail Goodman, Crown, 1993, Random House, 1994.

Seven Days in June: A Novel of the American Revolution, Carol Publishing, 1994.

FOR YOUNG PEOPLE

The Romance of a People, Hebrew Publishing, 1941.

Tony and the Wonderful Door, Blue Heron, 1952, illustrated by Imero Gobbato, Knopf, 1968, published as *The Magic Door,* illustrated by Bonnie Mettler, Peace Press, 1979, Avon, 1980.

April Morning, Crown, 1961, Bantam, 1976.

"THE IMMIGRANTS" SERIES

The Immigrants, Houghton, 1977.

The Second Generation, Houghton, 1978.

The Establishment, Houghton, 1979.

The Legacy, Houghton, 1980.

The Immigrant's Daughter, Houghton, 1985.

NOVELS; UNDER PSEUDONYM E. V. CUNNINGHAM

Sylvia, Doubleday, 1960, published under name Howard Fast, Thorndike Press, 1992.

Phyllis, Doubleday, 1962.

Alice, Doubleday, 1963.

Shirley, Doubleday, 1963.

Lydia, Doubleday, 1964.

Penelope, Doubleday, 1965.

Helen, Doubleday, 1966.

Margie, Morrow, 1966.

Sally, Morrow, 1967, (as Howard Fast) Chivers North America, 1994.

Samantha, Morrow, 1967.

Cynthia, Morrow, 1968.

The Assassin Who Gave Up His Gun, Morrow, 1969.

Millie, Morrow, 1973.

The Case of the One-Penny Orange, Holt, 1977.

The Case of the Russian Diplomat, Holt, 1978.

The Case of the Poisoned Eclairs, Holt, 1979.

The Case of the Sliding Pool, Delacorte, 1981.

The Case of the Kidnapped Angel, Delacorte, 1982.

The Case of the Angry Actress, Delacorte, 1984.

The Case of the Murdered Mackenzie, Delacorte, 1984.

The Wabash Factor, Doubleday, 1986.

NONFICTION

Haym Salomon, Son of Liberty, Messner, 1941.

Lord Baden-Powell of the Boy Scouts, Messner, 1941.

Goethals and the Panama Canal, Messner, 1942.

(With Bette Fast) *The Picture-Book History of the Jews,* Hebrew Publishing, 1942.

The Incredible Tito, Magazine House, 1944.

Tito and His People, Contemporary Publishers, 1948.

Intellectuals in the Fight for Peace, Masses and the Mainstream, 1949.

Literature and Reality, International Publishers, 1950.

Peekskill, U.S.A.: A Personal Experience, Civil Rights Congress, 1951.

Spain and Peace (second edition), Joint Anti-Fascist Refugee Committee, 1952.

The Passion of Sacco and Vanzetti: A New England Legend, Blue Heron, 1953, Greenwood Press, 1972.

The Naked God: The Writer and the Communist Party, Praeger, 1957.

The Howard Fast Reader (includes *The Golden River),* Crown, 1960.

The Jews: The Story of a People, Dial, 1968, Dell, 1992.

The Art of Zen Meditation, Peace Press, 1977.

War and Peace: Observations on Our Times, M. E. Sharpe, 1993.

Being Red: A Memoir (autobiography), Houghton, 1990, M. E. Sharp, 1994.

SHORT STORY COLLECTIONS

Patrick Henry and the Frigate's Keel and Other Stories of a Young Nation, Duell, Sloan and Pearce, 1945.

Departure and Other Stories, Little, Brown, 1949, Peace Press, 1980.

The Last Supper, and Other Stories, Blue Heron, 1955.

The Edge of Tomorrow, Bantam, 1961.

The General Zapped an Angel: New Stories of Fantasy and Science Fiction, Morrow, 1970.

A Touch of Infinity: Thirteen Stories of Fantasy and Science Fiction, Morrow, 1973.

Time and the Riddle: Thirty-One Zen Stories, Ward Ritchie Press, 1975, Houghton, 1980.

PLAYS, SCREENPLAYS, AND SCRIPTS

The Hammer, produced in New York, 1950.

Thirty Pieces of Silver (produced in Melbourne, 1951), Blue Heron, 1954.

George Washington and the Water Witch, Bodley Head, 1956.

(With Dalton Trumbo) *Spartacus* (screenplay based on novel of the same title; directed by Stanley Kubrick and produced by Universal Studios), 1960.

The Crossing, produced in Dallas, 1962.

The Hill (screenplay), Doubleday, 1964.

David and Paula, produced in New York City at American Jewish Theater, November 20, 1982.

Citizen Tom Paine: A Play in Two Acts (produced in Washington, D.C., at the John F. Kennedy Center for the Performing Arts, 1987), Houghton, 1986.

The Novelist, produced in Williamstown, Massachusetts, 1987.

The Second Coming, produced in Greenwich, Connecticut, 1991.

OTHER

(With William Gropper) *Never Forget: The Story of the Warsaw Ghetto* (poetry), Book League of the Jewish Fraternal Order, 1946.

(Editor) *The Selected Works of Tom Paine,* Modern Library, 1946.

(Editor) *Best Short Stories of Theodore Dreiser,* World Publishing, 1947.

Also author of *The Hessian* (screenplay), 1971; *What's a Nice Girl Like You . . . !* (television script; based on Fast's novel *Shirley); The Ambassador* (television script), 1974; with Edward Hume, *21 Hours at Munich* (television script), 1976. Author of weekly column, *New York Observer,* 1989—, and columns for the *Daily Worker.*

Author of "The Trap," in *The Human Almanac: People Through Time,* edited by Richard L. Burrill, Sierra Pacific Press, 1983. Author of introductions in Maxim Gorky's *Mother: The Great Revolutionary Novel,* Carol Publishing, 1992; Arthur J. Sabin's *Red Scare in Court: New York Versus the International Workers Order,* University of Pennsylvania Press, 1993; Bette Fast's *The Sculpture of Bette Fast,* M. E. Sharpe, 1995.

Fast's work has been translated into 82 languages. His manuscripts are collected at the University of Pennsylvania, Philadelphia, and the University of Wisconsin, Madison.

■ Adaptations

More than ten of Fast's novels and stories have been adapted for production as motion pictures, including *Man in the Middle,* based on his novel *The Winston Affair,* 1964; *Mirage,* based on a story he wrote as Walter Ericson, 1965; *Penelope,* based on his novel of the same title, 1966; *Jigsaw,* based on *The Fallen Angel,* 1968; *Freedom Road,* based on his novel of the same title, 1980. *The Immigrants* was broadcast as a television miniseries, 1979; *April Morning* was adapted as a television program, 1988. *The Crossing* (based on Fast's screenplay of the same title) was recorded on cassette, narrated by Norman Dietz, Recorded Books, 1988; *The Immigrant's Daughter* was recorded on cassette, narrated by Sandra Burr, Brilliance Corporation, 1991.

■ Sidelights

Howard Fast tirelessly worked his way from poverty to become one of the most widely read writers of the twentieth century. He was already an acclaimed writer by the mid-1940s, when he decided to formalize his support for the Communist party despite the anti-Communist sentiments that intensified at the conclusion of World War II. The decision not to deny his beliefs, as some other leftist intellectuals did at the time, changed his life. Fast was considered a "Red," and he was jailed for his refusal to cooperate with the House Un-American Activities Committee. He was blacklisted, and Federal Bureau of Investigation chief J. Edgar Hoover did what he could to prevent the publication of Fast's books. FBI agents were even sent to public libraries to remove Fast's published books—suddenly considered Communist propaganda—from the shelves.

Fast's persecution seemed ironic to some observers, because in the historical and biographical novels he had already published—like *Conceived in Liberty: A Novel of Valley Forge* and *The Unvanquished*—as well as in his work for the Office of War Information, Fast emphasized the importance of freedom and illuminated the heroic acts that had built American society. He made the relatively unknown or forgotten history of the United States accessible to millions of Americans in books like *The Last Frontier,* and as a correspondent for the radio program that would become the Voice of America, he was entrusted with the job of assuring millions of foreigners of the country's greatness and benevolence during World War II.

Yet even after Fast learned of Stalin's atrocities, which convinced him that he had been betrayed by the Communist party and caused him to break

his ties with it, he did not regret the decision he had made in 1944. His experience as the target of political persecution evoked some of his best and most popular works, including *Spartacus,* which became a major motion picture—directed by Stanley Kubrick and starring Kirk Douglas—as well as a best-selling book. It also led Fast to establish his own publishing house, the Blue Heron Press, and to write the first book in a well-received series of suspense novels under the pseudonym E. V. Cunningham.

Finally, Fast's time as a Communist in Cold War America provided him with an extraordinary story to share in his memoirs, *The Naked God* and *Being Red.* Charles C. Nash of *Library Journal* called *Being Red* "indispensable to the . . . literature on America's terrifying postwar Red Scare." As Fast explained to Jean W. Ross in a *Contemporary Authors* interview, "There is no way to imagine war or to imagine jail or to imagine being a father or a mother. These things can only be understood if you live through them. Maybe that's a price that a writer should pay."

Growing Up in Poverty

Fast's parents were immigrants, as he noted in an essay for *Something about the Author Autobiography Series (SAAS)*. His father, Barney Fastov, left Ukraine in 1878 and traveled to the United States, where immigration officials changed his last name to Fast. During the years that he worked in a tin factory on Long Island, Barney Fast fell in love with a photograph of a co-worker's sister who lived with her Lithuanian family in London. Fast sent this woman, Ida Miller, the money to travel to America, and she later agreed to marry him. Howard, born in 1914, was the fourth of their five children.

After a year-long battle with pernicious anemia, a severe blood disorder, Ida Fast died. Howard Fast, who was just eight-and-a-half years old at the time, recalled in *SAAS* that he repressed his memories of his mother when he learned of her death. "My mind chose forgetfulness so that I could remain sane. . . . it was not until years later that my memories of my mother began to return." While what Fast described as infantile amnesia helped him survive the emotional consequences of his mother's death, he had to rely on the companionship of his brother Jerome and his own resourcefulness to live through the physical ones.

As Fast remarked in *SAAS,* his mother made the poverty they lived in bearable. She made the children clothes of fine fabrics, cooked meals and cleaned, and told tales about her childhood in London with her English accent.

After Ida Fast's death, there was no one to ease the effects of poverty for the Fast children. Howard's life was miserable. Barney Fast descended into a deep depression which, coupled with the long hours he toiled at work, kept him blind to the fact that his children's clothes were falling apart and that their apartment was full of trash. Rena Fast, the oldest of Howard's siblings, hurried off to get married, while Julius, just four years old, was sent to live with Ida's mother. Since Arthur, the oldest boy, had died of diphtheria when he was six years old, Jerome and Howard were left on their own.

The boys did what they could to feed, clothe, and house themselves and managed to attend school like other children. At first, they stole the bread and dairy products delivered to middle-class people in the mornings, begged outside the Polo Grounds where the New York Giants used to play, and collected bottles to return for nickels. Howard Fast was ten and his brother was eleven when they found their first jobs; they jointly worked one route as delivery boys for the *Bronx Home News.* Later, they worked for the New York Public Library, where Fast was paid twenty-five cents an hour during the Great Depression. By the time he was fourteen, as Fast explained in *SAAS,* the boys "had arrived at an age where we could change things." The money they earned supplemented Barney Fast's income, and the sum was enough to care for the family (Julius had joined them) and pay to rent an apartment in a better part of town.

Becoming an Acclaimed Writer

Fast found a haven in the public library where he worked in Harlem. As he wrote in *SAAS,* "the walls gave me a sense of history, of order, of meaning in this strange world. . . . I read everything without discrimination, psychology, astronomy, physics, history, and more history—and some of it I understood and some of it I didn't." Fast also "began to think" during these years. He developed his own ideas based on various books he read on social theory, psychology, and science.

By the Author of
SECOND GENERATION
The all-time bestseller of a young man's baptism by fire during the bloody battle of Lexington.
April Morning by **Howard Fast**

This novel—one of Fast's most popular books—shows what it's like to be a raw, young soldier facing his first battle.

At this time, Fast decided to become a writer, and he intended to illustrate his own work. He earned a scholarship to the National Academy of Design, one of the best art schools in the country at the time. Fast was just sixteen, but he was determined to be successful in his chosen profession. "The question of ever being anything else never entered my mind; there was only one thing I could be in this life and that was what I was," he claimed in *SAAS.* He rose each morning at six to write before school and sent the stories he produced to various publishers. When *Amazing Stories* magazine bought "Wrath of Purple" in 1931 for thirty-seven dollars, Fast left the academy to devote himself to writing. While he worked to support his family and fund his brother Jerome's years in college, Fast wrote five unpublished novels. He kept writing even when his efforts met with rejection. He also took time to travel through the southern United States.

Fast's big break came when he was just nineteen. Dial Press purchased *Two Valleys* and he "was recognized as a bright new hope on the literary horizon" and received the Bread Loaf Literary Award, as Fast recalled in *SAAS.* Fast soon gained another feather in his cap with the publication of *The Children* in *Story* magazine. Fast had struggled to write this novel, based on the Halloween night when he saw a black boy just a year older than himself get lynched by a white gang. Several cities in New England, including Boston, banned that issue of *Story,* and the controversy called attention to his work. The young writer had made news and achieved literary success at the same time.

Fast married Bette Cohen, an artist he had met in 1936 on a blind date, after the publication of *The Children.* He began to write full-time, and he traveled throughout the United States with his wife. A visit to Valley Forge, Pennsylvania, inspired him to write *Conceived in Liberty,* which Fast called in *SAAS* "my first real break-through as a novelist." A stay on a Native American reservation in Oklahoma provided the background for *The Last Frontier,* which, according to Fast, "marked the end of our time of poverty and intermittent small riches."

Although *The Last Frontier* is written from the white man's perspective, Fast is frank about the United States' tyrannical treatment of the Native Americans. Readers gain an understanding of the Cheyenne people and, through an unsentimental narrative, come to sympathize with them. Some critics enthusiastically welcomed *The Last Frontier* as a historical novel and as an addition to literature on the history of Native Americans. Oliver La Farge, for example, described the book as "something new in Americana" in the *Saturday Review of Literature,* and exclaimed that it should be "hailed with joy." After noting the book's emphasis on the value of freedom, Joseph Henry Jackson of *New York Herald Tribune Books* suggested that "in the person of Mr. Fast we may have the next really important American historical novelist."

The Unvanquished, a novel written from the perspective of George Washington, was also praised for its use of little-known facts and events to explain Washington's greatness. In the words of Malcolm Cowley of *New Republic, The Unvanquished* "restores a great figure to our mythology." Fast's portrait of Thomas Paine in *Citizen Tom Paine* similarly highlighted the heroic aspects of a leader while offering readers a fictional account of his concerns, activities, and vision of America.

A bizarre death and an even stranger confession form the basis for this 1989 story of politics, morality, and destiny.

Work at the Office of War Information

Fast's plans for settling down in the cottage he and his wife had built near Tarrytown, New York, were disrupted with the intensification of World

War II. The couple moved back to the city, where Fast began to write pamphlets for the Office of War Information (OWI). Recognizing Fast's talents, executives there put him to work writing the propaganda that would be broadcast over British radio in a variety of languages throughout Europe every day. Fast's eyesight kept him out of the war, and he continued to work for what became known as the Voice of America until 1944.

Fast described the daily creation of a fifteen-minute script for the OWI as a nightmare in his *SAAS* essay. He was not even thirty years old when he became responsible for determining what people around the world would learn about the United States' war efforts. He was pressured by White House staff members, by bureaucracies including the Department of Agriculture and the Chamber of Commerce, and by private groups.

Fast continued to write, despite the frantic pace of his job at the OWI. *Freedom Road,* a novel which follows a group of freed slaves during the Reconstruction period after the Civil War, was published in 1944 and eventually sold one million copies. This bestseller was praised by the black leaders of the United States and recognized with the 1944 Schomburg Award for Race Relations.

Despite the success of *Freedom Road,* Fast's position at the OWI and his career as a writer were both in jeopardy in 1944. Word had spread that he was a Communist. As a result, many of his friends stopped seeing him, and J. Edgar Hoover had a pointed talk with Fast's OWI superiors. Fast was asked to resign instead of following the Voice of America when it moved to North Africa in 1944.

Fast could not deny his political orientation. The sense of justice that led him to favor socialism and then communism had its origins in his childhood. He had survived overwhelming poverty and witnessed the Great Depression. His father, who attempted to travel to Cuba in 1898 to fight in revenge for Spain's expulsion of Jews in 1492, was a dedicated unionist and was not afraid to picket despite the threat of injury. Fast's encounters with racism as a Jew growing up in a Protestant community, and various childhood memories like the one he wrote about in *The Children,* also shaped his understanding of what values were worth fighting for.

As Fast explained in *SAAS,* he had been fascinated with leftist social philosophy since reading Jack London's *The Iron Heel* as an adolescent, and later Karl Marx's *Communist Manifesto.* As his writing career took off, he realized that the authors and artists he most respected, like playwright Arthur Miller, held leftist political perspectives. The Communist party "was on the right side of all the causes he held dear: the union movement, civil rights and the fight against fascism," Ken Gross wrote in *People Weekly.* Nevertheless, it was not until after he was denied permission to travel with the Voice of America that Fast officially joined the Communist party, in 1944.

Consequences of Joining the Communist Party

Fast accepted work as a correspondent for *Coronet* magazine and the newspaper *P.M.* and traveled through India, North Africa, and Saudi Arabia for the rest of the war. As World War II ended, however, the Cold War began, and American Communists were treated as outcasts and even traitors. Fast soon became a victim of what Rhoda Koenig of *New York* magazine called the "anti-Communist mania" fueled by Senator Joseph McCarthy. In 1950, after Fast refused to provide the House Un-American Activities Committee with the names of people who provided money for medical aid to anti-fascist fighters in Spain, he was sentenced to jail for three months. In prison, Fast worked on the manuscript that would become *Spartacus* and developed terrible headaches that he still must treat with oxygen.

Upon Fast's release from prison, he was treated as a pariah. Although his previous novels had been appreciated for their messages about freedom and democracy, his next book, *The American,* "was denounced as Communist propaganda," as Fast recalled in *SAAS.* J. Edgar Hoover, the head of the FBI, blacklisted Fast and saw to it that no publishing company would touch his work. The FBI also tried to destroy Fast's books held in the New York Public Library.

When Fast brought *Spartacus* to his regular publishers, they rejected the novel. Instead of giving up, Fast boldly created his own publishing agency, the Blue Heron Press, and published *Spartacus* himself in 1951. The book eventually sold 40,000 copies in hardcover alone. Like many of Fast's previous novels, *Spartacus* tells the story of a small group of people fighting a seemingly impossible battle for their freedom. Yet this story is set in 71 B.C., in the Roman Empire, and the freedom fighters are escaped slaves. In addition to publishing his own books, Fast found another way to get his work published—he wrote under pseudonyms. He wrote *The Fallen Angel* as Walter Ericson, and he also wrote the first of a number of books under pseudonym E. V. Cunningham.

Fast's other reaction to the persecution he faced was to confront it with the political channels democracy afforded him. He exercised his freedom of speech to write for the *Daily Worker* and to write plays that were produced with the funds and influence of the Communist party. In 1952, Fast ran for a seat as the U.S. Congressman from New York's 23rd district as a member of the American Labor party. Fast's determination and the support of his wife were not enough to overcome the stigma attached to the party, however, and Fast lost the election. Finally, according to Ronald Radosh of *Commentary*, Fast contributed to the party's "propaganda campaign" and painted "a picture abroad of a United States in the grip of fascism, with Truman and then Eisenhower playing the role of Hitler."

Although Fast could not get his books published by mainstream publishers for many years during the 1950s, some of his books, including *Clarkton*, *My Glorious Brothers*, and *The Proud and the Free*, were translated and published in the Soviet Union. These books exalted labor and posited communism as the world's hope for the future. Fast was rewarded by the Soviet Union with the Stalin International Peace Prize in 1954.

Renouncing the Party

Fast's enchantment with the Communist party gradually wore off. According to Gross, the writer had "bridled at the party's ideological rigidity" for some time when he learned of the atrocities committed by Soviet Premier Joseph Stalin. Fast felt betrayed and decided to renounce communism. This was no small matter—his official withdrawal from the party in 1956 made the front page of the *New York Times*. It took Fast an entire book, *The Naked God*, to explain to himself and the nation how bitter he felt about the Communist party. According to Radosh, the book was "a strong indictment of American communism." Bernard Levin described *The Naked God* in *Specta-*

tor as "a tiny masterpiece of urgent, diamond-hard prose."

Over time, Fast rebuilt his reputation. While he continued to write serious novels with political messages, he found new outlets for his creativity. The Fast family moved to Los Angeles in 1974, where Fast wrote screenplays. The city also provided a setting for Fast's popular mystery series written under the pseudonym E. V. Cunningham. These crime novels feature Japanese-American Masao Masuto, who is a karate expert, a Zen Buddhist (as is Fast), and a detective for the Beverly Hills Police Department. Masuto uses his intellect, meditation, and his many relatives to solve mysteries. The Masao Masuto series has been well-received in the United States, and "Europeans are absolutely mad about them," as Fast told Ross. He continues to write the books "for fun," and considers them to be "almost a relaxation from the other books."

With the publication of *The Immigrants*, which became a bestseller in 1977, Fast began another popular series. Set in San Francisco, the five novels that make up the series follow four immigrant families (Catholic, Chinese, Jewish, and Protestant), tracing their interactions and charting their progress. In *The Immigrants*, Fast introduces the Italian-French Dan Lavette, whose determination to succeed leads him to power and wealth. *Second Generation*, *The Establishment*, *The Legacy* and *The Immigrant's Daughter* all focus on Barbara, Dan's daughter, while relating the stories of other characters as well.

The Immigrant's Daughter, the last book of the series, begins when Barbara is sixty years old and very much in control of her life. She makes a bid for a Congressional seat and has adventures in El Salvador. Fast told Ross that Barbara Lavette is an autobiographical character. "I had her born when I was born simply to have the chronology clear, and I immersed her in a lot of events that happened to me: the Spanish Civil War, the events of World War II, and so forth. So either through her or through her family the books are more or less a history of the sixty-eight years from 1914 to 1982."

Readers and critics alike have enjoyed the "Immigrants" series. Donald Newlove of the *New York Times Book Review* commented that *The Immigrants* allowed him to drop his guard, though he "always fear[s] that a Fast novel is proving a thesis." Joanne Leedom-Ackerman of *Christian Science Monitor* described *The Immigrants* as "a good, easy read" and asserted that "Fast is at his best as a storyteller."

Recalling the Past and Shaping the Future

In the later years of his career, Fast continued to write the kind of historical novels that made him famous. In a review of *Seven Days in June: A Novel of the American Revolution,* published in 1994, a *Publishers Weekly* critic remarked that Fast's unique approach to history enables him to create "genuine suspense from events whose outcome is a matter of historical fact."

Fast also continued to interpret current events, trends, and debates in realistic novels with contemporary and near-future settings. *New York Times Book Review* critic Morton Kondracke stated that *The Confession of Joe Cullen* "is virtually a novelization of the much-investigated, never-verified and often disputed conspiracy theory" in which the United States government "is involved in unethical activities in Central America." Sybil Steinberg of *Publishers Weekly* concluded that the book "delivers a resounding message about the decline of America's values."

Fast tackles the issue of abortion in *The Trial of Abigail Goodman.* As a *Publishers Weekly* critic noted, he views America's attitude toward abortion as "parochial" and is sympathetic to his protagonist, a college professor who has an abortion after the third trimester in a southern state with a retroactive law forbidding such acts. Ray Olson of *Booklist* observed that "every anti-abortion character" is stereotyped, and that Fast "undermines . . . any pretensions to evenhandedness." The *Publishers Weekly* critic, on the other hand, found *The Trial of Abigail Goodman* to be "electrifying" and called Fast "a master of courtroom pyrotechnics."

Fast recalled his experiences as a Communist in fiction as well as nonfiction. *The Pledge,* which prompted Sybil Steinberg of *Publishers Weekly* to state that "Fast's narrative sense has never been stronger," tells how a foreign correspondent becomes familiar with communism, loses his job, cannot get his book published, and spends time in jail. As Steinberg noted, Fast "captures the McCarthy-era atmosphere of suspicion and be-

In this 1994 novel, the Battle of Bunker Hill is presented through the eyes of fictional surgeon Evan Feversham.

trayal" and demonstrates how "demagogues" can undermine democracy.

Fast explains how his official embrace of communism changed his life in *Being Red: A Memoir,* published in 1990. Fast told Gross that he wrote the book with the inspiration of his son, Jonathan, who wanted to show it to his own children. Rhoda Koenig of *New York* magazine remarked that Fast's story is "a lively and gripping one," and that he "brings alive the days of parochial-school children carrying signs that read KILL A COMMIE FOR CHRIST."

With a critical eye, Ronald Radosh asserted in *Commentary* that *Being Red* contains information and perspectives that contradict portions of *The Naked God.* In Radosh's opinion, *Being Red* was the author's attempt to "rehabilitate" the Communist party he had admonished in *The Naked God.* "Now, nearly thirty-five years later, it almost sounds as though Fast wants to end his days winning back the admiration of those unreconstructed Communists," Radosh claimed, even calling them "some of the noblest human beings I have ever known."

In the early 1990s, Fast owned a large and comfortable house in Connecticut, where he lived with his wife, Bette, a sculptor. The Fasts' daughter, Rachel, had become a psychoanalyst and was writing her first book. Their son, Jonathan, was also a writer. Aside from his family's support, Fast has something else that no one—no matter their party affiliation—can take away from him. For sixty years he has toiled as a writer of historical fiction and biographies, plays, screenplays, scripts, short stories, poems, and even pamphlets. Fast's works have been translated into eighty-two languages, and worldwide sales of his novels were estimated at over eighty million copies.

Fast's voice has interpreted America's past and present, shaped its reputation at home and abroad, and perhaps even directed its future. One of his own favorites among his novels, *April Morning,* has been standard reading about the American Revolution in public schools for generations; the film *Spartacus* has become a popular classic; and *Being Red* offers an account of American history that Americans may never want to forget, whether or not they agree with Fast's perspectives. As Victor Howes commented in *Christian Science Monitor,* if Howard Fast "is a chronicler of some of mankind's most glorious moments, he is also a register of some of our more senseless deeds."

■ Works Cited

Cowley, Malcolm, "The Death of Debunking," *New Republic,* August 17, 1942, p. 203.

Fast, Howard, interview with Jean W. Ross, *Contemporary Authors New Revision Series,* Volume 3, Gale, 1981, pp. 132–137.

Fast, essay in *Something about the Author Autobiography Series,* Volume 18, Gale, 1994, pp. 167–87.

Gross, Ken, "Howard Fast," *People,* January 28, 1991, pp. 75–79.

Howes, Victor, "A Hard Flint Chip of a Story," *Christian Science Monitor,* August 23, 1972, p. 11.

Jackson, Joseph Henry, "An Important American Historical Novel," *New York Herald Tribune Books,* July 27, 1941, p. 3.

Koenig, Rhoda, "Party Time," *New York,* November 5, 1990, pp. 124–25.

Kondracke, Morton, "Uncle Sam Is the Heavy," *New York Times Book Review,* August 20, 1989, p. 25.

La Farge, Oliver, "Flight of the Cheyennes," *Saturday Review of Literature,* July 26, 1941, p. 5.

Leedom-Ackerman, Joanne, "Fast's Quick-Scene Novel: Grist for TV Drama Mill?," *Christian Science Monitor,* November 7, 1977, p. 18.

Levin, Bernard, "Hard and Fast," *Spectator,* August 15, 1958, p. 227.

Nash, Charles C., review of *Being Red, Library Journal,* October 1, 1990, p. 96.

Newlove, Donald, "Three Novels: 'The Immigrants,'" *New York Times Book Review,* October 2, 1977, p. 24.

Olson, Ray, review of *The Trial of Abigail Goodman, Booklist,* July, 1993, p. 1916.

Radosh, Ronald, "About-Face," *Commentary,* March, 1991, pp. 62–64.

Review of *Seven Days in June, Publishers Weekly,* July 11, 1994, p. 66.

Steinberg, Sybil, review of *The Pledge, Publishers Weekly,* July 22, 1988, p. 41.

Steinberg, Sybil, review of *The Confession of Joe Cullen, Publishers Weekly,* June 30, 1989, p. 84.

Review of *The Trial of Abigail Goodman, Publishers Weekly,* June 21, 1993, p. 83.

■ For More Information See

BOOKS

Meyer, Hershel D., *History and Conscience; The Case of Howard Fast,* Anvil-Atlas, 1958.

Newquist, Roy, *Counterpoint,* Rand McNally, 1964.

Rideout, Walter B., *The Radical Novel in the United States: Some Interrelations of Literature and Society,* Harvard University Press, 1956.

PERIODICALS

Atlantic, September, 1944, p. 127.

Bestsellers, September 1, 1973; November, 1979.

Book Week, May 9, 1943.

Christian Science Monitor, July 8, 1939.

Gentlemen's Quarterly, October, 1990, pp. 145–46.

Horn Book, June, 1973.

Nation, July 15, 1991, p. 88.

National Review, February 24, 1989, pp. 62–63.
New Statesman, August 8, 1959.
New York Times, July 14, 1963, p. 18.
Washington Post, October 4, 1979; March 3, 1987.
　　　　　—Sketch by Ronie-Rochelle Garcia-Johnson

Alan Dean Foster

■ Personal

Also writes as James Lawson; born November 18, 1946, in New York, NY; son of Maxwell Feinberg (a salesperson) and Helen (a homemaker; maiden name Smith) Foster; married JoAnn Oxley (a homemaker), July 5, 1975. *Education:* University of California, Los Angeles, B. A., 1968, M. F. A., 1969. *Politics:* "Adaptable." *Religion:* Jewish. *Hobbies and other interests:* Backpacking, basketball, body surfing, classical and hard rock music, collecting first–edition science fiction works and art, biking, scuba diving, weight lifting, world travel.

■ Addresses

Home and office—Prescott, AZ. *Agent*—(fiction) Virginia Kidd, Box 278, Milford, PA 18337; (scripts) Ilse Lahn, 5300 Fulton, Van Nuys, CA 91401.

■ Career

Writer. Headlines Ink Agency (public relations firm), Studio City, CA, head copywriter, 1970–71; Los Angeles City College, Los Angeles, CA, instructor in motion picture writing and history, 1971–76; University of California, Los Angeles, instructor in English and film, periodically beginning in 1971; Northern Arizona University, Flagstaff, AZ, adjunct faculty member, 1991—. City of Prescott Planning and Zoning Commission, vice–chairman, 1986–87. *Military service:* U. S. Army Reserve, 1969–75. *Member:* Science Fiction Writers of America (Nebula Awards chairman, 1973–74), Authors Guild, Writers Guild of America West.

■ Awards, Honors

Galaxy Award, 1979, for *Splinter of the Mind's Eye: From the Adventures of Luke Skywalker;* Southwest Book Award, 1990, for *Cyber Way.*

■ Writings

SCIENCE FICTION NOVELS

Splinter of the Mind's Eye: From the Adventures of Luke Skywalker (Science Fiction Book Club selection), Del Rey, 1978. *The Man Who Used the Universe,* (Science Fiction Book Club selection), Warner Books, 1983.

The I Inside, Warner Books, 1984.
Slipt, Berkeley Publishing, 1984.
Glory Lane (Science Fiction Book Club selection), Ace Books, 1986.

To the Vanishing Point (Science Fiction Book Club selection), Warner Books, 1988. *Quozl* (Science Fiction Book Club selection), Ace Books, 1989.

Cyber Way (Science Fiction Book Club selection), Ace Books, 1990.

Cat-a-Lyst, Ace Books, 1991.

Codgerspace, Ace Books, 1992.

Chorus Skating, Warner Books, 1994.

Design for Great-Day, Tor Books, 1995.

The Dig, Warner Books, 1995.

Montezuma Strip, Warner Books, 1995.

"THE DAMNED" SERIES

A Call to Arms, Del Rey, 1991.

The False Mirror, Del Rey, 1991.

Spoils of War, Del Rey, 1993.

"COMMONWEALTH" SERIES

The Tar-Aiym Krang, Ballantine, 1972.

Bloodhype, Ballantine, 1973.

Midworld, (Science Fiction Book Club selection), Ballantine, 1975.

Orphan Star (sequel to *The Tar-Aiym Krang*) Del Rey, 1977.

The End of the Matter (sequel to *Orphan Star*), Del Rey, 1977.

Cachalot (Science Fiction Book Club selection), Del Rey, 1980.

Nor Crystal Tears, Del Bey, 1982.

Flinx of the Commonwealth, three volumes, Ballantine, 1982.

For Love of Mother-Not, Del Rey, 1983.

Voyage to the City of the Dead, Del Rey, 1984.

Sentenced to Prism, Del Rey, 1985.

Flinx in Flux, Del Rey, 1988.

"ICERIGGER" TRILOGY

Icerigger, Ballantine, 1974.

Mission to Moulokin, Del Rey, 1979.

The Deluge Drivers, Del Rey, 1987.

"SPELL SINGER" SERIES

Spellsinger, Warner Books, 1981.

Spellsinger at the Gate (includes *Spellsinger* and *The Hour of the Gate;* also see below) Phantasia Press, 1983.

The Hour of the Gate (Science Fiction Book Club selection), Warner Books, 1984.

The Day of Dissonance (Science Fiction Book Club selection), Phantasia Press, 1984.

The Moment of the Magician (Science Fiction Book Club selection), Phantasia Press, 1964.

Season of the Spellsong (includes *Spellsinger, The Hour of the Gate,* and *The Day of Dissonance*), Doubleday, 1984.

The Paths of the Perambulator, Phantasia Press, 1985.

The Time of the Transference (Science Fiction Book Club selection), Phantasia Press, 1986.

Spellsinger's Scherzo (includes *The Moment of the Magician, The Paths of the Perambulator,* and *The Time of Transference*), Doubleday, 1987.

Son of Spellsinger, Warner Books, 1993.

NOVELIZATIONS

Luana (based on screenplay by Louis Road), Ballantine, 1974.

Dark Star (based on screenplay of the same title by Dan O'Bannon and John Carpenter), Ballantine, 1974.

Alien (based on the screenplay of the same title by O'Bannon; Science Fiction Book Club selection), Warner Books, 1979.

The Black Hole (based on screenplay of the same title by Jeb Rosenbrook and Gerry Day; Science Fiction Book Club selection), Del Rey, 1980.

Clash of the Titans (based on screenplay of the same title by Beverley Cross; Science Fiction Book Club selection), Warner Books, 1981.

Outland (based on the screenplay of the same title by Peter Hyams), Warner Books, 1981.

The Thing (based on the screenplay of the same title by Bill Lancaster; Science Fiction Book Club selection), Bantam, 1982.

Krull (based on the screenplay of the same title by Stanford Sherman), Warner Books, 1983.

The Last Starfighter (based on the screenplay of the same title by Jonathan Betuel), Berekley Publishing, 1984.

Starman (based on the screenplay of the same title by Ray Gideon, Bruce Evans, and Dean Riesner), Warner Books, 1944.

Pale Rider (based on the screenplay of the same title by Michael Butler and Dennis Shryak), Warner Books, 1985.

Aliens (based on the screenplay of the same title by James Cameron; Science Fiction Book Club selection), Warner Books, 1986.

Alien Nation (based on the screenplay of the same title by Roakne S. O'Bannon), Warner Books, 1988.

Alien 3, Warner Books, 1991.

"STAR TREK LOG" SERIES

Star Trek Log One, Ballantine, 1974.
Star Trek Log Two, Ballantine, 1974.
Star Trek Log Three, Ballantine, 1975.
Star Trek Log Four, Ballantine, 1975.
Star Trek Log Five, Ballantine, 1975.
Star Trek Log Six, Ballantine, 1976.
Star Trek Log Seven, Ballantine, 1976.
Star Trek Log Eight, Ballantine, 1976.
Star Trek Log Nine, Ballantine, 1977.
Star Trek Log Ten, Del Rey, 1978.

EDITOR

Animated Features and Silly Symphonies, Abbeville, 1980.

The Best of Eric Frank Russell, second edition, Ballantine, 1986.

(With Martin Greenberg) *Smart Dragons, Foolish Elves,* Ace Books, 1991.

Betcha Can't Read Just One, Ace Books, 1993.

The Soul of Liberty: The Universal Ethic of Freedom and Human Rights, Fred E. Foldvary, Gutenberg Press, 1980.

OTHER

With Friends Like These . . . (collection), Del Rey, 1977.

(Author of story) *Star Trek: The Motion Picture,* Paramount, 1979.

Who Needs Enemies? (collection), Del Rey, 1984.

Maori (historical novel), Berkley Publishing, 1988.

The Metrognome and Other Stories (collection), Del Rey, 1990.

(Afterword) *The Fantasy Art and Techniques of Tim Hildebrandt,* Avery Publishing Group, 1992.

Author of radio scripts for the "Episodes in American History" series produced by station KFIR, Oregon, including *The Age of Ice, Mystery of the North, Flip Wilson Did Not Discover America, But . . ., First in Space, Goodyear, Cream Cheese, and Rubber, The Monitor Was a Swede, The Battle We Almost Lost,* and *The Iroquois*

Confederacy. Contributor to anthologies, including *World's Best SF, 1972–72,* two volumes, edited by Donald A. Wollheim and Arthur W. Saha, DAW Books, 1972–73; and *Fellowship of the Stars: Nine Science Fiction Stories,* edited by Terry Carr, Simon & Schuster, 1974. Contributor of short stories to science fiction and fantasy magazines, including *Adam, Analog, Arkham Collector, Cog, Fantasy Book, Galaxy, Galileo, Issac Asimov's Science Fiction Magazine, Magazine of Fantasy and Science Fiction,* and *Worlds of If.* Author of media columns for the periodicals *Rigel,* 1981–83, and *Science Fiction Review,* 1991—.

Foster's work has been translated into numerous languages. The author's correspondence and manuscripts are housed at the Hayden Library, Arizona State University.

■ Sidelights

Alan Dean Foster once commented: "I write in order to meet people I'd like to meet but otherwise never will, and to visit places I otherwise never could. Faraway or imaginary worlds and people often filled my idle childhood hours. Today I share them with others." These fantastic worlds and the beings who inhabit them—such as the ostrich–like Wais, extra–dimensional Incas, and fierce fighting otters—have entertained readers of all ages for over twenty years. When not creating new peoples and universes, Foster and his family live with dogs, cats, fish, visiting javelina, porcupines, eagles and other animals native to the southwestern United States. An avid traveler and adventurer, the author has studied karate with Chuck Norris, and spent time in many exotic spots of the globe (including the Peruvian jungle). "All my travels, everyone I meet, eventually find their way into my stories," Foster noted. "Keep that in mind if you ever meet me. You might find yourself in the next tale I tell."

Foster was born in New York City. He grew up in Los Angeles, and eventually attended the University of California. As a child, Foster was exposed to science fiction and fantasy by his father and his uncle (both men were avid sf–fantasy readers). As he commented, Foster "started writing science fiction because it had been around the house since I was a kid." The author's other literary favorites included comic books about Scrooge McDuck, written by Carl Barks, and

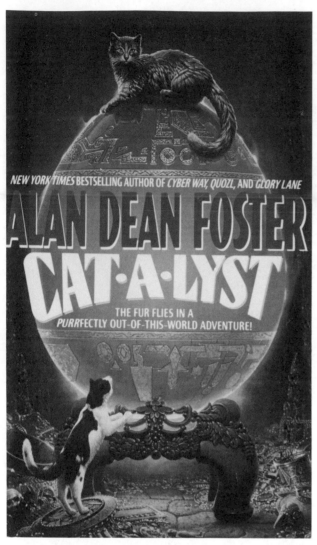

In this 1983 book, graduate student and musician Jonathan Thomas Meriwether is drawn into a world of magic and danger by a ragtag group of adventurers from another dimension.

Moby Dick, by Herman Melville. "From Barks I learned the value of education, research, honesty, and more importantly than anything else, the fact that getting old doesn't have to be a bad thing," he remarked.

Foster originally planned to be a lawyer, so he heavily emphasized the social sciences in his college studies. This strategy changed when Foster took some film writing courses when he was a senior. After concluding that he wanted entertain people—instead of wearing a suit and tie and going to an office every day—the author decided to pursue a graduate degree in cinema. While working on his studies, Foster published his first pro-

fessional piece, a short story in *The Arkham Collector.* Foster continued to write and publish short fiction in magazines throughout graduate school.

After graduation, Foster worked as a copywriter for a small advertising and public relations company in Studio City, California. He taught classes in motion picture writing and history from 1971 until 1976, all the while composing early "Commonwealth" novels and many of the "Star Trek Log" books. In 1976, Foster decided to devote himself fully to writing; he also began to studying the world, travelling to Tahiti, French Polynesia, Europe, Asia and parts of Africa. "When I can I travel as often as possible, seeking out the obscure parts of our planet as well as the

While on vacation in Peru, movie star Jason Carter discovers members of a lost civilization bent on taking over the planet.

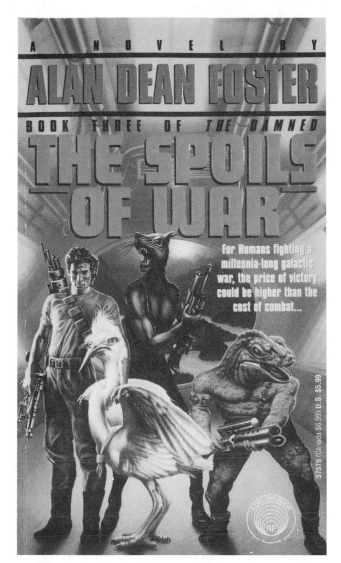

In the third volume of "The Damned" series, human nature comes under fire after a scholar predicts that earthling aggression could damage a fragile intergalactic union.

developed. I am fascinated by small things as well as by the great and impressive," he noted.

The author's decision to write full time was, in part, triggered by the publication of a number of works, including *Icerigger*—the first book in the "Icerigger" trilogy—and *Orphan Star,* the sequel to Foster's first "Commonwealth" novel, *The Tar–Aiym Krang.* In an essay for *Twentieth–Century Science Fiction Writers,* Foster described the Universe of Commonwealth as "a future society in which mankind has formed a close alliance with a race of insect–like creatures call the Thranx. . . . It is my eventual intention to tie all the Commonwealth stories together in one grand conclusion

(perhaps in 40 or so years)." One of Foster's most popular characters—the genetically enhanced orphan Flinx—appears in several of the "Commonwealth" books. Flinx, together with his pet minidragon, have numerous adventures as they travel in search of the orphan's parents. Describing the "Commonwealth" books as "fascinating" in a piece for *Twentieth–Century Science Fiction Writers,* John I. Lawson added that Foster's "plausible, scientifically sound settings combined with vivid, sensual descriptions make [the author's] world's come alive."

Foster's ability to create interesting new worlds—and characters—is apparent in many of his works. In *Nor Crystal Tears,* for example, the insect–like Thranx first come in contact with humans. Told through the eyes of Thranx agriculturalist Ryo, the tale explores how the two cultures struggle to form a community (a struggle that eventually leads to the formation of the Commonwealth). *Midworld* follows the trials of a lost space colony after it is forced to set up camp on a jungle–like planet. As the years go by, the colonists form a symbiotic relationship with their environment, a bond endangered by greedy industrialists. And in the "Icerigger" stories, a group of stranded people must use all their skills to survive on a cold, unfriendly planet.

Although a lot of Foster's work has been defined as "hard" science fiction, the author has also been lauded for his fantasy tales. The "Spellsinger" series, for example, takes place in an alternate world that sometimes intersects with modern Los Angeles. Jonathon Thomas Meriweather (or "Jon–Tom"), a UCLA student, is drafted by a rag–tag bunch of otherworldy adventurers to help battle an ancient evil. A large part of the success of the "Spellsinger" books is the humor that accompanies much of the action (such as the fact that Jon–Tom is a *most* reluctant hero).

When not working on original pieces, Foster keeps busy writing film novelizations. These titles, like much of the author's original fiction, cover a broad spectrum of subjects. There are science fiction works—like *Alien* and its two sequels—as well as fantasies such as *Clash of the Titans,* which explores the world of Greek mythology, and thrillers like the space crime drama *Outland.* Foster had even more "hands on" experience with film when he wrote the screenplay for *Star Trek: The Motion Picture.*

"I try to explore how people, especially ordinary people, react to extraordinary circumstances," Foster commented in his essay. Combined with themes like ecological deterioration, prejudice, war/peace and change, this exploration has helped the author create a body of work that is both unique and accessible to a wide audience. It is also, as Lawson suggested, why Foster "not only holds his old fans, but continues to attract new ones."

■ Works Cited

Foster, Alan Dean, essay in *Twentieth–Century Science Fiction Writers,* 3rd edition, St. James, 1991, p. 287.

Lawson, John I., "Alan Dean Foster," *Twentieth–Century Science Fiction Writers,* St. James, 1991, pp. 288–89.

■ For More Information See

PERIODICALS

Analog, May, 1983, p. 163; September, 1983, p. 105; December, 1983, p. 160; February, 1984, p. 163; November, 1984, p. 163; January, 1985, p. 176; June, 1985, p. 161; April, 1986, p. 173; August, 1987, p. 181; April, 1988, p. 177; April, 1989, p. 175; December 15, 1989, p. 177.

Fantasy Review, August, 1984, p. 10; September, 1984, p. 28; October, 1984, p. 30; November, 1984, p. 31; December, 1984, pp. 24–25; January, 1985, p. 13; March, 1985, p. 26; April, 1985, p. 20; November, 1985, p. 19; March, 1986, p. 18; January, 1987, p. 36.

Locus, October 23, 1974; June 3, 1975; June 30, 1976; February, 1990, p. 52; April, 1990, p. 21; August, 1990, p. 48; January, 1991, p. 75; April, 1991, p. 23; May, 1991, p. 47; June, 1991, p. 48; July, 1991, pp. 33 and 46.

Magazine of Fantasy and Science Fiction, August, 1982, p. 20; April 1987, p. 54; April, 1988, p. 46; April, 1989, p. 86; May, 1990, p. 65; March, 1991, p. 81.

Science Fiction Review, May, 1977; November/December, 1978; November, 1981, p. 58; February, 1983, p. 16; May, 1983, p. 54; November, 1984, p. 17.

—Sketch by Hollis Helmeci

Louis L'Amour

■ Personal

Also wrote under pseudonym Jim Mayo, and as Tex Burns, a house pseudonym. Born March 28, 1908, in Jamestown, ND; died June 10, 1988, of lung cancer in Los Angeles, CA; son of Louis Charles (a veterinarian and farm machinery salesman), and Emily (Dearborn) LaMoore; married Katherine Elizabeth Adams, February 19, 1956; children: Beau Dearborn, Angelique Gabrielle. *Education:* Self-educated.

■ Career

Author and lecturer. Held numerous jobs, including positions as longshoreman, lumberjack, miner, elephant handler, hay shocker, boxer, flume builder, and fruit picker. Lecturer at many universities including University of Oklahoma, Baylor University, University of Southern California, and University of Redlands. *Military service:* U.S. Army, 1942–46; became first lieutenant. *Member:* Writers Guild of America (West), Western Writers of America, Academy of Motion Picture Arts and Sciences, American Siam Society, California Writers Guild, California Academy of Sciences.

■ Awards, Honors

Western Writers of America Award—Novel, 1969, for *Down the Long Hills;* LL.D., Jamestown College, 1972; Theodore Roosevelt Rough Rider award, North Dakota, 1972; American Book Award, 1980, for *Bendigo Shafter;* Buffalo Bill Award, 1981; Distinguished Newsboy Award, 1981; National Genealogical Society Award, 1981; Congressional Gold Medal, 1983; Presidential Medal of Freedom, 1984; LL.D., Pepperdine University, 1984.

■ Writings

NOVELS

Westward the Tide, World's Work (Surrey, England), 1950.

Hondo (expanded version of his story, "The Gift of Cochise"; also see below), Gold Medal, 1953, reprinted with introduction by Michael T. Marsden, Gregg, 1978.

Crossfire Trail (also see below), Ace Books, 1954, reprinted with introduction by Keith Jarrod, Gregg, 1980.

Heller with a Gun (also see below), Gold Medal, 1954.

Kilkenny (also see below), Ace Books, 1954, reprinted with introduction by Wesley Laing, Gregg, 1980.

To Tame a Land, Fawcett, 1955.

Guns of the Timberlands, Jason, 1955.

The Burning Hills, Jason, 1956.
Silver Canyon (expanded version of his story, "Riders of the Dawn"), Avalon, 1956.
Last Stand at Papago Wells (also see below), Gold Medal, 1957.
The Tall Stranger (also see below), Fawcett, 1957.
Sitka, Appleton, 1957.
Radigan, Bantam, 1958.
The First Fast Draw (also see below), Bantam, 1959.
Taggart, Bantam, 1959.
Flint, Bantam, 1960.
Shalako, Bantam, 1962.
Killoe (also see below), Bantam, 1962.
High Lonesome, Bantam, 1962.
How the West Was Won (based on the screenplay by James R. Webb), Bantam, 1963.
Fallon, Bantam, 1963.
Catlow, Bantam, 1963.
Dark Canyon, Bantam, 1963.
Hanging Woman Creek Bantam, 1964.
Kiowa Trail (also see below), Bantam, 1965.
The High Graders, Bantam, 1965.
The Key-Lock Man (also see below), Bantam, 1965.
Kid Rodelo, Bantam, 1966.
Kilrone, Bantam, 1966.
The Broken Gun, Bantam, 1966.
Matagorda, Bantam, 1967.
Down the Long Hills, Bantam, 1968.
Chancy, Bantam, 1968.
Conagher, Bantam, 1969.
The Empty Land, Bantam, 1969.
The Man Called Noon, Bantam, 1970.
Reilly's Luck, Bantam, 1970.
Brionne, Bantam, 1971.
Under the Sweetwater Rim, Bantam, 1971.
Tucker, Bantam, 1971.
North to the Rails, Bantam, 1971.
Callaghen, Bantam, 1972.
The Ferguson Rifle, Bantam, 1973.
The Quick and the Dead, Bantam, 1973, revised edition, 1979.
The Man from Skibbereen, G. K. Hall, 1973.
The Californios, Saturday Review Press, 1974.
Rivers West, Saturday Review Press, 1974.
Over on the Dry Side, Saturday Review Press, 1975.
The Rider of the Lost Creek (based on one of his short stories), Bantam, 1976.
Where the Long Grass Blows, Bantam, 1976.
Borden Chantry, Bantam, 1977.
The Mountain Valley War (based on one of his short stories), Bantam, 1978.
Fair Blows the Wind, Bantam, 1978.
Bendigo Shafter, Dutton, 1978.
The Iron Marshall, Bantam, 1979.

The Proving Trail, Bantam, 1979.
The Warrior's Path, Bantam, 1980.
Comstock Lode, Bantam, 1981.
Milo Talon, Bantam, 1981.
The Cherokee Trail, Bantam, 1982.
The Shadow Riders, Bantam, 1982.
The Lonesome Gods, Bantam, 1983.
Son of a Wanted Man, Bantam, 1984.
The Walking Drum, Bantam, 1984.
Passin' Through, Bantam, 1985.
Last of the Breed, Bantam, 1986.
West of the Pilot Range, Bantam, 1986.
A Trail to the West, Bantam, 1986.
The Haunted Mesa, Bantam, 1987.

Also author of *Man Riding West,* Carroll & Graf, and of *The Turkey Feather Riders.*

"SACKETT FAMILY" SERIES; NOVELS

The Daybreakers, Bantam, 1960.
Sackett, Bantam, 1961.
Lando, Bantam, 1962.
Mojave Crossing, Bantam, 1964.
The Sackett Brand, Bantam, 1965.
Mustang Man, Bantam, 1966.
The Skyliners, Bantam, 1967.
The Lonely Men, Bantam, 1969.
Galloway, Bantam, 1970.
Ride the Dark Trail, Bantam, 1972.
Treasure Mountain, Bantam, 1972.
Sackett's Land, Saturday Review Press, 1974.
The Man from the Broken Hills, Bantam, 1975.
To the Far Blue Mountains, Dutton, 1976.
Sackett's Gold, Bantam, 1977.
The Warrior's Path, Bantam, 1980.
Lonely on the Mountain, Bantam, 1980.
Ride the River, Bantam, 1983.
Jubal Sackett, Bantam, 1985.

"HOPALONG CASSIDY" SERIES; PUBLISHED UNDER HOUSE PSEUDONYM TEX BURNS

Hopalong Cassidy and the Riders of High Rock, Doubleday, 1951, published as *The Riders of High Rock: A Hopalong Cassidy Novel,* Bantam, 1993.
Hopalong Cassidy and the Rustlers of West Fork Doubleday, 1951, published as *The Rustlers of West Fork: A Hopalong Cassidy Novel,* G. K. Hall, 1994.
Hopalong Cassidy and the Trail to Seven Pines, Doubleday, 1951, published as *The Trail to Seven Pines: A Hopalong Cassidy Novel,* G. K. Hall, 1994.
Hopalong Cassidy: Trouble Shooter, Doubleday, 1952.

UNDER PSEUDONYM JIM MAYO; REPRINTED UNDER AUTHOR'S REAL NAME

Showdown at Yellow Butte (also see below), Ace Books, 1954, reprinted with introduction by Scott R. McMillan, Gregg, 1980.

Utah Blaine (also see below), Ace Books, 1954, reprinted with introduction by Wayne C. Lee, Gregg, 1980.

OMNIBUS VOLUMES

Kiowa Trail [and] *Killoe*, Ulverscroft, 1979.

The First Fast Draw [and] *The Key-Lock Man*, Ulverscroft, 1979.

Four Complete Novels (includes *The Tall Stranger, Kilkenny, Hondo*, and *Showdown at Yellow Butte*), Avenal Books, 1980.

Five Complete Novels (includes *Crossfire Trail, Utah Blaine, Heller with a Gun, Last Stand at Papago Wells*, and *To Tame a Land*), Avenel Books, 1981.

L'Amour Westerns (four volumes), Gregg, 1981.

SHORT STORIES

War Party, Bantam, 1975.

Yondering, Bantam, 1980, revised edition, 1989.

The Strong Shall Live, Bantam, 1980.

Buckskin Run, Bantam, 1981.

Law of the Desert Born, Bantam, 1983.

Bowdrie, Bantam, 1983.

The Hills of Homicide, Bantam, 1984.

Bowdrie's Law, Bantam, 1984.

Riding for the Brand, Bantam, 1986.

Dutchman's Flat, Bantam, 1986.

The Trail to Crazy Man, Bantam, 1986.

The Rider of the Ruby Hills, Bantam, 1986.

Night over the Solomons, Bantam, 1986.

West from Singapore, Bantam, 1987.

Lonigan, Bantam, 1988.

The Outlaws of Mesquite, Bantam, 1991.

OTHER

Smoke from This Altar (poetry), Lusk (Oklahoma City, OK), 1939.

Frontier (essays), Bantam, 1984.

The Sackett Companion: A Personal Guide to the Sackett Novels (nonfiction), Bantam, 1988.

A Trail of Memories: The Quotations of Louis L'Amour (excerpts from L'Amour's fiction), compiled by daughter, Angelique L'Amour, Bantam, 1988.

The Education of a Wandering Man (autobiography), Bantam, 1989.

Also author of filmscripts and more than sixty-five television scripts. Author of foreword, Frank C. McCarthy, *Frank C. McCarthy: The Old West,* Greenwich Press, 1981. Contributor of more than four hundred short stories and articles to more than eighty magazines in the United States and abroad, including *Argosy, Collier's,* and *Saturday Evening Post.*

■ Adaptations

Feature films and television movies include *Hondo,* Warner Bros., 1953; *East of Sumatra,* Universal, 1953; *Four Guns to the Border,* Universal, 1954; *Treasure of the Ruby Hills,* Allied Artists, 1955; *Kilkenny,* Columbia, 1956; *The Burning Hills,* Warner Bros., 1956; *Utah Blaine,* Columbia, 1956; *Walk Tall,* Allied Artists, 1957; *Last Stand at Papago Wells,* Columbia, 1958; *Heller with Pink Tights* (based on his *Heller with a Gun*), Paramount, 1960; *Guns of the Timberlands,* Warner Bros., 1960; *Taggart,* Universal, 1964; *Kid Rodelo,* Paramount, 1966; *Shalako,* Cinerama Releasing Corp., 1968; *Catlow,* Metro-Goldwyn-Mayer, 1971; *The Broken Gun,* Warner Bros., 1972; *The Man Called Noon,* Scotia-Barber, 1973; *Down the Long Hills,* Disney Channel, 1986; *The Quick and the Dead,* Home Box Office, 1987; the *Sackett Family* series was made into a television miniseries entitled *The Sacketts.* Audio cassettes of L'Amour's work include *Riding for the Brand* (adapted from a short story from *Riding for the Brand*), Bantam, 1987; *Bowdrie Passes Through,* (adapted from a short story from *Bowdrie*), Bantam, 1988; *Keep Travelin' Rider* (adapted from a short story from *Dutchman's Flat*), Bantam, 1988; *One for the Mojave Kid* (adapted from a short story from *Dutchman's Flat*), Bantam, 1988, and *The Black Rock Coffin Makers.*

■ Sidelights

"It was May 14. In a few days my class back in Jamestown, North Dakota would be graduating from high school, and I was in Singapore."

With these words, Louis L'Amour introduces *Education of a Wandering Man,* his memoir that traces his self-education as he pursued it around the globe. Although he left home at the age of fifteen before finishing high school, L'Amour pursued his own destiny to become one of the world's most popular writers. His achievements were even more remarkable in light of the obstacles that he overcame to achieve his success. He had little formal education, never graduated from high school, spent much of his youth wandering from job to job, and was over forty by the time he published his first novel. Still, he sold more books than nearly every other contemporary novelist. He wrote more million-copy bestsellers than any other American fiction writer. He was the only novelist in this nation's history to be granted either of the country's highest honors—the Congressional Gold Medal and the Presidential Medal of Freedom. L'Amour received them both. "I thought it was very interesting," he told Mary Scott Dye in an interview for *Contemporary Authors New Revision Series,* "that over half of the other recipients of the Medal of Freedom who were on the platform with me had read my books."

A Frontier Life Commences

Louis Dearborn LaMoore was the seventh and youngest child of Louis Davenport La–Moore, a veterinarian, and his wife Emily. L'Amour (who changed the spelling of his name after he began his writing career) claimed that he could trace his ancestry in America back to the seventeenth century. His father was a state veterinarian who also served the community of Jamestown, North Dakota, as deputy sheriff, policeman, and alderman. Both L'Amour's parents were educated and adaptable beyond the demands of the North Dakota prairie. "As horses gave way to tractors for farm work," declared Robert L. Gale in his study *Louis L'Amour,* "Doc LaMoore began to sell steam threshers, soon finding himself able

to repair such implements. Emily LaMoore . . . is remembered as a quiet person, a passionate gardener, an avid reader, an amateur poetess, and a splendid storyteller."

Their youngest son Louis grew up in a household that appreciated education, enjoyed reading, and recognized the value of physical fitness. "From his earliest years," Gale related, "L'Amour was an unusual blend of Huck Finn-like physicality and Tom Sawyer-like bookishness. He attended school faithfully for about six years but decided at the age of twelve that doing so was interfering with his education. Thereafter, although he continued attendance until he was fifteen, he preferred both the outdoors and eclectic reading."

The oral tradition of storytelling permanently shaped L'Amour's narrative style. He identified himself as a storyteller in the tradition of Geoffrey Chaucer, the fourteenth-century author of *The Canterbury Tales,* and many of his stories came from ordinary people, as did Chaucer's. When the author's father inspected cattle, his son tagged along to listen to the cattlemen tell of their adventures on the trail. Other stories about the frontier came to him from his father, who learned Indian lore from a Huron Indian; his grandfather, a veteran of the Civil War; an uncle who, refusing to settle, travelled and worked throughout the West; and the miners, gunfighters, and cowboys he worked alongside after leaving home at the age of fifteen. One of L'Amour's other sources was an employer who had been raised as an Apache Indian, and

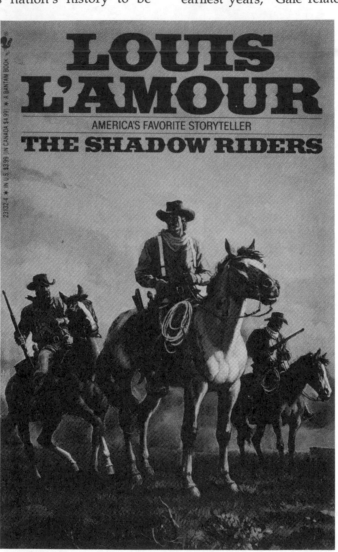

Dal unites with his two brothers and his uncle in a relentless pursuit of thirty killers who have kidnapped his sister and girlfriend.

who taught him much about the Indian experience in the American west.

L'Amour's tastes in reading and in exercise were very broad. An early job as a Western Union messenger boy led to an acquaintance with pulp fiction. "Like many youngsters," stated Robert Weinberg in *The Louis L'Amour Companion,* "Louis was fascinated by the science fiction stories he found in such titles as *Argosy* and *Science and Invention*. The strong thread of fantastic elements that ran through much of L'Amour's fiction probably had its roots in the heroic adventures of John Carter of Mars as related by Edgar Rice Burroughs." He also maintained a strong interest in boxing, a skill that proved very useful to him during his travels. "Right now, I can't remember a time when I wasn't boxing," L'Amour stated in Weinberg's book. "My father and my two brothers took a swing at it, and so I just about grew up with gloves on my hands. By the time I was thirteen, and already starting to grow up fast, I was working in the gym with professional fighters."

Far Places of the Earth

Despite their gifts, the LaMoores encountered hard times during the 1920s. "The relentless tide of progress," explained Weinberg, "put his father out of a job." At the end of 1923, Doc LaMoore sold his practice and moved his family to the Southwest. It was then that L'Amour struck out on his own. "I'd missed connections with my family," he stated in Weinberg's book, "and when they next heard from me, I was in Liverpool, England." L'Amour's "yondering" adventures also took him to California and around the world. By the time his former classmates were graduating, L'Amour related in *Education of a Wandering Man,* "I had skinned dead cattle in Texas, baled hay in New Mexico, worked as a roustabout with the Hagenbeck-Wallace Circus, and in between times had boxed a couple of exhibitions in small towns and won a few fights. I had hoboed across Texas on the Southern Pacific and shipped out to the West Indies as a seaman and, later, on another ship, to Liverpool and Manchester, England. Returning, I had planted fruit trees near Phoenix, worked as a caretaker of a mine in the Bradshaws, and spent three very rough months 'on the beach' in San Pedro." Later, after reestablishing contact with his family, L'Amour traveled in the Near and Far East. He stated in Weinberg's book that he "sailed

In this autobiographical work, L'Amour describes the events in his life that shaped him, as well as the people and places he saw that inspired his books.

a dhow from Aden to Port Twefik through the Red Sea. . . . In China, I boxed a couple of times, ran a machine gun for Chiang Kaishek, and left stoking coal on a British Blue Funnel boat bound for Balikpapan, Borneo."

L'Amour had fixed on writing as an occupation by the late 1930s, and soon realized that the only way he could become a full-time writer was to settle down. He joined his family, now located in Choctaw, Oklahoma, and began to teach himself how to be a writer. Despite a collection of more than 200 rejection slips, he kept working until more than 400 of them were published. Many of these were boxing or adventure stories sold to pulp magazines such as *True Gang Life, Sky Fight-*

ers, and *Thrilling Adventures.* "I also wrote some sport stories, some detective stories, and some Western stories," L'Amour told Dye. "It so happens that the Westerns caught on and there was a big demand for them. I grew up in the West, of course, and loved it, but I never really intended to write Westerns at all." With the publication of his first book in 1939, a volume of poetry entitled *Smoke from This Altar,* L'Amour became a recognized professional writer.

Despite the early publication date of *Smoke from this Altar,* L'Amour's first novel, *Westward the Tide,* did not appear until 1950. World War II interrupted L'Amour's literary ambitions. At the out-

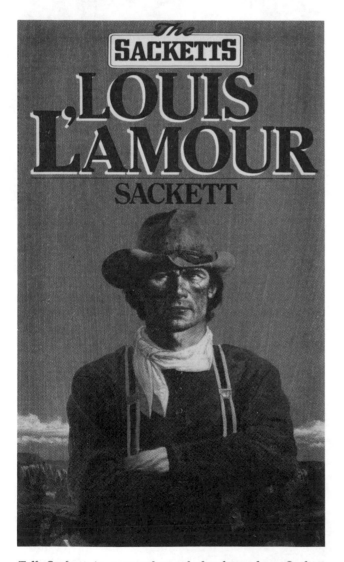

Tell Sackett is a member of the legendary Sackett family, known for uniting together whenever there is trouble and for not quitting until they have won the fight.

break of the war, according to an interview cited in Gale's book, "L'Amour was told he would be placed in navy intelligence where his knowledge of the Far East and Oriental languages would be useful. Instead, he found himself in Army khaki." From 1942 to 1944, L'Amour was kept in the States, "teaching winter-survival techniques in Michigan for part of the time," said Weinberg. "Eventually he was made officer of a tank destroyer," Gale continued, "and he finished up the war in Europe . . . commanding a platoon of the 'Red Ball Express,' the legendary unit of oil tankers that barreled along behind Patton's armor, bringing up the fuel the cavalry brigades gulped down to keep advancing." L'Amour received the Bronze Star four times for his services and was honorably discharged from the Army in January of 1946.

A Return to Writing

L'Amour began publishing again after the war, when a friend needed some stories for a magazine. L'Amour obliged. Soon he was writing Western novels, published under the pseudonym Jim Mayo. "My publisher at the time said nobody would ever buy a Western story written by a guy named L'Amour," the author told Dye, "and I'd have to use a different name. I had written some short stories about the Far East and a character named Pongo Jim Mayo. Jim Mayo was the only name I could think of on the spur of the moment, so I used it. As soon as I began to acquire some king of a following, I switched back to my own name. And I made them like it." By the time *Hondo,* his 1953 novel, became a successful John Wayne film, L'Amour's career was established.

Early in his career L'Amour determined to use this information in his work in a nontraditional way. "A long time ago," he told Dye, "when I was a small boy, I grew up hearing Indian stories. My great-grandfather was scalped by Indians, my grandfather fought Indians. I knew the stories very well and I knew a great deal about Indians. I came out of the movies one night with my father and I heard a man say to his wife, 'That's how it was.' And it wasn't at all—the movie was entirely false." "I thought that nobody had the right to mislead people that way," L'Amour continued. "From that time on I knew that when I wrote I was going to be authentic. The American frontier has never been properly written about. There's too much stress on the cowboys-and-Indi-

In this 1956 novel, a wounded man fights for his life while is trapped up on a canyon rim.

ans type of thing, the buckskins, the Daniel Boone types, when so much else was happening. . . . The Indian was never properly presented. He was both better and worse than the way he's been depicted."

Despite his growing readership, L'Amour's novels were often not even reviewed by critics. As Ned Smith of *American Way* noted, L'Amour suffered the same fate as the majority of Western writers who found themselves "largely greeted with indifference . . . by the critics." L'Amour ignored the criticism—or the lack of it—and decided to do what hardly anyone had ever done before: make a living as a Western writer. His determination to persevere led to increased critical interest in his work; the literary establishment eventually could no longer continue to ignore such a popular writer.

Under contract to produce three original paperbacks per year, L'Amour established a routine: he wrote five pages a day, seven days a week, using his afternoons to keep in shape, leaving evenings open for his voracious reading. He interrupted his schedule only when travelling for research purposes. L'Amour often duplicated journeys taken by characters in his novels, recording place names and landmarks in notebooks. He researched the other major elements of his books with equal intensity. A typical L'Amour novel often contained as many factual elements as fictional ones. Writing in *Arizona and the West* about L'Amour's novel *Lando,* Michael T. Marsden noted that in that book alone the writer "instruct[ed] his readers on the historical and cultural importance of Madeira wine, the nature of longhorn cattle, the Great Hurricane of 1844, and the several cultural functions of a Western saloon, all the while providing them with an entertaining romance."

In other L'Amour works readers learned such things as how Native Americans made moccasins, how to pan for gold, and the finer points of Elizabethan decor. The novelist's white characters also know much about Indian life, but the claims of their own culture exert a stronger hold. The title character of *Bendigo Shafter* describes the conflict felt by many of L'Amour's frontier heroes: "I could have lived the Indian way and loved it. I could feel his spirits move upon the air, hear them in the still forest and the chuckling water of the mountain streams, but other voices were calling me, too, the voices of my own people and their ways. For it was our way to go onward; to go forward and to try to shape our world into something that would make our lives easier, even if more complicated."

Some critics felt that all the factual material in L'Amour's novels detracted from their narrative continuity. They also felt that L'Amour's energies might have been better spent developing his characters or varying his plots rather than on research. Tom Nolan, reviewing *Jubal Sackett* for the *Los Angeles Times Book Review,* declared, "Much historical and cultural information is imparted as an organic part of a tale thick with plot. Where the book's tone seems to falter is in its occasionally jarring shifts of sensibility—from the plain speech of Jubal the woodsman to the more sophisticated discourse of Jubal the knowledgeable Englishman's son." Charles Champlin, assessing *The Lonesome Gods* for the *Los Angeles Times Book Review,* asserted that the novel's complicated plot, a "lengthy saga of the [protagonist] and his complicated pre-history, his friendship with a pioneering Los Angeles entrepreneur, the mystery of a giant in the desert, the good guys and the bad guys and the unrepentant old grandfather, seems so uncharacteristically diffuse and sprawling that the author as concocter keeps showing through the seams."

Other critics maintained that L'Amour's style was the key to his appeal. They applauded his ability to write quick-paced action novels filled with accurate descriptions of the Old West or other locales in which his protagonists found themselves. "Probably the biggest reason for L'Amour's success," wrote Ben Yagoda in *Esquire,* was ". . . his attention to authenticity and detail. . . . His books are full of geographical and historical information." Stuart Applebaum, quoted in an article for *Publishers Weekly* by Dennis E. Showalter, echoed Yagoda's assessment: "L'Amour's backgrounds were as solid as his story lines. He was a non-stop researcher of the history, the customs, the behavior he put into his books." "L'Amour is popular," concluded Gale, ". . . because he takes the two main types of Western stories—the formulary and the historical—and plays variations with them. He is also a master at giving the impression that he is sitting at a campfire with use, characterizing individual heroes and heroines and villains and many types in between, setting them into action, and above all placing them in locales that we are made to believe are real, and in times past to which we all wish we could escape for a while."

Another reason for L'Amour's popularity lies in his background as a pulp fiction writer. "Much of L'Amour's success was attributable to his style of writing," stated Weinberg. "His novels were fast-moving, entertaining Westerns with larger-than-life heroes and menacing villains. Most of his books were comparatively short and could be read in one sitting. Psychological insights were few and the books were free of gratuitous sex and violence. There was action but not senseless killing or gore. In reality, L'Amour's books were Western pulp novels done in paperback form." However, as Steve Berner declared in the *Lone Star Review,* "It [was], in fact, pointless to discuss the merits or weaknesses of L'Amour's writings . . . since it

[had] little or no effect on either author or his public." Readers bought his novels as fast as he could write them. In all, 200 million copies of his novels were in print in twenty different languages by the time he died.

Sacketts, Chantrys, Talons, and Others

In 1956, L'Amour changed his bachelor status for married life when he married Kathy Elizabeth Adams. The couple was introduced to each other by actress Julie Newmar. "Twenty-two when she wed the author," Weinberg explained, "Kathy Adams had been an actress with appearances on 'Gunsmoke' and 'Death Valley Days.' After their marriage, she left acting and devoted herself full-time to her husband and his career." "The marriage was the first for each," Gale related. "The couple honeymooned in the West Indies and on the northern coast of South America. Of his marriage L'Amour enthusiastically says, 'That . . . is when I *really* struck it rich!'" The L'Amours had two children: a son, Beau, born in 1961, and a daughter, Angelique, born in 1964.

Shortly after his marriage, L'Amour began one of his most successful series of related novels with *The Daybreakers,* the first volume in the Sackett family saga. L'Amour explained that he had gotten the idea from two events during his wandering years: two cousins, each from large families, who helped him escape a beating, and a desert watering-hole he came across in Arizona called Sackett's Well. "Much of American history has been the story of families moving westward," L'Amour declared in *The Sackett Companion,* "and after I had written *The Daybreakers,* I decided to tell the story of the opening of a continent as seen through the eyes of three families, the Sacketts, Chantrys, and Talons." "My stories are history of a kind," the author concluded. "The difference is that I write of the nameless ones, and when they have left no stories I write what must have been, what could have been, using knowledge of the country itself, how it was traveled, how many people lived by hunting and gathering, and what their relationships might have been with the Indians and others. Yet my stories or any others, as well as history itself, must always be read with the understanding that we know only a small part of the whole picture."

L'Amour continued the story of the Sackett family in seventeen novels. These books explore the lives of the two branches of the Sackett clan and, to a lesser extent, the Chantrys and the Talons, across three hundred years of history. "History and historical fiction have most often related the stories of kings, nobles, presidents, and generals," L'Amour declared in *The Sackett Companion*. "They have dealt, until recently, largely with wars and politics, or with exploration of the land through stories that have survived. . . . What we must remember when reading history is that we can never have more than a small part of the story, and it is a story often told in highlights." "The story of the West is our story, an American story," L'Amour concluded in *The Sackett Companion*, "but one for all the world, and all the world contributed. . . . Through the eyes of the Sacketts I invite you to see it happen in many of its phases."

Toward the end of his life L'Amour branched out in several directions. The publication of his 1984 novel, *The Walking Drum*, caused a stir in literary circles because its hero lived in medieval Europe instead of the American West. Apparently the author's change of locale did not intimidate his readers, for the book appeared on the *New York Times* hardcover bestseller list five days before its official publication date. He also wrote *The Sackett Companion: A Personal Guide to the Sackett Novels*, which includes a Sackett family tree as well as background information on the sources behind the novels in the series, and completed his long-planned autobiography, *The Education of a Wandering Man*.

L'Amour wrote three novels a year for his publisher for more than thirty years. Even so, by the late 1980s, he had come nowhere near to exhausting the store of research he had gathered as a connoisseur of historical details. At the time of his death in 1988, he had developed outlines for fifty more novels. A year before he died, L'Amour told Dye, "There's a lot of Western material out there that's very fresh. And the Western novel is not dying, it's doing very well. It's selling every place but in the movies. . . . There seem to be some misconceptions about me and my type of writing, which have been perpetuated by several articles that weren't written too well. . . . Too often people start with a cliched idea of a Western writer. That automatically eliminates an awful lot of things that interest me. There's no difference in the Western novel and any other novel, as I said earlier. A Western starts with a beginning and it goes to an end. It's a story about people, and that's the important thing to always remember.

Every story is about people—people against the canvas of their times."

■ Works Cited

Berner, Steve, review of *Comstock Lode, Lone Star Review*, May, 1981.

Champlin, Charles, "L'Amour: A Love of the Lore where the Ground Rules," *Los Angeles Times Book Review*, March 20, 1983, pp. 3, 10.

Gale, Robert L., *Louis L'Amour*, Twayne, 1985.

Jackson, Donald Dale, "World's Fastest Literary Gun: Louis L'Amour," *Smithsonian*, May, 1987, pp. 154–56, 158.

L'Amour, Louis, *Bendigo Shafter*, Dutton, 1978.

L'Amour, Louis, interview with Mary Scott Dye, *Contemporary Authors New Revision Series*, Volume 25, Gale, 1988, pp. 261–67.

L'Amour, Louis, *The Sackett Companion: A Personal Guide to the Sackett Novels*, Bantam, 1988.

L'Amour, Louis, *Education of a Wandering Man* (autobiography), Bantam, 1989.

Marsden, Michael T., *Arizona and the West*, autumn, 1978.

Nolan, Tom, review of *Jubal Sackett, Los Angeles Times Book Review*, August 25, 1985, p. 3.

Showalter, Dennis E., "Bringing Back the Western," *Publishers Weekly*, May 5, 1989, pp. 25–27.

Smith, Ned, "Louis L'Amour: He's No Rhinestone Cowboy," *American Way*, April, 1976.

Weinberg, Robert, *The Louis L'Amour Companion*, Andrews & McMeel, 1992.

Yagoda, Ben, review of *The Proving Trail* and *Bendigo Shafter, Esquire*, March 13, 1979.

■ For More Information See

BOOKS

Authors in the News, Volume 2, Gale, 1976.

Contemporary Literary Criticism, Volume 25, Gale, 1983.

Dictionary of Literary Biography Yearbook: 1980, Gale, 1981.

Elton, J. C., *Louis L'Amour: The Long Trail*, Amereon Ltd, 1976.

Hall, Halbert, *The Works of Louis L'Amour: An Annotated Bibliography and Guide*, Borgo Press, 1991.

Louis L'Amour: America's Storyteller, Bantam, 1983.

Pilkington, William T., editor, *Critical Essays on the Western American Novel*, G. K. Hall. 1980.

Author & Artists Volume 16

Phillips, Robert S., *Louis L'Amour: His Life and Trails*, Knightsbridge, 1990.

PERIODICALS

Chicago Tribune, June 5, 1984; June 23, 1985; February 25, 1987.

Chicago Tribune Book World, September 9, 1984.

Detroit News, March 31, 1978; June 30, 1985.

Globe and Mail (Toronto), May 19, 1984; October 17 1987.

Los Angeles Times, July 9, 1983; May 30, 1984; August 3 1986; November 7, 1989.

Los Angeles Times Book Review, March 20, 1983; August 25, 1985; April 3, 1986; August 3, 1986.

Newsweek, November 10, 1975; July 14, 1986.

New Yorker, May 16, 1983.

New York Times, October 21, 1971; September 23, 1983.

New York Times Book Review, November 24, 1974; April 6, 1975; November 30, 1975; January 2, 1977, March 22, 1981; April 24, 1983; July 1, 1984; June 2, 1985; July 6, 1986.

People, June 9, 1975; July 23, 1984.

Publishers Weekly, October 8, 1973; November 4, 1978; November 27, 1978.

Southwest Review, winter, 1984.

Time, April 29, 1974; December 1, 1980; August 19, 1985; July 21, 1986; August 4, 1986.

Times Literary Supplement, August 26, 1977.

Us, July 25, 1978.

USA Weekend, May 30-June 1, 1986.

Washington Post, March 20, 1981; June 23, 1983; November 30, 1989.

Washington Post Book World, December 12, 1976; March 1, 1981; April 17, 1983; December 2, 1984; June 16, 1985; July 6, 1986; June 14, 1987.

West Coast Review of Books, November, 1978.

Western American Literature, May, 1978; February, 1982.

■ Obituaries

PERIODICALS

Chicago Tribune, June 19, 1988.

Detroit News, June 13, 1988.

Los Angeles Times, June 13, 1988.

New York Times, June 13, 1988.

Times (London), June 14, 1988.

Washington Post, June 13, 1988.*

—*Sketch by Kenneth R. Shepherd*

Kevin Major

■ Personal

Born September 12, 1949, in Stephenville, Newfoundland, Canada; son of Edward (a fisherman and boiler-room worker) and Jessie (Headge) Major; married Anne Crawford (a librarian), July 3, 1982; children: Luke, Duncan. *Education:* Memorial University of Newfoundland, B.Sc., 1973. *Religion:* Anglican.

■ Addresses

Home—Box 85, Eastport, Newfoundland, Canada A0G 1Z0. *Agent*—Nancy Colbert, 303 Davenport Rd., Toronto, Ontario, Canada, M5R 1K5.

■ Career

Teacher in Roberts Arm, Newfoundland, 1971-72, and Carbonear, Newfoundland, 1973; Eastport Central High School, Eastport, Newfoundland, teacher of special education and biology, 1974-76; writer, 1976—. Substitute teacher, 1976—. Guest on television and radio programs. *Member:* Writers Union of Canada.

■ Awards, Honors

Children's Literature Prize from Canada Council, Book-of-the-Year Award from Canadian Association of Children's Librarians, and Ruth Schwartz Children's Book Award from Ruth Schwartz Charitable Foundation and Ontario Arts Council, all 1979, all for *Hold Fast*; *Hold Fast* was also named to the Hans Christian Andersen Honor List by the International Board on Books for Young People, and to the *School Library Journal* list of Best Books of the Year, both 1980; *Far from Shore* received the Canadian Young Adult Book Award from the Young Adult Caucus of the Saskatchewan Library Association, and was named to *School Library Journal* list of Best Books of the Year, both 1981.

■ Writings

FOR YOUNG ADULTS

Hold Fast, Clarke, Irwin, 1978, Delacorte, 1980.

Far from Shore, Clarke, Irwin, 1980, Delacorte, 1981.

Thirty-Six Exposures, Delacorte, 1984.

Dear Bruce Springsteen, Doubleday/Delacorte, 1987.

Blood Red Ochre, Doubleday/Delacorte, 1989.

Eating between the Lines, Doubleday, 1991.

OTHER

(Editor and contributor of illustrations) *Doryloads: Newfoundland Writings and Art,* Breawater Books, 1974.

(With James A. Tuck) *Terra Nova National Park: Human History Study,* Parks Canada, 1983.

■ **Sidelights**

BANNED FROM THE LIBRARY. FOUL LANGUAGE. EXCESSIVE SEX. These are the kind of comments that are made by some librarians regarding Kevin Major's, gritty, coming-of-age novels. His writing has become controversial enough that in his native Canada, some libraries refuse to carry his work. On the other hand, many critics and readers heartily applaud his work, claiming that the situations he sets up are realistic and speak to modern young adults. Major stated in *School Libraries in Canada* that "Sex and strong language play no greater or no lesser a part in my work than they do in real life. The truth is both are preoccupations of adolescents as is their family life, school, their relationships with their friends. So why the great fear?" Major's champions appear to outweigh his critics. His first novel, *Hold Fast,* about a young boy trying to find his way in Newfoundland, has been compared favorably to J.D. Salinger's coming-of-age story, *Catcher in the Rye,* and Mark Twain's seminal *The Adventures of Huckleberry Finn,* and is considered to be a young adult classic in Canada.

Major was the youngest child born to a large family in Newfoundland, a large island off the eastern coast of Canada. He was the first of the family's children to be born after Newfoundland became a province of Canada, so his father jokingly termed him the only true Canadian in the family. Major was able to see how confederation with Canada changed his home. "I . . . have seen the clash between [Newfoundland's] traditional way of life and the wave of new ideas, attitudes and values that swept in as Newfoundland came out of its long period of relative isolation. The changes that have resulted, particularly as reflected in the lives of its young people, is perhaps the central theme of my writing," he once commented.

Lobsters and Literature

Major's youth was tied to the land. His father was a fisherman, and the young Major would often help with the work, including the catching of lobsters. Yet the city they lived in, Stephenville, was close to a modern air force base set up by the United States during World War II. So, even while he was enjoying the natural beauty of his province, he was also influenced by the military base, taking classes there and sometimes watching the B-52 bombers.

Writing was always a hobby that Major enjoyed. "I even remember one high school teacher saying that he thought one day I would write a book," he related to *SATA.* That thought remained in his mind, but when he went off to attend college, he had his sights set on becoming a doctor—he was even accepted to medical school. A low-budget traveling sabbatical to the West Indies and Europe changed his mind. He had plenty of time to think, and when he returned to Canada, he told *SATA* that he had decided to "become a teacher and write in my spare time."

Upon graduation from college, he became a teacher in Newfoundland, in the small coastal villages that he knew so well. He realized immediately that there was a problem with the reading materials the children had. "There were no novels which had characters in them much like the junior high school students I was teaching," he told *SATA,* "nor did any portray the way of life they knew. To try writing a novel from the viewpoint of a Newfoundland teenager seemed a natural step." He wrote a novel which he could not get published. Undaunted, he began writing a second novel. He found a publisher for *Hold Fast* with relative ease. By the time it was published in 1978, he had given up teaching full time and was working on his writing projects. *Hold Fast* made a large and lasting impression on readers and critics alike. The book won three of Canada's major awards for books for young people and was also named a Hans Christian Andersen honor book.

In *Hold Fast,* Major was able to capture the clash between Newfoundland's traditional society and the encroaching modern American culture. The main character, Michael, a fourteen-year-old boy, loses both his parents when their car collides with a drunk driver's vehicle. Michael has been living in a small village where he fishes and hunts. After his parent's death, he is shipped off to a big city to stay with an aunt and uncle and their two children. Michael feels like an outcast in his new home. The city kids tease him mercilessly for his country accent and way of dressing. His uncle is a strict disciplinarian. Tired of this life, Michael runs away, taking his cousin Curtis with him. Then Michael's grandfather dies, and both boys attend the funeral. Michael is able to go live with an aunt and his younger brother in his old home town. However, Curtis must return to his dictatorial father with no certainty of his life changing.

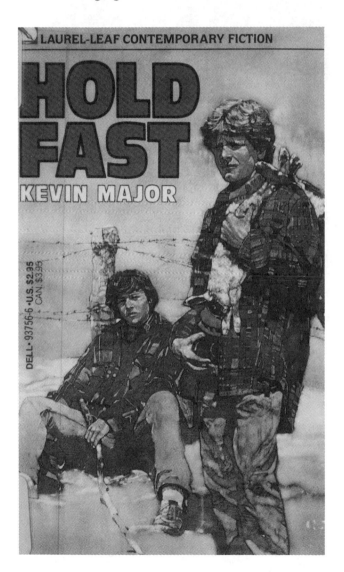

After losing his parents in a car accident and suffering abuse from his uncle, Michael runs away with his cousin and tries to survive without money, family, or friends.

Critics were very positive about this novel. Irma McDonough wrote in *In Review: Canadian Books for Children* that "*Hold Fast* is a landmark in Canadian writing for young people. It reaches other, profounder places than most realistic writing meant for them. . . . [Here is] a stunningly perceptive novel of family life in the outport and the city in his native province, and of one young person at the centre of it." Reviewers also compared the book to other coming-of-age stories. Robert Fulford commented in *Saturday Night* about the main character's strong presence: "Michael contains a bit of Holden Caufield [of *Catcher in the Rye*] and a bit of Huckleberry Finn, but there is also something authentically Newfoundland about him. *Hold Fast* . . . speaks honestly from a regional consciousness." Helen Porter, writing in *Atlantic Provinces Book Review* also commented on the similarity between Major's character and Holden Caufield and Huckleberry Finn: "Like them, [Michael] will be around for a long, long time." Major told Sherie Posesorski in an interview for *Books in Canada* that "I want my books to be relevant to the experience of growing up in Newfoundland. Newfoundland society is in the midst of tremendous changes. . . . My novels dramatize the conflicts that have developed between parents and children because of these changes." *Hold Fast* had achieved that accomplishment and propelled Major to a new position in Canadian literature.

Major's next novel, *Far from Shore,* was published in 1980. Once again, he returned to chronicling the ups and downs of life for teenage boys in Newfoundland. This book features Chris Slade, the son of two troubled parents. His father is a chronic alcoholic without a job. His mother starts working to help support the family and falls in love with her boss. Chris feels caught in an impossible situation, and his confusing feelings as an adolescent only add to it. Because of his unstable family situation, Chris starts to rebel. He joins up with the "wrong" crowd and loses a girlfriend he was beginning to rely on. His father moves to a far away province to find work, so Chris only feels more abandoned. Finally, he gets in trouble with the law. The local minister, trying to help out, finds him a job at a summer camp, where he irresponsibly almost causes another boy to drown. The end of the book features Chris's father returning home, and his parents reconciling. However, things are still rocky, and Chris has found no easy answers.

This book was very popular among young readers. Critical response was generally enthusiastic, although the unevenness of the plot was cited as a weakness. Janet Lunn in *Books in Canada* wrote that "Major's strength is not story-telling. His plot is trite and the story doesn't flow." However, she adds that "the weaknesses of plot do not destroy the book. This isn't just another fashionably slick tale of sex, violence, and drugs among young adults. It's an honest and deeply felt story." Irma McDonough in *Canadian Books for Children* writes that the book "fulfills the promise that was evident in *Hold Fast*. It is a satisfying literary experience that once again reveals Major's uncommon artistic integrity."

Narration and Experimentation

In the writing of this book, Major experimented with technique. He told the story of Chris Slade through the voices of five different narrators, including members of his family and the camp director. Major commented on this technique in his interview with Posesorski for *Books in Canada*: "In changing the point of view I wanted to go beyond the standard stylistic conventions employed in young adult fiction. Often, young adult novels are quite simplistic in their approach to story-telling. My books . . . require more involvement on the reader's part."

Major's next book, *Thirty-Six Exposures,* was to delve even deeper into the experimental narrative he had tried in *Far from Shore*. Major's main character Lorne is eighteen years old, a high-school photographer who also has deep interests in poetry. There are thirty-six chapters in the book, each offering a small story that centers around Lorne's senior year. In the book, Lorne goes through a difficult time trying to keep his best friend, Trevor from getting kicked out of school. He also attempts an unsuccessful sexual relationship with a girlfriend. Somehow, Lorne and Trevor, make it to graduation day, but a tragic car accident cuts short the life of one of the characters.

This book was described by some as having even more strong language and sexual situations than Major's first two. Some critics found it to be excessive. Jack Beidler, writing in *Best Sellers* concluded that *Thirty-Six Exposures* depends too much on strong language and sexual innuendoes and "as a result the story falls far short of Major's

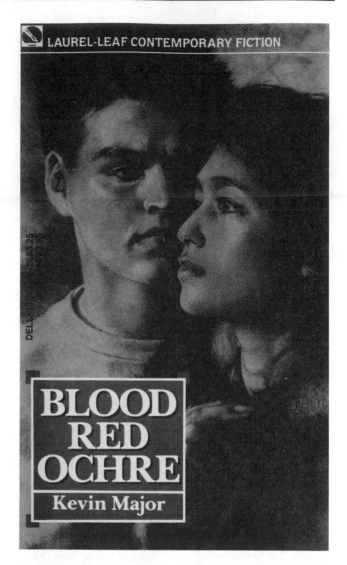

This 1989 novel alternates between the story of fifteen-year-old David who discovers that his father is not his birth parent, and Dauoodaset, one of the last Beothuk Indians and the main character of a book David is reading.

capabilities as a writer." In *School Library Journal,* Ellen M. Fecher explained that she thought the "book . . . tries hard to be contemporary but is too forced to be completely successful." John Lord, writing in *Voice of Youth Advocates* complained about the excessive use of sexual situations, and adds "the scenes were tame, but still they may cause eyebrows to raise." He concluded that *Thirty-Six Exposures* is "not a bad book, just not great."

In 1987, Major published *Dear Bruce Springsteen,* a novel that featured a series of letters from a fictional teenager named Terry Blanchard to his hero, the rock star. Terry is in an awkward situation. His father has deserted the family. His mother is seeing someone else and is asking for a divorce. With no one to talk to, Terry turns to his favorite rock star. Once again experimenting with narrative, Major presents this story solely as a series of letters written by the main character over a six-month period. During the novel, the letters seem to help Terry develop himself both socially and musically. He eventually overcomes most of his demons and finds more self-confidence. Less attention was given to *Dear Bruce Springsteen* than to Major's previous novels. *Publishers Weekly* commented that Major "understands well the inner workings of teenagers." However, Jack Forman, writing in *School Library Journal* took exception with the format of the novel, commenting that it takes away from "some of the novel's humor, and flattened out Terry's character."

Major's next novel, *Blood Red Ochre*, had an inventive and original narrative structure. David is a fifteen-year-old Newfoundland boy whose life at home is confusing to him. He finds out that the father he lives with is not his birth parent. He also begins a school project on the Beothuk Indians—a tribe that became extinct years before. Each chapter of *Blood Red Ochre* alternates between David's third-person narrative and the first-person narrative of the book he is reading, which is told from the viewpoint of Dauoodaset, one of the last Beothuk Indians. As David grows more and more estranged from his family, he becomes more interested in the history of the Beothuk. He befriends a girl in his school—the mysterious Nancy—who is also researching the Beothuk tribe. One day they canoe off to Red Ochre Island, a site of a Beothuk archeological find. On the island, his friend Nancy suddenly declares herself to be Shanawdithit, Dauoodaset's lover. The last chapter presents a confrontation between these two characters and the real (or imagined) historical counterparts. Yvonne A. Frey wrote in *School Library Journal* that "the book does provide good detail on Indian life and customs, [but] there are few insights into the characters of David and Nancy." Sarah Ellis commented in the *Horn Book* magazine on the structure of the novel: "Major achieves a remarkable balance between the two narratives, each with its own weight and energy." She concludes that "This novel is a troubling one, carefully crafted to prevent an easy dismissal of the issues it presents."

Magic Coins and More

Major's next novel, published in 1991, is more light-hearted than many of his previous efforts. *Eating between the Lines* chronicles the life of Jackson, a fun-loving teen with an appetite for food and other teenage distractions. Although a naturally happy kid, Jackson is not doing well in school, he can't get a girl he likes to notice him, and his parents marriage is not doing well. Through the assistance of a magical gold coin, Jackson finds himself able to project himself into all of his favorite stories. He then finds some adventure by romping around as different characters from stories, like Ulysses or Huck Finn. Virginia Beaton, writing in *Books in Canada* concludes that Major is "sending us a serious message about the importance of allowing children and young adults to experience literature in all its richness—including books that have scenes or language that may distress some."

Although controversies over language, sex, and other topics may never fade, Major has said that he would not choose to write his novels any other way. "I write this literature," he told *School Libraries in Canada*," . . . the way I do because, given the type of characters I've created, to do otherwise would be false and literature, after all, is one very important means by which we see how other people live." When critics attack his work, Major turns to his readers for solace. He added: "The comments about my work that I cherish the most are contained in some of the letters I have received from young people."

Another controversy for Major is the fact that his books are categorized for one certain age of reader. "I've never really been content with the term `young adult book,' which is usually how they're labeled," Major said in an interview with *Contemporary Authors,* "because it tends to place a limit on the readership, on the kind of audience the labelers think the books would appeal to. I'd like to think of them as being good novels to begin with, to be enjoyed by readers of any age; and it does seen that a fair number of adults are reading the books and enjoying them." This distinction appears to agree with John Moss's summary of Major's talents. He writes in his *A Reader's Guide to the Canadian Novel* that Major is "among the best Canadian writers of his generation. . . . he has established himself as a figure of singular importance in our literature."

■ Works Cited

Beaton, Virginia, review of *Eating between the Lines, Books in Canada,* December, 1991, pp. 38-9.

Beidler, Jack, review of *Thirty-Six Exposures, Best Sellers,* February, 1985, p. 439.

Review of *Dear Bruce Springsteen, Publishers Weekly,* January 29, 1988, p. 432.

Ellis, Sarah, "News from the North," *Horn Book,* February, 1984, pp. 99-103.

Fecher, Ellen M., review of *Thirty-Six Exposures, School Library Journal,* February, 1985, pp. 85-6.

Forman, Jack, review of *Dear Bruce Springsteen, School Library Journal,* May, 1988, p. 110.

Frey, Yvonne A., review of *Blood Red Ochre, School Library Journal,* April, 1989, p. 119.

Fulford, Robert, "Capturing Newfoundland Before It Goes Away," *Saturday Night,* October, 1978, pp. 14-15.

Lord, John, review of *Thirty-Six Exposures, Voice of Youth Advocates,* February, 1985, p. 329.

Lunn, Janet, "Huck Finn in Newfoundland," *Books in Canada,* December, 1980, pp. 21-3.

Major, Kevin, "Challenged Materials: An Author's Perspective," *School Libraries in Canada,* spring, 1984, pp. 15-16.

Major, Kevin, in an interview with Sherie Posesorski, *Books in Canada,* December, 1984, pp. 24-25.

Major, Kevin, in an interview with Jean W. Ross for *Contemporary Authors New Revision Series,* Volume 21, Gale, 1988, pp. 263-66.

McDonough, Irma, review of *Hold Fast, In Review: Canadian Books for Children,* summer, 1978, p. 70.

McDonough, Irma, review of *Far from Shore, In Review: Canadian Books for Children,* February, 1981, pp. 42-43.

Moss, John, "Kevin Major," *A Reader's Guide to the Canadian Novel,* McClelland & Stewart, 1981, p. 340.

School Libraries in Canada, spring, 1984, pp. 15-16.

■ For More Information See

BOOKS

Children's Literature Review, Volume 11, Gale, 1986.

Contemporary Literary Criticism, Volume 26, Gale, 1983.

Dictionary of Literary Biography, Volume 60: Canadian Writers since 1960, Gale, 1987.

Speaking for Ourselves: Autobiographical Sketches by Notable Authors of Books for Young Adults, edited by Donald R. Gallo, National Council of Teachers of English, 1990.

Twentieth-Century Children's Writers, 3rd edition, St. James, 1989.

PERIODICALS

Canadian Children's Literature, Volume 66, 1992.

—*Sketch by Nancy Rampson*

Bernard Malamud

68; Library of Congress, honorary consultant in American letters, 1972-75. *Member:* National Institute of Arts and Letters, American Academy of Arts and Sciences, PEN American Center (president, 1979).

■ Personal

Born April 26, 1914, in Brooklyn, NY; died of natural causes, March 18, 1986, in New York, NY; son of Max (a grocery store manager) and Bertha (Fidelman) Malamud; married Ann de Chiara, November 6, 1945; children: Paul, Janna.

■ Education

City College of New York (now City College of the City University of New York), B.A., 1936; Columbia University, M.A., 1942.

■ Career

Writer. Bureau of the Census, Washington, DC, clerk, 1940; Erasmus Hall Evening High School, New York City, and other evening high schools, instructor in English, 1940-49; Harlem High School, NY, instructor in English, 1948-49; Oregon State University, instructor, assistant professor, associate professor of English, 1949-61; Bennington College, Bennington, VT, faculty member of the Division of Language and Literature, 1961-68; Harvard University, Cambridge, MA, visiting lecturer, 1966-

■ Awards, Honors

Partisan Review fellow in fiction, 1956-57; Richard and Hinda Rosenthal Foundation Award, National Institute of Arts and Letters, and Daroff Memorial Fiction Award, Jewish Book Council of America, both 1958, both for *The Assistant;* Rockefeller grant, 1958; National Book Award in fiction, 1959, for *The Magic Barrel,* and 1967, for *The Fixer;* Ford Foundation fellow in humanities and arts, 1959-61; Pulitzer Prize in fiction, 1967, for *The Fixer;* O. Henry Award, 1968, for "Man in the Drawer"; Jewish Heritage Award, B'nai B'rith, 1976; Governor's Award for Excellence in the Arts, Vermont Council on the Arts, 1979; American Library Association Notable Book citation, 1979, for *Dubin's Lives;* Brandeis Creative Arts Award in fiction, 1981; Gold Medal in Fiction, American Academy and Institute of Arts and Letters, 1983; Elmer Holmes Bobst Award for fiction, 1983; honorary degree, City College of the City University of New York.

■ Writings

NOVELS

The Natural, Harcourt, 1952, reprinted, Avon, 1980.

The Assistant, Farrar, Straus, 1957, reprinted, Avon, 1980:

A New Life, Farrar, Straus, 1961, reprinted, 1988.

The Fixer, Farrar, Straus, 1966, reprinted, Pocket Books, 1982.

Pictures of Fidelman: An Exhibition, Farrar, Straus, 1969, reprinted, 1988.

The Tenant, Farrar, Straus, 1971.

Dubin's Lives, Farrar, Straus, 1979.

God's Grace, Farrar, Straus, 1982.

SHORT STORIES

The Magic Barrel, Farrar, Straus, 1958, reprinted, Avon, 1980.

Idiots First, Farrar, Straus, 1963.

Rembrandt's Hat, Farrar, Straus, 1973.

The Stories of Bernard Malamud, Farrar, Straus, 1983.

OTHER

(Contributor) John Fisher and Robert B. Silvers, editors, *Writing in America,* Rutgers University Press, 1960.

Philip Rahv, editor, *A Malamud Reader,* Farrar, Straus, 1967.

Robert Giroux, editor, *The People and Uncollected Stories,* Farrar, Straus, 1989.

Contributor of short stories to various magazines, including *Atlantic, Commentary, Harper's,* and *New Yorker.* Also contributor of articles to the *New York Times* and *New York Times Book Review.*

Some of Malamud's manuscripts are archived at the Library of Congress, Washington, DC, including *The Natural, The Assistant, A New Life, The Fixer, Pictures of Fidelman,* and parts of *The Magic Barrel, Idiots First,* and various short stories.

■ Sidelights

"The purpose of the writer is to keep civilization from destroying itself," Bernard Malamud remarked in 1958, quoting existential writer Albert Camus. Malamud managed to uphold this purpose during his half-century-long career, which was distinguished by his winning the Pulitzer Prize for *The Fixer,* and two National Book Awards, for *The Fixer* and *The Magic Barrel.* The final novel of his lifetime, *God's Grace,* shows some optimism even after civilization has self-destructed. When the last man left on earth after a nuclear holocaust cries out to God about injustice and gets pelted with lemons, an intelligent chimp makes lemonade. Like this imaginative transformation of hardship into a God-send, Malamud rose from his Depression-era young adulthood to become a major American writer.

Malamud was born and raised in Brooklyn, New York. His parents, Russian-Jewish immigrants, worked sixteen hours a day in their small grocery store. Reflecting back on his youth, Malamud recalled no books in his home. In fact, his only cultural nourishment came on Sundays, when sounds of piano playing filtered through the living room window. As a student at Brooklyn's Erasmus Hall High School in the late 1920s, he published his earliest stories in the school literary magazine. His first published story in high school described his family's grocery store. (Many critics have suggested that this knowledge of the urban world helped Malamud create the flesh-and-blood characters found in his best fiction.) Malamud graduated from the City College of New York in 1936 with a bachelor of arts degree.

Unable to find a job teaching English in the New York public schools after graduation, Malamud worked in a factory, various stores, and as a clerk for the Bureau of Census in Washington, D.C. He continued to write in his spare time and finally secured a position teaching at night at Erasmus Hall High School in 1940. Teaching evening classes in New York City high schools—which Malamud did until 1949—allowed him the freedom to work on his writing during the day and to complete his masters degree in 1942. In 1945, he married Ann de Chiara. Their son Paul was born in 1947, and their daughter Janna in 1952. By this time Malamud had begun publishing stories about Jews, Italians, and blacks—works reflecting the people he had come in contact with growing up in his East Side neighborhood.

The author moved his family to Oregon in 1949, where he taught English at Oregon State University until 1961. That year he became a professor at Bennington College in Vermont, where he remained on the faculty until his death in 1986. During his college teaching career, Malamud took occasional leaves of absence to travel in England, Italy, Russia, France, Spain, and Israel in the 1950s and 1960s. He also taught at Harvard University from 1966 to 1968 and served as a consultant at the Library of Congress from 1972 to 1975.

A Natural Storyteller

Malamud's writing career, spanning five decades, produced eight novels, four short-story collections, and an unfinished novel, which was published posthumously along with sixteen stories. *New York Times Book Review* writer Bette Pesetsky praises him as "a natural storyteller who seduced us with fable and myth and folklore and affirmed our astonishment at the possibilities of life." Malamud once said that he wrote about "simple people struggling to make their lives better in a world of bad luck," according to Mervyn Rothstein of the *New York Times*.

Prior to World War II, Malamud had not given much thought to what it really meant to be Jewish. By 1945, however, after the tragedy of the Holocaust was revealed, he began to wonder about his religious background and read many

THE STORIES OF BERNARD MALAMUD

25 STORIES CHOSEN BY THE AUTHOR AS HIS VERY BEST...
"STORIES THAT WILL BE READ AS LONG AS ANYONE CONTINUES TO CARE ABOUT AMERICAN FICTION WRITTEN IN THE TWENTIETH CENTURY."
—THE NEW YORK TIMES BOOK REVIEW

Malamud himself chose these twenty-five stories as his favorite and most popular.

books about Jewish tradition and history. Marrying a Christian woman also gave Malamud insight into his own identity and helped convince him that he had something to say as a Jewish writer. He admitted to Rothstein that "the suffering of the Jews is a distinct thing for me. . . . I for one believe that not enough has been made of the tragedy of the destruction of six million Jews. Somebody has to cry—even if it's a writer, 20 years later."

Although many of his works focus on the Jewish experience, Rothstein explains that for Malamud, "Jewishness was more a spiritual than a cultural or a religious quality." His most famous Jewish characters all learn more about what it means to be human. Writing in *Dictionary of Literary Biography*, Leslie Field interprets Malamud's famous quotation that "all men are Jews" as a reference to his belief that everyone has a "moral obligation to one's fellow man and the community, acceptance of responsibility, involvement in the suffering of others, and learning from one's own suffering." Malamud himself avoided social issues for many years, arguing that "writing was involvement enough," according to Rothstein. As president of the international writers' group PEN in 1979, however, he protested the repression of writers in the Soviet Union and South Africa.

The first major period of Malamud's career extends from 1949 to 1961, when he taught in Oregon and produced three novels and a collection of short stories. In Malamud's first novel, *The Natural*, baseball player Roy Hobbs longs to be the best in the game and to break all records for pitching and hitting. Although he possesses great natural talent, the American dream of becoming a hero and a superstar ultimately leads to Roy's undoing, since "he abandons the people who mean most to him as he furthers his own career," according to Field. Malamud stated in interviews that he viewed baseball as a metaphor for American society: when heroes are created, often the real people behind the myth are destroyed. Critical discussion of the book centered around Malamud's presentation of Hobbs as a mythic figure, similar to characters in Arthurian legends.

The Natural helped Malamud to develop a reputation as an expert in the quick change of scenes. His unique writing style, which often jumped from one scene to the next in a single sentence, made the novel a natural for movie adaptation. The 1984 film starred Robert Redford as Hobbs and preserved many of the mythic elements of the book. The movie was fairly successful at the box office, thanks in part to its "Hollywood ending," which was considerably different than the novel. As Jeffrey Helterman comments in *Dictionary of Literary Biography Yearbook,* "Robert Redford would be no Casey, and, instead of striking out as the novel requires, he hits the home run that wins the pennant."

Exploring Simple People's Struggles

The Assistant, Malamud's next novel, established his prominence among post-World War II writers. Jewishness became a prevalent motif he continued

AVON BOOKS • 0-380-51474-5 • (CANADA $5.95) • U.S. $4.95

"REMARKABLY REAL...
ALIVE AND MOVING."
CHICAGO TRIBUNE

Bernard Malamud
The Assistant

In this 1957 novel, Frank Alpine is wracked by guilt and converts to Judaism after he robs the grocery store where he works and rapes his employer's daughter.

to explore for the rest of his life. *Commonweal* contributor Jonathan Baumbach sees *The Assistant* as a "more realistic novel than *The Natural* but also fantastic, lyrical, dark, magical." Unlike Roy Hobbs, who repeats his mistakes, the similarly self-destructive main character in *The Assistant,* Italian-American Frank Alpine, learns from his and moves toward moral illumination to become a good man. Frank's transformation from thief to would-be saint grows out of his guilt and atonement for robbing Morris Bober, the Jewish proprietor of a run-down Brooklyn grocery store. Having fallen in love with the Bobers' daughter Helen, Frank betrays her friendship by raping her. Eventually, the death of Bober allows Frank to purify himself through pain and suffering; he converts to Judaism through ritual circumcision and takes over managing the Bobers' store. "Malamud's people are memorable and real as rock," William Goyen states in the *New York Times Book Review.* "He knows his people and keeps them free with the kind of writer's control that one does not find often enough in the myriad novels about simple people."

A New Life, Malamud's third novel, shares some of the magical, touching, and funny qualities of his earlier work, but also represents an ambitious change of pace. The book is set in the Pacific Northwest, and marks the author's first attempt at social satire. S. Levin, who once lived a bleak life as an alcoholic in a New York tenement, starts his life over again as an instructor of composition at Cascadia College, an agricultural and technical college in the Pacific Northwest. "Levin believes wholeheartedly the metaphors about America as a New World Garden of Eden," Sheldon J. Hershinow states in *Bernard Malamud.* "By going west he feels he can recapture his lost innocence and escape the past—become the New World Adam." At first, however, Levin struggles comically in his new environment. For instance, he teaches his first class with his fly open and then muddles his way through an affair with Nadalee, a student who wrote an essay on nude bathing. Later, Levin falls in love with Pauline, the Gentile wife of a colleague, and is forced to leave academia. Though the novel received praise for its characterizations and its biting satire of academic life, it was not among the best-received of Malamud's works.

In addition to these three novels, Malamud produced some of his greatest stories in the early part of his career—especially "The Magic Barrel" in his 1958 collection of the same name, which received the National Book Award. In the story, matchmaker Pinye Salzman tricks student rabbi Leo Finkle into falling in love with his daughter Stella, a prostitute. Writer Chaim Potok, in a tribute published in *Dictionary of Literary Biography Yearbook*, praises the stories collected in *The Magic Barrel* as "boldly hued canvases of language and imagination, that linger longest, that grow richer and more resonant with each rereading, and that will be permanent in our literature."

The second major period of Malamud's career began in 1961, when he moved back East to teach at Bennington College in Vermont. His work took on a more cosmopolitan and international direction, as well as a somewhat bleaker cast. His final major work of this period, *Pictures of Fidelman: An Exhibition,* collected six stories that Malamud had published from 1958 to 1969 about Arthur Fidelman, a Bronx artist who goes to Italy to find himself. A *Publishers Weekly* reviewer considers these stories "richly comic, sometimes terrifying," concluding that "whatever Fidelman's failures as a painter and a lover, he is a memorable human being." Among the many lessons the character learns is that the essence of being human is understanding that people are responsible for each other.

The Universal Sufferer

In many of his novels, Malamud draws upon traditional Yiddish literature to create a character known as a "schlemiel," or inept bungler. According to Field, the range of his characters includes "the born loser, the hard-luck guy, the poignant misfit." Despite being a comic figure, the schlemiel in Jewish myth and in Malamud's works ends up achieving "the moral victory often denied to others," Field concludes.

The Jewish hero of Malamud's fourth novel, the Pulitzer Prize-winning *The Fixer,* fits this profile of a victim who is victorious in the end. Yakov Bok, an unemployed "fixer" (handyman) in Kiev, is falsely accused of ritualistically murdering a twelve-year-old boy in order to use his blood to bake Passover matzos. The story was inspired by a famous case in Czarist Russia, in which Mendel Beiliss was falsely accused and acquitted of a 1911 murder. Yakov faces an absurd trial and is imprisoned for a long period of time, but this hard-

Now a Major Tri-Star Motion Picture Starring **Robert Redford**

All he ever wanted was to be the best.

The Natural — *Bernard Malamud*

AVON BOOKS • 0-380-50809-2 •(CANADA $5.99) • U.S. $4.99

Baseball player Roy Hobbs longs for the American dream of becoming a heroic superstar, but it proves his undoing in this 1952 novel that was later made into a movie starring Robert Redford.

ship eventually makes his spirit stronger. He becomes heroic in "accepting the role thrust upon him by circumstance, by choosing the integrity of his destiny," according to Baumbach. The critic goes on to praise Malamud for writing such a "passionate novel" about "the dignity of the individual." Similarly, a *Booklist* reviewer comments upon the "poetry of man's self-discovery and irreducible dignity in spite of the most cynical injustice and brutality." *The Fixer* was made into a movie which was released in 1968.

The Tenants marks the beginning of the last period in Malamud's career, which began in 1971 and continued through his death in 1986. Prior to 1971, his typical Jewish characters move toward responsibility rather than toward achievement; with this 1971 novel, his characters become extraordinary achievers. Harry Lesser, an undistinguished Jewish novelist who is unable to complete a book, lives in an apartment building that his landlord Levenspiel wants to demolish. Then Willie Spearmint, a black writer, moves into the building. The two provide a perfect contrast to one another: Harry's writing concentrates on form, while Willie's is all style. The novel reaches a frenetic and violent conclusion, as Harry steals Willie's girlfriend and destroys his typewriter, Willie burns Harry's manuscript and clobbers Harry, and finally Harry castrates Willie. Malamud claimed in an interview that he intended the novel to be a warning against fanaticism.

Malamud's next novel, *Dubin's Lives,* achieved much greater critical praise than *The Tenants.* Again the hero is a writer, biographer William Dubin, who is working on a biography of D. H. Lawrence. During a protracted inner struggle, Dubin "loses his memory, his sexual powers, his ability to work, even his ability to relate to his family," as Helterman remarks. After he is betrayed in Venice by his voluptuous young lover Fanny Bick, Dubin retreats to his barn as the isolated overachiever still in love.

God's Grace, Malamud's final completed novel, tells the story of Calvin Cohn, a paleontologist doing research undersea who survives an atomic Holocaust and finds himself the last man on earth. Reviewers found this novel quite puzzling. Patricia Blake, in a review for *Time,* calls it "an astonishment: a fable of the last man so bizarre that it defies explication." She advises readers to give up any notion of figuring out "symbols that fall as thick and fast as the hailstones of God's wrath." Writing in the *Los Angeles Times,* Elaine Kendall concludes that Malamud's "grim" fable of beasts learning from man offers "neither hope for salvation nor much in the way of comfort or diversion."

Chronicler of the Human Struggle

Before he died in 1986, Malamud had nearly completed the first draft of a novel about a Russian Jewish peddler among Indians in the West. The novel was published in 1989 along with sixteen stories written from 1943 to 1985. The hero of *The People,* Yozip, is kidnapped by Indians in the Pa-

cific Northwest after the Civil War. When the chief dies, Yozip (renamed Jozip) succeeds him. The tribe is defeated in battle and forced to leave their land, rounded up and put into freight cars to be incarcerated. According to Janet Hadda of the *Los Angeles Times,* the work's biographical elements and its allusions to persecution in Jewish history show that Malamud continued to the end with "his own literary and psychological struggle for self-expression."

Malamud's place as a major writer in American literature is secure, according to Helterman. Though he likely will continue to be labelled as a Jewish-American novelist, Malamud also followed in the tradition of Russian writers, such as

DELL · 2573 · 95c

THE YEAR'S BIG WINNER!

Bernard Malamud

The FIXER

PULITZER PRIZE

NATIONAL BOOK AWARD FOR FICTION

Yakov Bok is falsely accused and imprisoned for ritualistically murdering a twelve-year-old boy in this Pulitzer Prize-winning novel.

Chekhov and Dostoevski, as well as various Yiddish writers. Still, Helterman claims that Malamud is an original—"wise, comic, and moral." In a tribute published in *Dictionary of Literary Biography Yearbook,* Leslie Fiedler calls Malamud "one of the few writers of his generation who will be read and appreciated a hundred years from now." In addition to the Jewish tradition that is present in his work, Malamud is known for his recurrent theme of suffering. As the author stated in a *New York Times* interview: "People say I write so much about misery, but you write about what you write best. As you are grooved, so you are grieved. And the grieving is that no matter how much happiness or success you collect, you cannot obliterate your early experience."

Despite his remarkable success, writing was never easy for Malamud. "The idea is to get the pencil moving quickly," the author said, describing his writing process to Rothstein. "Once you've got some words looking back at you you can take two or three—or throw them away and look for other. I go over and over a page. Either it bleeds and shows it's beginning to be human, or the form emits shadows of itself and I'm off." Malamud attributed his trademark swift transitions to the influence of Charlie Chaplin movies. The author told Rothstein that he especially appreciated "the rhythm and snap of his comedy and his wonderful, wonderful mixture of comedy and sadness."

An intensely private man, Malamud rarely granted extensive interviews. His friend the writer Philip Roth, however, used Malamud as the model for the character E. I. Lonoff in his novel *The Ghost Writer.* Roth describes Lonoff to Rothstein as a novelist "deeply skeptical of the public world . . . whose ideas of work and aesthetic purity obliged him to live a life of solitude." Malamud firmly believed, as he explained to Rothstein, that "the story will be with us as long as man is. You know that, in part, because of its effect on children. It's through story they realize that mystery won't kill them. Through story they learn they have a future."

■ Works Cited

Baumbach, Jonathan, "Malamud's Heroes," *Commonweal,* October 28, 1966, pp. 97-9.

Blake, Patricia, "Genesis II," *Time,* September 13, 1982, p. K8.

Field, Leslie, "Bernard Malamud," *Dictionary of Literary Biography,* Volume 28: *Twentieth-Century American-Jewish Fiction Writers,* Gale, 1984, pp. 166-175.

Review of *The Fixer, Booklist,* October 15, 1966, p. 237.

Goyen, William, "A World of Bad Luck," *New York Times Book Review,* April 28, 1957, p. 4.

Hadda, Janet, "Chosen for Another People," *Los Angeles Times Book Review,* November 26, 1989, p. 3.

Helterman, Jeffrey, "Bernard Malamud," *Dictionary of Literary Biography Yearbook 1986,* Gale, 1987, pp. 240-44.

Hershinow, Sheldon J., *Bernard Malamud,* Ungar, 1980.

Kendall, Elaine, review of *God's Grace, Los Angeles Times Book Review,* September 12, 1982, pp. 1, 8.

Pesetsky, Bette, "Schlemiel of the Golden West," *New York Times Book Review,* November 19, 1989, p. 7.

Review of *Pictures of Fidelman, Publishers Weekly,* February 24, 1969, p. 63.

Rothstein, Mervyn, "Bernard Malamud Dies at 71; Chronicled Human Struggle," *New York Times,* March 19, 1986, pp. A1, D27.

■ For More Information See

BOOKS

Abramson, Edward A., *Bernard Malamud Revisited,* Twayne, 1993.

Alter, Iska, *The Good Man's Dilemma: Social Criticism in the Fiction of Bernard Malamud,* AMS Press, 1981.

Astro, Richard, and Jackson J. Benson, editors, *The Fiction of Bernard Malamud,* Oregon State University Press, 1977.

Avery, Evelyn G., *Rebels and Victims: The Fiction of Richard Wright and Bernard Malamud,* Kennikat, 1979.

Baumbach, Jonathan, *The Landscape of Nightmare: Studies in the Contemporary American Novel,* New York University Press, 1965.

Bilik, Dorothy Seldman, *Immigrant-Survivors: Post-Holocaust Consciousness in Recent Jewish-American Literature,* Wesleyan University Press, 1981.

Bloom, Harold, editor, *Bernard Malamud,* Chelsea House, 1986.

Cohen, Sandy, *Bernard Malamud and the Trial by Love,* Rodopi, 1974.

Concise Dictionary of American Literary Biography: The New Consciousness, 1941-1968, Gale, 1987.

Contemporary Authors Bibliographical Series, Volume 1: *American Novelists,* Gale, 1986.

Contemporary Literary Criticism, Gale, Volume 1, 1973; Volume 2, 1974; Volume 3, 1975; Volume 5, 1976; Volume 8, 1978; Volume 9, 1978; Volume 11, 1979; Volume 18, 1981; Volume 27, 1984; Volume 44, 1987.

Dictionary of Literary Biography, Volume 2: *American Novelists since World War II,* Gale, 1978.

Dictionary of Literary Biography Yearbook, Gale, 1980, 1981, 1986, 1987.

Ducharme, Robert, *Art and Ideas in the Novels of Bernard Malamud: Toward "The Fixer,"* Mouton, 1974.

Fiedler, Leslie, *Love and Death in the American Novel,* Criterion, 1960.

Field, Leslie A., and Joyce W. Field, editors, *Bernard Malamud and the Critics,* New York University Press, 1970.

Field, Leslie A. and Joyce W. Field, editors, *Bernard Malamud: A Collection of Critical Essays,* Prentice-Hall, 1975.

Helterman, Jeffrey, *Understanding Bernard Malamud,* University of South Carolina Press, 1985.

Klein, Marcus, *After Alienation: American Novels in Mid-Century,* World, 1962, pp. 247-93.

Kosofsky, Rita Nathalie, *Bernard Malamud: An Annotated Checklist,* Kent State University Press, 1969.

Kostelanetz, Richard, editor, *American Writing Today,* Whitston, 1991, pp. 155-65.

Lasher, Lawrence, editor, *Conversations with Bernard Malamud,* University Press of Mississippi, 1991.

Meeter, Glenn, *Bernard Malamud and Philip Roth: A Critical Essay,* Eerdmans, 1968.

Ochshorn, Kathleen G., *The Heart's Essential Landscape: Bernard Malamud's Hero,* Peter Lang, 1990.

Richman, Sidney, *Bernard Malamud,* Twayne, 1966.

Salzberg, Joel, *Bernard Malamud: A Reference Guide,* Hall, 1985.

Schulz, Max F., *Radical Sophistication: Studies in Contemporary Jewish-American Novelists,* Ohio University Press, 1969, pp. 56-68.

PERIODICALS

American Literature, March, 1990, pp. 102-4.

American Scholar, winter, 1990, pp. 67-79.

Critique, winter, 1964-65, pp. 110-22; summer, 1989, pp. 252-60.

Essays in Literature, spring, 1988, pp. 87-101.

Explicator, spring, 1990, pp. 224-26.

Kenyon Review, summer, 1963, pp. 438-57.

Library Journal, July, 1982, p. 1345; November 1, 1989, p. 112.

Linguistics in Literature, fall, 1977.

New Republic, May 12, 1986, pp. 40-1.

New York Review of Books, January 19, 1984, pp. 14-6.

New York Times Book Review, August 29, 1982, p. 1; April 20, 1986, p. 1; November 5, 1989, pp. 1, 43-4.

Notes on Contemporary Literature, November, 1993, pp. 4-5.

Partisan Review, 1986, pp. 464-6.

Publishers Weekly, December 25, 1978, p. 54; June 25, 1982, p. 108.

Studies in American Fiction, spring, 1992, pp. 57-73.

Studies in American Jewish Literature, spring, 1978.

Studies in Short Fiction, winter, 1986, pp. 19-24; summer, 1993, pp. 359-66.*

—Sketch by Laura M. Zaidman

Carolyn Meyer

90; guest lecturer at various organizations, and at elementary, junior high, and high schools. *Member:* Authors Guild, Phi Beta Kappa.

■ Personal

Full name, Carolyn Mae Meyer; born June 8, 1935, in Lewiston, PA; daughter of H. Victor (a businessman) and Sara (Knepp) Meyer; married Joseph Smrcka, June 4, 1960 (divorced, 1973); married E. A. "Tony" Mares (an historian, poet, and playwright), May 30, 1987; children: Alan, John, Christopher, one daughter. *Education:* Bucknell University, B.A. (cum laude), 1957. *Politics:* Liberal. *Religion:* Episcopal.

■ Addresses

Home—202 Edith Boulevard, N.E., Albuquerque, NM 87102. *Agent*—Amy Berkower, Writers House Inc., 21 West 26th St., New York, NY 10010.

■ Career

Freelance writer, 1963—. Worked as a secretary, late 1950s; book columnist for *McCall's* magazine, 1960s-1970s; Institute of Children's Literature, instructor, 1973-79; Bucknell University, Alpha Lambda Delta Lecturer, 1974; reviewer of children's and young adult books, *Los Angeles Times,* 1989-

■ Awards, Honors

Notable book citations, American Library Association (ALA), 1971, for *The Bread Book: All about Bread and How to Make It,* 1976, for *Amish People: Plain Living in a Complex World,* and 1979, for *C.C. Poindexter; New York Times* Best Book citation, 1977, for *Eskimos: Growing Up in a Changing Culture;* Best Book for Young Adults citations, ALA, 1979, for *C.C. Poindexter,* 1980, for *The Center: From a Troubled Past to a New Life,* 1986, for *Voices of South Africa: Growing Up in a Troubled Land,* 1992, for *Where the Broken Heart Still Beats: The Story of Cynthia Ann Parker,* and 1993, for *White Lilacs; Voice of Youth Advocates* YASD Best Books citations, 1988, for *Denny's Tapes* and *Voices of South Africa;* Pennsylvania School Librarians Association Author of the Year Award, 1990; several books chosen as Junior Library Guild selections.

■ Writings

YOUNG ADULT FICTION

C.C. Poindexter, Atheneum, 1979.
Eulalia's Island, Atheneum, 1982.
The Summer I Learned about Life, Atheneum, 1983.
The Luck of Texas McCoy, Atheneum, 1984.

Elliott & Win, Atheneum, 1986.
Denny's Tapes, Macmillan, 1987.
Wild Rover, Macmillan, 1989.
Killing the Kudu, Macmillan, 1990.
Where the Broken Heart Still Beats: The Story of Cynthia Ann Parker, Harcourt, 1992.
White Lilacs, Harcourt, 1993.
Rio Grande Stories, Harcourt, 1994.
Drummers of Jericho, Harcourt, 1995.

"HOTLINE" SERIES

Because of Lissa, Bantam, 1990.
The Problem with Sidney, Bantam, 1990.
Gillian's Choice, Bantam, 1991.
The Two Faces of Adam, Bantam, 1991.

YOUNG ADULT NONFICTION

People Who Make Things: How American Craftsmen Live and Work, Atheneum, 1975.
Amish People: Plain Living in a Complex World, photographs by Michael Ramsey, Gerald Dodds, and the author, Atheneum, 1976.
Eskimos: Growing Up in a Changing Culture, with research assistance by Bernadine Larsen, photographs by John McDougal, Atheneum, 1977.
The Center: From a Troubled Past to a New Life, Atheneum, 1980.
Rock Band: Big Men in a Great Big Town, Atheneum, 1980.
(With Charles Gallenkamp) *The Mystery of the Ancient Maya*, Atheneum, 1985, revised edition, 1995.
Voices of South Africa: Growing Up in a Troubled Land, Harcourt, 1986.
Voices of Northern Ireland: Growing Up in a Troubled Land, Harcourt, 1987.
A Voice from Japan: An Outsider Looks In, Harcourt, 1988.

JUVENILE

Miss Patch's Learn-to-Sew Book, illustrated by Mary Suzuki, Harcourt, 1969.
(Self-illustrated) *Stitch by Stitch: Needlework for Beginners*, Harcourt, 1970.
The Bread Book: All about Bread and How to Make It, illustrated by Trina Schart Hyman, Harcourt, 1971.
Yarn: The Things It Makes and How to Make Them, illustrated by Jennifer Perrott, Harcourt, 1972.
Saw, Hammer and Paint: Woodworking and Finishing for Beginners, illustrated by Toni Martignoni, Morrow, 1973.
Christmas Crafts: Things to Make the 24 Days before Christmas, illustrated by Anita Lobel, Harper, 1974.

Milk, Butter and Cheese: The Story of Dairy Products, illustrated by Giulio Maestro, Morrow, 1974.
Rock Tumbling: From Stones to Gems to Jewelry, photographs by Jerome Wexler, Morrow, 1975.
The Needlework Book of Bible Stories, illustrated by Janet McCaffery, Harcourt, 1975.
Lots and Lots of Candy, illustrated by Laura Jean Allen, Harcourt, 1976.
Coconut: The Tree of Life, illustrated by Lynne Cherry, Morrow, 1976.
Being Beautiful: The Story of Cosmetics from Ancient Art to Modern Science, illustrated by Marika, Morrow, 1977.
Mask Magic, illustrated by Melanie Gaines Arwin, Harcourt, 1978.
Japan: How Do Hands Make Peace?, McGraw, 1990.
Multicultural Sing & Learn: Folk Songs and Monthly Activities, Good Apple, 1994.

OTHER

Author of columns, "Cheers and Jeers," 1967-68, "Chiefly for Children," 1968-72, and of multi-part series on crafts and women, and consulting editor for "Right Now" section, *McCall's*, 1972. Contributor of articles and book reviews to periodicals, including *Family Circle, Redbook, Golf Digest, Los Angeles Times, Accent on Leisure, Town and Country, Publishers Weekly*, and *Americana*.

■ Work in Progress

In a Different Light: Growing Up in a Yup'ik Eskimo Village in Alaska, juvenile nonfiction for Simon & Schuster; *Gideon's People*, a young adult novel for Harcourt.

■ Sidelights

After years of hard work while striving to attain the title of published author, Carolyn Meyer, a young housewife and mother, finally sold her first short story to a secretarial magazine. Her family and friends, however, could not read this first published work—it was printed in shorthand. From this inauspicious beginning Meyer built what eventually turned into two writing careers—one in nonfiction and one in fiction. With the exception of several magazine articles, her work has primarily been directed towards children and young adults, numbering over fifteen novels and over twenty nonfiction books. And the range of these works covers everything from craft how-to books for younger readers, to teen novels with both historical and contemporary settings that utilize such foreign settings as Northern Ireland and South Africa.

In writing about teens, Meyer often focuses on kids who feel themselves to be misfits, feelings she herself associates with from her own childhood. In an essay for *Something about the Author Autobiographical Series* (*SAAS*), she describes herself as "an only child, a homely child, and an intelligent child" who wore thick glasses and didn't know how to play with other children. As early as kindergarten she was labelled odd, and grew up with few close friends her own age. "Everybody played softball and roller-skated and climbed trees and skinned the cat," she notes in *Fifth Book of Junior Authors*, "while I sat inside and read and wrote and daydreamed." Even though she had few social skills, Meyer *was* skilled at getting out of events she hated, like birthday parties and school picnics. Whenever a dreaded event occurred, she simply became sick, allowing her loving, overprotective parents to indulge her every need. Thus Meyer describes her early school years in *SAAS* as being spent "at home in bed, surrounded by my books, a little radio my grandfather brought me, and a lot of hovering attention from my mother."

Social ineptitude aside, Meyer shined academically. She was very bright—bright enough to tutor a few of the slower children in her small country school. This gave her some status in the classroom, but it was status that eluded Meyer when she and her classmates stepped out onto the playground. One insensitive classmate even dubbed her "Professor Pisspot," figuring, Meyer explains in *SAAS*, "that there wasn't a thing wrong with me except that I was too smart for my own good."

By the time Meyer reached junior high she was tired of feigning illness for every important event, and her sicknesses—which had all seemed real in their times—miraculously disappeared. It was harder to shed her role as a social outcast, however, in spite of the fact that she graduated at the head of her high school class and became valedictorian. Meyer went to her senior dinner dance alone, and attended the school prom with "some poor soul who . . . certainly didn't want to go with me any more than I wanted to go with him," she remembers in her *SAAS* essay. This isolation was made even harder to bear by the fact

In this 1995 novel, a Jewish girl spending her freshman year of high school in a small town learns the importance of friendship and exercising one's rights.

that her mother, Sara Knepp, also an only child, had attended the same high school, only she had been pretty and popular, so much so that some of Meyer's teachers were surprised to find out she was Sara's daughter. She was, as her mother often said, a late bloomer.

By college things began to change, and at the end of her senior year, Meyer graduated with an engagement ring on her finger. During one summer vacation, she had also learned to type and take shorthand. This was done at her father's insistence, since Meyer had no desire to go on to graduate school or to teach English, the subject of her major. At this point no one, including Meyer herself, took her stated desire—to become a writer—very seriously. The secretarial course was intended to make her employable, at least until she married. As it turned out, Meyer's first engagement fell through and she found herself working at a secretarial job that she disliked from the start. As Meyer notes in *SAAS*, the myth at the time was that "persistent girls who didn't get sidetracked into marriage and family could eventually work their way into interesting jobs—but not as interesting as the jobs the boys got, and probably not as interesting as marriage."

Writing as Antidote to Housework

So Meyer let herself be sidetracked into marriage at the earliest opportunity, and set out to become a perfect housewife and mother. Within a few years she had three sons as well as a husband, and devoted herself to caring for them. It was during this time that she began writing in earnest, using her afternoon hours to sharpen her skills while her children took naps. "[It was] a way to stay sane and alive after the housework was done," she explains in *Junior Literary Guild.* After making numerous submissions to the *New Yorker* (all rejected) and writing a novel that never sold, Meyer had her first success with the secretarial magazine. As time went on she sold more short pieces, and finally acquired an agent who sold her first book, *Miss Patch's Learn-to-Sew Book,* which was published in 1969.

Several more how-to-books followed, mostly to favorable reviews. *Rock Tumbling: From Stones to Gems to Jewelry* was called "a superior how-to book" by a reviewer in *Appraisal,* and *Saw, Hammer and Paint: Woodworking and Finishing for Beginners,* was described as "everything a how-to book ought to be" by a *Bulletin of the Center for Children's Books* contributor. While the books generally reflected Meyer's interests in cooking and crafts, she also began to include some history, another of her avocations. For example, *The Bread Book: All about Bread and How to Make It* is as much about the history and myths of bread as it is about baking bread. As time went on, Meyer found herself growing more interested in the people who made the crafts than in the crafts themselves, and as a result wrote *People Who Make Things: How American Craftsmen Live and Work.* In *SAAS,* Meyer describes the book as "transitional," in that, for the first time, the research took her beyond her local library. By this

time, Meyer had divorced, and, exploring her new independence, she traveled around the country visiting potters, weavers, woodworkers, glassblowers, and several others to learn what their lives and work were like.

This interest in history and the way people live soon came together in Meyer's next journalistic book, *Amish People: Plain Living in a Complex World.* Meyer was first inspired to write about the Amish while visiting her mother in her old hometown of Lewiston, Pennsylvania. Although she had grown up surrounded by the Amish and shared some ancestors with them, Meyer knew little about them, and so was again required to do substantial research. Her efforts paid off, and the book was well-received critically, including being described by Edward Hoagland in the *New York Times Book Review* as "an excellent introduction to Amishism."

Amish People uses the device of showing the Amish way of life through the eyes of a fictional seventeen-year-old boy. Shortly afterwards Meyer moved into fiction wholeheartedly with *C.C. Poindexter,* her first novel. C.C.'s parents are recently divorced, leaving C.C. bewildered and mistrusting of the adults in her life. As far as she can see, they are as confused as she is, which leads her to conclude that "being an adult was really not that much different from being a teenager, except that you were expected to act as though you knew at least some of the answers, and when you didn't know, you couldn't admit it but had to fake it." Adding to C.C.'s distress is the fact that she is six-foot-one and still growing. C.C. is one of Meyer's misfits, and Meyer has said that she found it very easy to identify with her. Nevertheless, the book is not autobiographical. In it, C.C. admires her ultra-feminist aunt and considers joining a commune—things the young Meyer could scarcely have imagined.

"What's It Like?"

Whether fiction or nonfiction, much of Meyer's work stems from her desire to answer the question, "What's it like?" As she says in *Fifth Book of Junior Authors,* "In order to learn the answer to that basic question, 'What's it like?', I've spent a lot of time in different places—in an Eskimo village near the Bering Sea, on an Amish farm, in a therapeutic community, in rock-and-roll clubs, on a small Caribbean island." That two-month visit was to St. Lucia, and it inspired several different "what's it like?" questions. It was an exceptionally productive time for Meyer; *C.C. Poindexter* was begun during the visit, and Meyer also collected material for her next novel, *Eulalia's Island* (what's it like for a white teenage boy to become friends with a black St. Lucian family?), as well as research for a book on coconuts. In addition, Meyer began corresponding with a caucasian woman who had married into the Eskimo culture, a correspondence that eventually evolved into research for *Eskimos: Growing Up in a Changing Culture.*

In looking for situations and personalities that provoke interesting "what's it like?" questions, Meyer is often inspired by people close to her, especially when writing fiction. For example, *The Summer I Learned about Life* grew out of the diaries Meyer's father kept when he was a young man, *Elliott & Win* stemmed from a bachelor friend's experience with a "big brother" program, and the idea for *The Luck of Texas McCoy* developed after Meyer learned about ranch life from a young riding instructor in New Mexico.

Different locations also inspired some of Meyer's "what's it like?" questions. After her divorce, the author moved several times, first from suburban Connecticut to New York City, then to New Mexico (first Santa Fe and then Albuquerque), later to Denton, Texas, and finally back to Albuquerque. Each location inspired different versions of the question, and each has figured prominently in her novels. The move to New Mexico provided the background not only for *The Luck of Texas McCoy,* but also for *Elliott & Win, Wild Rover,* and *Rio Grande Stories.* The move to Denton inspired two other novels: *White Lilacs,* the story of a girl growing up in a black community that was forcibly moved by their white neighbors to make room for a park, and *Where the Broken Heart Still Beats: The Story of Cynthia Ann Parker,* which is based on the true story of a white woman who was kidnapped and raised by Comanches and then kidnapped back by the Texas Rangers twenty-five years later.

In looking for inspiration for her nonfiction, for many years Meyer felt that the topics she pursued had to be self-generated. "If they weren't my ideas in the first place, I might have trouble working up a genuine passion for somebody else's inspiration," she comments in *SAAS.* This changed when she developed a severe case of writer's block. After recovering from serious surgery in 1984, Meyer suddenly found that nothing happened when she faced a blank computer screen. "In those black days in the winter of 1984 and 1985, whatever I forced myself to write didn't work," the author explains in *SAAS.* "After more than twenty years of writing almost every day, I seemed to have nothing more to say. I came to the conclusion that I might not be a writer after all. . . . it was very painful, one of the most depressing times in my life." In her essay for *Fifth Book of Junior Authors,* Meyer writes that "eventually I learned that I have to look in different places than I did before and to listen to different sounds."

These different sounds came through loud and clear in 1985 when Meyer was asked to write a book about South Africa by an editor who had read and enjoyed *The Mystery of the Ancient Maya.* At the time, apartheid was very much in the news, and the idea of writing a book for teenagers about growing up in South Africa appealed to Meyer immensely. She spent five weeks in the country, interviewing as many people as she could, both black and white, in order to be able to draw a convincing portrait of a country about which she had previously known very little. And so the writing of *Voices of South Africa: Growing Up in a Troubled Land* brought an end to Meyer's writer's block.

As the author notes in *SAAS,* obtaining the interviews that helped her answer the question, "What's it like to grow up in South Africa?," was no easy feat. Because the South African government had no sympathy for American journalists, Meyer identified herself only as a children's author. Nevertheless, it was difficult to get people to open up to her. "I was variously considered a bloody Yank, a communist agitator, and a CIA agent," she remembers in her *SAAS* essay. In spite of the difficulties she encountered, Meyer succeeded in impressing the critics with *Voices of South Africa.* The book was hailed as "articulate and insightful . . . a fine book," by a *Horn Book* contributor; "an engrossing personal account," by Cathi McRae in *Wilson Library Bulletin;* and a *Kirkus Reviews* contributor describes *Voices of South Africa* as "[a] brilliant study."

Voices of Northern Ireland: Growing Up in a Troubled Land, the author's next book, was developed through similar research, by visiting the country and speaking with as many adults and young people as possible in the short span of six weeks. Again, Meyer's techniques proved successful. A *Horn Book* reviewer praises Meyer for being "a shrewd observer [who] appears to have had the gift of encouraging the young to talk to her," and a *Kirkus Reviews* contributor calls the book "outstanding," adding that it is "a lively, thought-provoking study."

Despite their success, Meyer found the type of research necessary to answer the "what's it like?" questions for these two books to be both drain-

ing and depressing. In addition to the strain of traveling alone in countries that are not accustomed to independent women, she was dismayed by the hopelessness that seemed to pervade the lives of many of the countries' citizens. Her next book, *A Voice from Japan: An Outsider Looks In*, involved similar research, but this time it was further complicated by the language barrier and the constraints of a vastly different culture. She had also recently remarried, to poet and playwright E. A. "Tony" Mares, and found herself longing to be home rather than traveling in a foreign country alone.

Crafting Fiction and Nonfiction

Since then, Meyer has turned her energy and attention mainly to answering her "what's it like?" questions in fiction, where most of her research is done close to home. One exception is the revision of *Eskimos: Growing Up in a Changing Culture*; retitled *In a Different Light: Growing Up in a Yup'ik Eskimo Village in Alaska*, the new book required Meyer to track down her collaborator on the original version. When Meyer found her, she was no longer living in Alaska, but in New Hampshire, and the two arranged to meet in Chefornak, a village in southwestern Alaska (and the model for the early book). Meyer stayed for three weeks, sleeping on the floor of the kindergarten schoolroom and eating peanut butter sandwiches and dehydrated soup heated up in the school microwave.

Fifteen students decide to write and sell a book to raise money for their school, so each contributes a story that celebrates their unique heritage, resulting in a portrayal of the diverse cultures and people of New Mexico.

Whatever Meyer's subject matter may be, though, she always approaches her work by beginning with a very rough first draft on her computer. (When she first began to write, the author did her first drafts in longhand, but over the years learned to write at the typewriter, and later, with a word processing program.) Meyer doesn't stop to refine her work as she gets her ideas on paper; sometimes a character's name changes from one chapter to the next, or a character who has been male suddenly becomes female. It doesn't matter, since this draft will go through several rewrites before it becomes a finished manuscript. Still, Meyer confesses in her *SAAS* entry, "I occasionally worry that I will be run over by a trolley before I have a chance to put it all together in a second draft, and that one of my sons, going through my desk . . . will find this wretched first draft, glance at it, and say to his brothers, 'Poor Ma. She really lost it there at the end. This isn't even readable.'"

The second draft goes more slowly, as Meyer irons out the details, comes to know her characters well, and organizes her material. But she still isn't finished; one more draft is required to fine-tune the language and "polish, polish, polish," as she writes in *SAAS*. Only then does the manuscript go to her editor, inevitably to come back with more changes to be made. It's a long process, and when a work is finally finished, Meyer says, she has symptoms of withdrawal. What had seemed elegantly written when she first wrote it often suddenly appears leaden and dull. Not until Meyer receives her editor's approval can she truly relax and begin to devote herself to the next project. Whatever that next project turns out to be, it will almost certainly involve answering a "what's it like?" question that some new location or story has brought to Meyer's attention, and she will be more than willing to explore the answer.

■ **Works Cited**

Hoagland, Edward, review of *Amish People: Plain Living in a Complex World, New York Times Book Review,* May 9, 1976, p. 14.

McRae, Cathi, "The Young Adult Perplex," *Wilson Library Bulletin,* December, 1988, pp. 92-3.

Meyer, Carolyn, *C.C. Poindexter,* Atheneum, 1979.

Meyer, Carolyn, in an interview for *Fifth Book of Junior Authors,* edited by Sally Holmes Holtze, Wilson, 1983, p. 214.

Meyer, Carolyn, in an essay for *Something about the Author Autobiography Series,* Volume 9, Gale, 1990.

Review of *People Who Make Things: How American Craftsmen Live and Work, Literary Guild,* March, 1975.

Review of *Rock Tumbling: From Stones to Gems to Jewelry, Appraisal,* winter, 1976.

Review of *Saw, Hammer and Paint: Woodworking and Finishing for Beginners, Bulletin of the Center for Children's Books,* October, 1973.

Review of *Voices of Northern Ireland: Growing Up in a Troubled Land, Horn Book,* January/February, 1988, p. 87.

Review of *Voices of Northern Ireland, Kirkus Reviews,* September 1, 1987, p. 1323.

Review of *Voices of South Africa: Growing Up in a Troubled Land, Horn Book,* May/June, 1987, p. 359.

Review of *Voices of South Africa, Kirkus Reviews,* September 1, 1986, p. 1377.

■ **For More Information See**

PERIODICALS

New York Times Book Review, December 18, 1977, p. 23.

Publishers Weekly, November 21, 1986, p. 48.

School Library Journal, November, 1990, p. 50; January, 1991, p. 114; July, 1991, p. 88.

Voice of Youth Advocates, August, 1991, pp. 173-74.

Wilson Library Bulletin, June, 1991, p. 109; October, 1991, p. 102; March, 1994, pp. 126-27.

—Sketch by Sarah Verney

Tim O'Brien

■ Personal

Full name, William Timothy O'Brien; born October 1, 1946, in Austin, MN; son of William T. (an insurance salesman) and Ava E. (a teacher; maiden name, Schultz) O'Brien; married Ann Elizabeth Weller (a magazine production manager), 1973 (divorced). *Education:* Macalester College, B.A. (summa cum laude), 1968; graduate study at Harvard University.

■ Addresses

Home—Boxford, MA. *Agent*—Lynn Nesbit, International Creative Management, 40 West 57th St., New York, NY 10019.

■ Career

Writer. *Washington Post*, Washington, DC, national affairs reporter, 1973-74; Bread Loaf Writers' Conference, Ripton, VT, teacher. *Military service:* U.S. Army, 1968-70, served in Vietnam, promoted to sergeant, received Purple Heart. *Member:* Phi Beta Kappa.

■ Awards, Honors

O. Henry Memorial Awards, 1976 and 1978, both for chapters of *Going After Cacciato,* and 1982; National Endowment for the Arts fellow, 1976 and 1987; Best American Short Stories fellow, 1977 and 1987; National Book Award, 1979, for *Going After Cacciato;* Guggenheim Foundation fellowship, 1981; Vietnam Veterans of America award, 1987; National Magazine Award in Fiction, 1987, for "The Things They Carried"; Heartland Prize, *Chicago Tribune,* 1990, Melcher Book award, National Book Critics Circle nomination, and Pulitzer Prize nomination, all 1991, all for *The Things They Carried: A Work of Fiction;* L.H.D., Miami University (Ohio), 1990; has also received awards from the Massachusetts Arts and Humanities Foundation and the Bread Loaf Writers' Conference.

■ Writings

If I Die in a Combat Zone, Box Me Up and Ship Me Home, Delacorte, 1973.

Northern Lights, Delacorte, 1975.

Going After Cacciato, Delacorte, 1978.

The Nuclear Age, limited edition, Press-22, 1981; first trade edition, Knopf, 1985.

The Things They Carried: A Work of Fiction, Houghton, 1990.

In the Lake of the Woods, Houghton, 1994.

Contributor to magazines, including *Playboy, Esquire, Redbook,* and *New York Times Magazine.*

■ **Sidelights**

"It's incredible, it really is, isn't it? Ever think you'd be humping along some crazy-ass trail like this one, jumping up and down out of the dirt, jumping like a goddamn bullfrog, dodging bullets all day? Don't know about you, but I sure as hell never thought *I'd* ever be going all day like this. Back in Cleveland I'd still be asleep."

Thus begins Tim O'Brien's 1973 book, *If I Die in a Combat Zone, Box Me Up and Ship Me Home,* the first of many critically acclaimed works that describe his horrifying experiences in Vietnam and their lasting impact on his life. O'Brien served in the United States Army for two years (1968-70) during the Vietnam War. A radio-telephone operator for the 198th Infantry Brigade stationed in the Quang Ngai Province of Vietnam, he saw friends, villagers, and enemy soldiers alike fall during his tour of duty. He was wounded himself and received a Purple Heart. After returning to the United States, O'Brien began his career as a novelist. In works such as *Going After Cacciato, The Things They Carried: A Work of Fiction,* and *In the Lake of the Woods,* he has skillfully described the experiences of American soldiers in Vietnam and the physical and emotional toll that the war exacted on its participants. O'Brien explained in a *Publishers Weekly* interview with Michael Colley that "my passion as a human being and as a writer intersect in Vietnam, not in the physical stuff but in the issues of Vietnam—of courage, rectitude, enlightenment, holiness, trying to do the right thing in the world."

Tim O'Brien was born in the small town of Austin, Minnesota, on October 1, 1946. The son of an insurance salesman and a schoolteacher, he described himself in a 1994 *New York Times Magazine* article as a "chubby and friendless and lonely" child. As a kid he learned to do a variety of magic tricks in front of a little stand-up mirror down in the basement of his house. Magic became his principal hobby, in part because exercising this talent brought him applause and a sense of power. "There's a real appeal in that for a lonely little kid in a lonely little town, to get that kind of love and applause and to feel you have some control," O'Brien recalled in an interview with John Mort in *Booklist.*

After graduating from high school, O'Brien attended Macalester College in Saint Paul, Minne-

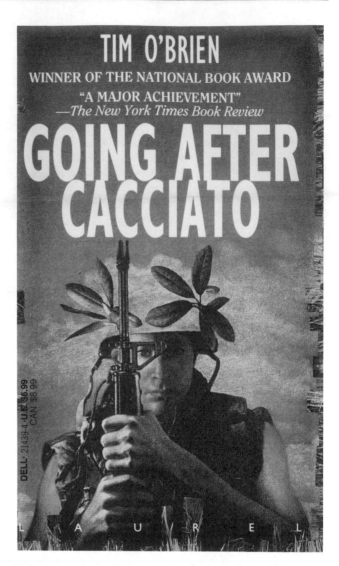

Recipient of the National Book Award in 1979, this novel tells both the trials of a troop in Vietnam and an infantryman's fantasy about chasing down a private who has deserted.

sota. At Macalester he discovered that, even though his grades were good, his other school activities gave him a reputation as a radical. As student body president his senior year, O'Brien pressed for a wide range of reforms to school rules and regulations that he thought were discriminatory or flawed. He graduated summa cum laude in 1968 with a bachelor's degree in political science and was promptly drafted into the army. "In college, I stood in peace vigils. I rang doorbells for Gene McCarthy [a presidential candidate who opposed U.S. involvement in Vietnam], composed earnest editorials for the school newspaper," O'Brien wrote in the *New York Times Magazine.* "But when the draft notice arrived after graduation, the old demons went to work almost instantly. I thought about Canada. I thought about jail. But in the end I could not bear the prospect of rejection: by my family, my country, my friends, my hometown. I would risk conscience and rectitude before risking the loss of love. . . . I was a coward. I went to Vietnam."

O'Brien Goes to Vietnam

"In February 1969 . . . I arrived as a young, terrified [private first class] on this lonely little hill in Quang Ngai Province. Back then, the place seemed huge and imposing and permanent," O'Brien recalled in the *New York Times Magazine.* "I remember a tar helipad, a mess hall, a medical station, mortar and artillery emplacements, two volleyball courts, numerous barracks and offices and supply depots and machine shops and entertainment clubs. [It] was our castle. Not safe, exactly, but far preferable to the bush. No land mines here. No paddies bubbling with machine-gun fire." O'Brien and the rest of his Alpha Company outfit were able to spend three or four days a month at this location, where "there were hot showers and hot meals, ice chests packed with beer, glossy pinup girls, big, black Sony tape decks booming 'We gotta get out of this place' at decibels for the deaf." But the majority of their time was spent out in the bush, where at any moment they could be hit by sniper fire or mortar attacks.

The territory patrolled by Alpha Company was frightening and forbidding. The terrain was unfamiliar to the soldiers and the enemy Viet Cong proved elusive—except when they attacked. And all around them they could see the aftermath of previous attacks. "Back in 1969," O'Brien commented in the *New York Times Magazine,* "the wreckage was all around us, so common it seemed part of the geography, as natural as any mountain or river. Wreckage was the rule. Brutality was S.O.P. [standard operating procedure]. Scalded children, pistol-whipped women, burning hooches, free-fire zones, body counts, indiscriminate bombing and harassment fire, villages in ash, M-60 machine guns hosing down dark green tree lines and any human life behind them."

For two long years O'Brien endured the harsh, merciless conditions of the Quang Ngai Province. During that period the war repeatedly tested his sense of right and wrong. *New York Times Book Review* contributor Jon Elsen wrote that "once in

Vietnam, [O'Brien] committed what he considers to be sins to gain the love and respect of his comrades. 'If friends are burning hooches, you don't want to be thought of as a bad person, so you burn along,' he said. 'You'll do bad things to be loved by your friends, realizing later that you've made a horrible mistake.'"

Even so, O'Brien wrote in the *New York Times Magazine,* "Vietnam was more than terror. For me, at least, Vietnam was partly love. With each step, each light-year of a second, a foot soldier is always almost dead, or so it feels, and in such circumstances you can't *help* but love. You love your mom and dad, the Vikings, hamburgers on the grill, your pulse, your future—everything that might be lost or never come to be." As his service continued, the sights of death and destruction further nurtured his love of life. "Intimacy with death carries with it a corresponding new intimacy with life," he said in the *New York Times Magazine.* "Jokes are funnier, green is greener. You love the musty morning air. You love the miracle of your own enduring capacity for love. You love your friends in Alpha Company—a kid named Chip, my buddy. He wrote letters to my sister, I wrote letters to his sister. . . . In May of 1969, Chip was blown high into a hedge of bamboo. Many pieces. I loved the guy, he loved me. I'm alive. He's dead. An old story, I guess."

Writing about Vietnam

After returning to America, O'Brien spent a couple years working at the *Washington Post,* first as an intern and then as a national affairs reporter for the newspaper. He also enrolled in a number of graduate courses at Harvard University in the early 1970s. He studied there until 1976, when he left to pursue a full-time career as a novelist. His first book, *If I Die in a Combat Zone, Box Me Up and Ship Me Home* (1973), was part-novel, part-diary. The chapters of *If I Die* chronicled in gritty detail the experiences of a young man who is drafted, trained, and sent to war. In many ways the book mirrored the author's own thoughts and emotions before and during his stint in Vietnam. Critics took note of the novel and hailed O'Brien as a powerful new interpreter of the lives of American soldiers in Vietnam.

O'Brien's second novel was *Northern Lights* (1975), a tale of two brothers and their evolving relationship. One of the brothers, Harvey, is a Vietnam

War hero who is the apple of his father's eye. His brother Paul, though, is an unremarkable man who has lived a quiet and fearful life. During a long and ultimately perilous cross-country ski trip, however, the two brothers slowly change places. Harvey proves far more vulnerable than anyone imagined, and Paul ultimately saves his brother's life by tapping into reserves of courage and cunning that he did not know he possessed. *Northern Lights* received mixed reviews from critics, many of whom pointed to the book's similarity to several of Ernest Hemingway's works. John Deck wrote in the *New York Times Book Review* that O'Brien told "the story modestly and neatly . . . [in] a crafted work of serious intent with themes at least as old as the Old Testament."

This 1973 novel is an account of O'Brien's year as a foot soldier in Vietnam.

O'Brien's third novel was published in 1978. *Going After Cacciato,* which received the National Book Award in 1979, "told two different stories," noted James Marcus in the *Nation.* "One detailed the life, times and steady decimation of the First Platoon of Alpha Company, 198th Infantry Brigade, stationed in Quang Ngai in late 1968. . . . Next to this narrative O'Brien placed a second, the long and fabulous story of the deserter Private Cacciato, who is pursued by members of the platoon from the jungle all the way to Paris." This section of the novel is a dreamlike tale told from the perspective of Paul Berlin, an infantryman who fantasizes about chasing Cacciato while standing guard one evening at a station by the South China Sea. While a few reviewers were critical of *Going After Cacciato,* the vast majority echoed the sentiments of *Washington Post Book World* reviewer Robert Wilson, who said that "Tim O'Brien knows the soldier as well as anybody, and is able to make us know him in the unique way that the best fiction can." And John Romano wrote in the *Atlantic Monthly* that *Going After Cacciato* "strikes me as the best novel about Vietnam and one of the best war novels that I know."

By the early 1980s O'Brien's musings on the nature of human frailty and courage within the context of war had established him as one of America's most eloquent voices on the Vietnam War. His fourth book, however, explored new territory. *The Nuclear Age* (1985) told the story of William Cowling, a man who in the year 1995 has succumbed to long-held feelings of paranoia about nuclear annihilation that date back to his childhood in the 1950s. O'Brien employs a series of extended flashbacks to flesh out his protagonist's unhappy childhood and days as a campus radical and to explain his present fear of nuclear war. As with *Northern Lights,* reviews of *The Nuclear Age* were mixed. Many critics complained about leaden characterizations and stereotypical cliches in the novel. *New York Times* reviewer Michiko Kakutani called the book "bereft of originality or persuasive passion," while Romano wrote that *The Nuclear Age* "is in truth less a book about living with the abominable than an abominable book, abominably written and underconceived in every important respect." Others such as *Washington Post Book World* critic Richard Lipez, however, contended that "flawed as it is, *The Nuclear Age* is still in many ways a wonderful novel."

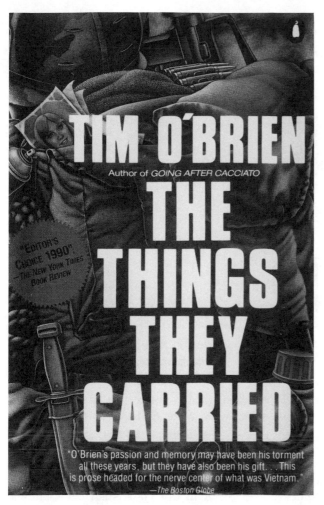

A Pulitzer Prize nominee, this 1990 novel is a collection of the childhoods and dreams of soldiers and the effects the Vietnam War had on them.

The Things They Carried

O'Brien's next book—*The Things They Carried* (1990)—returned to the rice fields and burning villages of the Vietnam War with devastating effect. A "compassionate, complex, magnificent novel of self-acceptance and renewal," according to Mort, *The Things They Carried* was hailed as perhaps the author's greatest work.

The work, composed of a series of chapters that can be easily read as separate short stories, once again puts readers in the shoes of an American foot soldier tramping through the jungles of Vietnam. The title story reflects on the many things that a soldier carries into combat with him—weapons, fears, memories, and hopes—while "On the Rainy River" relates a draftee's agonized weighing of his options: report for duty or flee to

Canada. These and other chapters in the book, such as "How to Tell a True War Story" and "Sweetheart of the Song Tra Bong," moved Richard Eder of the *Los Angeles Times* to write that "the best of these stories—and none is written with less than the sharp edge of a honed vision—are memory as prophecy. . . . It is an ultimate, indelible image of war in our time, and in time to come." Verlyn Klinkenborg of the *New York Times Book Review* called *The Things They Carried* "one of the finest books, fact or fiction, written about the Vietnam War." A *Publishers Weekly* contributor agreed and added that "O'Brien's meditations—on war and memory, on darkness and light—suffuses the entire work with a kind of poetic form, making for a highly original, fully realized novel. . . . The book is persuasive in its desperate hope that stories can save us." *The Things They Carried* won the 1990 *Chicago Tribune* Heartland Award in fiction and was nominated for a Pulitzer Prize.

O'Brien Turns to My Lai

In 1994 O'Brien's sixth book was published. *In the Lake of the Woods* concerns John Wade, a young politician from Minnesota whose political career has been destroyed by revelations that he was present at the My Lai massacre that actually took place in Vietnam on March 16, 1968. On that date more than one hundred U.S. soldiers entered the village of My Lai. Although they encountered no resistance or enemy fire the soldiers turned their guns on the animals and people of the village. Estimates of the number of villagers murdered in the attack range from three hundred to five hundred, many of whom were infants, children, women, and old men. The massacre that took place at My Lai was not made public until 1969, and only five U.S. soldiers were court-martialed. Only one soldier—Lt. William L. Calley—was convicted of crimes connected to that attack, but his conviction was overturned, and he was set free in 1974. This lack of punishment outraged O'Brien, who wrote in the *New York Times Magazine* that he felt betrayed by a "military judicial system that treats murderers and common soldiers as one and the same. Apparently we're all innocent—those who exercise moral restraint and those who do not, officers who control their troops and officers who do not."

In his interview with Mort, O'Brien explained that "I served in the My Lai area a few months after the massacre. It scared the shit out of me, to be honest with you. It was a spooky, evil place on the earth. . . . It scared everybody, and that was before we knew what had gone on." After O'Brien and the other members of Alpha Company heard about the massacre, "we all understood why the people in that place were so hostile, why they had such looks of obvious hatred. I'd always wanted to write about it but didn't know how. I didn't want to write just a My Lai book but a deeper book about life and secrecy in general. . . . Nam and atrocity and evil are not just to be found in war—they're in our hearts every day of our lives." He went on to note that of all the U.S. soldiers who took part in the murder of the My Lai villagers, most remain largely anonymous. Still, O'Brien says, they are out there, carrying around their dark secret. "Who knows what they've told their girlfriends and their wives?"

O'Brien noted in the *New York Times Magazine* that even when the full horror of the events at My Lai became known, "most Americans seemed to shrug it off as a cruel, nasty, inevitable consequence of war. There were numerous excuses, numerous rationalizations. . . . Now, more than 25 years later, the villainy of that Saturday morning in 1968 has been pushed off to the margins of memory. . . . Evil has no place, it seems, in our national mythology."

Although John Wade, the main character in the novel, was not a leading figure in the atrocities at My Lai, "Wade's presence there was a secret Wade had kept from his wife, from his campaign manager and, in a sense, from himself," remarked Klinkenborg. After learning of her husband's dark secret, Kathleen Wade disappears. The novel includes sections devoted to John Wade's search for his wife and speculation about her whereabouts, but also includes chapters containing quotes, interviews, press reports, and trial testimony concerning Wade, the My Lai incident, and other historical military actions.

O'Brien called *In the Lake of the Woods* his "stab at trying to understand evil" in his interview with Mort. *Los Angeles Times Book Review* reviewer Richard Eder pointed to the following footnote as the book's key passage, the one that most closely sought to consider the nature of evil: "I know how [the massacre] happened. I know why. It was the sunlight. It was the wickedness that soaks into your blood and slowly heats up and begins to

Tim O'Brien received a Purple Heart for wounds he received as a young soldier in Vietnam.

boil. Frustration, partly. Rage, partly. The enemy was invisible. They were ghosts. . . . But it went beyond that. Something more mysterious. The smell of incense, maybe. The unknown, the unknowable. The blank faces. The overwhelming otherness. This is not to justify what occurred on March 16, 1968, for in my view, such justifications are both futile and outrageous. Rather, it's to bear witness to the mystery of evil."

Return to Vietnam

In February 1994 O'Brien returned to Quang Ngai Province in Vietnam, the place where he had witnessed so much bloodshed and horror. "I was more than reluctant—I was petrified, I looked for excuses" not to go, he admitted in the *New York Times Magazine*. But he returned to walk the same ground he had trod twenty-five years before. He met with men who had been officers in the very Viet Cong forces that Alpha Company had been trying to track down. He ate dinner with women who had survived the My Lai massacre only to discover that the rest of their families had been slain. The journey proved to be a time of healing. O'Brien commented in his interview with Mort that "going to Vietnam took the Nam out of me, at least some of it. There was a new Vietnam in my thoughts. . . . It's a nice feeling to find the geography, to walk in the backyard again and not really remember what happened so much as feel blown away by the utter peace that's replaced what was horror . . . to feel the rice in your hands and see the tree line and that little village over there. You're standing looking at these things and part of you is trying to remember those bodies, but all you're seeing is geese. You come away with the rice blowing and the sun hitting it and everything's golden."

After returning to the United States, O'Brien indicated that he planned to stop writing fiction for a while. "With *In the Lake of the Woods,* I feel like I've completed the things I have to say about myself and the world I've lived in, and also I've completed a kind of search," he explained to Mort. "I'm just gonna head north. See what happens."

■ Works Cited

Colley, Michael, interview with Tim O'Brien, *Publishers Weekly,* February 16, 1990, pp. 60-1.

Deck, John, review of *Northern Lights, New York Times Book Review,* October 12, 1975, p. 42.

Eder, Richard, review of *The Things They Carried, Los Angeles Times,* March 11, 1990.

Eder, Richard, "Vanishing Act," *Los Angeles Times Book Review,* October 2, 1994, p. 3.

Elsen, Jon, "Doing the Popular Thing," *New York Times Book Review,* October 9, 1994, p. 33.

Kakutani, Michiko, "Prophet of Doom," *New York Times,* September 28, 1985, p. 12.

Klinkenborg, Verlyn, "A Self-Made Man," *New York Times Book Review,* October 9, 1994, pp. 1, 33.

Lipez, Richard, "In the Shadow of the Bomb," *Washington Post Book World,* October 13, 1985, p. 9.

Marcus, James, "A Hole Is to Dig," *Nation,* November 2, 1985, pp. 450, 452-3.

Mort, John, "The Booklist Interview: Tim O'Brien," *Booklist,* August, 1994, pp. 1990-91.

O'Brien, Tim, *If I Die in a Combat Zone, Box Me Up and Ship Me Home,* Delacorte, 1973.

O'Brien, Tim, *In the Lake of the Woods,* Houghton, 1994.

O'Brien, Tim, "The Vietnam in Me," *New York Times Magazine,* October 2, 1994, pp. 48-57.

Romano, John, "Blue Over the Bomb," *Atlantic Monthly,* October, 1985, pp. 105-6.

Wilson, Robert, "Dreaming of War and Peace," *Washington Post Book World,* February 19, 1978, p. E4.

■ For More Information See

BOOKS

Contemporary Literary Criticism, Gale, Volume 7, 1977, Volume 19, 1981, Volume 40, 1986.

Dictionary of Literary Biography Documentary Series, Gale, Volume 9, 1991.

Dictionary of Literary Biography Yearbook: 1980, Gale, 1981.

Kaplan, Steven, *Understanding Tim O'Brien,* University of South Carolina Press, 1994.

PERIODICALS

English Journal, January, 1994, p. 82.

Library Journal, August, 1994, p. 132.

Los Angeles Times Book Review, November 3, 1985, p. 16.

Publishers Weekly, July 11, 1994, p. 61.*

—Sketch by Kevin Hillstrom

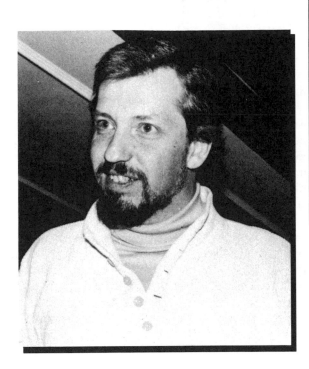

Dan Simmons

■ Personal

Born in the United States in 1948.

■ Addresses

Agent—c/o Putnam, 200 Madison Avenue, New York, NY 10016.

■ Career

Writer. Elementary school teacher who works with gifted children.

■ Awards, Honors

Fulbright scholarship, 1977; *Twilight Zone* magazine award for first published work, "The River Styx Runs Upstream," 1982; World Fantasy Award for Best First Novel, 1985, for *Song of Kali;* Hugo Award for Best Novel, 1989, for *Hyperion;* Locus Award for Best Science Fiction Novel, 1989, for *Hyperion;* Bram Stoker Award, 1990, for *Carrion Comfort;* Locus Award for Best Horror Novel, 1990, for *Carrion Comfort;* Locus Award for Best Science Fiction Novel, 1990, for *The Fall of Hyperion;* Science Fiction Chronicle Award for Best Novel, 1990, for *The Fall of Hyperion.*

■ Writings

NOVELS

Song of Kali, Tor Books, 1985.

Hyperion, Doubleday, 1989.
Phases of Gravity, Bantam, 1989.
Carrion Comfort, Warner Books, 1989.
The Fall of Hyperion, Doubleday, 1990.
Summer of Night, Putnam, 1991.
Children of the Night, Putnam, 1992.
The Hollow Man, Bantam, 1992.
Pele's Fire, Putnam, 1994.
Fires of Eden, Putnam, 1994.

COLLECTED SHORT STORIES

Hyperion Cantos, Guild America Books, 1990.
Banished Dreams, Roadkill Press, 1990.
Entropy's Bed at Midnight (chapbook), Lord John Press, 1990.
Prayers to Broken Stones: A Collection (includes "Vanni Fucci is Alive and Well and Living in Hell" and "The Death of the Centaur"), Dark Harvest, 1990.
Lovedeath, Warner Books, 1993.

OTHER

Going After the Rubber Chicken (nonfiction collection), Roadkill Press, 1991.

Contributed writings to a number of science fiction and fantasy anthologies, including *Night Visions V,* edited by Stephen King, Dark Harvest,

1988. Has also contributed material to periodicals of the genre, including *Galaxy, Omni,* and *Twilight Zone.*

■ Sidelights

Dan Simmons got his first big break as a writer of horror and science fiction stories with the 1982 publication of his short story "The River Styx Runs Upstream," which appeared in Rod Serling's *Twilight Zone* magazine. Encouraged in the early 1980s by science fiction writers Harlan Ellison and Edward Bryant, Simmons' stories and novellas soon began appearing in many of the major sci-

In this 1985 novel, an American novelist learns first-hand that the Cult of Kali—a group of fanatical followers who kill to give the evil Goddess of Destruction life—still exists.

ence fiction magazines of the day, including *Twilight Zone, Omni,* and *Galaxy.* (Indeed, it wasn't long before "The River Styx" would earn the author the first of many science fiction/fantasy writing awards.)

Simmons credits Ellison with a crucial piece of encouragement in early 1981: "Harlan told me in his usual tactful way," says Simmons, "that if I didn't keep writing he would personally rip my nose off." The following year Simmons completed the manuscript of what was to become his first novel, *Song of Kali,* which Tor Books published in 1985. *Song of Kali* is a grisly tale involving the kidnapped daughter of an American journalist in Calcutta, India and a deranged band of bloodthirsty worshippers of the Hindu goddess Kali. At first the journalist and his family are terrorized by the sect, and later his daughter is kidnapped by them for use in a ritual of human sacrifice. According to Simmons, the germ of the novel began in 1977, when he was travelling through India on a Fulbright scholarship: "I've lived in cities before, and wasn't afraid of them, but Calcutta was different. The cultural chaos and poverty there make it hard to be objective."

Critics of the first novel found its use of gruesome scenes of death and mutilation to be cutting-edge in the genre, along the lines of horror fiction pioneered by the likes of Stephen King and Clive Barker. But in Simmons' case the use of shocking and grisly story elements have a serious intention: a strong message of nonviolence is meant to be communicated. According to Simmons, that commitment to delivering a serious message put a lot of publishers off: "Several editors wanted a shoot-em-up, get-revenge ending, which I refused to do. I was trying to show a way for [the journalist hero] to *break* the cycle of violence, without making the ending of the novel anticlimactic."

Simmons' efforts paid off with the critics, who commended both his exploration of moral themes and his evocation of the horrific Indian city. Bob Collins, a critic writing for *Fantasy Review,* observed that "Simmons' vision of Calcutta is stunningly realistic, yet horrifyingly suggestive of a world rendered catatonic through brutalization, where the 'unthinkable' has become routine." Edward Bryant, who as a friend and mentor to Simmons was instrumental in encouraging him in the early years of his career, described *Song of*

DAN SIMMONS

HYPERION

"EXTRAORDINARY."
—ISAAC ASIMOV'S
SCIENCE FICTION MAGAZINE

This tale of seven pilgrims on a voyage to Hyperion to find the answers to the questions in their lives won the Hugo Award for Best Novel and the Locus Award for Best Science Fiction Novel in 1989.

Kali as "gripping" in his review of the novel for *Mile High Futures*. The book, wrote Bryant, "is a suspense novel of terror in which the monster is a city: Calcutta. Simmons presents this Indian metropolis as a teeming, festering, purely evil hellhole."

Collins described the experience of reading *Song of Kali* as being akin to "spending an evening in the rotting heart of a human compost heap." Bryant declared in his review that he couldn't put the book down and read it in one sitting. Faren Miller, critiquing the novel for *Locus* magazine, observed that its tale of an American family's involvement with a cult of the dreaded bloodthirsty

goddess could easily descend to a lower literary level, but Simmons elevates it ""with fine characterization, prose that rarely escapes control, and—above all—a keen moral sense." Kali's evil, Miller concludes, is a reflection of the present day, immediate and current. A writer for *Science Fiction Chronicle* added to the chorus of praise, observing that "there is no question that the novel is a powerful experience, and frequently a repulsive one. Simmons is an author to watch." It was an impressive horror debut by all accounts: gory, suspenseful, thrilling, and meaningful.

Off and Running

Simmons' impressive debut left little doubt of his ability to handle the horror genre, so with his next novel the author worked with a stronger science fiction underpinning than the reality-based Calcutta setting of the first. *Carrion Comfort,* published in 1989, tells the tale about mutant human beings, eaters of carrion, who have the supernatural ability to control other human beings via direct psychic access to their brains, making it possible for them to feast psychically on the experiences they compel their victims to have. Again, using an exploration of morality to weave the subtle underpinnings of his tale, the vampire-like creatures of *Carrion Comfort* lose control of their reality when they become addicted to pain and death.

Phases of Gravity, also published in 1989, is yet another departure for the writer—whose work exemplifies a spirit of experimentation that serves serious themes. With *Phases,* which narrates the tale of the psychic rejuvenation of a grounded astronaut, Simmons may have become the first science fiction writer of his generation to write an historical novel about the space program. With *Hyperion,* also published in 1989, and *The Fall of Hyperion,* published in 1990, Simmons returned to the full-blown realm of science fiction. The two books, which also are published together as the *Hyperion Cantos,* constitute a single, powerful tale set in a future time when a black hole has destroyed the planet Earth. *Cantos* is classically rich, complex, space-opera science fiction that explores many themes, including time travel, religious quests, cyberspace, ecology, bioengineering, and more.

In the first volume, *Hyperion,* Simmons uses a structure taken from Chaucer's *The Canterbury*

Winner of the Science Fiction Chronicle Award for Best Novel in 1990 and sequel to *Hyperion*, this novel describes the changes wrought by the opening of the mysterious Time Tombs.

Tales, telling the tale of a journey by seven pilgrims to a planet called Hyperion. During the course of their journey, each pilgrim recounts the story of his or her life, revealing significant experiences that define who they are and how they came to be on this quest for transcendence. The form of the novel gave Simmons the opportunity to showcase his short story writing talents. Indeed, one of the pilgrim's tales, "Remembering Siri," was first published separately in 1983 as a short story. The form also gives Simmons the nifty opportunity to use different science fiction idioms for each tale— to literally play with forms within the genre. The effect is a growing mosaic of styles and disparate tales that together form one cohesive whole.

In addition to Chaucer, Simmons also took inspiration from the poet Keats. Each of the two volumes that comprise *Cantos* take the titles of Keats's long but never completed poems about the displacement of the old gods and the victory of a new pantheon. That theme is intricately woven into the futuristic, space-opera world of *Cantos,* for the pilgrims are travelling to Hyperion to secure a transcendence (possibly of Time itself) that will save the war-torn, apocalypse-threatened Galaxy. Critics overall found that the intellectual brilliance of the conception of the twin novels made them a possibly definitive example of the devices and impulses of 1980s science fiction. But, regardless of their place in the history of the genre, the two novels affirmed a trend in Simmons' work toward highly literate yet highly entertaining science fiction.

Going for the Big Stakes

It is a hallmark of Simmons' writing that he works with complex themes. As Gregory Feeley put it in a review of *The Hollow Man* in the *Washington Post Book World,* Simmons "goes for the big stakes." In the 1992 novel, Simmons' themes included the nature of consciousness, the nature of the universe, the responsibility of the individual, the redemptive power of love—all classic themes in the science fiction genre—and, as Feeley puts it, "all of them not merely dramatized but firmly explained."

The Hollow Man, again with a title inspired by great poetry (in this case T. S. Eliot), tells the story of a man, Jeremy Bremen, who following the death of his wife liquidates his life and sets off on a random journey that soon becomes a nightmare. Blessed with the ability to read peoples' minds, Bremen's hollowness leaves him incapable or unwilling to use that power to help either himself or others, and the result is a downward spiral into violence and near madness. Though Feeley found the novel ultimately "unsatisfying and ersatz," a reviewer for *Voice of Youth Advocates* cited the work as one that "should take its place next to other masterpieces of horror in older young adult collections."

Originally published by *Omni* magazine as a short story entitled "Eyes I Dare Not Meet in Dreams," the much-expanded novel is pure science fiction in rationale: structured to resemble a metaphysical journey into hell, along the lines of Dante's

Inferno, and it contains numerous references to the Eliot poem in addition to the title. In addition to tributes to Dante and Eliot, Simmons takes the opportunity in *The Hollow Man* to use quantum physics and Chaos-theory mathematics as a means of explaining and making real the possibility of ESP.

In *Children of the Night* Simmons turned to classic vampire tales of Romania to construct a novel about AIDS. A major character in the novel, a priest named O'Brien, had appeared as a child in Simmons' novel of the previous year *Summer of Night,* a novel set in 1960—featuring giant lamprey eels, evil adults and a heroic boy who wants to become a writer when he grows up—that tells a tale about a small midwestern town where something is eating all the children who live there. In *Children of the Night,* Father O'Brien helps an American doctor to adopt a baby in Romania. When Kate Neuman, an American CDC research hematologist, adopts the Romanian orphan, she discovers that the boy has a unique ability to absorb transfused blood—and she becomes convinced that her adopted son's genetic mutation holds the key to a cure for AIDS.

Unfortunately, someone tries to fake the murder of Kate's son (substituting a body that she exposes as a fake), and events lead her to follow a trail back to Romania, where with Father O'Brien's help she discovers that her son is about to be consecrated as successor to Count Dracula of Transylvania. Mary K. Chelton, reviewing the novel for *Voice of Youth Advocates* magazine, found that the story's "progress from the initial scientific plausibility of the baby's rare blood disorder to a wonderfully melodramatic but equally plausible denouement is nonstop, well-written horror fantasy entertainment by a master of the genre." A *Publisher's Weekly* contributor described the book as a "mesmerizing revival" of the classic Dracula tale.

With *Lovedeath,* Simmons returned to the familiar starting point of his career: the short story or novella. The 1993 collection, according to *Booklist* reviewer Elliott Swanson, "demonstrates the full range of one of the most gifted writers in the psychological horror field." Among the stories included in the collection are "Entropy's Bed at Midnight," which contrasts the loss of a child with the impersonal nature of actuarial tables, "The Man who Slept with Teeth Women," which uses

Vampire-like beings use their psychic powers to enjoy the pain and agony felt by their human victims in this recipient of the 1990 Bram Stoker Award.

the voice of a Native American to recount a coming-of-age tale that involves humor, magic and horror, and "The Great Lover," which recreates the experiences of a World War I poet-soldier. "Simmons is one of the few authors associated with genre fiction who commands significant respect among literati," wrote Swanson. Barbara Conaty, writing a review of the collection for the *Library Journal,* added: "These fine novellas mark the newest epiphany in a career that spans some dozen books." The collection illustrates Simmons' abiding obsession with themes of love, death, and loss. Other notable story collections that Simmons has published include *Prayers to Broken Stones,* which includes "Vanni Fucci is Alive and Well and

Living in Hell," a story about religious hypocrites, and "The Death of the Centaur," which explores the lives of children in a flawed education system. Edward Bryant, in a review for *Locus* magazine, described the collection as "a marvelous range of intellectual concerns, passionate commitments, keenly honed artistic blades—and stretching exercises. . . . This book is an architectural plan for the construction of a major literary career."

Among Simmons' more recent novels is *Fires of Eden,* a 1994 novel that explodes with the author's trademark imagination and intellectual style. Described by *Publishers Weekly* as a "fractured horror novel," *Fires of Eden* features among other

A group of sixth-grade boys enjoy the summer of 1960 until an evil force emerges from the depths of the Old Central School.

things a talking hog with a bad attitude, a hunchback with a shark's mouth protruding from his hump, Mark Twain, and Byron Trumbo, a Donald Trump-like tycoon who has recently offended the Hawaiian volcano gods. The novel makes use of a double narrative, one a third-person chronicle of the volcano gods' revenge on a Hawaiian resort, and the other the first-person, 19th-century-diary-style account of similar difficulties undergone by a young woman travelling the country with a young Mark Twain. This post-modern-style science fiction tale, like so many of Simmons' prior works, assembles disparate but fascinating elements. Though a critic in *Publishers Weekly* thought the novel would have been better off focusing on the 19th-century Twain story (rather than the modern-day revenge of the volcano gods), A. M. B. Amantia's review for the *Library Journal* found the book to be "as rich in Hawaiian mythology as it is in suspense."

Although they may differ in their opinions of the relative success of his efforts, critics recognize both Simmons' contributions to science fiction and his success in developing and expanding the genre. Most of all, however, they recognize his greatest strengths: the ability to tell a story that commands the reader's full and undivided attention, and to explore the darkest passions and terrors of the soul. "Come with Dan Simmons," urges Sister Mary Veronica in a review of *The Hollow Man* published in the *Voice of Youth Advocates,* "into the uncharted depths of tortured human minds."

■ Works Cited

Amantia, A. M. B., review of *Fires of Eden, Library Journal,* October 15, 1994, pp. 88-9.

Bryant, Edward, review of *Song of Kali, Mile High Futures,* December, 1985, pp. 19-20.

Chelton, Mary K., review of *Children of the Night, Voice of Youth Advocates,* December, 1992, pp. 295-96.

Review of *Children of the Night, Publishers Weekly,* April 26, 1993, p. 71.

Collins, Bob, "Dan Simmons: 'New Frontiers' in the Cult of Violence," *Fantasy Review,* October, 1986, pp. 13-4.

Conaty, Barbara, review of *Lovedeath, Library Journal,* October 15, 1993, p. 92.

Feeley, Gregory, review of *The Hollow Man, Washington Post Book World,* September 27, 1992, p. 11.

Review of *Fires of Eden, Publishers Weekly,* August 29, 1994, p. 60.

Miller, Faren, review of *Song of Kali, Locus,* February, 1986, p. 13.

Review of *Song of Kali, Science Fiction Chronicle,* July, 1986, p. 40.

Swanson, Elliott, review of *Lovedeath, Booklist,* October 15, 1993, p. 419.

Veronica, Sister Mary, review of *The Hollow Man, Voice of Youth Advocates,* April, 1993, p. 46.

■ For More Information See

BOOKS

Contemporary Literary Criticism, Volume 44, Gale, 1987, pp. 273-75.

PERIODICALS

Analog Science Fiction/Science Fact, December 15, 1989, pp. 179-80.

Locus, October, 1990, pp. 23-4.

—Sketch by Mindi Dickstein

Jean Thesman

■ Personal

Married; children: two daughters, one son.

■ Addresses

Agent—c/o Houghton Mifflin, Children's Books Division, 1 Beacon St., Boston, MA 02108.

■ Career

Writer.

■ Awards, Honors

American Library Association (ALA) Recommended Book for the Reluctant Young Adult Reader, Children's Choices Book, and Young Adult Choices Book, all for *Who Said Life Is Fair?*; ALA Recommended Book for Reluctant Readers, for *Running Scared*; ALA Best Book for Young Adults, Recommended Book for the Reluctant Young Adult Reader, Children's Choices Book, Young Adult Choice Book, and Pick of the List, all for *The Last April Dancers*; Children's Choices Book, and Young Adult Choices Book, both for *Was It Something I Said?*; Sequoyah Young Adult Award, ALA Recommended Book for the Reluctant Young Adult Reader, and IRA Young Adult Choice Book, all for *Appointment with a Stranger*; ALA Notable Children's Book, and ALA Best Book for Young Adults, both for *Rachel Chance*; ALA Recommended Book for the Reluctant Young Adult Reader, and Phantom's Choice Award, both for *Erin*; Golden Kite Award, Society of Children's Book Writers and Illustrators, 1991, ALA Best Book for Young Adults, *School Library Journal* Best Book, and *Booklist* Editor's Choice, all for *The Rain Catchers*; ALA Notable Book, for *When the Road Ends*.

■ Writings

YOUNG ADULT NOVELS

Who Said Life Is Fair?, Avon, 1987.

Running Scared, Avon/Flare, 1987.
The Last April Dancers, Houghton, 1987.
Was It Something I Said?, Avon/Flare, 1988.
Appointment with a Stranger, Houghton, 1989.
Couldn't I Start Over?, Avon/Flare, 1989.
Rachel Chance, Houghton, 1990.
The Rain Catchers, Houghton, 1991.
When Does the Fun Start?, Avon/Flare, 1991.
When the Road Ends, Houghton, 1992.
Molly Donnelly, Houghton, 1993.
Cattail Moon, Houghton, 1994.
Nothing Grows Here, HarperCollins, 1994.
Summerspell, Simon & Schuster, 1995.

"WHITNEY COUSINS" SERIES

Heather, Avon, 1990.

Amelia, Avon, 1990.
Erin, Avon, 1990.
Triple Trouble, Avon, 1992.

"BIRTHDAY GIRLS" SERIES

I'm Not Telling, Avon/Camelot, 1992.
Mirror, Mirror, Avon/Camelot, 1992.
Who Am I, Anyway?, Avon/Camelot, 1992.

■ **Sidelights**

Jean Thesman is an accomplished author of young adult novels whose hallmark is a realistic yet sensitive portrayal of the difficulties of growing up. Her novels show young girls encountering death, war, suicide, old age, life inside dysfunctional families, as well as the typical social problems associated with being a teen. Marked by an unusually strong sense of time and place, Thesman's books also employ a lyrical use of language that gives strength to the emotional life and depth of her characters. A *Publishers Weekly* contributor, reviewing Thesman's "Whitney Cousins" Series, observes that it is the author's "perceptive characterizations and keen explorations of social issues that make her books notable." Chief among these notable books are *The Last April Dancers, Appointment with a Stranger, Rachel Chance, The Rain Catchers, Molly Donnelly,* and *Cattail Moon.*

Thesman first achieved recognition for her work in 1987, when she published three books: *Who Said Life is Fair?, Running Scared,* and *The Last April Dancers.* In *Who Said Life is Fair?,* sixteen-year-old Teddy has a crush on a boy at school, but the boy who loves her is Bill, a childhood friend. Over the course of the novel Teddy, who is editor of the school newspaper, faces several personal tests as she deals with the school administration and traverses the difficult path of first love. Margaret Mary Ptacek, reviewing the novel in *Voice of Youth Advocates,* writes that the result is a book "better than your average teen romance." Anne Saidman, writing in the *School Library Journal,* finds Teddy "a likeable heroine who's not afraid to speak up for herself."

In *Running Scared,* the protagonist is fifteen-year-old Caroline Cartwright, who has an adventure

A fourteen-year-old meets the mother who abandoned her in this winner of the Golden Kite Award.

while on her way to visit her grandmother. Travelling by bus with her bug-loving younger cousin Jasper, the two discover a mysterious box, the possession of which causes them to become prisoners of a militant survivalist group who are after the box and its contents. Susan Ackler, reviewing the novel for *Voice of Youth Advocates,* maintains: "There is enough suspense here to keep pages turning." And a *Kliatt* contributor dubs the book's adventure story "a cut above the usual."

The Last April Dancers, like the other two books published that same year, takes on themes of romance and responsibility, though in this case the story also explores suicide and death. The heroine of the story is Catherine St. John, known as Cat, who becomes concerned about her father's erratic behavior and, over the course of the story, attempts to help him and to get others to help too. For the most part she fails, and one night, after a fight with Cat when he forgets to take her for her driver's license test on her sixteenth birthday, her father commits suicide. Racked with guilt and the belief that her father's suicide is her fault (for having gotten angry at him), Cat is helped through her grief by her Aunt Leah, who helps the girl's growing determination to take control of her future.

Critics applauded *The Last April Dancers* for its stunning ability to convey a wide range of emotion and to handle a difficult subject matter. Blair Christolon, reviewing the novel for *School Library Journal,* declares that "readers will share Cat's bewilderment, frustration, humiliation, anger, and pain." A reviewer in the *Bulletin of the Center for Children's Books* complements Thesman's impressive sensitivity in developing "Cat's ambivalence, her courage, and her resolution of sorrow." And a *Publishers Weekly* reviewer describes the novel as "powerful" and "disturbing."

Themes of Self and Family

In 1988 Thesman published *Was It Something I Said?,* and in 1989 her award-winning *Appointment with a Stranger* was released. *Appointment with a Stranger* features a teenage girl, Keller, whose severe asthma condition so embarrasses her that she has become reclusive in order to hide the illness from her classmates in a new hometown. Though her reclusion achieves the desired effect, the consequences are loneliness and isolation. Then one day while swimming in a pond she is saved from drowning by a local boy, Tom, and she falls in love with him. He is not like the other boys she knows and, in fact, she realizes she never sees him except when they are in the woods.

A boy at school, Drew, becomes suspicious of Keller's story and, after doing some research, discovers that "Tom" is the name of a boy who drowned in that same pond more than 40 years ago. *Appointment with a Stranger* is an "unabashedly romantic tale" that at the same time conveys "a contemporary message about conquering self-pity and forming realistic relationships," asserts a *Publishers Weekly* reviewer. A *Kirkus Reviews* contributor applauds Thesman's "engaging narrative style."

Several subsequent books by Thesman deal with family dynamics. *Couldn't I Start Over?,* which concerns the trouble between a teenage girl,

Shiloh, and her shifty new friend, Lovey Sullivan, showcases the ways that families help each other through personal crises. *Rachel Chance,* Thesman's next book, explores the dynamics of an unconventional family as it struggles to stay together. The novel's characters include Rachel Chance's bad-tempered grandfather, his psychic companion Druid Annie, a mentally disabled cousin, and Rachel's widowed mother (who has an illegitimate second child by a migrant worker). The story is set in the state of Washington during the 1940s, its events surrounding the kidnapping of Rachel's illegitimate baby brother. When local townspeople refuse to help the Chance family find Rachel's brother, Rachel sets out to do so herself and succeeds. Along the way to finding the boy, Rachel meets and falls in love with Hank, a local farmhand. Barbara Chatton, reviewing the novel in *School Library Journal,* finds Rachel, "who fights to protect [her family] against all odds, is a charac-

This 1992 story concerns three children in foster care who ultimately form their own family.

Thesman describes the effect World War II had on a young girl and her American family through excerpts from the girl's diary.

ter to be remembered." And a *Horn Book* critic points out: "The underlying theme, which pits the irresistible force of rugged individualism against the immoveable nature of local mores, has seldom been more entertainingly explored."

In *The Rain Catchers,* another award-winning novel, Thesman turns her focus to a story about a girl, Grayling, who derives strength from a circle of women in her family who meet every day at her grandmother's Seattle home for tea and chat. Inspired by the women's talk of life and history, Grayling decides to get to know more about her own past. She journeys to San Francisco, where her estranged mother lives, and attempts both to get to know her mother better and to learn more about the death of her father. Though her efforts to get to know her mother fail, Grayling returns to the warmth of her grandmother's family circle. Barbara Chatton, reviewing the novel for *School*

Library Journal, writes: "It is a beautiful story, with elderly characters who exhibit a loving and gracious reaction to life." A *Publishers Weekly* contributor similarly finds Thesman's work to be "lucid, sensual writing."

In *When the Road Ends,* a group of misfits consisting of three foster children and a child-like adult (sister to the children's foster father) find themselves on their own for the summer when the housekeeper who was supposed to look after them absconds with all their money. Their joint efforts to survive together prove a maturing experience for all. A reviewer for the *Wilson Library Bulletin* praises the book's "unusual story, full of warmth and quiet humor." A *Horn Book* reviewer applauds "the book's weighty theme of children forced before their time to behave like adults," and a *Publishers Weekly* contributor asserts that *When the Road Ends* is "Thesman at her best."

Capturing Time and Place

Molly Donnelly is the story of a young teenage girl whose life is rendered chaotic by the 1941 bombing of Pearl Harbor. The story follows Molly's life as she deals with the effects of this catastrophic event, including not only her emotions relating directly to the bombing, but also those associated with the repercussions that this historical event had on American daily life: namely, a backlash of racism against Japanese families. When Molly's best friend's family is abruptly taken away because of their Japanese heritage, Molly gets her first lesson in coping with the realities of a quixotic and changing world.

The novel charts Molly's life as she comes of age during the World War II years of 1941 to 1945, and deals not only with the difficulty of losing a best friend to deportation, but also describes rationing, blackouts, the intense fear and paranoia that comes with war, women leaving home to work in factories, and men leaving home to fight wars. Inevitably, the war brings death to Molly's family, too, and she must learn to cope with that tragedy along with all the others. The teenage Molly grows up fast, taking on responsibility for her home and for her younger brother, though she remains an intrepid, intelligent, sensitive, and winning heroine. "The war has been like a magnifying glass," she writes toward the end of the novel, "the best and the worst of us shows up, bigger than ever."

Along with the exploration of issues dealing directly with war, hatred and death, Thesman's story also embraces the beginnings of feminism in postwar America when Molly's mother finds that she likes working better than being a housewife. Susan Ackler, reviewing *Molly Donnelly* for *Voice of Youth Advocates,* observes that the book "creates an authentic picture of the American homefront during World War II and reflects the feelings of the people at that time." A critic for *Horn Book* similarly maintains that "the manner in which [the war years] altered social and political attitudes is shown in a skillfully written novel of a young girl's growth to maturity. What is most impressive is the author's style and sense of story: her focus remains true to her subject—Molly."

A *Publishers Weekly* contributor calls *Molly Donnelly* "raw and bittersweet, possibly Thesman's best work to date. . . . Once again, the author of *Rachel Chance* and *When the Road Ends* effortlessly evokes the tastes and textures of life in the Northwest." Carol A. Edwards, reviewing the book for the *School Library Journal,* asserts: "this is one [story] that will quietly catch readers up and take them to another place and time. Realistic and rich, Thesman's story of a young woman coming-of-age in a difficult time is historical fiction at its best." Stephanie Zvirin, writing for *Booklist,* similarly describes the novel as "part sweet nostalgia and part bitterness," concluding: "Wartime America is a fitting and compelling backdrop for this sturdy coming-of-age tale . . . and Thesman sifts the history through Molly's perspective in a way that gives readers a real sense of the turbulent times."

Cattail Moon is another coming-of-age story concerning an almost-fifteen-year-old girl, Julia Foster. In the beginning of the story Julia is living in Seattle with her somewhat shallow, superficial mother. Where Julia is more interested in her budding music career and close friends, her mother wants her to concentrate on cheerleading and outward appearance. Desperate to make Julia care about looks and social position, her mother even stoops so low as to take Julia to an "imagemaker." But the constant pushing and fighting between them over how Julia will live her life results only in a lowered sense of self-esteem for Julia.

Deciding that she will be happier living with her father and grandmother in the Cascade Mountains of Washington State, Julia chooses to leave her

In this 1994 novel, Julia is interested in her budding music career and close friends, while her mother wants her to concentrate on her outward appearance.

mother's home and take up residence with her paternal family in a place called Moon Valley. Moon Valley may have the blessing of an emotionally secure and supportive environment, but being a small, mountain town it lacks piano and voice teachers—as well as the best friends that Julia has left behind in Seattle.

The story follows Julia's acclimation to Moon Valley—making friends and finding pursuits that interest her—including falling in love with a local boy whose parents do not permit him to date yet. She also discovers the local legend (and ghost) of Moon Valley, and learns about the haunting woman in white who people say is the ghost of Christine Woodmark, a singer and novelist who once lived there. As Julia learns more about Christine's life, including a difficult choice between love and career, she draws parallels with her own.

In the end, she decides she must return to Seattle (where she can resume studying music) to live with her best friend's family.

Ellen Fader, reviewing the novel in *Horn Book*, observes that "Thesman succeeds in combining themes of the supernatural, mystery, romance, and friendship in an extremely readable and compelling novel that also presents a highly realized Northwest setting." A *Publishers Weekly* contributor points out that *Cattail Moon* has a "lump-in-the-throat urgency. Recounted with Thesman's exuberant sense of humor and keen ear for dialogue, the scenes of Julia searching for a niche in her new school provide a satisfyingly down-to-earth counterpoint to the story's ghostly goings-on." And *Booklist* critic Carolyn Phelan finds that "for a while, the supernatural element threatens to overcast the realistic tenor of the story with an almost gothic tone, but in the end, it works as another piece of a puzzle. Thesman's many well-crafted characters and their conflicts make this novel quite readable and believable."

Thesman once commented that she grew up in a house full of books, "around people who were accomplished storytellers. It didn't take me long to see that bookworms, storytellers, and people who laugh easily are never bored. There is only one logical occupation for a storytelling bookworm with a sense of humor, so I write books for young people. It's the best job in the world."

■ Works Cited

Ackler, Susan, review of *Running Scared, Voice of Youth Advocates*, December, 1987, pp. 238-39.

Ackler, Susan, review of *Molly Donnelly, Voice of Youth Advocates*, August, 1993, p. 158.

Review of *Appointment with a Stranger, Kirkus Reviews*, March 15, 1989, p. 470.

Review of *Appointment with a Stranger, Publishers Weekly*, March 10, 1989, p. 90.

Review of *Cattail Moon, Publishers Weekly*, April 4, 1994, p. 81.

Chatton, Barbara, review of *Rachel Chance, School Library Journal*, April, 1990, pp. 145-46.

Chatton, Barbara, review of *The Rain Catchers, School Library Journal*, March, 1991, p. 218.

Christolon, Blair, review of *The Last April Dancers, School Library Journal*, October, 1987, p. 142.

Edwards, Carol A., review of *Molly Donnelly, School Library Journal*, May, 1993, p. 130.

Fader, Ellen, review of *Cattail Moon, Horn Book*, July/August, 1994, p. 461.

Review of *The Last April Dancers, Bulletin of the Center for Children's Books*, September, 1987.

Review of *The Last April Dancers, Publishers Weekly*, September 25, 1987, p. 112.

Review of *Molly Donnelly, Horn Book*, September/October, 1993, p. 606.

Review of *Molly Donnelly, Publishers Weekly*, March 1, 1993, p. 58.

Phelan, Carolyn, review of *Cattail Moon, Booklist*, April 1, 1994, p. 1437.

Ptacek, Margaret Mary, review of *Who Said Life Is Fair?, Voice of Youth Advocates*, August, 1987, p. 123.

Review of *Rachel Chance, Horn Book*, September/October, 1990, p. 610.

Review of *The Rain Catchers, Publishers Weekly*, February 22, 1991, p. 219.

Review of *Running Scared, Kliatt*, September, 1987, p. 20.

Saidman, Anne, review of *Who Said Life Is Fair?, School Library Journal*, May, 1987, p. 118.

Thesman, Jean, *Molly Donnelly*, Houghton, 1993.

Review of *When the Road Ends, Horn Book*, May/June, 1992, p. 342.

Review of *When the Road Ends, Publishers Weekly*, February 17, 1992, p. 64.

Review of *When the Road Ends, Wilson Library Bulletin*, September, 1992, p. 94.

Review of *The Whitney Cousins: Heather, Amelia, and Erin, Publishers Weekly*, April 27, 1990, p. 63.

Zvirin, Stephanie, review of *Molly Donnelly, Booklist*, April 1, 1993, p. 1425.

—Sketch by Mindi Dickstein

Yoshiko Uchida

■ Personal

Surname is pronounced "oo-*chee*-da"; born November 24, 1921, in Alameda, CA; died June 21, 1992, in Berkeley, CA; daughter of Dwight Takashi (a businessman) and Iku (a poet; maiden name, Umegaki) Uchida. *Education:* University of California, Berkeley, A.B. (cum laude), 1942; Smith College, M.Ed., 1944. *Politics:* Democrat. *Religion:* Protestant. *Hobbies and other interests:* Folk crafts, theater, visiting museums, taking walks, writing poetry.

■ Career

Full-time writer, 1952-57, 1962—. Elementary school teacher in Japanese relocation center in Topaz, UT, 1942-43; Frankford Friends' School, Philadelphia, PA, teacher, 1944-45; Institute of Pacific Relations, membership secretary, 1946-47; United Student Christian Council, New York City, secretary, 1947-52; Lawrence Radiation Laboratory, University of California, Berkeley, secretary, 1957-62. *Exhibitions:* Oakland Museum, 1972.

■ Awards, Honors

Ford Foundation Foreign Area research fellowship in Japan, 1952; Children's Spring Book Festival Honor Book, *New York Herald Tribune,* 1955, for *The Magic Listening Cap;* Notable Book citation, American Library Association (ALA), 1972, for *Journey to Topaz;* Silver Medals for best juvenile book by a California author, Commonwealth Club of California, 1972, for *Samurai of Gold Hill,* and 1982, for *A Jar of Dreams;* Award of Merit, California Association of Teachers of English, 1973, for body of work; Contra Costa chapter of Japanese American Citizens League citation, 1976, for outstanding contribution to the cultural development of society; International Reading Association Children's Choice citations, 1979, for *Journey Home,* and 1985, for *The Happiest Ending;* Notable Children's Trade Books in the Field of Social Studies, National Council for Social Studies and the Children's Book Council, 1979, for *Journey Home,* 1982, for *A Jar of Dreams,* and 1985, for *The Happiest Ending;* Morris S. Rosenblatt Award, Utah State Historical Society, 1981, for article, "Topaz, City of Dust"; Distinguished Service Award, University of Oregon, 1981, for significant contribution to the cultural development of society; award from Berkeley chapter of Japanese American Citizens League, 1983, for "her many books which have done so much to better the understanding of Japanese culture and Japanese American experiences in America"; Best Book of 1985 citation, Bay Area Book Reviewers, 1985, for *The Happiest Ending;* Young Author's Hall of Fame Award, San Mateo and San Francisco Reading Associations, 1985; Bay Area Book Reviewers Association Book Award for Children's Literature, 1986, for *The Happiest Ending;* Friends of Children and Literature Award,

1987, for *A Jar of Dreams. Journey to Topaz, The Best Bad Thing,* and *The Happiest Ending* were all ALA Notable Books; *Journey Home, A Jar of Dreams, The Best Bad Thing,* and *The Happiest Ending* were all Junior Library Guild selections.

■ Writings

FOR CHILDREN

The Dancing Kettle and Other Japanese Folk Tales, illustrations by Richard C. Jones, Harcourt, 1949, reprinted as *The Dancing Kettle,* Creative Arts, 1986.

New Friends for Susan, illustrations by Henry Sugimoto, Scribner, 1951.

(And illustrator) *The Magic Listening Cap: More Folk Tales from Japan,* Harcourt, 1955, new edition, Creative Arts, 1987.

(And illustrator) *The Full Circle* (junior high school study book), Friendship, 1957.

Takao and Grandfather's Sword, illustrations by William M. Hutchinson, Harcourt, 1958.

The Promised Year, illustrations by Hutchinson, Harcourt, 1959.

Mik and the Prowler, illustrations by Hutchinson, Harcourt, 1960.

Rokubei and the Thousand Rice Bowls, illustrations by Kazue Mizumura, Scribner, 1962.

The Forever Christmas Tree, illustrations by Mizumura, Scribner, 1963.

Sumi's Prize, illustrations by Mizumura, Scribner, 1964.

The Sea of Gold, and Other Tales from Japan, illustrations by Marianne Yamaguchi, Scribner, 1965.

Sumi's Special Happening, illustrations by Mizumura, Scribner, 1966.

In-Between Miya, illustrations by Susan Bennett, Scribner, 1967.

Hisako's Mysteries, illustrations by Bennett, Scribner, 1969.

Sumi and the Goat and the Tokyo Express, illustrations by Mizumura, Scribner, 1969.

Makoto, the Smallest Boy: A Story of Japan, illustrations by Akihito Shirakawa, Crowell, 1970.

Journey to Topaz: A Story of the Japanese-American Evacuation, illustrations by Donald Carrick, Scribner, 1971, revised edition, Creative Arts, 1985.

Samurai of Gold Hill, illustrations by Ati Forberg, Scribner, 1972, revised edition, Creative Arts, 1985.

The Birthday Visitor (picture book), illustrations by Charles Robinson, Scribner, 1975.

The Rooster Who Understood Japanese (picture book), illustrations by Robinson, Scribner, 1976.

Journey Home (sequel to *Journey to Topaz*), illustrations by Robinson, McElderry Books, 1978, 2nd edition, Macmillan Children's Books, 1992.

A Jar of Dreams, McElderry Books, 1981, 2nd edition, Macmillan Children's Books, 1993.

The Best Bad Thing (sequel to *A Jar of Dreams*), McElderry Books, 1983, 2nd edition, Macmillan Children's Books, 1993.

Tabi: Journey through Time, Stories of the Japanese in America, United Methodist Publishing House, 1984.

The Happiest Ending (sequel to *The Best Bad Thing*), McElderry Books, 1985.

The Two Foolish Cats: Suggested by a Japanese Folktale, illustrations by Margot Zemach, McElderry Books, 1987.

The Terrible Leak, Creative Education, 1989 (originally published in 1955).

The Invisible Thread: An Autobiography, Simon & Schuster, 1991.

(Reteller) *The Magic Purse,* illustrations by Keiko Narahashi, McElderry Books, 1993.

The Bracelet, illustrations by Joanna Yardley, Philomel, 1993.

(Reteller) *The Wise Old Woman,* illustrations by Martin Springett, McElderry Books, 1994.

Also contributor of short stories for children to anthologies, including *Flight Near and Far,* Holt, 1970; *Scribner Anthology for Young People,* Scribner, 1976; *Arbuthnot Anthology of Children's Literature,* 4th edition, Scott, Foresman, 1976; *Courage to Adventure,* Crowell, 1976; *Sense,* Scott, Foresman, 1977; *Image,* Scott, Foresman, 1977; *Sharing Literature with Children,* D. McKay, 1977; *Clues and Clocks,* Harper, 1977; *Echoes of Time: A World History,* McGraw, 1977; *The Secret Life of Mr. Mugs,* Ginn, 1978; *With the Works,* Scott, Foresman, 1978; *Riding Rainbows,* Allyn & Bacon, 1978; *Handstands,* Allyn & Bacon, 1978; *The Big Ones 2,* Allyn & Bacon, 1978; *Standing Strong,* Allyn & Bacon, 1978; *Question and Form in Literature,* Scott, Foresman, 1979; *Literature and Life,* Scott, Foresman, 1979; *Changing Scenes,* Harcourt, 1979; *And Everywhere Children,* Greenwillow, 1979; *Many Voices,* Harcourt, 1979; *Tell Me How the Sun Rose,* Ginn, 1979; *Japan: Change and Continuity,* Rigby, 1980; *Full Circle,* Macmillan, 1980; *Fairy Tales of the Sea,* Harper, 1981; *Here and There,* Holt, 1981; *Spinners,* Houghton, 1981; *Banners,* Houghton, 1981; *The Abracadabras,* Addison-Wesley, 1981; *Wingspan,* Allyn & Bacon, 1981; *Another Earth, Another Sky,* Harcourt, 1982; *Understanding Literature,* Macmillan, 1983; *Anthology of*

Children's Literature, Scott, Foresman, 1984; *Strategies for Reading*, Harcourt, 1984; *Exploration*, Houghton, 1986.

FOR ADULTS

We Do Not Work Alone: The Thoughts of Kanjiro Kawai, Folk Art Society (Japan), 1953.

(Translator of English portions) Soetsu Yanagi, editor, *Shoji Hamada*, Asahi Shimbun Publishing, 1961.

The History of Sycamore Church, Sycamore Congregational Church, 1974.

Desert Exile: The Uprooting of a Japanese-American Family, University of Washington Press, 1982.

Picture Bride (novel), Northland Press, 1987.

Contributor of adult stories and articles to newspapers and periodicals, including *Woman's Day*, *Gourmet*, *Utah Historical Quarterly*, *Far East*, *Craft Horizons*, *Nippon Times* (Tokyo), *Motive*, and *California Monthly*.

OTHER

Contributor to exhibit catalog, *Margaret da Patta*, Oakland Museum (Oakland, CA), 1976. Author of regular column, "Letter from San Francisco," in *Craft Horizons*, 1958-61. Uchida's manuscripts are kept at the Kerlan Collection at the University of Minnesota; the University of Oregon Library, Eugene (manuscript collection prior to 1981); Bancroft Library, University of California, Berkeley (manuscripts, papers, and all published materials since 1981).

■ Adaptations

"The Old Man with the Bump" (cassette; based on the story from *The Dancing Kettle*), Houghton, 1973; "The Two Foolish Cats" (filmstrip with cassette; based on the story from *The Sea of Gold*), Encyclopedia Britannica Educational, 1977; "The Fox and the Bear" (cassette; based on a story from *The Magic Listening Cap*), Science Research Associates, 1979.

■ Sidelights

After the attack on Pearl Harbor in 1942, the United States had declared war on Japan and, in a move that would later be considered by many one of the lowest points in American social justice, President Franklin D. Roosevelt imprisoned some 80,000 innocent American citizens. These men, women, and children were not traitors, but because their parents or grandparents—who were also imprisoned—were immigrants from Japan they were considered a risk to national security. In all, 120,000 Japanese-Americans were sent to prisoner-of-war camps. One of these people, future award-winning author Yoshiko Uchida, would later turn her experiences with this injustice into her acclaimed book, *Journey to Topaz: A Story of the Japanese-American Evacuation*. Yuki Sakane, the eleven-year-old girl in the story, echoes the author's frustration over how she and her family were treated: "Both the Fifth and Fourteenth Amendments to the Constitution providing for 'due process of law' and 'equal protection under the law for all citizens,' were flagrantly ignored in the name of military expediency, and the forced eviction was carried out purely on the basis of race."

Yet *Journey to Topaz* is not a bitter account of Japanese internment. Instead, the story focuses on how Japanese Americans managed to overcome their hardship, and in this way it is a book that, according to *Journal of Home Economics* reviewer Laurence E. Smardan, "Japanese-Americans could benefit considerably from . . . for it would enable them to come to grips with" what had happened. In many ways, all of Uchida's writing serves the purpose of helping young Japanese Americans understand their origins better, not just with regard to the war, but also with what it means in general to be an American of Japanese descent. She accomplished this with books like *Journey to Topaz* and its sequel, *Journey Home*, as well as her retellings of Japanese folk tales and her fiction featuring such beloved characters as Sumi, Miya, and Hisako. With these books, which offer honest viewpoints, suspense, and humor, Uchida educated her readers about aspects of Japanese life on both sides of the Pacific.

Growing Up as an Outsider

Born in 1921 in Alameda, California, Uchida was the younger of two daughters born to Japanese immigrants. Her father had found a good job working for a Japanese business firm in America, and her mother later came to this country to fulfill her part in a prearranged marriage. The young couple had their first daughter, Keiko, not long after they were married in 1916. A little later, Uchida was born, and the family moved to Ber-

Yoshiko Uchida (far left) and her sister (far right) with their parents on the day they left the United States' concentration camp at Topaz in 1943.

keley, California, where they made their home for some twenty years before the beginning of the war. Despite the fact that she was born in America—and therefore a citizen—and spoke flawless English, Uchida encountered prejudice from an early age. "Although we had several close white American family friends," Uchida writes in her *Something about the Author Autobiography Series (SAAS)* entry, "I lived in a society that in general made me feel different and not as good as my white peers. . . . All I longed for in those early years was to be like everyone else and to be viewed as an American."

At home, however, Uchida found happiness in the love of her family and the richness of the culture they kept alive there. Uchida's parents, who were both educated at one of Japan's first Christian universities, Doshisha University, had a strong religious faith, which they passed along to their children. In addition to this, Uchida's mother, who liked to write poetry and whom Uchida describes in her *SAAS* essay as a "gentle dreamer," taught her to appreciate literature. "My mother . . . loved books," the author remembers, "and our

house was filled with them. Although she didn't find time to read much for herself, she often read Japanese stories to Keiko and me. Many of these were the Japanese folktales which I later included in my first published book, *The Dancing Kettle*."

Adapting the stories her mother had told her so that they would be more understandable to American children, Uchida completed *The Dancing Kettle and Other Japanese Folk Tales* in 1949, and it was followed in 1955 with a similar collection, *The Magic Listening Cap: More Folk Tales from Japan*, as well as 1965's *The Sea of Gold, and Other Tales from Japan*. Several critics noted the value of Uchida's first collection as a retelling of popular tales, many of which had not been in print in the United States for decades. While *New York Times Book Review* contributor Irene Smith lauds Uchida's approach as "directness and economy in good storytelling style," another reviewer, Louise S. Bechtel, says in the *New York Herald Tribune Weekly Book Review* that Uchida's writing is an expression of her hope for "the possible meeting of East and West through mutual understanding of cultural heritages."

Cultural understanding had a long way to go when Uchida was young, however. "Junior high and high school were not very happy times," she recalls in *SAAS*, "for those were the years when I felt more and more alienated and excluded, especially from the social activities of my white classmates. I couldn't wait to get out of high school." In order to get out of high school as quickly as possible, Uchida studied twice as hard as most of her classmates. She finished high school early and was accepted to the University of California at Berkeley at the young age of sixteen. But escaping high school didn't solve Uchida's problem; she found prejudice and exclusion just as common at the university. "There the exclusion of Japanese Americans from the social activities of white students was even greater than in high school, and my social life was confined to activities of the Japanese students clubs."

"My Whole World Fell Apart"

Uchida was a senior in college when Japan attacked Pearl Harbor. It was final exams time, and Uchida went to study for her tests after hearing the news on the radio. The thought of war breaking out was so incredible to her and her family that they didn't believe the reports at first. That evening she returned home to discover that her father had been taken into custody by the FBI. For three days they heard nothing about what had become of him; then, three days after the bombing, the Uchidas learned that he had been sent to a prisoner-of-war camp in Missoula, Montana.

Uchida, her mother, and sister were not immediately apprehended. For the next several months, they waited anxiously while travel restrictions and curfews were imposed and rumors spread about Japanese American traitors who had committed acts of sabotage. Uchida found herself— and anyone who looked like her—becoming an object of hatred by whites, many of whom lashed out verbally and physically against the perceived threat of Japanese living in America. Uchida had to drop out of college and put her life on hold; on May 1, 1943, all Japanese Americans living in Berkeley were evacuated from their homes.

Living in a horse stall at the Tanforan Racetrack (where her diploma was later mailed to her), Uchida was eventually reunited with her father when he was given permission to leave prison

and rejoin his family. That September the Uchidas were moved again; this time they were sent to a concentration camp in Topaz, Utah, a desolate place located in the middle of the Great Basin. In both camps, Uchida kept herself busy by teaching second grade students, while her sister Keiko organized nursery schools, and her father worked on committees that helped to keep camp life running smoothly, if not entirely comfortably. The barracks they were forced to live in were not insulated against the winter cold and, as Uchida describes them in *SAAS*, "the lack of inner sheetrock walls allowed white powder-like dust to sift into the rooms from every crack in the siding as well as the hole in the roof where the stovepipe was to fit." The desert winds also brought deluges of dust into the barracks rooms, creating a constant mess for the occupants to clean up and often making it difficult to breathe.

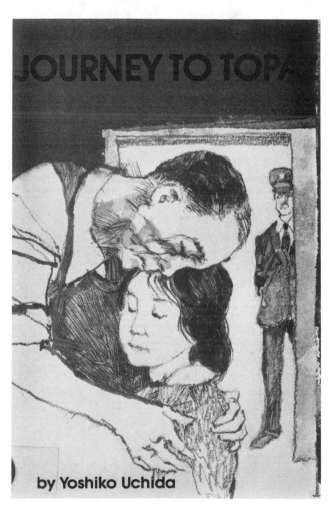

Uchida's twelve-year-old character echoes the author's feelings about what it was like to be forced into an internment camp.

"The Eight-Headed Dragon" is just one of the fourteen authentic folk stories retold in this collection.

Existence in the concentration camp was unbearable, and Uchida looked for ways she could get out. Working with the American Friends Service Committee, in May, 1943, she was able to get a fellowship to attend graduate school at Smith College in Northampton, Massachusetts, where she received a master's in education the next year. Keiko was also allowed to leave to teach nursery school, and, not long afterwards, her parents managed to get permission to go to Salt Lake City. The experience of being sent to a concentration camp would stay with Uchida. "It had been a devastating and traumatic year," she writes in *SAAS,* "which left a lasting impact on my life, but it was many years before I could write about the experience."

Journey to Topaz

She later did write about it, however, and created four books based on what had happened to her and her family: the two fictionalized accounts for children ages nine to twelve, *Journey to Topaz* and *Journey Home;* a picture book, *The Bracelet,* for children four to eight; and a book for adults, *Desert Exile. The Invisible Thread: An Autobiography,* which was written for students in grades five through nine, also includes her reminiscences of her family's imprisonment. Uchida wrote the novelized accounts first. *Journey to Topaz* was written after Uchida's mother had passed away and her father was suffering from the effects of a stroke. "I felt moved to write a book especially for them and the other first-generation Japanese (the Issei), who had endured so much and been so strong," she explains in her autobiographical essay.

Journey to Topaz concludes when the Sakane family is reunited and allowed to leave the concentration camp. Uchida would have allowed the tale to end there, but "because so many children wanted to know what happened to Yuki and her family after the war, I wrote a sequel entitled *Journey Home."* Since the character Yuki is years younger than Uchida was at the time, instead of going to graduate school like the author did she accompanies her parents to Salt Lake City and then back to Berkeley. With the war over, the Sakanes must try to put their lives back together. All their possessions have been taken away from them, and they have suffered emotionally from their long separation from relatives and friends. Uchida adds another factor that is not based on her actual life when she gives Yuki a brother, who fights in the war and later has to go through fierce emotional anguish to come to terms with his personal involvement in killing Japanese. *Journey Home* ends happily, however. Working with other Japanese American families, Yuki's father starts a grocery store, and, through the support of the family and comfort of Japanese traditions, the family manages to build a loving home once more.

School Library Journal reviewer Dora Jean Young comments that *Journey Home* "fills a great need in describing the cruel treatment inflicted upon Japanese-Americans." Although critics have generally praised Uchida's efforts, several reviewers have voiced concerns regarding the characterization. In a *New York Times Book Review* critique of *Journey to Topaz,* for example, Sidney Long observes that "the characters are overshadowed by the situation," concluding that "their lack of depth makes the book seem predictable and flat." A *Booklist* reviewer makes a similar remark about the characters in *Journey Home,* commenting that they could have been "more fully explored and developed," but adding that Uchida provides "many sensitive touches and interesting glimpses" into an "important historical episode."

After she received her degree in education from Smith College, Uchida found a job teaching first and second graders at a Quaker school near Philadelphia. But she soon found that teaching left her with no spare time to pursue writing, so she quit her job and moved to New York City. Earning living expenses by working as a secretary, at night Uchida wrote short stories, which she submitted to several magazines. Like most writers, Uchida received many rejection slips at first, including one

for an article she wrote for the *New Yorker* about Topaz, an article that later formed the basis for *Desert Exile*. Uchida eventually discovered that she could find greater success writing for children than for adults. Then, in 1952, she received a Ford Foundation fellowship that enabled her to spend two years in Japan conducting research on Japanese culture. While in Japan, Uchida gained a new appreciation for that ancient land, especially for its poetry and pottery.

Writings Explore Japanese Heritage

When she returned from her stay overseas, Uchida decided that, although she had no great talent for

THE **Magic** PURSE

retold by Yoshiko Uchida
illustrated by Keiko Narahashi

A retelling of an old story about a poor farmer who, through his good and noble acts, becomes wealthy.

creating Japanese crafts, she was good at writing about them. "I soon discovered potters turning up in some of my children's books . . . [such as] *Takao and Grandfather's Sword, Rokubei and the Thousand Rice Bowls,* and *Makoto, the Smallest Boy,*" she writes in *SAAS.* "And of course many of my subsequent books incorporated aspects of Japanese life that I had absorbed during my two years there—*The Forever Christmas Tree, Sumi's Prize, Sumi's Special Happening, Sumi and the Goat and the Tokyo Express, In-Between Miya,* and *Hisako's Mysteries.*

"Most important, however, my years in Japan had made me aware of a new dimension to myself as a Japanese American and deepened my respect and admiration for the culture that had made my parents what they were."

Many of Uchida's early stories are set in Japan and have young children as protagonists. These tales are useful for relating details of Japanese culture, as well as enjoyable for their memorable characters, such as Sumi, who is featured in a number of books, Miya in *In-Between Miya,* and Hisako in *Hisako's Mysteries.* The books allow readers to see what life in Japan's cities and countryside is like, as well as observe some of the contrasts between ancient traditions and the modern, post-war culture. In the Sumi books, Uchida presents "an appealing little girl of modern Japan," as a *Virginia Kirkus' Service* reviewer describes her, and her various adventures in Japan. *In-Between Miya* offers a special opportunity to see these contrasts when twelve-year-old Miya—the middle child of three children—travels from the countryside to Tokyo to take care of her ailing aunt. Over the course of the story, the adventure of the big city becomes a lesson in growing up for Miya, who must take on some unexpected responsibilities. Reviewers such as Helen B. Crenshaw have compared Miya favorably to Sumi. Crenshaw states in a *Horn Book* review that "friends of Sumi . . . will want to become acquainted with Miya."

As with *In-Between Miya,* in which the relationship between a young girl and her aging aunt is portrayed, *Hisako's Mysteries* illuminates old traditions through the eyes of a young girl. In this case, thirteen-year-old Hisako is an orphaned girl who must live in Kyoto with her old-fashioned grandparents, whose lives are tied to the traditional Japanese ways. Just as Miya does, Hisako travels to Tokyo to visit relatives. When an accident sends Hisako to the hospital, a mysterious visitor leads her to discover facts about her family that had been kept hidden from her all her life. While several critics have found that the mystery in the story creates some interesting suspense, a *Library Journal* reviewer especially appreciates "its picture of family life in modern Japan." Ethel L. Heins similarly comments in *Horn Book* that she enjoyed "the authentic presentation of a land and a people."

Focus on Immigrants

After Uchida finished *Journey to Topaz,* the focus of her writing changed somewhat. Instead of always setting her tales in Japan, many of her books since 1972 have been about Japanese Americans. "I saw the need to reinforce the self-knowledge and pride of young Japanese Americans," Uchida tells Catherine E. Studier Chang in *Language Arts,* "to give them a remembrance of their culture and their own particular history." Her first book initiating this new agenda was *Samurai of Gold Hill,* a historically based tale of the Japanese colonists who came to California in the 1850s to found the Wakamatsu Colony. Uchida tells her story through the eyes of Koichi, a young boy who comes to the colony with his father to work on a tea and silk farm. The colony faces great adversity, however, as a result of natural catastrophes and the prejudice of some of the immigrants' new neighbors. Koichi suffers, too, and achieves manhood when he decides not to use his grandfather's samurai sword as a violent solution to their problems, selling it instead to get money to feed the other colonists. Reviewers found the story to be well researched and balanced in the sense that it shows both good and bad Japanese and white characters. Zena Sutherland notes in her *Bulletin of the Center for Children's Books* review that Uchida is good at portraying her characters' relationships, "especially in Koichi's growing understanding of his father."

Uchida's trilogy of books—*A Jar of Dreams, The Best Bad Thing,* and *The Happiest Ending*—return to a study of Japanese American life in Berkeley during the Great Depression of the 1930s. "I wanted to convey in my trilogy the *values* that gave those early immigrant families their strength, and to convey the strong sense of family that sustained them," Uchida once told *Something about the Author (SATA).* "These books are not based on my own life," the author says in her *SAAS* entry, "for [main character Rinko Tsujimura's] family had

The Magic Listening Cap

More Folk Tales From Japan
Retold and Illustrated by Yoshiko Uchida

Uchida's second collection of folk tales portrays the Japanese countryside.

more of a struggle to survive in those difficult times than we did. Still, there is much of me in Rinko."

The trilogy begins with *A Jar of Dreams,* in which Rinko tells what happens when her Aunt Waka arrives from Japan for a visit. Aunt Waka is shocked by the prejudice she observes and encourages all of Rinko's family members to pursue their dreams: for Rinko's father, this means starting a new garage business; for her mother, it means making the family laundry business a success; and for Rinko it means overcoming her poor self-image and saving up money for a good education. While some critics have complained about a lack of well-defined characters in the story—*School Library Journal* reviewer Sally Holmes Holtze offers the unflattering comparison that the book "has the depth and style of most TV shows"—other critics have been more enthusiastic about *A Jar of Dreams.*

In *Booklist* Denise M. Wilms praises the manner in which Uchida tells the story using Rinko's voice, "allowing the author to get her message across unobtrusively." Heins also likes Rinko, calling her, in another *Horn Book* review, a "genuine and refreshing" character whose "worries and concerns seem wholly natural, honest, and convincing."

While prejudice is mentioned in several places in the trilogy, it often takes a back seat to characterization and Uchida's efforts to draw a complete picture of what life was like for Japanese Americans during the 1930s. Critics have not missed this point. Kate M. Flanagan, for example, says in her *Horn Book* review that *The Best Bad Thing* "is essentially about an appealing young girl's unique way of interpreting life's vicissitudes." And *School Library Journal* contributor Anne L. Okie notes that "despite the unfamiliar setting . . . the rich warmth and complexity of family and community" lend a unique flair to *The Best Bad Thing.*

While Uchida acknowledges similarities between herself and Rinko in *SAAS,* she writes that Rinko "discovers pride in herself as a Japanese American much earlier than I did." The shy young girl who had once only wanted to be like all other Americans eventually grew up to be a talented author, proud of her heritage and happy to share that heritage through her writings. When she was a young girl and kept a journal, she "was trying to hold on to and somehow preserve the magic as well as the joy and sadness of certain moments in my life." As an adult, Uchida still drew "from the memories of the past. I also find bits and pieces of my child self turning up in my writing." The author, who died of a stroke in 1992, maintained in *SAAS* that preserving these bits of her life experiences was "really what books and writing are all about."

■ Works Cited

Bechtel, Louise S., "Fairy Stories," *New York Herald Tribune Weekly Book Review,* May 8, 1949, p. 13.

Chang, Catherine E. Studier, "Profile: Yoshiko Uchida," *Language Arts,* February, 1984 (amended by the author).

Crenshaw, Helen B., review of *In-Between Miya, Horn Book,* December, 1967, pp. 755-56.

Flanagan, Kate M., review of *The Best Bad Thing, Horn Book,* October, 1983, p. 578.

Heins, Ethel L., review of *Hisako's Mysteries, Horn Book,* June, 1969, p. 309.

Heins, Ethel L., review of *A Jar of Dreams, Horn Book,* December, 1981, p. 666.

Review of *Hisako's Mysteries, Library Journal,* May 15, 1969.

Holtze, Sally Holmes, review of *A Jar of Dreams, School Library Journal,* August, 1981, p. 72.

Review of *Journey Home, Booklist,* December 15, 1978, p. 691.

Long, Sidney, review of *Journey to Topaz, New York Times Book Review,* May 12, 1972, p. 8.

Okie, Anne L., review of *The Best Bad Thing, School Library Journal,* November, 1983, p. 83.

Smardan, Laurence E., review of *Journey to Topaz, Journal of Home Economics,* December, 1972, p. 54.

Smith, Irene, "From Japan," *New York Times Book Review,* April 24, 1949, p. 34.

Review of *Sumi's Special Happening, Virginia Kirkus' Service,* September 15, 1966, p. 979.

Sutherland, Zena, review of *Samurai of Gold Hill, Bulletin of the Center for Children's Books,* May, 1973, p. 18.

Uchida, Yoshiko, *Journey to Topaz: A Story of the Japanese-American Evacuation,* revised edition, Creative Arts, 1985.

Uchida, Yoshiko, entry in *Something about the Author Autobiography Series,* Volume 1, Gale, 1986, pp. 269-78.

Wilms, Denise M., review of *A Jar of Dreams, Booklist,* October 15, 1981, pp. 312-13.

Young, Dora Jean, review of *Journey Home, School Library Journal,* January, 1979, p. 58.

■ For More Information See

BOOKS

Children's Literature Review, Volume 6, Gale, 1984, pp. 250-59.

Twentieth-Century Children's Writers, 3rd edition, St. James Press, 1989.

PERIODICALS

Booklist, December 1, 1965, pp. 365-66; January 15, 1970, p. 623; January 1, 1972, p. 395; September 15, 1976, p. 182; September 15, 1982, p. 90; April 1, 1987, p. 1211; March 1, 1992, p. 1272.

Horn Book, December, 1976, p. 622; May/June, 1987, p. 351.

Library Journal, October 15, 1965, p. 237; November 15, 1967, p. 71.

Los Angeles Times Book Review, November 7, 1965, p. 40; October 31, 1982, p. 6; August 9, 1987, p. 11.

New York Times Book Review, November 14, 1993, p. 21.

School Library Journal, November, 1976, p. 52; April, 1992, p. 144; December, 1993, pp. 95-6.

Times Literary Supplement, October 3, 1968, p. 1121.

Voice of Youth Advocates, August, 1982, p. 49.*

—Sketch by Janet Hile

Jules Verne

■ Personal

Born February 8, 1828, in Nantes, France; died of complications of diabetes, March 24, 1905, in Amiens, France; buried in La Madeleine cemetery, Amiens; son of Pierre (a lawyer) and Sophie (Allotte de la Fuye) Verne; married Honorine Anne Marie (de Viane) Morel, January 10, 1857; children: Michel (son); Valentine, Suzanna (stepdaughters). *Education:* Received law degree, 1850. *Religion:* Roman Catholic.

■ Career

Novelist. Theatre Lyrique, Paris, France, secretary, 1852-1857; Eggly & Cie., Paris, stockbroker, 1857-1863. Served on Municipal Council, Amiens, France, 1883-1905. *Military service:* Served with French Coast Guard during Franco-Prussian War, 1870-71.

■ Awards, Honors

Chevalier of the Legion of Honor (France), 1870; received special award from the French Academy, 1872.

■ Writings

"LES VOYAGES EXTRAORDINAIRES" SERIES; NOVELS, EXCEPT AS NOTED

Five Weeks in a Balloon; or, Journeys and Discoveries in Africa, by Three Englishmen, Appleton, 1869 (originally published as *Cinq Semaines en ballon: Voyage de decouvertes en Afrique par trois anglais,* Hetzel, 1863).

A Journey to the Centre of the Earth, H. L. Shepard, 1874, (originally published as *Voyage au centre de la terre,* Hetzel, 1864); also translated as *A Journey to the Interior of the Earth;* and *A Trip to the Center of the Earth.*

From the Earth to the Moon: Passage Direct in Ninety-seven Hours and Twenty Minutes, Newark Printing and Publishing, 1869 (originally published as *De la terre a la lune: Trajet direct en 97 heures 20 minutes,* Hetzel, 1865); also translated as *The Baltimore Gun Club;* and *The American Gun Club.*

The Voyages and Adventures of Captain Hatteras, J. R. Osgood, 1874 (originally published as *Voyages et aventures du Capitaine Hatteras,* 2 volumes, Hetzel, 1866).

At the North Pole; or, The Adventures of Captain Hatteras, Porter & Coates, 1874, (originally published as Volume I of *Voyages et aventures du Capitaine Hatteras: Les Anglais au Pole Nord,* 1866); also translated as *A Journey to the North Pole;* and *The English at the North Pole.*

The Field of Ice, Routledge, 1876 (originally published as Volume II of *Voyages et aventures du Capitaine Hatteras: Le Desert de glace*, 1866); also translated as *The Wilderness of Ice*; and *The Desert of Ice*.

A Voyage Round the World, Lippincott, 1873 (originally published as *Les Enfants du Capitaine Grant: Voyage autour du monde*, Hetzel, Volume I: *Amerique du Sud*, 1867, Volume II: *Australie*, 1867, Volume III: *Ocean Pacifique*, 1868); also translated as *Among the Cannibals; The Castaways, or, A Voyage Round the World; Captain Grant's Children;* and *The Mysterious Document.*

All Around the Moon, Catholic Publication Society, 1876 (originally published as *Autour de la lune*, Hetzel, 1870); also translated as *Round the Moon: A Sequel to "From the Earth to the Moon";* and *Around the Moon.*

Twenty Thousand Leagues under the Sea, Douglas & Myers, 1874 (originally published as *Vingt Mille Lieues sous les mers*, Hetzel, 1870).

The Mysterious Island, J. W. Lovell, 1883 (originally published as part of *L'Ile mysterieuse*, three volumes, Hetzel, 1870); individual volumes also translated as *Abandoned; Dropped from the Clouds; The Secret of the Island;* and *Wrecked in the Air.*

"A Floating City" and *"The Blockade Runners,"* Scribner, 1875 (novel and short story; originally published as *"Une Ville flottante" suivi de "Les Forceurs de blocus"* Hetzel, 1871).

Around the World in Eighty Days, S. Low, 1874, (originally published as *Le Tour du monde en quatre-vingts jours*, Hetzel, 1872); also translated as *The Tour of the World in Eighty Days;* and *Round the World in Eighty Days.*

Meridiana: The Adventures of Three Englishmen and Three Russians in South Africa, Scribner, 1873 (originally published as *Aventures de trois russes et de trois anglais dans l'Afrique australe*, Hetzel, 1872); also translated as *Adventures in the Land of the Behemoth; The Adventures of Three Englishmen and Three Russians in South Africa;* and *Measuring a Meridian.*

The Fur Country; or, Seventy Degrees North Latitude, W. L. Allison, 1873 (originally published as *Le Pays des fourrures*, two volumes, Hetzel, 1873).

Doctor Ox, and Other Stories, J. R. Osgood, 1874 (originally published as *Le Docteur Ox; Maitre Zacharius; Un Hivernage dans les glaces; Un Drame dans les airs*, Hetzel, 1874); also translated as *From the Clouds to the Mountains: Comprising Narratives of Strange Adventures by Air, Land and Water; Dr. Ox's Experiment, and Other Stories;* and *A Winter Amid the Ice, and Other Thrilling Stories.*

The Wreck of the Chancellor, J. R. Osgood, 1875 (originally published as *Le Chancellor*, Hetzel, 1875); also translated as *The Survivors of the Chancellor: Diary of J. R. Kazallon, Passenger;* and *The Chancellor.*

Martin Paz (originally published as part of *Le Chancellor*), translation from the original French, S. Low, 1876, published as *The Pearl of Lima*, G. Munro, 1879.

Michael Strogoff; or, The Courier of the Czar, G. Munro, 1877 (originally published as *Michel Strogoff*, two volumes, Hetzel, 1876).

Hector Servadac: Travels and Adventures Through the Solar System, G. Munro, 1877 (originally published as *Hector Servadac: Voyages et aventures a travers le monde solaire*, two volumes, Hetzel, 1877); also translated as *To the Sun! A Journey Through Planetary Space; Off on a Comet! A Journey Through Planetary Space;* and *To the Sun? Off on a Comet!*; portions published as *The Anomalous Phenomena* and *Homeward Bound.*

The Child of the Cavern; or, Strange Doings Underground, S. Low, 1877 (originally published as *Les Indes-noires*, Hetzel, 1877); also translated as *The Black-Indies; Underground City, or, The Child of the Cavern;* and *Black Diamonds.*

A Captain at Fifteen, G. Munro, 1878, (originally published as *Un Capitaine de quinze ans*, Hetzel, 1878; also translated as *Dick Sand, or, A Captain at Fifteen;* and *Dick Sands: The Boy Captain.*

The Begum's Fortune, With an Account of the Mutineers of the "Bounty," S. Low, 1887 (novel and short story; originally published as *"Les Cinq Cents Millions de la Begum," suivi de "Les Revoltes de la 'Bounty,'"* Hetzel, 1879); also translated as *The Five Hundred Millions of the Begum;* and *The Begum's Fortune.*

The Tribulations of a Chinaman in China, G. Munro, 1879 (originally published as *Les Tribulations d'un Chinois en Chine*, Hetzel, 1879); also translated as *The Tribulations of a Chinaman;* and *The Tribulations of a Chinese Gentleman, Associated Booksellers.*

The Steam-house; or, A Trip Across Northern India, G. Munro, 1880-81 (originally published as *La Maison a vapeur: Voyage a travers l'Inde septentrionale,* Hetzel, 1880); portions published as *The Demon of Cawnpore* and *Tigers and Traitors.*

The Jangada; or, Eight Hundred Leagues over the Amazon, G. Munro, 1881-82 (originally published as *La Jangada: Huit Cents Lieues sur l'Amazone,* Hetzel, 1881); also translated as *The Giant Raft;* and *Eight Hundred Leagues on the Amazon;* portions published as *Down the Amazon* and *The Cryptogram.*

Robinsons' School, G. Munro, 1883 (originally published as *L'Ecole des Robinsons,* Hetzel, 1882); also translated as *Godfrey Morgan: A Californian Mystery (partial);* and *The School for Crusoes.*

The Green Ray, S. Low, 1883 (originally published as *Le Rayon-vert,* Hetzel, 1882).

The Headstrong Turk, G. Munro, 1883-84 (originally published as *Keraban-le-tetu,* Hetzel, 1883); also translated as *Keraban the Inflexible.*

The Southern Star; or, The Diamond Land, G. Munro, 1885 (originally published as *L'Etoile du sud: Le Pays des diamants,* Hetzel, 1884); also translated as *The Vanished Diamond: A Tale of South Africa;* and *The Southern Star Mystery.*

Mathias Sandorf, G. Munro, 1885 (originally published by Hetzel, 1885).

Robur the Conqueror; or, A Trip Round the World in a Flying Machine, G. Munro, 1887 (originally published as *Robur-le-conquerant,* Hetzel, 1886); also translated as *Clipper of the Clouds.*

The Flight to France; or, The Memoirs of a Dragoon, G. Munro, 1889 (originally published as *Le Chemin de France,* Hetzel, 1887).

Texar's Vengeance; or, North Versus South, G. Munro, 1887 (originally published as *Nord contre sud,* Hetzel, 1887); also translated as *North against South;* portions published as *Burbank the Northerner* and *Texar the Southerner.*

A Two Years' Vacation, G. Munro, 1889 (originally published as *Deux Ans de vacances,* Hetzel, 1888); also translated as *Two Years' Holiday;* and *A Long Vacation;* portions published as *Adrift in the Pacific* and *Second Year Ashore.*

Topsy-Turvy (sequel to *From the Earth to the Moon*), J. S. Ogilvie, 1890 (originally published as *Sans dessus dessous,* Hetzel, 1889); also translated as *The Purchase of the North Pole.*

A Family Without a Name, J. W. Lovell, 1889 (originally published as *Famille sans-nom,* Hetzel, 1889); portions published as *Leader of the Resistance* and *Into the Abyss.*

Caesar Cascabel, Cassell, 1890 (originally published as *Cesar Cascabel,* Hetzel, 1890); portions published as *The Travelling Circus* and *The Show on Ice.*

Claudius Bombarnac, the Special Correspondent, Hurst, c. 1894 (originally published as *Claudius Bombarnac,* Hetzel, 1892); also translated as *The Special Correspondent; or, The Adventures of Claudius Bombarnac.*

Captain Antifer, R. F. Fenno, 1895 (originally published as *Mirifiques Aventures de Maitre Antifer,* Hetzel, 1894).

Floating Island; or, The Pearl of the Pacific, S. Low, 1897 (originally published as *L'Ile a helice,* two volumes, Hetzel, 1895); also translated as *Propeller Island.*

Clovis Dardentor, S. Low, 1897 (originally published by Hetzel, 1896).

Facing the Flag, F. T. Neely, 1897 (originally published as *Face au drapeau,* Hetzel, 1896); also translated as *For the Flag.*

An Antarctic Mystery, Lippincott, 1900 (originally published as *Le Sphinx des glaces,* two volumes, Hetzel, 1897); also translated as *The Mystery of Arthur Gordon Pym by Edgar Allan Poe and Jules Verne.*

The Village in the Tree Tops, Associated Booksellers, 1964 (originally published as *Le Village aerien,* Hetzel, 1902).

The Sea Serpent: The Yarns of Jean Marie Cabidoulin, Associated Booksellers, 1967 (stories; originally published as *Les Histoires de Jean-Marie Cabidoulin,* Hetzel, 1902).

The Master of the World: A Tale of Mystery and Marvel, S. Low, 1914 (originally published as *Maitre du monde,* Hetzel, 1904).

The Lighthouse at the End of the World, G. H. Watt, 1924 (originally published as *Le Phare du bout du monde,* Hetzel, 1905).

The Golden Volcano, Arco, 1962 (originally published as *Le Volcan d'or,* Hetzel, 1906); portions published as *The Claim on Forty Mile Creek* and *Flood and Flame.*

The Thompson Travel Agency, Associated Booksellers, 1965 (originally published as *L'Agence Thompson & Co.,* Hetzel, 1907); portions published as *Package Holiday,* and *End of the Journey.*

The Chase of the Golden Meteor, G. Richards, 1909 (originally published as *La Chasse au meteore,* Hetzel, 1908); also translated as *The Hunt for the Meteor.*

The Danube Pilot, Arco, 1967 (originally published as *Le Pilote du Danube,* Hetzel, 1908).

The Survivors of the "Jonathan," Associated Booksellers, 1962 (originally published as Les Naufrages du "Jonathan," two volumes, Hetzel, 1909); portions published as The Masterless Man and The Unwilling Dictator.

Yesterday and Tomorrow, Associated Booksellers, 1965 (short stories; originally published as Hier et demain: Contes et nouvelles, Hetzel, 1910).

The Secret of Wilhelm Storitz, Associated Booksellers, 1963 (originally published as Le Secret de Wilhelm Storitz, Hetzel, 1910).

The Barsac Mission, Associated Booksellers, 1960 (originally published as L'Etonnante Aventure de la mission Barsac, two volumes, Hachette, 1920); portions published as Into the Niger Bend and The City in the Sahara.

FICTION; IN ENGLISH TRANSLATION

The Archipelago on Fire, G. Munro, 1885 (originally published as L'Archipel en feu, Hetzel, 1884).

(With Andre Laurie [a pseudonym of Paschal Grousset]) The Waif of the "Cynthia," G. Munro, 1886 (originally published as L'Epave du Cynthia, Hetzel, 1885); also translated as Salvage from the "Cynthia"; or, The Boy on the Buoy.

Ticket No. 9672, G. Munro, 1886 (originally published as Un Billet de loterie, Hetzel, 1886); also translated as The Lottery Ticket: A Tale of Tellemarken.

Mistress Branican, Cassell, 1891 (published in French under same title, Hetzel, 1891).

The Castle of the Carpathians, Merriam, 1892 (originally published as Le Chateau des Carpathes, Hetzel, 1892); also translated as Carpathian Castle.

Foundling Mick, S. Low, 1895 (originally published as P'tit Bonhomme, Hetzel, 1893).

The Will of an Eccentric, S. Low, 1902 (originally published as Le Testament d'un excentrique, Hetzel, 1899).

Their Island Home: The Later Adventures of the Swiss Family Robinson, S. Low, 1923, G. H. Watt, 1924 (originally published as volume 1 of Seconde Patrie, Hetzel, 1900).

The Castaways of the Flag: The Final Adventures of the Swiss Family Robinson, S. Low, 1923, G. H. Watt, 1924 (originally published as volume 2 of Seconde Patrie, Hetzel, 1900).

A Drama in Livonia, Arco, 1967 (originally published as Un Drame en Livonie Hetzel, 1904).

Paris in the Twentieth Century, Random House, 1996 (undiscovered manuscript from 1863; originally published as Paris au XXe Siecle, [Paris], 1994).

UNTRANSLATED FICTION

Le Superbe Orenoque, Hetzel, 1898.

Les Freres Kip (title means "The Kip Brothers"), Hetzel, 1902.

Bourses de voyage (title means "Traveling Scholarships"), Hetzel, 1903.

L'Invasion de la mer (title means "Invasion of the Sea"), Hetzel, 1905.

NONFICTION; IN ENGLISH TRANSLATION

Great Voyages and Great Navigators, G. Munro, 1879, (originally published as Histoire des grands voyages et des grands voyageurs, Hetzel, Volume I: Decouverte de la terre, 1878, Volume II: Les Grands Navigateurs du XVIIIe siecle, 1879, Volume III: Les Voyageurs du XIXe siecle, 1880); also translated as Celebrated Travels and Travellers, Volume I: The Exploration of the World; and Famous Travels and Travellers, Volume II: The Great Navigators of the Eighteenth Century, Volume III: The Great Explorers of the Nineteenth Century.

UNTRANSLATED NONFICTION

Geographie illustree de la France et de ses colonies (description and travel; title means "Illustrated Geography of France and of the Colonies"), Hetzel, 1867.

Decouverte de l'Amerique: Christophe Colomb (1436-1506), Hetzel, 1883.

Voyage a reculons en Angleterre et en Ecosse (title means "Voyage Backward to England and Scotland"), Le Cherche Midi, 1989.

PLAYS

Les Pailles rompues (title means "The Broken Straws"; produced in Paris, 1850), Beck, 1850.

(With Michel Carre and Aristide Hignard) Le Colin-Maillard (title means "Blindman's Bluff"), Michel Levy, 1853.

(With Carre and Hignard) *Les Compagnons de la Marjolaine* (title means "The Companions of the Marjolaine"), Michel Levy, 1855.

(With Carre and Hignard) *L'Auberge des Ardennes* (operetta; title means "The Inn of the Ardennes"; produced in Paris, 1859), Michel Levy, 1857.

(With Carre and Hignard) *Monsieur de Chimpanze* (musical comedy), produced in Paris, 1858.

(With Charles Wallut) *Onze jours de siege* (three-act comedy; title means "Eleven Days' Siege"; produced in Paris, 1861), Michel Levy, 1861.

(With Edouard Cadoul and Wallut) *Un Neveu d'Amerique; ou, Les Deux Frontignac* (title means "A Nephew From America; or, The Two Frontignacs"), Hetzel, 1873.

(With d'Ennery) *Le Tour du monde en quatre-vingts jours* (adapted from Verne's novel; produced in Paris, 1874), F. Debons, 1875.

(With d'Ennery) *Le Docteur Ox* (adapted from Verne's novel), produced in Paris, 1877.

(With d'Ennery) *Les Enfants du Capitaine Grant: Voyage autour du monde* (adapted from Verne's novel), Mesnil, 1879.

(With d'Ennery) *Michel Strogoff* (adapted from Verne's novel), Mesnil, 1880.

(With d'Ennery) *Les Voyages au theatre*, Hetzel, 1881.

(With d'Ennery) *Voyage a travers l'impossible: Piece fantastique en 3 actes, inedite* (three-act; first produced at Theatre de la Porte Saint Martin, 1882), Pauvert, 1981.

Keraban-le-Tetu, produced in Paris, 1883.

(With William Busnach and Georges Maurens) *Mathias Sandorf* (adapted from Verne's novel), produced in Paris, 1887.

COLLECTIONS; IN ENGLISH

Works of Jules Verne, fifteen volumes, edited by Charles F. Horne, V. Parke, 1911.

The Omnibus Jules Verne, Lippincott, 1931, published as *The Omnibus*, Blue Ribbon Books, 1933.

The Fitzroy Edition of Jules Verne, edited by I. O. Evans, B. Hanison, 1958.

Space Novels, Dover, 1960.

Jules Verne, edited by Armand Goupil, Larousse, 1975.

The Best of Jules Verne: Three Complete, Illustrated Novels, With Original Illustrations, edited by Alan K. Russell, Castle Books, 1978.

Jules Verne: Classic Science Fiction, edited by Russell, Castle, 1981.

Works of Jules Verne, edited by Claire Boss, Avenel Books, 1983.

OTHER

(With Aristide Hignard) *Les Gabiers: Chanson maritime* (title means "Seamen: Maritime Song"), J. Meissonier, 1851.

(With Alfred Dufresne and Jules Lefort) *En avant les Zouaves! Chanson guerriere* (title means "Forward Zouaves! War Song"), Ledeulu, 1855.

(With Hignard) *Daphne: Melodie*, E. Heu, 1857.

(With Hignard) *Rimes et melodies: Douze morceaux de chant par Aristide Hignard*, E. Heu, 1863.

(With Hignard) *Les Clairons de l'armee* (title means "Army Clarions"), Leon Gras, 1870.

(With Georges Alary) *Chanson groenlandaise* (title means "Greenland Song"), Durdilly, 1905.

Le Livre de Jules Verne, Hachette, 1928.

La Journee d'un journaliste americain en 1890, Atelier du "Gue," 1978.

Histoires inattendues (short stories; includes "L'Eternel Adam"), edited by Francis Lacassin, Union Generale, 1978.

Textes oublies: 1849-1903 (complete texts), Union Generale, 1979.

Poesies inedites (poetry), edited by Christian Robin, Le Cherche Midi, 1989.

Contributor to *Musee des Familles* and *Memoires de l'Academie d'Amiens*.

■ Adaptations

FILMS

Les enfants du Capitaine Grant, Societe Francaise des Films et Cinematographes Eclair, 1914; adapted as *Captain Grant's Children*, Amkino/Mosfilm (U.S.S.R.), 1939; also adapted as *In Search of the Castaways*, Walt Disney Productions, 1962.

Around the World in Eighty Days, Lewis Pennant Features, 1914; and United Artists, 1956.

Twenty Thousand Leagues under the Sea, Universal Films (also based on *The Mysterious Island*), 1916; Walt Disney Productions, 1954; and Argyle Enterprises/Telemated Motion Pictures (short film with teacher's guide), 1967; also adapted as *Dream One*, Diffusion Films, 1984.

Michael Strogoff; or, The Courier of the Czar, Universal, 1926; Continental, 1960; also adapted as *The Soldier and the Lady,* RKO Radio Pictures, 1937.

Mysterious Island, Metro-Goldwyn-Mayer (MGM), 1929; Gorki Films (U.S.S.R.), 1941; and Ameran Films, 1961; also adapted as *The Mysterious Island of Captain Nemo,* Cite-Cameroons Cinerama (Spain), 1973..

From the Earth to the Moon, Warner Brothers, 1958; and MGM (animated), 1979.

Journey to the Center of the Earth, Twentieth Century-Fox, 1959; MGM (animated), 1976; also adapted as *Where Time Began,* 1977.

The Fabulous World of Jules Verne (adapted from *Facing the Flag*), Warner Brothers, 1960.

Master of the World (adapted from *The Master of the World* and *Robur the Conqueror*), Warner Brothers, 1961; and MGM (animated), 1976.

Valley of the Dragons (based on *Hector Servadac*), Columbia, 1961; also adapted as *On the Comet* (also known as *Hector Servadac's Ark*), Studio Barrandor (Czech), 1968.

Five Weeks in a Balloon, Twentieth Century-Fox, 1962.

Mathias Sandorf, Procusa (France), 1963

Up to His Ears (based on *The Tribulations of a Chinaman in China*), Lopert Pictures, 1965.

Those Fantastic Flying Fools (inspired by various writings of Verne), American International Pictures, 1967.

Monster from under the Sea (excerpted portions from *Twenty Thousand Leagues under the Sea*), Walt Disney Home Movies, 1968.

The Southern Star, Columbia, 1968.

Strange Holiday (based on *A Two Years' Vacation*), Mass-Brown Pictures, 1969.

Captain Nemo and the Underwater City, MGM, 1971.

Indian Fantasy (animated; based on portions of *Around the World in Eighty Days*), Films Incorporated, 1971.

The Light at the Edge of the World (based on *The Lighthouse at the Edge of the World*), National General, 1971.

Monster Island (based on a Verne story; also known as *Mystery on Monster Island*), Fort Films, 1981.

OTHER

Rodney Dawes, *Around the World in Eighty Days* (three-act play), Dramatic Publishing, 1957.

Twenty Thousand Leagues under the Sea (filmstrips), Eye Gate House (includes teacher's manual), 1958; Encyclopaedia Britannica Films, 1961; Brunswick Productions, 1971; and Walt Disney Educational Materials (includes teacher's guide), 1974.

Adventures in Search of the Castaways and *The End of the Search for the Castaways* (filmstrips; adapted from *Les enfants du Capitaine Grant*) Encyclopaedia Britannica Films, 1964; also adapted as *In Search of the Castaways* (includes teacher's guide), Walt Disney Productions, 1975.

Pierre Thareau, *Michel Strogoff* (three-act play), Art et comedie, 1970.

The Mysterious Island (animated television special), CBS-TV, 1975.

The Return of Captain Nemo (three pilot television episodes), CBS-TV, 1978.

Around the World in Eighty Days (television miniseries), NBC-TV, c. 1990.

■ Sidelights

"From now on I will travel only in my imagination." So said an embarrassed eleven-year-old to his mother after being returned home after a failed runaway attempt. The year was 1839; the boy had crept from his bedroom and through the dark streets of Nantes, a French port on the Loire River, dreaming of life on the high seas. After meeting up with a less adventurous child already serving as cabin boy on the *Coralie,* a grand three-masted schooner, the two switched places. But the runaway's father snatched him from the vessel just as it was about to head off into the open waters of the Atlantic, bound for the West Indies. Although his parents put an end to his naval daydreams, they may have unwittingly started their son on a journey of another kind, a journey that would make life on a schooner tame in comparison. Hovering over the jungles of Africa in a passenger balloon, tangling with a gigantic squid at the bottom of the ocean, orbiting the moon—these were just some of the imaginary travels created by Jules Verne, a name that would come to mean adventure to countless readers around the world in the years ahead.

Although Verne's parents expected their eldest child to become a lawyer like his father, by the time Jules reached his thirties it was clear that writing was his true vocation. Verne hoped to become a famous playwright, but is remembered

THE
MYSTERIOUS ISLAND

by JULES VERNE

Illustrated by N. C. WYETH

Verne creates adventure after strange adventure for the group of people stranded on an island in the Pacific.

today as the author of "Les Voyages Extraordinaires," or "The Extraordinary Voyages." This truly extraordinary series encompasses more than sixty volumes, published over a period of about sixty years (including nine published after Verne's death). Hailed by some critics as the "father of science fiction," Verne referred to his works as "scientific romances," for they combined science fact with romantic conjecture and adventure. Possibly the most astounding feature of Verne's writing was his ability to accurately predict technological advances that were merely the stuff of laboratory dreams at the time his books were written.

A popular literary figure during his lifetime, after his death Verne's fiction drifted in and out of style. First, his works suffered at the hands of several incredibly inept translators of the English versions of his works; film versions of several of his novels produced by Disney Studios and others caused a minor resurgence in interest during the

1950s. This was followed by a period of intense critical study, especially in France, that has continued to this day. In 1994, when a long-lost Verne manuscript, *Paris au XXe Siecle* (*Paris in the Twentieth Century*) was published, it immediately became a best-seller in Verne's native France, with many translations in the works. Its spectacularly accurate predictions of gasoline-powered cars, subways, and fax machines made headlines around the world, serving as a reminder to a new generation of readers that many other exciting discoveries await them in the writings of Jules Verne.

While many of Verne's works became best-sellers, he was far from being an overnight sensation. Success certainly did not come quickly or easily; Verne was thirty-five before his first "Extraordinary Voyage" was published. Wishing to please his father, he had studied law in Paris but found himself unable to resist being part of the city's cultural crowd. Living in the same city with such literary giants as the poet Theophile Gautier and the novelists Victor Hugo and Alexandre Dumas (the elder) served only to strengthen his long-felt desire to be a writer—even his father had been known to compose a few verses of poetry once in a while. When the elder Verne suggested that Jules take over his law practice, the son had to finally admit that he was not going to put his law degree into operation. In *Jules Verne: His Life, His Work,* Marguerite Allotte de la Fuye (Verne's niece by marriage) included an excerpt from one of the many letters sent between father and son during this period. In one, Jules writes to his father: "The only career for which I am really suited is the one I am already pursuing: literature. I am deeply moved by your suggestions, but surely I must trust to my own judgment in this matter. If I took it over, your practice would only wither away." Perhaps Jules never had any intention of being a lawyer, for as he noted in an 1895 interview with Marie A. Belloc, a British journalist (reprinted in *The Best of Jules Verne*), "I cannot remember the time, when I did not write, or intend to be an author."

Alexandre Dumas the elder, famous as the author of *The Three Musketeers* and other swashbuckling novels, was instrumental in helping Verne's dream of being a writer come true. Verne's first taste of success came when he gathered up the courage to show Dumas—whom he had met at a party—several plays he had written. Dumas took an immediate liking to the shortest of Verne's pieces, a one-act comedy, *Les Pailles rompues* ("The Broken Straws"). After suggesting a few revisions, Dumas presented the play at his Theatre Historique in Paris. It was well-received and, as an added bonus, a former classmate of Verne's offered to publish it. Although Verne's father considered the play somewhat trivial, his mother was more receptive. A few months later, when Jules asked his parents for their permission to have the play produced at the Nantes Municipal Theater, they consented and attended the play's local premiere with their son. Verne was finally able to show them proof of his literary talents.

Struggling for Survival

Unfortunately, although he had been working hard at his craft, Verne was just barely managing to survive on his father's allowance and his meager income from writing. Long days doing research for his scientific articles in the National Library saved him the discomfort of sitting in his ill-heated rented room; he was so poor that for nights at the theatre and other special occasions, he and his roommate shared a set of evening clothes between them. Seeing Verne's haggard and thread-bare condition, Dumas came to his aid. This time he secured a position for the aspiring author as a secretary at the Lyric Theater. To supplement his income, Verne contributed short stories—many influenced by the works he knew in translation of James Fenimore Cooper and Edgar Allan Poe—to a Parisian periodical, *Musee des Familles.*

On January 10, 1857, Verne married Honorine Morel, a twenty-six-year-old widow with two young daughters. Knowing that he would need more money to support a family of four, Verne persuaded his father to buy him a partnership on the French stock exchange. He rose each morning to write before going to the exchange, where he worked as a stockbroker. He was able to have several of his works for theater produced during this period, including a musical comedy, *Monsieur de Chimpanze,* in 1858 and an operetta, *L'Auberge des Ardennes* ("The Inn in the Ardennes"), in 1860. He was determined to expand some of his short story ideas into novels. Money was even more of a concern now that he and his wife had a baby boy named Michel. Looking for some new form of literature that would capture the imagination of large numbers of readers, Verne spoke at length with the friends he had met through a local literary club, *Le Cercle de la Presse Scientifique,* about his idea of basing a series of novels on scientific facts. He was especially intrigued with the activities of one of the members of the group, Felix Tournachon, a well-known photographer under the name Nadar, who was planning to build *The Giant,* a colossal passenger balloon with a two-story cabin. Never one to let an idea go unexplored, Verne decided his next topic of research would be the possibility of using balloons to explore the unknown areas of the earth.

Inspired by Nadar's work, as well as by two Poe stories which featured balloon travel, Verne excitedly drew on his knowledge of geography and love of exploring to write a nonfiction manuscript. Hoping to increase interest in the work by linking it to current events of the day, he attempted to show how a balloon could be used to discover the source of the Nile. Reports of the true-life adventures of the likes of Sir Samuel Baker, Sir Richard Burton, John Speke, and other explorers in Africa made the region extremely popular in France at the time. Enthusiastic about what he had written, Verne sent his book to a publisher. It was soon returned, rejected. Verne sent it to another publisher and it was again rejected. After receiving the fifteenth rejection notice on that same manuscript, Verne had had enough. Filled with rage, he took the precious papers and tossed them into the fireplace. Luckily, Honorine came into the room at that moment, discovered what was happening and snatched the manuscript from the flames. She kept it safely hidden until her husband calmed down. During this difficult period, Verne poured his frustration into a letter to his father, reprinted in Peggy Teeters' biography of the author, *Jules Verne: The Man Who Invented Tomorrow.* "If I write a play for a particular theater director," Verne complained, "he moves elsewhere; if I think of a good title, three days later I see it on the billboards announcing someone else's play; if I write an article, another appears on the same subject. Even if I discovered a new planet, I believe it would at once explode, just to prove me wrong." He was beginning to think that maybe writing wasn't for him after all.

At a crossroads in his life, Verne decided to once again turn to Dumas for help. The older man suggested Verne contact a novelist friend. The friend sent Verne to see Pierre-Jules Hetzel, a publisher. When Verne saw the publisher shake his head as he finished reading the manuscript, he prepared himself for the worst. Instead, Hetzel said he liked what he read. He made numerous helpful suggestions to Verne about how to improve the manuscript, however, and encouraged him to rewrite it as a novel. In two weeks, the tale was ready to submit to Hetzel for his final approval or disapproval. The publisher proclaimed the manuscript to be exactly the type of story he wanted to acquire for his new bi-monthly family magazine, *Le Magazine d'Education et de Recreation* ("Magazine of Education and Recreation") and offered Verne a ten-year contract to produce at least two novels a year. Thrilled, Verne signed the contract; under terms of the agreement at least one of Verne's novels per year would be serialized in Hetzel's magazine before being published in book form. The novels were also expected to fill Hetzel's desire to provide reading material that could be enjoyed both by parents and their children, providing entertainment as well as educational and moral insights. After returning home to share the fantastic news with Honorine, Verne went immediately to quit his job on the stock exchange.

A Novel in a New Form

Verne was finally able to realize his dream of writing full-time. Even better, Hetzel's interest in an educational/recreational form of literature meshed perfectly with Verne's desire to write scientific fiction. When *Five Weeks in a Balloon* was published in January, 1863, it became a best-seller, widely read by adults as well as younger readers. The adventure begins as Dr. Samuel Ferguson, an erudite English explorer, leaves exotic Koumbeni (a tiny islet off the eastern African island of Zanzibar) in his balloon *Victoria* to take advantage of the trade-winds in his east to west flight over Africa. Although in real life there was no device yet available for steering passenger balloons, Verne's professor devises an ingenious furnace that controls the temperature of the hydrogen gas inside the balloon. As the gas is heated, it expands, and causes the balloon to rise; as it cools, the reverse happens. Although this setup would be actually very dangerous to use (since hydrogen gas is very flammable), it was sufficient for Verne's purposes. Accompanying Ferguson are Joe Wilson, his servant, and Dick Kennedy, a Scottish hunter. Although the three explore Africa from above the treetops, their story is full of excitement. Incredible adventures keep the story moving: the balloon's trail rope becomes wrapped around the tusks of an elephant who takes it for a wild ride, the balloon appears stuck in the middle of a torrential downpour, and the cabin of the balloon is lost and the crew is forced to hang onto the netting covering the balloon. Actual geographical references are given throughout the story so the exact route of the expedition can be plotted on a real map. During it all, Ferguson instructs his companions—and Verne's readers—on a variety of topics.

The book was the first of Verne's *Voyages Extraordinaires* and the beginning of a remarkable literary career. Although certainly not a masterpiece, the work gives a hint of Verne's great ability. The work's scientific focus spawned a revolution in literature that would continue to the present day. According to John J. Pierce, writing in *Foundations of Science Fiction : A Study in Imagination and Evolution,* Verne himself seemed to realize the importance of what he was doing. "I have just written a novel in a new form, one that is entirely my own," Pierce quoted Verne as saying about *Five Weeks in a Balloon.* "If it succeeds, I will have stumbled upon a gold mine." For Pierce, and many other critics, the book marks the beginning of what would develop into the modern genre of science fiction. Of course, Verne wasn't the first to write science fiction, but rather the first to systematically develop it over the course of a body of work. With Verne, Pierce noted: "Science and technology, which had been peripheral to the traditional travel tale when they appeared at all, were now placed at the center and combined with the elementary appeal of romantic action and adventure." He found the importance of *Five Weeks in a Balloon* in "the pervasive spirit of scientific enterprise in the novel. For Ferguson and his comrades, science is not simply a scholarly pursuit, but a means of expanding human experience and achievement as they soar over the obstacles that have frustrated previous explorations of Africa."

The very next year Verne published one of his most famous novels, *A Journey to the Center of the Earth.* This first-person narrative tells the story of Axel, a young German student, and his mineralogist uncle, Professor Otto Lidenbrock. In the novel's first scene, the professor is excitedly showing his nephew a newly purchased book by a "celebrated Icelandic author of the twelfth century." Suddenly, a small scrap of parchment covered with a series of words in ancient Icelandic falls out of the book. Converting the runic letters to our own modern alphabet presents no problem for the polyglot professor, but even then the words do not make sense. Reminiscent of Poe's famous cryptograms, the message appears to be in some sort of code. Lidenbrock surmises that it was written by Arne Saknussemm, a sixteenth-century Icelandic alchemist, but it is Axel who breaks the code. Reading the message, the two discover that Saknussemm had traveled inside the earth by entering through the crater of an extinct Icelandic volcano. Soon, Lidenbrock has convinced his nephew and Hans, an Icelandic guide, to follow the alchemist's route to the underground world. Not only do they discover vast caverns, like we might expect, but they also encounter a host of marvels too numerous to list. They pass a forest of mushrooms forty feet high, witness two creatures from the age of dinosaurs in mortal combat, and view from afar a strange human-like creature that stands about twelve feet tall. The journey under the earth is cut short when an earthquake throws the men up on to the surface through the Stromboli Island volcano in the Mediterranean Sea, near Italy.

As with his first novel, Verne chose the topic of *A Journey to the Center of the Earth* from the pages of the various scientific journals and newspapers he read. At that time, the true composition of the earth's interior was still hotly debated by scientists. One faction believed that perhaps all the world's volcanoes were connected by an underground network of caverns. Gathering background material, Verne met and talked with a French seismologist, Charles Saint-Claire Deville, an expert in volcanoes, who had actually entered the crater on Stromboli Island. With public curiosity about the subject high, Verne saw an underground journey as perfect both as an adventure story and as an opportunity to educate his readers in geology, archeology and the fledgling field of evolution. True to Verne's expectations, the book was well-accepted and remains one of his most popular works. "The story can still be enjoyed," I. O. Evans maintained in *Jules Verne and His Work*, "even now that we are hardened to 'strange journeys' and know its central idea to be fallacious, we can well imagine what enthusiasm it aroused when its theoretical basis was credible and science fiction was otherwise unknown!" Modern critics have delighted in the novel's mythic overtones, finding the center of the earth

to be a magical spot. Mark Rose in *Coordinates: Placing Science Fiction and Fantasy* saw the trio's pilgrimage as "a journey into the abyss of evolutionary time, and this fusion of the spatial and temporal modes is one of the fiction's sources of power. Temporarily projected, the quest for the center, the heart of the mystery, becomes the pursuit of origins, the quest for an ultimate moment of beginning."

Capturing the Moon

For his next novel, Verne chose to write about another magical place: the moon. About a century before the U.S. National Aeronautics and Space Agency, Verne developed a scheme for sending man to the moon. *From the Earth to the Moon* was published in 1865, followed by its sequel, *Around the Moon,* three years later. Verne, like many of his countrymen, had read with horror of

Adapted for both the stage and screen, this adventure novel–first published in 1873–is about a man's attempt to race around the world in only eighty days in order to win a bet.

the battles of the American Civil War during the previous few years. Shocked by the reported carnage in the fields, Verne wondered if some of the large artillery developed for the war couldn't be adapted for shooting a rocket into outer space instead of blowing other humans to bits. This "extraordinary voyage" follows the exploits of the members of the Gun Club of Baltimore, a group of Civil War veterans led by Impey Barbicane. Bored by life after the war, the veterans decide to construct a giant cannon to shoot a manned projectile to the moon. International news reports of the development of the vehicle induce a Frenchman, Michel Ardan (his surname is an anagram of the name of Verne's friend Nadar) to travel to the United States to offer his advice in return for a spot as one of the crew. The first novel ends with the capsule orbiting around the moon instead of landing on it. The sequel clears up the mystery of why the men couldn't land and shows how they eventually get back to earth. "Many of Verne's readers believed," Teeters reported, "that he was writing about a spaceship that actually existed and that a trip to the moon was indeed being planned. Hundreds of them wrote to Jules begging him to take them along on this fantastic voyage."

From the Earth to the Moon and *Around the Moon,* cover a topic—travel to the moon—not unique to those two volumes. Verne, for example, was familiar with the seventeenth-century story by Cyrano de Bergerac about a man who travels to the moon in a device powered by exploding firecrackers. He also admired a Poe story, *The Unparalleled Adventure of One Hans Pfaal,* which told of a man ascending to the moon in a balloon. While the theme that Verne had chosen was not new, he dealt with it in a scientific manner missing from the other works. In the end, he created a book that was astonishingly prophetic; he accurately predicted the location for the launch site (Florida), the velocity necessary for exiting the earth's atmosphere, the bullet-shaped capsule made of aluminum, weightlessness, the use of rockets to change orbit, and the splashdown in the Pacific (two and a half miles from the landing site of Apollo 8). What technical errors there were—we know that the men in the spacecraft could never have survived a return to earth going 115,200 miles an hour—are not enough to subtract from the enjoyment of the story. "What is important is that Verne recognized the necessity of being scientifically correct," declared science

fiction novelist Isaac Asimov in his forward to a dual edition of Verne's *Twenty Thousand Leagues Under the Sea* and *Around the Moon.* "He made a point of studying the scientific publications of his day, and tried to live up to the rules of the scientific game. Most of the time he *did,* and the amazing thing is that he could be so extraordinary *inside* those rules."

By this time, Verne's writings had made him an international celebrity constantly beleaguered by enthusiastic readers. In the summer of 1866, hoping to find the quiet he needed to write, Verne rented a cottage for his family in Le Crotoy, a village at the mouth of the Somme on the northern coast of France. While there, he planned to work on *Around the Moon* and another book tentatively entitled "Voyage under the Oceans." For complete privacy, he purchased a small boat, christened *St. Michel* in honor of his son, and set up a small workroom on board. Verne enjoyed being by the seaside so much—he said the sound of the breaking waves calmed him—that he eventually moved there with his family. Another opportunity for relaxation came in March the following year when Verne's brother Paul asked him to accompany him on a trip to the United States aboard the *Great Eastern,* then the largest steamship in the world. Always an admirer of modern technology, Jules was thrilled to go on the trip. As an additional incentive, he also learned that Cyrus Field, who had been responsible for the laying of the first telegraph cable between the United States and England, would be on board. With his mind on possible details that would be useful for his upcoming fictionalized undersea voyage, Verne spoke at length with Field and the workmen aboard the ship who had also been involved in placement of the cable. Of much interest to Verne were the colorful details the men supplied about the time a giant squid had become entangled in the cable. A similar episode would be found in his great undersea adventure, published in 1870 as *Twenty Thousand Leagues under the Sea.*

Considered by many to be his masterpiece, *Twenty Thousand Leagues under the Sea* includes two of Verne's most intriguing inventions: a submarine called the *Nautilus* and a character named Captain Nemo. Verne based his vessel on records of underwater craft already in existence, most notably a hand-powered submarine (also called the *Nautilus*) built by American inventor Robert Fulton in 1797. If Verne's idea of an underwater

In this novel, Michael Strogoff journeys across hostile country to warn the Grand Duke of an impending rebellion.

vehicle was not original, the craft itself definitely was. In *Foundation*, M. Hammerton likened it "to a modern nuclear attack submarine, though rather smaller and slimmer. No nuclear submarine, however—indeed, no millionaire's yacht—boasts the luxurious splendours with which Verne endowed his creation." The submarine, for example, offers a library of 12,000 volumes, a bar, a pipe organ, and picture windows looking out onto the watery scenery. Not only that, but the *Nautilus* is also powered, heated and illuminated by electricity, this at a time when a steam engine was far more powerful than any available electric motor, and years before Thomas Edison perfected his incandescent lamp.

Nemo (his name means "nothing" in Latin) is just as fascinating as his ship. He is one of the few Vernean characters that critics seem to admire. Compared to other Verne creations, Arthur B. Evans wrote in *Jules Verne Rediscovered*, Nemo is "much less one-dimensional as a fictional character and infinitely more intriguing—his mysterious and oxymoronic personality identifying him as a quite unique specimen in Verne's roster of

protagonists." In Walter James Miller's afterword to *The Annotated Jules Verne: Twenty Thousand Leagues under the Sea*, he contended that Nemo would be viewed even more favorably if many scenes and dialogue in the original French that show how "Nemo . . . grows as a personality" hadn't been omitted from the earliest and most widely reprinted English translations. Errors made by early English translators of *Twenty Thousand Leagues under the Sea* and other Verne titles have been highlighted in recent years by many critics. Hammerton, for instance, pointed out what he calls his "favorite howler": when a captain calls for a more skilled person the translator confuses the French words for "adept" and "right" and has the captain say, "another, more to the right." Fortunately, unabridged, accurate translations are now available for nearly all Verne's books.

"There I Am Free!"

Twenty Thousand Leagues under the Sea, like many of Verne's other novels, features a trio of adventurers: Professor Pierre Aronnax, an internationally famous French biologist; Conseil, his servant; and Ned Land, a French-Canadian harpooner. When their ship sinks while on a mission attempting to track down the source of reports of a sea monster terrorizing ships in the Atlantic, the three are taken aboard the *Nautilus*. With a mixture of horror and awe they discover that the incredible submarine has actually been behind the inexplicable sinkings and other incidents that caused their journey. Its captain is a recluse who for unknown reasons has fled the world of men, preferring to be under the sea. Although Nemo never reveals his quarrel with the surface world (Verne saves the secret for a later volume in which Nemo appears, *The Mysterious Island*), he tries to make his guests understand why he has chosen life under the ocean: "The sea does not belong to despots. Upon its surface men can still exercise unjust laws, fight, tear one another to pieces, and be carried away with terrestrial horrors. . . . Ah! sir, live—live in the bosom of the waters! There only is independence! There I recognise no masters! There I am free!" Not wanting his hideaway revealed, soon after the Professor and the others enter the *Nautilus*, Nemo lets them know they are now his prisoners and will never leave the submarine. Verne fills the rest of his novel with a series of adventures, including the attack by the gigantic squid. At the end of the story, the three prisoners are able to escape from the *Nautilus* but are left wondering if Captain Nemo is still alive.

Although Verne continued writing novels for the rest of his life, a combination of many events seemed to keep him from ever achieving the same measure of success that he enjoyed with his early novels. While both *Twenty Thousand Leagues under the Sea* and *Round the Moon* were published in 1870 and the prestigious Chevalier of the Legion of Honor medal was given to Verne that same year, the outbreak of the Franco-Prussian War in July changed Verne's life drastically. After sending his family to the comparative safety of Amiens, he was asked to form a French coast guard patrol at the mouth of the Somme at Le Crotoy. He carried out his duties with a cannon mounted on the back of the *St. Michel.* The short war sent the country into disarray; Verne's publisher fled the country and all other publishing houses were closed. Needing to support his family and the lifestyle the income from his writing afforded him, Verne went to live with relatives in Paris and took up his old stockbroker position for a few weeks after the war ended. A bright spot that came out of his war experience was his discovery one day of a Thomas Cook travel poster announcing that technological advances, such as the opening of the Suez Canal, had made it possible to go around the world in ninety days. Suddenly Verne was plotting what became his next novel, *Around the World in Eighty Days.*

The novel features a colorful character, Mr. Phileas Fogg. He's an Englishman who stands to win 20,000 pounds if he can circle the world in eighty days. He and Passepartout, his valet, leave on their journey, only to be closely followed by Detective Fix, who thinks Fogg is a bank robber leaving England to escape arrest. The novel caused a worldwide sensation when it was serialized in the Parisian newspaper, *Le Temps.* No one could wait for the next installment of the story to find out what was happening to Fogg and if he would make it back to London in the appointed time. Steamship lines even contacted Verne promising to pay the author a good deal of money if he used their line to get Fogg back to England. Verne refused. He arranged numerous close calls for his characters: in India a funeral procession holds Fogg up for a while, as does his having to travel by elephant for fifty miles; in the United States, Fogg must rescue Passepartout after he is captured by members of the Sioux Nation, is forced to cross

a rickety railroad bridge, and loses time when a herd of buffalo wander on to the railroad track. As usual, Verne keeps his readers in suspense until the very end: Fogg apparently arrives back in London five minutes late, but after careful calculations realizes that because he gained hours as he traveled from east to west through time zones, he is actually a day early! When published in 1873 in book form, anxious readers bought more than a half-million copies. Verne quickly gave permission for the novel to be adapted into a play that ran for two years in Paris and had successful engagements in cities all over the world.

The book and the play made Verne a very wealthy man. At the insistence of his wife, he moved his family permanently to Amiens. There

Written a quarter of a century before underwater travel was actually accomplished, Verne's most famous novel is about the enigmatic Captain Nemo and his submarine crew.

An illustration by William McLaren of a giant squid attack described in *Twenty Thousand Leagues under the Sea.*

he bought a mansion with a two-story turret from which he could look out over the city. He purchased two successively larger yachts, the *St. Michel II* and the *St. Michel III,* and took his first trip to the Mediterranean. There he was honored as a foreign dignitary and even had a private audience with the pope. He served on the Amiens Municipal Council and joined the Amiens Academy. He kept on writing and published many more books, but his outlook seemed more pessimistic than before. Not only was France severely depressed economically for over a decade, but during that same period Verne had to deal with problems with his son Michel (including a time when he had his son sent to jail), the death of his good friend and publisher, Hetzel, and, in 1886, a bizarre incident in which he was shot in the leg by his nephew Gaston and left partially crippled. Ill health added to his misery during his last decade as he suffered from cataracts, deafness and diabetes. Complications of the latter ended his life on March 24, 1905. Four days later, a throng of nearly five thousand mourners gathered at his funeral.

Verne's legacy lives on, not just in his books but also in the deeds they inspired. A remarkable number of famous scientists, explorers, and other men of science acknowledge their debt to the French novelist. Just a few of those inspired by the writer include Admiral Richard Byrd, who explored Antarctica in the 1920s and 1930s; Yuri Gagarin, the Soviet cosmonaut who became the first man in space; and Isaac Asimov, the prolific science-fiction writer. When the U.S. Navy launched the world's first nuclear submarine in 1954, it was named the U.S.S. *Nautilus.* In his writings, Verne amazingly predicted everything from television (he dubbed it the phono-tele-photo) to helicopters to guided missiles to seaplanes. In his recently published *Paris in the Twentieth Century* we discover he also accurately described the gasoline-powered car nearly three decades before it existed and anticipated fax machines by more than one hundred years. "He took the best and most up-to-date ideas of his times," wrote Alan K. Russell in his introduction to *The Best of Jules Verne,* "when new worlds in science were being discovered almost daily, and made them into novels peopled by memorable characters. As the stories take you racing along with Verne's imagination it is difficult to believe he was born one hundred and fifty years ago." Perhaps more inspiring than Verne's amazing predictions, however, was his belief in science and his ability to portray the wonders of technology. Verne himself recognized that his imagination could scarcely approach the realities of scientific invention that he found so fascinating, as he wrote in a letter reprinted in *Jules Verne, His Life, His Work:* "Everything that I invent, everything that I imagine, will always fall short of the truth, because there will come a time when the creations of science will outstrip those of the imagination."

■ Works Cited

Allotte de la Fuye, Marguerite, *Jules Verne: Sa vie, son oeuvre,* Simon Kra, 1928, translated by Erik de Mauny as *Jules Verne: His Life, His Work,* Staples, 1954, Coward-McCann, 1956.

Asimov, Isaac, "Father Jules," foreword to *Twenty Thousand Leagues under the Sea* [and] *Around the Moon,* by Jules Verne, Platt & Munk, 1965, pp. 9-13.

Belloc, Marie A., "Jules Verne at Home," in *The Best of Jules Verne,* edited by Alan K. Russell, Castle Books, 1978, pp. 460-467.

Evans, Arthur B., *Jules Verne Rediscovered,* Greenwood Press, 1988.

Evans, I. O., *Jules Verne and his Work,* Twayne, 1966.

Hammerton, M., "Verne's Amazing Journeys," in *Foundation,* winter, 1986-87, pp. 30-38.

Miller, Walter James, "Jules Verne Rehabilitated," afterword to *The Annotated Jules Verne: Twenty Thousand Leagues under the Sea,* by Jules Verne, Crowell, 1976, pp. 356-359.

Pierce, John J., "Verne and the Verneans," in *Foundations of Science Fiction: A Study in Imagination and Evolution,* Greenwood Press, 1987, pp. 33-49.

Rose, Mark, "Jules Verne: Journey to the Center of Science Fiction," in *Coordinates: Placing Science Fiction and Fantasy,* edited by George E. Slusser, Eric S. Rabkin, and Robert Scholes, Southern Illinois University Press, 1983, pp. 31-41.

Russell, Alan K., "The World of Jules Verne," introduction to *The Best of Jules Verne,* Castle Books, 1978, pp. vii-viii.

Teeters, Peggy, *Jules Verne: The Man Who Invented Tomorrow* (young adult), Walker, 1992.

Verne, Jules, *The Annotated Jules Verne: Twenty Thousand Leagues under the Sea,* Crowell, 1976.

Verne, Jules, *Journey to the Center of the Earth,* Airmont, 1965.

■ For More Information See

BOOKS

Barthes, Roland, *Mythologies,* translated by Annette Laver, Hill & Wang, 1972.

Butcher, William, *Verne's Journey to the Centre of the Self: Space and Time in the Voyages Extraordinaires,* with foreword by Ray Bradbury, St. Martin's Press, 1991.

Dictionary of Literary Biography, Volume 123: *Nineteenth-Century French Fiction Writers: Naturalism and Beyond,* Gale, 1992.

Lynch, Lawrence W., *Jules Verne,* Twayne, 1992.

Martin, Andrew, *The Mask of the Prophet: The Extraordinary Fictions of Jules Verne,* Clarendon Press, 1990.

Savater, Fernando, *Childhood Regained: The Art of the Storyteller,* translated by Frances M. Lopez-Morillas, Columbia University Press, 1982.

Twentieth Century Literary Criticism, Volume 52, Gale, 1994.

Verne, Jules, *A Journey to the Centre of the Earth,* with introduction by Isaac Asimov, Heritage Press, 1966.

Verne, Jules, *From the Earth to the Moon and Round the Moon,* with introduction by Arthur C. Clarke, Dodd, Mead, 1962.

Verne, Jules-Jean, *Jules Verne,* Hachette, 1973, translated from the French by Roger Greaves as *Jules Verne: A Biography,* Taplinger, 1976.

PERIODICALS

Nation, March 30, 1905.

Newsweek, October 10, 1994.

People, February 13, 1995.*

—Sketch by Marian C. Gonsior

John Waters

eration of Television and Radio Artists, Screen Actors Guild.

■ Awards, Honors

John Waters Day named by the State of Maryland, 1985; John Waters Week named by City of Baltimore, 1988.

■ Writings

SCREENPLAYS

(And director and producer) *Mondo Trasho,* New Line Cinema, 1969.

(And director and producer) *Multiple Maniacs,* New Line Cinema, 1970.

(And director and producer) *Pink Flamingos,* New Line Cinema, 1972.

(And director and producer) *Female Trouble,* New Line Cinema, 1974.

(And director and producer) *Desperate Living,* New Line Cinema, 1977.

(And director) *Polyester,* New Line Cinema, 1981.

(And director and actor) *Hairspray,* New Line Cinema, 1988.

(And actor) *Something Wild,* 1988.

(And actor) *Homer and Eddie,* 1990.

(And director) *Cry–Baby,* Universal, 1990.

(And director) *Serial Mom,* Savoy Pictures, 1994.

Author and director of short films "Hag in a Black Leather Jacket," 1964, "Roman Candles," 1966–67, "Eat Your Makeup," 1968, and "The

■ Personal

Born April 22, 1946, in Baltimore, MD; son of John Samuel (owner of a fire–protection equipment business) and Patricia Ann (a homemaker; maiden name, Whitaker) Waters. *Education:* Attended University of Baltimore, 1965, and New York University, 1966.

■ Addresses

Home—Baltimore, MD.

■ Career

Producer, director, and writer of films; actor. Worked in book stores; teacher of English and film, 1983–86, at Patuxent Institution, a psychiatric prison in Maryland. Lecturer at comedy clubs and colleges in the United States, Europe, and Australia; has raised funds for AIDS Action Baltimore; spokesperson for Anti–Violence Campaign in New York City, 1991. *Member:* Directors Guild of America, Writers Guild of America, Academy of Motion Picture Arts and Sciences, American Fed-

Diane Linkletter Story," 1970. Actor in episode of television series *21 Jump Street*, Fox, 1990.

OTHER

Shock Value: A Tasteful Book about Bad Taste (autobiography), Dell, 1981.

Crackpot: The Obsessions of John Water (essays), Macmillan, 1986.

Trash Trio: Three Screenplays (contains *Pink Flamingos*, *Desperate Living*, and *Flamingos Forever* [unproduced]), Vintage Books, 1988.

(Author of introduction) William Castle, *Step Right Up: I'm Gonna Scare the Pants off America*, World Almanac, 1992.

Contributor to periodicals, including *Rolling Stone*, *Vogue*, *Vanity Fair*, *American Film*, and *Film Comment*.

■ Sidelights

Vomit, hairspray, and the consumption of dog excrement are all to be expected when viewing the movies of writer–director John Waters. Raised by "normal" Catholic parents, at an early age Waters was inexplicably drawn to tacky, sleazy and trashy movies playing far from his suburban Baltimore neighborhood. After being kicked out of college on a drug bust, Waters returned home to his parents and, with their concerned blessing, began making sleazy movies. He reached what many consider to be his peak of underground "trash" filmmaking with the 1972 release *Pink Flamingos*—a work that continues to play on midnight movie circuits. He turned slightly more mainstream with the comedies *Polyester* and *Hairspray* in the 1980s. Still, Waters's mainstream hits are farther out than most other movie–house hits, because his main goal, he told William Geist in *People*, is to "leave them gagging in the aisles."

Early in his life, Waters started displaying characteristics that were different from other youngsters his age. Growing up in affluent surroundings in a very standard Baltimore suburb, Waters picked up the hobby of venturing to junkyards to see cars being smashed. He recreated this melee at home with his own toy cars. Waters was also obsessed with getting acne as a teenager—he wanted to see what it was like—and was quite disappointed when his skin turned out to be smooth and clear throughout his life.

It didn't take long for Waters to find his first true love—bad movies. At his Catholic high school, the nuns would make a list of all the movies that would send kids to hell if they saw them. It was at this point that Waters knew the reason he was attending this school. After scanning the list, he told Sally A. Lodge in *Publishers Weekly*, "I'd run to see them." Attending a conservative high school also worked wonders for Waters. He told Gerald L'Ecuyer of *Egg* magazine that every morning at the Calvert school, "you had to shake hands with the principal. Girls had to curtsy. There were two full theatre productions every year. . . . A good school, except for too much sports." In high school, Waters continued his search for sensational movies, often prowling the seedier areas of his town in search of horror and soft–core porno films. Some of his favorites included *Door to Door Maniac, I Dismember Mama,* and the works of the "King of Shock," William Castle.

In high school Waters ventured into the arena of moviemaking himself. His grandmother, trying to nurture a creative talent that his family felt could lead him astray, gave Waters a movie camera as a gift. Waters was soon underway producing a movie titled "Hag in a Black Leather Jacket," a romp featuring the trials of Ku Klux Klansman performing an interracial wedding ceremony. Waters commented to Lodge that "It was terrible. It was shot on the roof of my parents' house, and I never even edited it." Waters eventually arranged for a showing of his work at a coffee house in Baltimore and was able to turn a profit of $20.00.

Around this time, Waters was entranced by a neighborhood boy named Glenn Milstead, who was fond of dressing in women's outfits (Waters eventually dubbed Milstead "Divine"). Unfortunately Milstead was almost run out of town because of his behavior—he was constantly beaten up at his school. "I knew of Divine a long time before I met him," Waters told J. Hoberman and Jonathan Rosenbaum in *Midnight Movies*. "My father used to drive us to school and we'd see this creature with dyed red hair. My father would just shudder. I figured anyone who could get that reaction just by standing there I had to know. . . . I met him through a girl living up the street who had a green bee–hive hairdo." The two struck up a friendship that was to become a lifelong one,

Two groups compete for the title of "The Filthiest People Alive" in the 1972 movie *Pink Flamingos*.

and Divine became a fixture in many of Waters's films.

With high school behind him, Waters went to the University of Baltimore to attend college. He was attracted to the film school at New York University, and transferred there after his first year in Baltimore. His schooling didn't last long. Shortly before he was to complete his first semester, he was caught smoking marijuana in a dormitory drug bust. His punishment was to be expelled from school, and he was returned to his parents' custody.

His expulsion from school was a fortuitous event. Back in his hometown, he seemed to be nearer the creative inspiration he needed to make his movies. And make movies he did. With the financial help of his father, he soon returned to moviemaking. He was especially interested in the short films by Andy Warhol, George Kuchar, and Kenneth Anger he had seen. In 1966 Waters debuted "Roman Candles," another of his low–budget flicks, shot in the seedier areas of Baltimore. Using an innovative triple–screen projection tech-

nique, the movie portrays a nun and a priest in a romantic tangle, a junkie shooting up, and an overweight woman consuming fruit. This film marked the first time that Waters and Divine would work together. The film premiered in the hall of Emmanuel Episcopal church with the help of a very tolerant priest.

Divine Intervention

Divine was the star of Waters's next film, "Eat Your Make–Up." At a weight of three hundred pounds and dressed in outrageous drag, Divine was the focal point of the movie. "Eat Your Make–Up" concerns a crazed governess who kidnaps young women and forces them to model until they die of exhaustion. Once again, the home of Waters's parents was used as the set.

Undaunted by the lack of commercial success he was receiving, Waters borrowed two thousand dollars from his father to make his next film, *Mondo Trasho*. The now familiar Divine was cast in the lead role as a woman who accidentally hits a female pedestrian while driving. The unconscious girl ends up in Divine's trunk while a series of odd escapades unfold. Eventually, Divine takes the victim to a drug–addicted doctor, who decides to remove the victim's feet and replace them with chicken feet. Gunslingers invade the doctor's waiting room, mortally wounding Divine, who is able to escape and crawl into a muddy pigsty before expiring. The young victim ends up safe on a Baltimore street corner where she has to endure the angry insults of two unknown women. *Mondo Trasho* was the first of Waters's films to escape the small theatrical world of Baltimore, where it received modest praise for its zany satire.

"The Diane Linkletter Story" was Water's next venture. It was a short film starring Divine as the daughter of Art Linkletter, who had committed suicide after getting high on LSD. Waters moved on quickly after this effort to make his second feature–length film, *Multiple Maniacs*. This film was perhaps the pinnacle of Waters's genius for depravity. Once again, Divine had the lead role, this time as the woman in charge of "Lady Divine's Cavalcade of Perversions," a veritable circus that features drug addicts, pornographers, and homosexuals, as well as novelty acts such as a vomit–eater and a person who joys in smelling bicycle seats. Divine progresses into deeper and deeper levels of depravity during the film, often times resorting to murdering members of her entourage. Finally, some of her cohorts attempt to kill her; she retaliates by stabbing them, and then feasts upon their internal organs. Divine meets her match when she is raped by a giant lobster, but she survives to horrify people in her neighborhood. Finally, Divine's cruelty is ended when the National Guard comes in and shoots her dead. Waters commented in *Midnight Movies* that "Violence [is] this generation's sacrilege, so I wanted to make a film that would glorify carnage and mayhem for laughs." *Multiple Maniacs* was re-

Waters' 1981 film *Polyester* employed scratch-and-sniff cards to allow audiences to experience the smells of the movie, along with the sights and sounds.

leased on a sixteen–city tour of the underground movie circuit, further spreading Waters's scandalous vision.

Pink Flamingos was Waters's next effort, a film that turned into his first underground masterpiece and gave the filmmaker a massive national following. Divine stars in this movie where the main characters compete for the title of "The Filthiest People Alive." Divine portrays Babs Johnson, the leader of a strange group of perverts who live in a trailer park outside of Baltimore. Her competitor for the title is Connie Marble (played by Mink Stole), an uptight woman whose hobby is kidnapping girls, chaining them in her basement, getting them pregnant via artificial insemination, and selling their infants to lesbian couples. To ensure obtaining the title, the characters perform many disgusting acts, such as drooling over an entire house, decapitating live chickens, and—as the *piece de resistance* of the film—eating dog feces.

Waters was able to debut the film at his alma mater, the University of Baltimore. The film was such a hit that a commercial distributor picked it up and screened it in Boston. It bombed there, but Waters believed that it would do well in the midnight theaters in New York City. He was right. *Pink Flamingos* became one of the most popular underground films of the 1970s, grossing more than one hundred times the amount of its filming budget, and becoming one of the most profitable films ever released. This cult classic still plays in movie houses around the country. Waters later claimed in a *Contemporary Authors* interview that the success of *Pink Flamingos* proves that he has always been a mainstream movie producer. "*Pink Flamingos,* when you think about it, was a very, very commercial movie. It only cost ten–thousand dollars and it had to compete with every major studio production, so I put in something that no one would ever do. That's commercial. When you have no money, you have to do something completely different to get anybody to come see the film."

Many critics lambasted *Pink Flamingos,* unable or unwilling to see any humor in this parade of depravity. Joseph Gelmis of *New York Newsday* claimed that the film "is bottom–of–the–barrel bathroom humor, juvenile perversity, amateurishly written, acted, and directed." The filmmaker was undaunted by the opinions of the mainstream critics, however; as he told *Contemporary Authors,*

The lovable, if tacky Turnblads--played by Jerry Stiller, Ricki Lake, and Divine--are one of two families highlighted in Waters' 1988 offering *Hairspray.*

"The right kind of negative reviews were a very big help. In the late 1960s and early 1970s, there was a cultural war going on, and when you got a bad review from Rex Reed, it helped." In addition, alternative publications such as the *Village Voice* and *Interview* praised the director's work, adding to his cult status. Waters himself felt that he had created a whole new genre of films—those with "good bad taste." Generally, his definition of good bad taste was simple: campy mass culture was good bad taste, while prime–time television, an entertainment media that took itself too seriously, was not.

Waters raced through the rest of the 1970s, furiously writing and producing movies. *Pink Flamingos* helped him gain the momentum he needed to complete three films before 1982. The first of these was *Female Trouble,* a 1974 release that highlighted Divine as Dawn Davenport, a teenage runaway who lands a job at a beauty salon and becomes obsessed with beauty and glamour. She turns to murder as her obsession drives her mad, and is eventually sentenced to death by the electric chair.

Desperate Living premiered in 1977. It was the first film in many years that did not do well at the box office; it also did not feature Divine, as the actor did not appear in the film due to another job offer. *Desperate Living* takes place in the tacky town of Mortville, where the depraved residents secretly try to overthrow their evil queen. Other memorable characters include a four–hundred–pound housekeeper and a scarred lesbian. This film marked a turning point for Waters. Feedback from the critics indicated that most, including many of his past supporters, considered the film only for hard–core cult film fans. Well past thirty when the film was released, Waters re–thought what messages he wanted to champion in his films. He told *Midnight Movies* that "I had this nightmare of myself at 80, making movies about people eating colostomy bags."

Beyond Midnight Showings

Waters toned down the disgust factor for his 1981 picture, *Polyester*. Once again, the film featured Divine in the lead role. However, *Polyester* was sufficiently mainstream to earn an R rating, whereas his other films had consistently been rated X, keeping them out of regular movie theaters. One of the interesting points about the movie was that it employed a process Waters called "Odorama." Moviegoers were given scratch–and–sniff cards when they entered the theater. They received cues on the screen as to when to scratch the appropriate areas of the card, releasing such distinct odors as foods, sweaty shoes, and intestinal gas. In the picture, Divine stars as Francine Fishpaw, a Baltimore homemaker with many family troubles. Her daughter, Lulu, is trying to get an abortion, her son is suspected of being insane, and to top it off, the family dog decides to commit suicide. And, in order to revenge herself on her unfaithful husband, she decides to have an affair of her own—with movie heartthrob Tab Hunter.

Polyester was greeted with enthusiasm by the viewing public, further spreading Waters's vision. This was exactly what the filmmaker had intended. He related to Lodge that "I wanted to make a film that would . . . reach those who would be frightened to see my other films. I wanted to infect a larger group of people . . .

make the cancer grow." By all accounts, he accomplished his goal, for the movie was more widely distributed and put his name into the national media. Mainstream critics, too, were impressed with the film; *Newsweek*'s David Ansen, for instance, remarked that "this suburban tale is a rancidly hilarious piece of Americana." Vincent Canby likewise observed in the *New York Times* that *Polyester* "demonstrates gifts for social satire that were largely lost in . . . [Waters'] earlier work." While the filmmaker "still celebrates the seedy, the tacky and the second–rate," the critic explained, in *Polyester* Waters's work has "a coherence and a wit that sharpen the point of view."

Once Waters got a taste of the mainstream (or the "M" word, as he jokingly called it), he couldn't be stopped. His next film, *Hairspray,* carried the even less extreme rating of PG, and enjoyed a relatively widespread release to enthusiastic audiences. *Hairspray* is a satire that is half teen flick and half message movie. Talk show host Ricki Lake stars as Tracy Turnblad, the obese daughter of the equally obese Edna (played by Divine). Tracy becomes popular when she appears on *The*

"Drapes" Ricki Lake and Johnny Depp lure "Square" Amy Locane to take a ride on the wild side in Waters' 1990 musical *Crybaby.*

Sam Waterston and Kathleen Turner starred in *Serial Mom*, which tells the story of a normal suburban mother with one flaw: she kills people who fail to live up to her rather stringent personal standards.

Corny Collins Show, an afternoon television dance show featuring teens with large, lacquered hairdos. Tracy soon gets a reputation as the girl with the right dance moves and becomes queen of the show, displacing her pretty, thin, and rich rival, Amber. She decides that she will use her newfound power to racially integrate the show. "Waters treats the message movie as a genre to be parodied, just like the teenpic," Pauline Kael of the *New Yorker* stated. "Combining the two, he comes up with an entertainingly imbecilic musical comedy—a piece of pop dadaism."

Despite the success the movie enjoyed, critics still knew Waters had a twist that other filmmakers lacked. David Ansen commented in *Newsweek* that "Waters cult–followers needn't fear a sellout: mainstream Waters is still like nothing else on the block." About his new–found popularity, Waters joked to Geist: "I'd love to sell out completely. It's just that nobody has been willing to buy." The success of *Hairspray,* however, brought the filmmaker to the attention of Hollywood, making it

easier for him to obtain financing for his work. Sadly, just two short weeks after *Hairspray* debuted, Divine died of a heart attack. Waters commented upon the tragedy to *Contemporary Authors:* "His death really stunk. You work for more than twenty years, and you deserve more than a week to enjoy it. He knew the movie was a hit; he'd sit in his bed and ask me to read him all the good reviews. But he had a lot of plans. There's nothing good I can say about it."

Waters returned to the screen in 1990 with a new not–far–from–mainstream movie musical, *Crybaby.* This time he had an "almost big–time budget" to film his vision. The movie takes place in 1954, when teenagers in Baltimore were divided roughly into two camps—"Squares," the cleancut do-gooders; and "Drapes," the punks with greased–back hair and a tough attitude. Johnny Depp stars as the lead Drape. As the son of two executed bombers, he sports an electric–chair tattoo and is prone to crying spells (hence he acquires the nickname "Cry–Baby"). He clamors for the attention of Allison (Amy Locane), a Square, and eventually wins her love as she turns into a Drape.

Campy Casting

Once again, Waters's casting was beyond unique. He combined his favorite old movie stars, such as Troy Donahue, with rocker Iggy Pop and kidnapped heiress Patricia Hearst. In this send–up of the "wild kid" or "rebel" movie, Waters moved one step further into the mainstream. Still, he feels that he hasn't compromised his alternative roots. Waters told Robert Seidenberg in *Entertainment Weekly* that "There are some people that hate the fact that I made a Hollywood movie, but for me, that's getting the last laugh. It's the ultimate subversive thing to do."

Critical reaction to *Cry–Baby* was less enthusiastic than that for *Hairspray,* as was audience response. While *Time*'s Richard Corliss found the film a "parody paradise" that "once it gets revved up . . . is keen fun," Owen Gleiberman commented in *Entertainment Weekly* that "the satire is muted and scattershot," and the film "a little tiresome." A *Variety* reviewer noted that Waters's "old and new intentions don't always mix comfortably," with the worn plot of star–crossed lovers failing to support the director's "wicked sense of humor." But while Suzanne Moore wrote in *New Statesman and Society* that the film is "a bit too knowing, too self–consciously culty to be really successful," she added that the film is "all good, clean fun, which is the last thing I thought I'd ever say about a John Waters movie."

In 1994, Waters released another twisted film, *Serial Mom,* this time with a major Hollywood star in the lead. Kathleen Turner plays the excessively normal, suburban mother with a dark side. As Waters explained it to Eve Golden in *Movieline:* "She's the mother most of my friends wish they'd had. She just has this one problem. She overreacts and kills people." She murders for a variety of reasons—seeing someone who refuses to recycle or witnessing another person being cruel to her children. When she finally gets caught, she is excessively homespun and polite even to her jury.

Critical reception of *Serial Mom* was mixed. Anthony Lane wrote in the *New Yorker* that "it's worth catching *Serial Mom* to get a buzz of enjoyment off Kathleen Turner," yet he adds that "Waters' determination to shock—the one true motor of his movies—is getting tame and tired." *Time*'s Corliss, however, called the film "a spiffy new farce," particularly in "Mom's delirious trial and exploitation." Waters explained the movie's aim to Golden: "I'm asking you to laugh at something that basically isn't funny in real life. I'm always tryin' to get away with murder—this time, literally!" He later added, however, that "I don't think [serial killers] are funny. What *Serial Mom* is about is the fame that happens from it. I think *that* is funny."

Waters has also become well known for his lectures and books on various tacky topics. *Crackpot: The Obsessions of John Waters* is a collection of fifteen essays that originally appeared in a variety of magazines. He contemplates such things as the actress Pia Zadora, his 101 top loves and hates, and his reasons to enjoy the tabloid *National Enquirer.* Patrick Goldstein commented in the *Los Angeles Times Book Review* that in the book, "Waters proves just as gifted as a satirist as a film maker." *Booklist* reviewer Ray Olson called this collection of "ferociously, loonily hilarious" essays "incredibly good," while Jonathan Yardley commented in the *Washington Post* that "Waters is the ultimate connoisseur of pop culture gone berserk."

"Everybody has great secrets, and I want to know them all," Waters told Richard Corliss in *Time.* "I like to find things that can surprise me and confuse me and scare me and make me laugh." Waters has had an amazing career of airing out the tawdry secrets of the world on film, and has received much success from it. Yet, there is also a side to his filmmaking that vaguely innocent. He told Pat Aufderheide in *American Film* that "All my movies are very moral. The underdogs always win. The bitter people are punished, and people who are happy with themselves win." He further explained to Corliss why his humor is successful: "Here's the reason people can laugh about it. I've had a long day, you've had a long day, other people have been fired, they've been hurt in a relationship—*but they were not eaten today by Jeffrey Dahmer!*"

■ Works Cited

Ansen, David, review of *Polyester, Newsweek,* June 1, 1981.

Ansen, David, "A Shock Artist Goes Mainstream," *Newsweek,* February 29, 1988, p. 70.

Aufderheide, Pat, "The Domestication of John Waters," *American Film,* April, 1990, pp. 32–27.

Canby, Vincent, review of *Polyester, New York Times,* June 7, 1981.

Corliss, Richard, "Teen Tough," *Time,* April 23, 1990, pp. 90–1.

Corliss, Richard, "Sultan of Shock," *Time,* April 18, 1994, p. 74.

Review of *Cry–Baby, Variety,* April 2, 1990, pp. 2, 12.

Geist, William, "John Waters," *People,* March 14, 1988, pp. 61–2, 65.

Gelmis, Joseph, review of *Pink Flamingos, New York Newsday,* August 1, 1973.

Gleiberman, Owen, review of *Cry–Baby, Entertainment Weekly,* April 6, 1990, p. 18.

Golden, Eve, "Does This Man Look Like a Child Molester?," *Movieline,* April, 1994, pp. 57–91.

Goldstein, Patrick, review of *Crackpot, Los Angeles Times Book Review,* November 16, 1986, p. 4.

Hoberman, J. and Jonathan Rosenbaum, *Midnight Movies,* Harper & Row, 1983.

Kael, Pauline, review of *Hairspray, New Yorker,* March 7, 1988, pp. 87–88.

Lane, Anthony, review of *Serial Mom, New Yorker,* May 2, 1994, p. 108.

L'Ecuyer, Gerald, interview with Waters, *Egg,* April, 1990.

Lodge, Sally A., interview with Waters, *Publishers Weekly,* July 17, 1981.

Moore, Suzanne, review of *Cry–Baby, New Statesman and Society,* July 27, 1990.

Olson, Ray, review of *Crackpot, Booklist,* September 15, 1986, p. 97.

Robert Seidenberg, "Setting up Camp on Main Street," *Entertainment Weekly,* April 6, 1990, pp. 48–53.

Waters, John, interview in *Contemporary Authors,* Volume 130, Gale, 1990.

Yardley, Jonathan, review of *Crackpot, Washington Post,* September 24, 1986.

■ For More Information See

PERIODICALS

New York, February 29, 1988, pp. 117–18.

New York Times Book Review, November 6, 1986, p. 33.

People, March 12, 1990, p. 102.

Premiere, August, 1993, p. 25.

Publishers Weekly, September 5, 1986, p. 94.

Time, February 29, 1988, p. 101.

—Sketch by Nancy E. Rampson

August Wilson

■ Personal

Born Frederick August Kittel in 1945, in Pittsburgh, PA; son of Frederick August (a baker) and Daisy (a cleaning woman; maiden name, Wilson) Kittel, and stepfather, David Bedford; married second wife, Judy Oliver (a social worker), 1981 (marriage ended); married Constanza Romero (a costume designer); children: (first marriage) Sakina Ansari.

■ Addresses

Home—Seattle, WA. *Office*—c/o John Breglio, Paul Weiss Rifkind Wharton & Garrison, 1285 Avenue of the Americas, New York, NY 10019.

■ Career

Playwright. Black Horizons on the Hill (a theater company), Pittsburgh, PA, cofounder (with Rob Penny), scriptwriter, and director, 1968–78; Science Museum of Minnesota, St. Paul, MN, scriptwriter, 1979.

■ Awards, Honors

New York Drama Critics' Circle Award for best play of 1984–85, Antoinette Perry (Tony) Award nomination for best play, 1985, and Whiting Writers Award, Whiting Foundation, 1986, all for *Ma Rainey's Black Bottom;* American Theatre Critics Outstanding Play Award, 1986, Drama Desk Award for best new play of 1986–87, New York Drama Critics' Circle Award for best play of 1986–87, Pulitzer Prize for drama, 1987, Antoinette Perry Award for best play, 1987, and Outer Critics Circle Award for best Broadway play, 1987, all for *Fences;* John Gasner Award for best American playwright, Outer Critics Circle, 1987; named Artist of the Year by *Chicago Tribune,* 1987; New York Drama Critics' Circle Award for best play of 1987–88, and Antoinette Perry Award nomination for best play, 1988, both for *Joe Turner's Come and Gone;* named to list of Literary Lions by New York Public Library, 1988; Drama Desk Award for Outstanding New Play of 1989–90, New York Drama Critics' Circle Award for best play of 1989–90, Pulitzer Prize for drama, 1990, Antoinette Perry Award nomination for best play, 1990, and American Theatre Critics Outstanding Play Award, 1990, all for *The Piano Lesson;* Black Filmmakers Hall of Fame award, 1991; Antoinette Perry Award nomination for best play, and American Theatre Critics' Association Award, both 1992, both for *Two Trains Running;* Clarence Muse Award, 1992. Also recipient of Bush and Guggenheim Foundation fellowships.

■ Writings

PLAYS

Jitney (two-act), first produced in Pittsburgh, PA, 1982.

Ma Rainey's Black Bottom (first produced at Yale Repertory Theatre, New Haven, CT, 1984; produced on Broadway, 1984), New American Library, 1985.

Fences (first produced at Yale Repertory Theatre, 1985, produced on Broadway, 1987), New American Library, 1986.

Joe Turner's Come and Gone (first produced at Yale Repertory Theatre, 1986; produced on Broadway, 1988), New American Library, 1988.

The Piano Lesson (first produced at Yale Repertory Theatre, 1987; produced on Broadway, 1990; also see below), Dutton, 1990.

Three Plays (contains *Ma Rainey's Black Bottom, Fences,* and *Joe Turner's Come and Gone*), University of Pittsburgh Press, 1991.

Two Trains Running (first produced at Yale Repertory Theatre, 1990, produced on Broadway, 1992), New American Library/Dutton, 1993.

Seven Guitars, first produced in Chicago, IL, 1995.

The Piano Lesson (teleplay; adapted from his play), "Hallmark Hall of Fame," CBS-TV, 1995.

Also author of the plays *The Homecoming,* 1979, *The Coldest Day of the Year,* 1979, *Fullerton Street,* 1980, *Black Bart and the Sacred Hills,* 1981, and *The Mill Hand's Lunch Bucket,* 1983. Author of the book for a stage musical about jazz musician Jelly Roll Morton.

OTHER

Poetry represented in anthologies, including *The Poetry of Blackamerica.* Contributor of poems to periodicals, including *Black Lines* and *Connection.*

■ Sidelights

When playwright August Wilson was in his late teens he heard, for the first time, the blues as recorded by singer Bessie Smith. "I was literally stunned," he told Ben Brantley of *New York Times.* "And I listened to it again and again for 22 straight times. And I said, '. . . this belongs to me. This is mine.'" In the blues Wilson found a genuine, reliable expression of the African experience in America which shaped his understanding of black identity. Wilson began to perceive something of Bessie Smith's soulfulness and honesty in every black individual, something he attributed to the shared African-American legacy of cultural dislocation, slavery, and racism. "Blacks' cultural response to the world is contained in blues," Wilson asserted in a *New York Newsday* interview.

Beginning with the blues, then, Wilson has set out to document and confirm the African-American experience. He has launched an ambitious cycle of ten plays, one set in each decade of the twentieth century, which depict the hardships faced by blacks in America. With six of the plays complete, Wilson's work has been widely hailed by critics. Among his numerous awards, including an Antoinette Perry Award, or "Tony," Wilson has garnered two Pulitzer Prizes for drama. As Frank Rich proclaimed in *New York Times,* "August Wilson continues to rewrite the history of the American theater by bringing the history of black America—and with it the history of white America—to the stage."

August Wilson was born Frederick August Kittel in Pittsburgh, Pennsylvania, in 1945. His father, Frederick August Kittel, was a white baker of German descent. Wilson's father did not live with the family, and his infrequent visits failed to establish him as a fixture in Wilson's life. As a result, Wilson never really connected to his father, or to his father's European heritage. Instead, it was his mother Daisy Wilson's world in which Wilson grew up. Wilson's mother had migrated to Pittsburgh from rural North Carolina in 1937. She settled in a predominantly poor, black neighborhood known as the Hill. Wilson's mother worked as a cleaning lady to support him and his five siblings. Despite their poverty, Wilson's mother kept her family fed and optimistic, and managed to shield her children from the abuses she had suffered in the segregated south.

Pittsburgh, however, was not free of racism. Wilson struggled through a series of setbacks as a student, many of which were the result of racist attitudes. In high school, Wilson was accused of handing in the work of another when a teacher judged that Wilson's term paper on Napoleon was too good to be his own. "The next day," Wilson recounted in *Time,* "I went and played basketball outside the principal's window, obviously in the unconscious hope that someone would ask why I wasn't in class. No one did, and that was that." At fifteen, Wilson quietly dropped out of school and began working.

Discovers the Harlem Renaissance

Determined to educate himself, Wilson spent spare hours in the public library. There, in a section labeled "Negro," Wilson discovered the writers of the Harlem Renaissance, including Ralph Ellison, Langston Hughes, Richard Wright, and Arna Bontemps. These writers had addressed the African-American experience with a clarity that Wilson found compelling. "Those books were a comfort," Wilson told Samuel G. Freedman of the *New York Times*. "Just the idea that black people would write books. I wanted my book up there, too. I used to dream about being part of the Harlem Renaissance." Inspired by the work of these writers, Wilson began to split his time between working and writing. He concentrated his early efforts on poetry, some of which was published in the reviews *Black Lines* and *Connection*.

"Extraordinary...a major find for the American theatre."
—Frank Rich, The New York Times

Ma Rainey's Black Bottom

A Play By
August Wilson

PLUME Ⓟ

In this 1985 work, Wilson tells a fictional story about the legendary blues singer, Ma Rainey, and her rehearsal at a recording studio in 1927.

Not long after his crucial exposure to the blues, Wilson began to frequent a gathering place for former railroad porters, believing that the experiences of ordinary blacks were essential to any legitimate African-American art. "I kept quiet," he told Brantley of the *New York Times*. "For the most part, I still do. I kept quiet and listened to all kinds of philosophy, ideas, and attitudes." Some of these conversations impressed themselves on Wilson's memory, others he noted on a pad. While Wilson grasped the value of these narratives, and the lives they described, he still had to come to terms with their language. "I thought in order to make art out of it you had to change it around," he confessed.

When he was twenty, Wilson moved out of his mother's house. In the same year he wrote a term paper for his sister, who was in college at the time, titled "Two Violent Poets—Robert Frost and Carl Sandburg." In return, Wilson's sister sent him twenty dollars. He promptly bought a used Royal typewriter. Including his mother's maiden name, Wilson typed out all the permutations of his given name, finally adopting the name August Wilson. "When I bought the typewriter, that meant I was not going to be a bus driver and I was not going to be a lawyer," Wilson informed Brantley. "It meant I was going to write." Wilson was writing poetry at the time, and was strongly influenced by Welsh lyric poet Dylan Thomas and American poet John Berryman. He was also beginning to explore the short story as a form of literature. Wilson's writing gained him access to a group of black writers and artists from the Hill who were attempting to create, and support, an African-American art movement. Wilson, who had not attempted writing for theatre, encountered an issue of the *Tulane Drama Review* devoted to the black theatre movement. It was the beginning of his career as a playwright.

Founds Black Theatre Company

During this period of upheaval and reform in American society Wilson became involved with the Black Power movement, and was initially attracted to theatre as a vehicle for advancing its political agenda. In 1968, with playwright and professor Rob Penny, Wilson founded Black Horizons on the Hill, a theatre company committed to the production of work by black writers. The company determined to raise political consciousness by appealing to the broadest possible segment of the

A PLAY BY
AUGUST WILSON
Author of
Ma Rainey's Black Bottom

WITH AN INTRODUCTION BY
LLOYD RICHARDS

WINNER OF THE 1987 PULITZER PRIZE FOR DRAMA

FENCES

This 1987 winner of the Pulitzer Prize for drama examines the life of a man denied the opportunity to play major league baseball because of his race, and the difficulty he has accepting the liberation of the 1960s.

neighborhood population. Original work not only had to be produced, it had to be seen to realize its intentions. In the opinion of Freedman of the *New York Times,* Wilson did not fit comfortably into this solely political format. His interests in the presentation of drama went beyond propaganda, and he was still wrestling with the voices and dialogue of his characters, which, he hoped, would be the true voice of the Hill. Under Penny's direction, Wilson learned the fundamentals of play writing. For the next ten years Wilson was associated with Black Horizons, and was completely immersed in the vigorous black cultural scene developing in Pittsburgh, a scene that encompassed not only theatre, but jazz and art.

In 1978 Wilson visited friend and former Black Horizons associate Claude Purdy in St. Paul, Minnesota, where Purdy directed a black theatre called Penumbra. Wilson found the relaxed atmosphere of Minnesota to his liking, and moved to St. Paul. He took a job as a scriptwriter for the Science Museum of Minnesota, writing dialogue for presentations at the museum. With Purdy's encouragement, Wilson pursued his literary ambitions through the Playwrights Center in Minneapolis. With some distance between himself and his native Pittsburgh, Wilson's writing underwent a remarkable transformation: he grasped the artistic potential of black speech. "Being removed was what enabled me to hear," Wilson explained to Jack Kroll of *Newsweek.* "All those voices came back to me in a rush. I sat down to write a play called *Jitney* and the characters just talked to me. In fact they were talking so fast that I couldn't get it all down."

Jitney is set at a cab station illegally situated in a vacant Pittsburgh storefront. The realistic drama explores the lives of the cabbies, and was first produced at the Allegheny Repertory Theatre in Pittsburgh in 1982. The play had a popular run at the theatre, but Wilson's follow-up, *Fullerton Street,* failed to advance his reputation. Wilson then resumed work on an unfinished manuscript, which he submitted to the O'Neill Theatre Center's Playwrights Conference as *Ma Rainey's Black Bottom.* The play was given a staged reading, and Lloyd Richards, the conference director, was sufficiently impressed to mount a production at Yale's Repertory Theatre, which he also directed. Throughout production, Richards worked with Wilson to refine the play and tighten the dialogue.

First Major Production

Ma Rainey's Black Bottom, the first play in Wilson's planned ten-play cycle, is a fictional episode in the life of legendary blues singer Ma Rainey set in the late 1920s. The action takes place in a rehearsal room and recording studio in Chicago, and is focused mainly on the conversation of four musicians who are waiting for Ma to begin a recording session. As the drama unfolds, the marks that racism has left on each of these talented performers is revealed; each has his own method of dealing with injustice. The bandleader, a trombonist, is resigned to the indignities of racism and avoids confrontation. The pianist seeks intellectual solutions to racial division, while the self-indulgent bassist simply ignores the systematic abuse. It is the group's trumpeter, Levee, who is most painfully scarred by the experience of racism. Levee's memory of his mother's rape by a gang of white men has convinced him that reconciliation between the races isn't possible. When Levee is fired by Ma Rainey for promoting a more upbeat version of the tune "Ma Rainey's Black Bottom" and is subsequently cheated out of his share of the recording pay, a seemingly trivial incident sparks a violent outburst against one of his bandmates. Levee has suffered too much at the hands of those around him, both white and black, to avoid destruction.

With its Yale premier, *Ma Rainey's Black Bottom* was recognized by critics as the work of a noteworthy new voice in American theatre. Wilson's control of poetic language was recognized, and his ability to combine humor and tragic realism convincingly also received praise. The play moved onto Broadway where it was produced at the Cort Theatre. The *Chicago Tribune*'s Richard Christiansen characterized this production as "a work of intermittent but immense power." The play received the New York Drama Critics' Circle Award for best play, the Whiting Writers' Award, and a nomination for the Antoinette Perry Award, or "Tony," for best play.

In addition to establishing Wilson as a significant figure in American drama, *Ma Rainey's Black Bottom* marked the commencement of a collaboration between Lloyd and Wilson that was to continue through Wilson's next four plays. Wilson's work thereafter received its first staged reading at the O'Neill Theatre, and then premiered at Yale under Lloyd's direction before moving unto Broadway. Throughout the years of their working relationship, Lloyd exerted considerable critical influence, often compelling Wilson to craft and hone his work.

Fences Captures Pulitzer Prize for Drama

Wilson's second major play proved an even greater success than *Ma Rainey*. *Fences* earned Wilson his first Pulitzer Prize as well as the Antoinette Perry Award for best play. Set in the 1950s, *Fences* examines the life of Troy Maxson, a Pittsburgh garbage collector who was denied the opportunity to play major league baseball as a young man because of his race. When Troy's son,

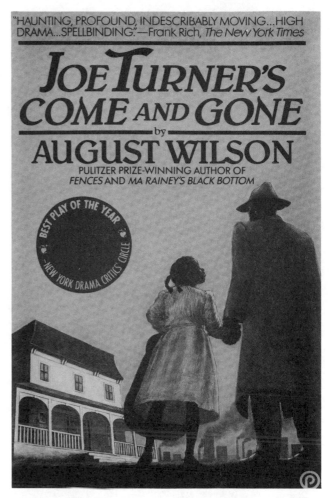

"HAUNTING, PROFOUND, INDESCRIBABLY MOVING...HIGH DRAMA...SPELLBINDING."—Frank Rich, *The New York Times*

JOE TURNER'S COME AND GONE
by
AUGUST WILSON
PULITZER PRIZE-WINNING AUTHOR OF
FENCES AND *MA RAINEY'S BLACK BOTTOM*

BEST PLAY OF THE YEAR
—NEW YORK DRAMA CRITICS CIRCLE

A man illegally sold into a chain gang struggles to regain his identity and place in society when he is freed seven years later.

Cory, is presented with a football scholarship, Troy insists that he refuse the offer. Troy is guided in his decision by a misplaced desire to protect his son from potential racism, a reluctance to believe that opportunities once closed to him are now available to his son, and finally, simple jealousy. Nonetheless, Troy is a strong-willed man who has toiled to become the first black employed in the Pittsburgh sanitation department. "Troy Maxson can turn gales of rage on the son who adores him," observed Freedman in the *New York Times Magazine*, "but he also feeds him, clothes him, teaches him." Troy's dependability as a family man is further eroded, however, when an affair with another woman is exposed. The pregnant girlfriend dies in childbirth, and it is Troy's wife Rose who demonstrates her strength when she agrees to raise the child as her own. In the final confrontation between father and son, Cory brandishes a baseball bat, symbol of all Troy's lost aspirations. Frank Rich of the *New York Times* noted that *Fences* "leaves no doubt that Mr. Wilson is a major writer, combining a poet's ear for vernacular with a robust sense of humor . . . , a sure instinct for cracking dramatic incident and passionate commitment to a great subject."

Wilson's next play, *Joe Turner's Come and Gone,* came to Broadway while *Fences* was still running. Set in 1911, *Joe Turner* presents the loss of culture, family, and identity suffered by blacks who migrated from the Southern United States to the North in the years following the Civil War. The play opens in a boardinghouse in Pittsburgh, where several migrants have taken residence. Dressed in black and desperately clutching his

In Wilson's second Pulitzer Prize winner, a sister and brother argue over the fate of a piano which she thinks should be saved as a family legacy and which he would like to sell so that he can buy the property where his ancestors were slaves.

eleven-year-old daughter, Herald Loomis appears at the boardinghouse door seeking the wife who abandoned him a decade earlier. At that time, Loomis, a former churchman, had been illegally sold into bondage by the notorious bounty-hunter Joe Turner. For seven years Loomis labored as a virtual slave. Shortly after the ominous arrival of Loomis, the residents gather for Sunday dinner. During the meal they spontaneously break into an African *juba.* Only Loomis stays apart, refusing to join the communal singing and dancing. During the celebration Loomis is overcome by an extraordinary vision, one of skeletons crossing an ocean, and collapses. He is revived by Bynum Walker, a resident with an inclination for the supernatural, who advises Loomis that he must come to terms with his past if he is ever to be free. With Walker's guidance, Loomis gradually recovers the spirit that was nearly extinguished by oppression and alienation.

Joe Turner's Come and Gone is "not about slavery," noted *New York Post* reviewer Clive Barnes. "It's about the results of slavery; it is about separation. Separation from roots, separation from kith and kin, separation within one's own psychic self." Frank Rich of the *New York Times* considered the play Wilson's best to date, and reserved special praise for Wilson's handling of the relationship between Loomis and Walker. "An American writer in the deepest sense," Rich declared, "August Wilson has once again shown us how in another man's freedom we find our own."

The Piano Lesson Earns Second Pulitzer

In 1990, Wilson was awarded his second Pulitzer Prize for *The Piano Lesson.* Set in the depression-era 1930s, the play pits brother against sister in a contest to decide the future of a valuable heirloom. Decades ago, a white slave-owner exchanged Doaker Charles' grandmother and father for the piano that now sits in Doaker's livingroom. At the time of the trade, Doaker's grief-stricken grandfather, the plantation carpenter, carved African-style portraits of his lost wife and son onto the piano. Years later, Doaker's older brother successfully plotted the theft of the piano and was killed in the aftermath. Doaker's son, Boy Willie, now wants to finance the ironic dream of purchasing the property in Mississippi where his ancestors were slaves by selling the piano. His sister Berniece, however, vehemently opposes the sale, the very thought of which she considers a

This play focuses on the reactions of a diner's regular customers when they learn that the restaurant will be torn down to make room for the city's renovation project.

depiction of racism in America as socially worthy but artistically "monotonous, limited, locked in a perception of victimization." Brustein expressed hope that Wilson would "develop that radical poet strain that now lies dormant in his work." Barnes of the *New York Post,* however, called the work the "best and most immediate" play of Wilson's cycle, adding: "This is a play in which to lose yourself—to give yourself up . . . to August Wilson's thoughts, humors and thrills, all caught in a microcosm largely remote for many of us from our own little worlds, yet always talking the same language of humanity." The critic concluded: "This is a wonderful play that lights up man. See it, wonder at it, and recognize it."

Wilson later adapted *The Piano Lesson* for a "Hallmark Hall of Fame" television production starring Charles Dutton as Boy Willie. John J. O'Connor of *New York Times* concluded that the adaptation successfully maintained the tensions of the original stage play. "If anything, *The Piano Lesson* is even more effective in this shortened version," asserted O'Connor.

Wilson continued his ten-play cycle with *Two Trains Running,* which came to Broadway in 1992. Set in a run-down diner in the late 1960s, the play involves the regular patrons' reactions to the pending sale of the diner. Some critics found the play had less subtlety and dramatic action than its predecessors, but *Newsweek*'s David Ansen praised the "musical eloquence" of Wilson's language, which he felt enhanced a "thematically rich" work. In 1995, Wilson premiered the sixth play of the cycle, *Seven Guitars.* Occupying the decade of the 1940s, *Seven Guitars* recounts the tragic undoing of blues guitarist Floyd Barton. The play opens with a gathering of friends who have come to mourn Floyd's untimely death. The action of the play then flashes back to recreate the events of Floyd's last week of life. Floyd has recently recorded his first hit and has the opportunity to record another if he can reach a Chicago studio. Floyd, however, has neither the money to buy a new guitar or a bus ticket to Chicago. While Floyd tries to find the money necessary for the trip, he also attempts reconciliation with his former girlfriend, Vera. The play "bristles with symbolism, with rituals of word and action that explode into anguished eloquence and finally into violence," wrote *Newsweek* reviewer Jack Kroll.

desertion of the family legacy. The ghost of the former slave owner mysteriously inhabits Doaker's house, and it also appears to have designs on the piano. The conflict between Willie and Berniece escalates, threatening violence, until Willie's final attempt to remove the piano is foiled by the ghost. After confronting the spirit Willie decides to leave the piano where it is. In Willie's final speech, he tells Berniece to keep playing the piano, otherwise he and the ghost are likely to return for it.

While acclaim for *The Piano Lesson* was wide-ranging, *New Republic* reviewer Robert Brustein, Richard Lloyd's predecessor as director of the Yale Repertory Theatre, considered the supernatural elements an intrusion in the otherwise realistic play. Brustein also characterized Wilson's ongoing

Seven Guitars was the first Wilson play produced without the direction of Richards, who was forced to abandon the project due to illness. The task of directing fell to Walter Dallas, whose staging at the Goodman Theatre in Chicago William Tynan characterized as "skillful" in a *Time* review. Tynan concluded that the play needed refining—Wilson is well-known for frequently revising his work during early stagings—but expressed confidence that Wilson would find solutions for the play's problem areas. "Given all that's right with play, it deserves no less," Tynan added.

Throughout his career Wilson has stressed that his main priority is getting his work produced. His exceptional skill and success in bringing the African-American experience to the American theatre are certain to ensure future productions. As Robert L. King wrote in *Massachusetts Review*: "Wilson sees the images of the past as layered truth; to peel away or to penetrate is to distort, yet as a playwright he has challenged himself to explore the black American heritage, a heritage of conflicting, sometimes self-serving voices greater than the sum of its historical facts."

■ Works Cited

Ansen, David, review of *Two Trains Running*, *Newsweek*, April 27, 1992, p. 70.

Barnes, Clive, "O'Neill in Blackface," *New York Post*, March 28, 1988.

Barnes, Clive, "'Piano Lesson' Hits All the Right Keys," *New York Post*, April 17, 1990.

Brantley, Ben, "The World That Created August Wilson," *New York Times*, February 5, 1995, pp. H1, H5.

Brustein, Robert, "The Lesson of 'The Piano Lesson,'" *New Republic*, May 21, 1990, pp. 28–30.

Christiansen, Richard, review of *Ma Rainey's Black Bottom*, *Chicago Tribune*, October 15, 1984.

Freedman, Samuel G., "A Voice from the Streets," *New York Times Magazine*, June 10, 1987, pp. 36, 40, 49, 70.

King, Robert L., "Recent Drama," *Massachusetts Review*, spring, 1988, pp. 87–97.

Kroll, Jack, "August Wilson's Come to Stay," *Newsweek*, April 11, 1988, p. 82.

Kroll, Jack, "August Wilson's Gritty Guitars," *Newsweek*, February 6, 1995, p. 60.

O'Connor, John J., "'The Piano Lesson': A Family Elegy," *New York Times*, February 3, 1995, p. D26.

Rich, Frank, review of *Fences*, *New York Times*, March 27, 1987, p. C3.

Rich, Frank, "Panoramic History of Blacks in America in Wilson's 'Joe Turner,'" *New York Times*, March 28, 1988, p. C15.

Tynan, William, "Death and the Blues," *Time*, February 6, 1995, p. 71.

Wilson, August, interview in *New York Newsday*, April 20, 1987, p. 47.

Wilson, August, interview in *Time*, April 11, 1988, pp. 77–78.

■ For More Information See

BOOKS

Black Literature Criticism, Gale, 1992.

Contemporary Literary Criticism, Gale, Volume 39, 1986, Volume 50, 1988, Volume 63, 1991.

Drama Criticism, Volume 2, Gale, 1992.

Elkins, Marilyn, editor, *August Wilson: A Casebook*, Garland, 1994.

Nadel, Alan, editor, *May All Your Fences Have Gates: Essays on the Drama of August Wilson*, University of Iowa Press, 1994.

Pereira, Kim, *August Wilson and the African American Odyssey*, University of Illinois Press, 1995.

PERIODICALS

Chicago Tribune, June 8, 1987; December 17, 1987; December 27, 1987.

Chicago Tribune Book World, February 9, 1986, pp. 12–13.

Christian Science Monitor, October 16, 1984, pp. 29–30.

Ebony, January, 1985; November, 1987, pp. 68–74.

Esquire, April, 1989, pp. 116–127.

Essence, August, 1987, pp. 51, 111, 113.

Los Angeles Times, November 24, 1984; November 7, 1986; April 17, 1987; June 7, 1987; June 8, 1987; June 9, 1987; February 6, 1988.

Maclean's, May 28, 1990, p. 62; May 18, 1992, pp. 56–57.

Nation, April 18, 1987, p. 518; June 1, 1990, pp. 832–33; June 8, 1992, pp. 799–800.

Newsweek, April 6, 1987.

New York, April 6, 1987, pp. 92, 94.

New Yorker, April 6, 1987, p. 81; April 11, 1988, p. 107; April 30, 1990, p. 85; April 27, 1992, p. 85.

New York Times, April 11, 1984; April 13, 1984; October 12, 1984; October 22, 1984; May 6, 1986; May 14, 1986; June 20, 1986; March 27, 1987; April 5, 1987; April 9, 1987; April 17, 1987; May

7, 1987; December 10, 1987; December 11, 1987; March 27, 1988, pp. 1, 34.

Saturday Review, January/February, 1985.

Theater, fall-winter, 1984, pp. 50–55.

Time, April 6, 1987, p. 81; April 27, 1987; January 30, 1989, p. 69; April 27, 1992, pp. 65–66.

Times (London), November 6, 1984; April 18, 1987; April 24, 1987.

Washington Post, May 20, 1986; April 15, 1987; June 9, 1987; October 4, 1987; October 9, 1987.

—Sketch by D. P. Johnson

Tobias Wolff

Personal

Born Jonathan Ansell Wolff, June 19, 1945, in Birmingham, AL; son of Arthur Saunders Wolff (an aeronautical engineer) and Rosemary (a secretary; maiden name, Loftus) Hutchins; married Catherine Dolores Spohn (an art history teacher and social worker), November 1, 1975; children: Michael, Patrick. *Education:* Oxford University, B.A. (first-class honors), 1972, M.A., 1975; Stanford University, M.A., 1978.

Addresses

Home—214 Scott Ave., Syracuse, NY 13244. *Office*—Syracuse University, Department of English, Syracuse, NY 13244-0002.

Career

Writer. Stanford University, Stanford, CA, writer-in-residence, 1975-78; Goddard College, Plainfield, VT, faculty member; Arizona State University, Tempe, faculty member, 1978-80; Syracuse University, NY, faculty member, 1980—. Also worked as a reporter, *Washington Post,* Washington, DC. *Military service:* U.S. Army, Special Forces, 1964-68; served in Vietnam; became first lieutenant. *Member:* PEN, Associated Writing Programs.

Awards, Honors

Wallace Stegner fellowship in creative writing, 1975-76; National Endowment for the Arts fellowship in creative writing, 1978 and 1985; Mary Roberts Rinehart grant, 1979; Arizona Council on the Arts and Humanities fellowship in creative writing, 1980; O. Henry short story prizes, 1980, 1981, and 1985; Guggenheim fellowship, 1982; St. Lawrence Award for Fiction, 1982, for *In the Garden of the North American Martyrs;* PEN/ Faulkner Award for Fiction, 1985, for *The Barracks Thief; Los Angeles Times* Book Prize, 1989, for *This Boy's Life;* Rea Award, 1989; Whiting Writers Award, 1989; National Book Award nomination, 1994, for *In Pharaoh's Army.*

Writings

BOOKS

Ugly Rumours, Allen & Unwin, 1975.

In the Garden of the North American Martyrs (short stories), Ecco Press, 1981 (published in England as *Hunters in the Snow,* Cape, 1982).

(Editor) *Matters of Life and Death: New American Stories,* Wampeter, 1982.

This Boy's Life: A Memoir, Atlantic Monthly, 1989.

The Barracks Thief (novella), Ecco Press, 1984.

Back in the World (short stories), Houghton, 1985.
The Best American Short Stories, Houghton, 1994.
In Pharaoh's Army: Memories of the Lost War, Knopf, 1994.
(Editor and author of introduction) *The Vintage Book of Contemporary American Short Stories,* Vintage Books, 1994.

UNCOLLECTED SHORT STORIES

"The Other Miller," *The Best American Short Stories,* edited by Ann Beattie and Shannon Ravenel, Houghton, 1987.
"Smorgasbord," *The Best American Short Stories,* edited by Mark Helprin and Ravenel, Houghton, 1988.
"Migrane," *Antaeus,* spring-autumn, 1990.
"Sanity," *Atlantic,* December, 1990.

Works also included in *Buying Time: An Anthology Celebrating Twenty Years of the Literature Program of the National Endowment for the Arts,* edited by Scott Walker, Graywolf, 1985. Contributor of short stories and book reviews to periodicals, including *TriQuarterly, Missouri Review, Ploughshares, Atlantic Monthly, Esquire, Vanity Fair,* and *Antaeus.*

■ Adaptations

This Boy's Life has been recorded on audio cassette, and released as a film starring Leonardo DiCaprio and Robert De Niro, Warner Bros., 1994.

■ Sidelights

"I was a liar myself when I was a kid. I'm still a liar, really, and I don't mean just in terms of telling stories and being a story writer. I wouldn't ever want to be held to a literal version of the facts when I tell people a story," Tobias Wolff told Jean W. Ross in a *Contemporary Authors* interview. "I don't know that I'm really capable of it."

Unlike a naughty child inventing stories, or an executive falsifying credentials, Wolff is praised and lauded for his imaginative lies. As enthralled critics have so often observed, Wolff is a master storyteller. His short stories, novels, and memoirs (which are, in themselves, expertly packaged collections of stories) have earned him an assortment of sought-after fellowships and grants, three O. Henry short story prizes, and the prestigious PEN/Faulkner Award for Fiction.

Despite his success in telling lies, however, truthfulness, or at least truthfulness as interpreted through memory, is important to Wolff as well. Much of his fiction is built from reworked recollections, and his memoirs—supposedly works of nonfiction—are embellished or edited versions of his personal history. "All my stories are in one way or another autobiographical," Wolff explained to Ross. "Sometimes they're autobiographical in the actual events which they describe, sometimes more in their depiction of a particular character. In fact, you could say that all of my characters are reflections of myself."

Wolff tries to treat his characters honestly once he has developed them. He revealed to Francine Prose of the *New York Times Magazine* that he felt an "affinity" for Raymond Carver's "standards of honesty and exactness," and his refusal "to destroy his characters with irony that proved his own virtue." Accordingly, with sparse prose, Wolff dwells on realistic, telling moments that represent or challenge the lives of his own characters. As often as not, they are left in the abyss of the daily existence in which they were introduced; they are not allowed happy endings or forced to suffer terrible, moral-proving consequences. Wolff is thus described as a realist and minimalist.

Learning to Lie

As Wolff demonstrates in his memoir, *This Boy's Life,* his childhood was difficult, but ultimately rewarding. His mother, Rosemary Loftus, was the daughter of a navy man who beat her every day. Although she provided security for Wolff, she also accepted a number of violent, unstable, or otherwise destructive men into her life. Tobias Wolff's father, Arthur Samuels Wolff, was a charming and talented liar who concocted a false history for himself and settled down with Loftus in Connecticut.

Prose noted that Arthur Wolff was a con man who, while "charming, charismatic, endlessly inventive," was also "a forger, a passer of bad checks, a car thief, a deadbeat extraordinaire, a compulsive spender, a dandy and a heavy drinker." His deceptions were numerous. Arthur Wolff was the son of a Jewish doctor, but he presented himself as an Episcopalian. Although he had been expelled from various boarding schools, he convinced people that he had degrees from Yale and Oxford. Wolff had also been rejected from the military because of his dental record, but he claimed he'd been a fighter pilot for the Royal Air Force. "Some of Arthur Wolff's schemes worked astonishingly well," commented Prose. "Using faked credentials, he fast-talked himself into a job as an aeronautical engineer and became a top-ranking executive in the booming postwar aviation industry." Eventually, though, his slippery maneuvering resulted in multiple arrests, three jail terms, and two ruined marriages.

The elder Wolff's storytelling talents influenced Tobias. In fact, as he told Ross, "Both my father and my mother were great raconteurs, and my brother is also a wonderful storyteller. It's always been the most natural kind of thing for me to do." Wolff began to write stories when he was just six years old. "I don't know exactly at what time the idea hardened in me to become a writer, but I certainly never wanted to be anything else."

Rosemary left Arthur Wolff when Toby, as Tobias was called, was just five years old. Geoffrey, the couple's elder son, stayed with his father on the East Coast. Rosemary and Toby made their way to Florida, where they lived with her lover, Roy. When Roy's abuse became overwhelming, Rosemary and Toby fled to Utah, where Rosemary thought that she could get rich picking up uranium. Instead, Rosemary found an office job, and her boyfriend from Florida found her. They lived together until he proposed marriage, and then she decided to flee from him once again, this time to Phoenix, Arizona. But instead of waiting for the Phoenix bus at the station, she and Toby took the bus that came before it. That bus deposited the two of them in Seattle, Washington.

After a time in Seattle, where Wolff renamed himself Jack (in honor of novelist Jack London) and made trouble at school, Rosemary married Dwight, a mechanic and house painter with three chil-

Woolf (second from left) pictured in 1958 with other Boy Scouts from his Newhalen, Washington troop.

dren of his own. They moved to the small town of Chinook, Washington, where Wolff was determined to work harder in school and create an entirely new reputation. Dwight's attitude and behavior, however, precluded that possibility. As Richard Eder of *Los Angeles Times Book Review* pointed out, Dwight treated Tobias "as a perpetual interloper and rival."

Dwight tormented and humiliated Wolff with continuous lectures and constant harassment. "Tobias's stepfather assigned him a battery of tedious jobs," related Prose, "stole Tobias's paper-route earnings, [and] traded Tobias's beloved rifle for an ugly, incontinent, gun-shy hunting dog." When Wolff joined the Boy Scouts, Dwight volunteered as an assistant scoutmaster and thus extended his influence beyond his home. Incredibly, as Wolff wrote in *This Boy's Life,* Dwight once painted the interior of their entire house, including the Christmas tree and the piano, white.

It is in this environment, wrote Joel Conarroe in the *New York Times Book Review,* that Wolff "gets an informal education in humiliation, betrayal and injustice, and learns how to fight, cheat, steal, gamble and, especially, lie." Life at home with Dwight and at Concrete High School became increasingly unbearable. Finally, at the age of sixteen, Wolff contacted his brother, Geoffrey, who had not even known where Wolff and his mother had been living. Geoffrey began to write to his younger brother, and Arthur Wolff invited his younger son to visit him in La Jolla, California. The day after Tobias arrived, Wolff left for a trip to Las Vegas with his girlfriend, and left Tobias alone. Later, when Tobias's brother Geoffrey arrived, Arthur had a serious nervous breakdown and was hospitalized. Tobias and Geoffrey used the time to get acquainted.

"Geoffrey was the first person I'd ever met for whom books were the only way in which you could in good conscience spend your life. I already had the notion that I wanted to be a writer, but I'd never been with people to whom books mattered, people who had a sense that this was something a sane person would want to be," Wolff told Prose. In fact, Geoffrey Wolff is an accomplished novelist as well.

This collection of ten short stories examines what life is like for people from various demographic areas.

Wolff Tells a Whopper

Geoffrey had been to Choate and was in school at Princeton. Tobias wanted those things for himself, too, but he knew that his poor grades would not help his cause. Aware that he needed an outstanding academic record to gain acceptance to top schools, he invented one. Wolff forged his transcript and improvised enthusiastic letters of recommendation on school stationary. Noted Wolff in *This Boy's Life,* "I wrote . . . in the words my teachers would have used if they had known me as I knew myself. . . . And on the boy who lived in their letters, the splendid phantom who carried all my hopes, it seems to me I saw, at last, my own face."

Wolff's fabricated history was convincing enough to get him a scholarship to the prestigious Hill School, far from his horrible stepfather in Washington. Unfortunately, Wolff's education had not prepared for him for the rigors of scholarship at the private institution, and he was eventually expelled.

Instead of finishing high school, Wolff eventually joined the army. As he explains in his book *In Pharaoh's Army,* he became a member of the Special Forces, learned Vietnamese, and was sent to Vietnam as an adviser. After serving in the Vietnam War, he visited England. Wolff set his sights on attending Oxford University. He managed to pass the entrance tests after months of study, and, fascinated with his courses, became a serious student. He graduated with a first class honors degree and stayed at Oxford to pursue a master's degree.

After a short stint working as a *Washington Post* reporter, Wolff settled in California. He supported himself with odd jobs and concentrated his efforts on his writing. Wolff's talents were recognized with a Wallace Stegner Fellowship, which allowed him to write in residence at Stanford. He eventually earned another master's degree at that university.

Wolff published *Ugly Rumours* in 1975, then sold several stories to various magazines and journals. Perhaps the most notable of these stories was "Smokers," published in *Atlantic*. In 1981 he unveiled *In the Garden of the North American Martyrs*. This collection of twelve stories was received with praise and enthusiasm by critics. The characters in these collections, from a boy who lies about his family at school to a shy professor who finally manages to speak her mind, are presented within the contexts of the daily lives they have created for themselves. As Le Anne Schreiber of *New York Times Book Review* remarked, Wolff's range in *In the Garden of the North American Martyrs* "extends from fastidious realism to the grotesque and the lyrical." She congratulated Wolff on his ability to allow his characters "scenes of flamboyant madness as well as quiet desperation."

The Barracks Thief Wins Critical Acclaim

Wolff's *The Barracks Thief* earned the writer more praise from critics and readers alike, and was recognized as the best work of fiction in 1984 with the PEN/Faulkner Award. Although, as Walter

Kendrick of *the New York Times Book Review* pointed out, the character of Philip Bishop "plays a minor role in the events that give" the story its title, *The Barracks Thief* is "principally" Bishop's story. The work begins by describing Bishop's childhood, while the conclusion discusses how that childhood led to Bishop's decision to become a soldier. The core of the novella features Bishop's haunting memory of a reckless moment in his past.

The histories of Bishop, Lewis, and Hubbard, three young paratroopers, merge forever in Bishop's mind on the day in 1967 when they are ordered to guard an ammunition dump at Fort Bragg. The three soldiers perversely consider allowing a forest fire to reach the dump and explode it. Lewis later becomes a thief and is thrown out of the army, while Hubbard deserts the force. Bishop, though, goes on to become a "conscientious man, a responsible man, maybe even what you'd call a good man . . . a careful man, addicted to comfort, with an eye for the safe course. . . . I would never do what we did that day at the ammunition dump, threatening people with rifles, nearly getting ourselves blown to pieces for the hell of it."

In the *New York Times Book Review*, Kendrick explained that the characters in *The Barracks Thief* "are portrayed with clear-eyed generosity" and that Wolff leaves it up to his readers to decide whether it is best to live and die in "safe conventionality" or recklessness. *Times Literary Supplement* reviewer Linda Taylor observed that readers may want to take in the book "all at once—the ingenuousness of the narration and the vulnerability of the characters are disarmingly seductive."

Wolff's next book was *Back in the World*. The title alludes to the shared daydreams of American soldiers in Vietnam who told each other about what they would do when they returned home, known as "back in the world." *Back in the World,* a collection of ten short stories, presents an interpretation of what that world is like for many people. In the words of *New York Times Book Review* contributor Russell Banks, *Back in the World* reveals "the inner lives of middle-class loners in the Sun Belt . . . lapsed materialists in a material world trying to ignite a spiritual flame despite being cut off from all traditional sources of the spirit—family, church, art, even politics." While Banks commented that *Back in the World* was not as accomplished as Wolff's first story collection and *The Barracks Thief,* he declared that "Leviathan" and "The Rich Brothers" are "as fine as anything Mr. Wolff has written."

Library Journal critic Shelley Cox called Wolff's grim collection a "brilliant examination of life." She noted that the protagonists in these stories are "cut off" from reality "until a seemingly random" occurrence shakes their perceptions of the world. In "Coming Attractions," a teenager who works in a theater demonstrates a detached emotional state that is almost cruel, yet she summons great strength to fetch a bicycle from the freezing waters of the family swimming pool. The protago-

nist of "Desert Breakdown" is burdened with a pregnant wife but doesn't have the means to support her; when their car won't start, he considers abandoning her. "Leviathan" features the thirtieth birthday party of a cocaine-snorting woman who is just beginning to understand her mortality.

This Boy's Life: A Memoir was an autobiographical book that described, according to Eder, how Wolff "masked and masqueraded his way through a childhood and adolescence that might otherwise have unhinged him." The story begins in 1955 with the flight of Tobias and his mother from Florida and concludes soon after his concoction of a glowing school record has won him admission to the Hill School.

According to *Publishers Weekly,* Wolff "characterizes the crew of grown-up losers with damning objectivity." Eder commented that *This Boy's Life* "is a desperate story. The desperation is conveyed in a narration that is chilly and dispassionate on the whole, vivid in detail, and enlivened by disconcerting comedy." *Times Literary Supplement* critic John Clute reminded readers that *This Boy's Life* is a story about lying, and implied that it demonstrates the benefits of stretching the truth in writing fiction. According to Clute, an episode in which Wolff plays on his mother's emotions to get his way "illuminates something of the deeply engaging craft of the older Wolff's way with a tale." Clute wrote that Wolff's "polishings" and "adroit manipulation of time" allow him to transform "inchoate raw materials into shining fables."

Some critics compared *This Boy's Life* to *The Duke of Deception,* Geoffrey Wolff's memoir about the writers' father, Arthur Wolff. They pondered the fact that both of the Wolff brothers have established themselves as writers of merit despite their divergent childhoods, and noted that they maintain a warm relationship with their mother, Rosemary, even though their books throw a bright spotlight on her sometimes difficult life.

Wolff "Disarms" Vietnam Memories

In Pharaoh's Army: Memories of the Lost War is a long-awaited account of Wolff's memories of his year in Vietnam. Wolff told Ron Fletcher of *Bloomsbury Review* that he hadn't intended to write another memoir after he finished *This Boy's Life,* but a story he wrote about Vietnam was a catalyst for the generation of the memoir. He ex-

"I have not read a book of stories in years that has given me such a shock of amazement and recognition—and such pleasure!"
—RAYMOND CARVER

THE BARRACKS THIEF
and Selected Stories

TOBIAS WOLFF

The author's PEN/Faulkner Award-winning novella and six short stories are featured in this 1984 collection.

plained that to "bring out" such memories "is, in some ways, to disarm" them, and "with any luck you understand the experience better." The first version of the manuscript was a long one, and Wolff found it necessary to shorten it. "A lot of writing is recognizing what should be mentioned and what should go unsaid," he told Fletcher.

In Pharaoh's Army describes the author's training for the special forces and his experiences as an army adviser to a Vietnamese division in the Mekong Delta. His tour of duty is neither glorious nor exciting. While his life is threatened on occasion, he spends most of his time in a muddy village where he performs mundane jobs (like arranging the trade of a rifle for a color television for a superior officer). Wolff does not excel as a soldier. When he is ordered to lead a company on a jump, he misses the target by five miles. *Publisher's Weekly* noted that the book "records his sense of futility and growing disillusionment with the war." The book details the author's decision to leave the army and depart for San Francisco. Later, at Oxford University, his study of English literature allows him to regain his sense of direction.

Although *In Pharaoh's Army* focuses on Wolff's year as a soldier in Vietnam and its aftermath, flashbacks recall other memories and explore other experiences, including those with his father. He also remembers the year he spent in Washington, D.C., studying Vietnamese and conducting a romance (which ultimately failed) with a Russian aristocrat. *Publishers Weekly* praised *In Pharaoh's Army* and the "great candor" with which he "charts . . . his evolution as a human being and a writer." *Booklist* reviewer John Mort wrote that the work is "full of rueful, gracefully rendered anecdotes," expressed in "immaculate prose."

Wolff's Writing Process

In addition to writing his own works, Wolff has edited two short story collections featuring the work of other writers. He also shares his craft with aspiring writers as a teacher at Syracuse University. Working as a teacher has its advantages, Wolff told Ross in *Contemporary Authors*. "I still consider myself lucky to be in a profession where I am given a lot of time to write—a lot more than I would be in any other profession—and not only that, but where people care about writing and give you room to breathe if you're a writer; where you're with other people for whom writing is the most important thing."

When he is not teaching, Wolff writes in a sound-proof room in the Syracuse home he shares with his wife and two sons. Although he has to discipline himself to do so, Wolff works even when he is not in the mood to write. As Wolff told Fletcher of *Bloomsbury Review,* "The very act of working is for me a generative act—that's what gets everything going."

Wolff also spends months writing and revising each story. He explained his need to write and rewrite in his *Contemporary Authors* interview with Ross. "Obviously by the time I come to write the last draft I know where every word is going to go, and every comma. It's in my mind from beginning to end, but there have been lots of surprises along the way that I hope the reader will feel even if I don't feel them when I'm writing the last draft."

■ Works Cited

Banks, Russell, "Aging Clay and the Prodigal Son," *New York Times Book Review,* October 20, 1985, p. 9.

Clute, John, review of *This Boy's Life, Times Literary Supplement,* May 12-18, 1989, p. 508.

Conarroe, Joel, review of *This Boy's Life, New York Times Book Review,* January 15, 1989, pp. 1, 28.

Cox, Shelley, review of *Back in the World, Library Journal,* October 15, 1985, p. 104.

Eder, Richard, "The Boy Lost, the Writer Found," *Los Angeles Times Book Review,* January 8, 1989, pp. 3, 6.

Fletcher, Ron, "Surveying the Shape of the Terrain: A Conversation with Tobias Wolff," *Bloomsbury Review,* March/April, 1995, pp. 13, 16.

Kendrick, Walter, "Men with Rifles," *New York Times Book Review,* June 2, 1985, p. 42.

Mort, John, review of *In Pharaoh's Army, Booklist,* September 1, 1994, p. 2.

Prose, Francine, "The Brothers Wolff," *New York Times Magazine,* February 5, 1989, pp. 22-28.

Review of *In Pharaoh's Army, Publishers Weekly,* August 29, 1994, p. 55.

Schreiber, Le Anne, review of *In the Garden of the North American Martyrs, New York Times Book Review,* November 15, 1981.

Taylor, Linda, "Disarmingly Armed," *Times Literary Supplement,* November 6-12, 1987, p. 1227.

Review of *This Boy's Life, Publishers Weekly,* December 9, 1988, p. 50.

Wolff, Tobias, *The Barracks Thief,* Ecco Press, 1984.

Wolff, Tobias, interview with Jean W. Ross, *Contemporary Authors,* Volume 117, Gale, 1986, pp. 494-98.

Wolf, Tobias, *This Boy's Life: A Memoir,* Atlantic Monthly, 1989.

■ **For More Information See**

BOOKS

Contemporary Authors Autobiography Series, *Volume 22, Gale, 1996.*

PERIODICALS

America, September 8, 1984.

Booklist, October 1, 1985, p. 230.

Chicago Tribune Book World, October 18, 1981.

Christian Science Monitor, June 7, 1985, p. B7.

Hudson Review, August, 1986, pp. 487-488.

Library Journal, September 15, 1994, p. 93.

Los Angeles Times Book Review, November 17, 1985, p. 3.

Kirkus Reviews, November 15, 1988, p. 1666.

Mother Jones, January, 1989, p. 50.

Time, December 2, 1985, p. 99.

Times Literary Supplement, May 13, 1988, p. 532.

Voice of Youth Advocates, February, 1990, p. 368.

—Sketch by R. Garcia-Johnson

Robert Zemeckis

premiere episode of the television series *Johnny Bago,* CBS, 1993. Worked as a film editor on television commercials and for NBC News, Chicago; appeared as a guest on several television specials, including *Roger Rabbit & the Secrets of Toontown,* CBS, 1988, *Premiere Presents: Christmas Movies '89,* Fox, 1989, *American Cinema,* PBS, 1995, and *Inside the Academy Awards,* TNT, 1995. *Member:* Directors Guild of America.

▪ Personal

Born in 1952, in Chicago, IL; married Mary Ellen Trainor (an actress); children: Alex. *Education:* Received professional training at the University of Southern California (USC) Film School.

▪ Addresses

Agent—Jack Rapke, Creative Artists Agency, 1888 Century Park E., Suite 1400, Los Angeles, CA 90067-1768; or 9830 Wilshire Blvd., Beverly Hills, CA 90212.

▪ Career

Director, screenwriter, producer, and editor. Director and executive producer of numerous episodes of the television series *Tales from the Crypt,* HBO, 1989-95; character creator for the television series *Back to the Future,* CBS, 1991; executive producer of the films *The Frighteners, The Public Eye,* 1992, and *Tales from the Crypt Presents Demon Knight,* Universal, 1995; producer and creator of the television series *Tales from the Cryptkeeper,* ABC, 1993; creator, executive producer, and director of

▪ Awards, Honors

Special jury award, Second Annual Student Film Awards of the Academy of Motion Picture Arts and Sciences, and fifteen international honors, all for *A Field of Honor;* Academy Award nomination (with Robert Gale), best original screenplay, 1986, for *Back to the Future;* Golden Globe Award, best director, Academy Award, best director, and NATO/ShoWest's Director of the Year Award, all 1995, all for *Forrest Gump.*

▪ Films

DIRECTOR

(And writer with Robert Gale) *I Wanna Hold Your Hand,* Universal, 1978.

(And writer with Gale) *Used Cars,* Columbia, 1980.

Romancing the Stone, Twentieth Century-Fox, 1984.

(And writer with Gale) *Back to the Future,* Universal, 1985.

Who Framed Roger Rabbit?, Buena Vista, 1988.
Back to the Future Part II, Universal, 1989.
Back to the Future Part III, Universal, 1990.
(And producer with Steve Starkey) *Death Becomes Her*, Universal, 1992.
Forrest Gump, Paramount, 1994.

OTHER

Also screenwriter, with Gale, and executive producer of *Trespass*, Universal, 1992; screenwriter, with Gale, of *1941*, 1979; writer, director, and producer of the short film *A Field of Honor*. Television writer, with Gale, of episodes for *McCloud*, NBC, and *Kolchak: The Night Stalker* and *Get Christie Love*, both ABC.

■ Sidelights

"If raw, irrepressible energy has a name, it must be Bob Zemeckis," writes Steven Spielberg in the *Hollywood Reporter*. "Working, laughing, storytelling with Bob is a little like hanging on to someone who has a finger stuck in an electrical outlet. . . . Audiences for any Zemeckis movie earn their pleasure."

Among the Robert Zemeckis films that bring this pleasure to both audiences and critics alike are the box-office hits *Romancing the Stone, Back to the Future, Who Framed Roger Rabbit?*, and *Forrest Gump*. As a director, Zemeckis maintains common threads in all his films, as diversely different as they may seem. The latest technological advances are utilized to create difficult special effects, comedic elements are often let loose, and Zemeckis always remains true to the main component of all his films—the characters. While focusing on the characters, he also strives to create a movie in which his work as a director goes unnoticed by the audience. "The camera always follows the actors and the story," explains Zemeckis in an interview with Mark Horowitz in *American Film*. "If you have two actors who are cooking together—really burning—and you've got a great scene on paper, then, as a director, why impose technique on something that doesn't need it? I don't want to do anything that reminds the audience that there is a director standing behind the camera. It's all supposed to be invisible. I've always said that good directing is good writing and good casting, and that's all."

The Road to California

Growing up on Chicago's south side, Zemeckis remembers the event that made him realize he wanted to be a film director. Up until the age of fifteen, his main interest in movies was in the mechanics of the actual filming process, at least until he saw *Bonnie and Clyde* in 1967. "I went to see it because everybody was talking about the incredibly gory machine-gunning at the end, and I thought that was worth seeing," relates Zemeckis to Stephen Galloway in *Hollywood Reporter*. "Suddenly, there was this scene where Gene Hackman got his brains blown out. The film had made me love these characters so much—and here he was dead. At that moment, I realized that this film was moving me emotionally, and I sensed this was an incredible power. I thought, I have really got to check into this. From then on I was driven (to direct)."

This at first seemed an unattainable goal—Chicago was worlds away from Hollywood. But Zemeckis remained determined and was accepted into the University of Southern California Film School, and it was as an undergraduate here that he first met Bob Gale. The two were the minority in a college filled with graduate students; "we were juniors, so we did not have the pseudointellectual veneer that comes with being a graduate student," Gale recalls to Galloway in the *Hollywood Reporter*. "We weren't there to learn about the intricacies of 'Last Year at Marienbad' or the world of Jean-Luc Godard. We were there to learn about Clint Eastwood movies."

The friendship between Zemeckis and Gale developed into a partnership and the two began making films together. They, along with several other students, would pull all-nighters while creating their not-always-legal student film projects. "It was very much guerrilla filmmaking," Zemeckis states to Galloway in the *Hollywood Reporter*. "We did incredibly wonderful and illegal things, and it was very good training for making feature films. For my last student film, we staged these car stunts and gunplay that were completely illegal. We'd just go around and scramble and hustle. We hustled a police car at Universal. We didn't get in any trouble. But we did have fun driving it down the freeway, turning the lights on and pulling people over."

Their last student film, *Field of Honor*, won Zemeckis many awards, but these were not enough to land him a professional directing job after leaving school. At this point, he sought out the advice of fellow USC alumnus George Lucas by sending him a copy of his film and asking to

Zemeckis cowrote and directed *I Wanna Hold Your Hand*, a film about a group of teenagers and their attempts to see the Beatles.

meet with him. "So I flew up to San Francisco, and we had this long conversation," explains Zemeckis in an interview with Randall Tierney and Duane Byrge in the *Hollywood Reporter.* "He said, 'So you want to be a movie director, right?' I said: 'That's right. How do I do it?' And he said: 'Somehow, you'll do it. There's no pattern. Everybody's got their own story. There's no chain of command. You just work your way up.' It was the most true advice I've ever been given. It was a Yoda answer."

Rough Cuts

Zemeckis' passion for directing mirrored Gale's desire to be a writer, so the two developed a plan of attack. First, they would make a low-budget horror film featuring a whorehouse of vampires, *Bordello of Blood.* Unable to develop this, however, the pair turned to their second plan: writing for television. Writing together, Zemeckis and Gale

sold an outline for the series *Kolchak: The Night Stalker,* a two-hour script for *McCloud,* and an episode for another series, *Get Christie Love,* to Universal TV. Despite the fact that none of these scripts were ever filmed, Zemeckis and Gale were offered a seven-year contract to write for television based on this work. But they wanted to make movies, and after hiring both an agent and an attorney for advice they turned down the offer.

Very low on money at this point, Zemeckis and Gale moved on to their third and final strategy— to write films for big studios. Their break came when they sent a script entitled *Tank* to John Milius, a USC graduate who also had a four-picture deal with Metro-Goldwyn-Mayer. Admiring the script for *Tank,* Milius offered to let Zemeckis and Gale write one of the four films he was developing. "The result was *1941,* a project that brought them attention in unexpected ways but almost proved the undoing of their soon-to-be-mentor Spielberg," points out Stephen Galloway in the *Hollywood Reporter.*

1941 is based on a little-known historical event during World War II. After a Japanese submarine made it to the Santa Barbara coast a state of hysteria broke out in California, which was further amplified when a Japanese plane was reported over Los Angeles only two nights later. That same night, the people of California lit up the skyline with gunfire as they shot into an empty sky for approximately six hours. Zemeckis and Gale portrayed these events with humor in *1941,* which was Spielberg's biggest-budgeted film at the time and which also included a large cast headed by John Belushi.

"Although *1941* did not do as badly as legend has it, for a director coming fresh from the smash hit *Jaws* it was considered a disaster," observes Galloway in the *Hollywood Reporter.* "Zemeckis and Gale emerged mostly unscathed, but when their next two projects also flopped, it appeared that they'd had three strikes and were out." *I Wanna Hold Your Hand,* a film centered around a group of teenagers desperate in their pursuit to see the Beatles, and *Used Cars,* a comedy about rival used car lots, were strikes two and three against Zemeckis and Gale, and the team entered one of the lowest points in its career. During this period, they wrote *Back to the Future,* a movie that every studio in Hollywood quickly turned down.

The biggest lull in Zemeckis' career followed, and his wife, actress Mary Ellen Trainor, recalls how lost and depressed her husband was during this period. "Bob is a very simple person in his presentation to the outside world," observes Trainor in an interview with Galloway in the *Hollywood Reporter.* "He is a very levelheaded guy, not the least bit temperamental, and he has a tremendous clarity about what he wants. But (underneath) he is far more complex—and very few people know that. He also—which is true of every real artist—has a very big dark side. The demons are really there. Bob is still uncomfortable with waking up in the morning and not feeling he has much value unless he is going to tell 225 people what to do."

The Future Begins

It took five years from the release of *1941* to the release of Zemeckis' next directorial effort—*Ro-*

Christopher Lloyd stars as Doc Brown, a scientist who creates a time machine out of a DeLorean sports car, and Michael J. Fox stars as teenager Marty McFly, who inadvertently alters his present life and Brown's future in *Back to the Future.*

mancing the Stone. This opportunity, which made Zemeckis a viable director, came out of nowhere; Michael Douglas, who admired the movie *Used Cars,* called and asked Zemeckis to direct his new action-comedy. And once studio approval of both the director and the actor was granted, *Romancing the Stone* was made and released in 1984 to worldwide boxoffice success. "The narrative of *Romancing the Stone* was a perfect match with Zemeckis," maintains Duane Byrge in the *Hollywood Reporter.* "The story of a somewhat reclusive [romance] novelist who becomes sucked into her own adventure in South America, the film was a rip-roaring adventure yarn with plenty of action thrills and a lot of laughs."

This success had every studio suddenly clamoring to make *Back to the Future,* but Zemeckis and Gale took their movie back to Spielberg, who had originally wanted to produce it. Released in 1985, *Back to the Future* features Michael J. Fox as teenager Marty McFly and Christopher Lloyd as eccentric Doc Brown, the inventor of a time machine made out of a DeLorean sports car. In this adventure story, Marty finds himself travelling back to the 1950s, where he alters Doc Brown's future and inadvertently changes his current life when he meets his parents as teenagers. Achieving box-office and critical success, this science fiction comedy shows off both Zemeckis' cutting edge use of special effects and his penchant to develop believable and likeable characters. Byrge asserts in the *Hollywood Reporter:* "Watching *Back to the Future* gave you the feeling you had a kid at the throttles and, even better, made everyone feel like a kid again."

The years 1989 and 1990 brought two sequels to the original *Back to the Future,* building on the story and on Zemeckis' special effects skills and testing the director's stamina. The filming for *Back to the Future Part III* started while Zemeckis was still editing *Back to the Future Part II;* days were spent on the set, followed by nights in the editing room. And both of these films were more technologically advanced, challenging the crew with shots in which Fox would be playing three or four characters all interacting together. The first sequel takes Marty McFly and Doc Brown into the future (where Marty meets his future children), back to the present, and then back to the 1950 scenes of the first movie. The last film in the trilogy uses the Old West as its setting, offering a much slower pace and a romance between Doc Brown and a school teacher. The ending, however, picks up the pace of the first two movies as a

racing train is employed to start the time machine one final time.

"Like its predecessor," maintains Richard Schickel in *Time,* "*Back to the Future Part II* does not merely warp time; it twists it, shakes it and stands it on its ear. . . . Satirically acute, intricately structured and deftly paced, it is at heart stout, good and untainted by easy sentiment." Schickel goes on to conclude that *Back to the Future Part II* establishes Zemeckis "as today's most exciting young director." David Denby, writing in *New York,* welcomes the slower pace of *Back to the Future Part III,* pointing out: "Bob Gale (writer) and Robert Zemeckis (director) offer some genially goofy, sometimes even graceful, play with the clichés of Westerns." Denby also sees similarities in this concluding movie with the first in the series. "Zemeckis and Gale occasionally hit the mood that was so haunting in the first film of the series, the strangeness of the past as a chrysalis of the present."

The overflowing schedule tackled by Zemeckis while making the last two *Back to the Future* movies demonstrates just how well the director organizes and runs all the processes that go into making a film. "I feel that I have a very calm set," asserts Zemeckis in his interview with

Who Framed Roger Rabbit? challenged Zemeckis to combine cartoon characters with live actors.

Tierney and Byrge. "I don't thrive on chaos; there's enough of that anyway."

All this expertise can make for boring work stories at the end of a long day on the job, though. "People always ask me about anecdotes," Zemeckis tells Marc Shapiro in an interview in *Starlog,* "and I *never* have anything unusual or unexpected to tell them. I guess, because my movies are so meticulously planned and so complicated to execute, that nothing funny *ever* happens. There's basically no room for the unexpected and unplanned things that end up making good anecdotes. What my films are is just a lot of hard work."

Technological Wizardry

In between the hard work involved in his *Back to the Future* films, Zemeckis tackled the difficulties of marrying cartoons with live actors in *Who Framed Roger Rabbit?* "Everything about that film was difficult to do and it became more difficult as the filming progressed," explains Zemeckis in *Starlog.* "We weren't dealing with minutes and seconds like you do in normal films. In *Roger,* we were dealing with frames all the time. It was one of those things that if you knew it was going to be that hard, you *never* would have done it." *Who Framed Roger Rabbit?* begins with a traditional cartoon that ends with a new twist—the "toon" ac-

Death Becomes Her contains many special effects, such as this one where Meryl Streep's head appears to twist around on her neck.

tors walk off the set after filming, right into the world of regular people. In this world where toons and humans mix, the toon actor Roger Rabbit finds himself accused of a crime he didn't commit. He seeks out human detective Eddie Valiant, whose brother was killed by a toon, to help clear his name. Along the way, they must face characters like Judge Doom, played by Christopher Lloyd, whose evil scheme to eliminate Toontown and all its inhabitants almost succeeds.

Byrge writes of *Who Framed Roger Rabbit?* in the *Hollywood Reporter:* "Experiencing it, you get the feeling that this is a real kid let loose in a candy store of cartoon characters and wizardry. It's slippery and slick in all the best ways. And, once again, although the effects were polished by rigorous discipline and a cutting-edge resourcefulness, the characters sported that appealing rough-around-the-edges quality." Reviewing the film in *People Weekly,* Peter Travers exclaims, "Here is historic, hot-ziggety entertainment with humans and Toons blending seamlessly and three-dimensionally." Travers adds that "adults may better appreciate the film's oddball humor. But all ages will thrill to the pure enchantment of the visuals. . . . Your eyeballs have no choice but to go boinnnnng."

Visuals are also an important element in Zemeckis' 1992 film *Death Becomes Her.* In this black comedy, two women obsessed with their bodies and cosmetic appearances make a deal with the devil to remain youthful-looking for all eternity. Along for the ride is a plastic surgeon who learns to do makeup for these newly-dead women as they manage to mangle each other during their many battles. Although only mildly successful, *Death Becomes Her* was recognized for its amazing visual effects and for its satirical look at a culture obsessed with youth. Richard Corliss states in *Time* that "you can have a good, mean time at this movie, in synch with the cartoonish comedy . . . and elaborate special effects." And *Newsweek* reviewer David Ansen points out that "it's nice to see Zemeckis making a comedy with teeth again."

Simple Success

All of these early films shaped and molded Zemeckis as a director, building up to what he considers his best film to date, the 1994 Academy Award-winning *Forrest Gump.* In this character-driven, technically-challenging comedy the myriad

Director Zemeckis with Tom Hanks on the set of the 1994 Academy Award-winning film *Forrest Gump.*

talents of Zemeckis are all at work. A slow and simple man, Forrest Gump fumbles through the major events of the sixties, seventies, and eighties. Harassed as a child because of his slowness, he starts running and keeps right on running all the way through college and the Vietnam War. As the years pass, Forrest has a hand in several famous historical events and eventually becomes a very successful businessman. He does not achieve complete happiness, though, until he marries his childhood friend and love Jenny, who has also given him a son.

"Zemeckis' successful handling of the emotional, character-driven narrative of *Forrest Gump* caught many observers off guard because of his reputation as a technorat," explains Galloway in the *Hollywood Reporter.* "Yet many of the film's ingredients are to be found throughout Zemeckis' work: the merging of inventive technology with humanism, an emphasis on the simple values of decency and honesty, and the focus on one character grappling with a world he doesn't entirely understand." After his first reading of the screenplay for *Forrest Gump,* Zemeckis knew he had to make this movie because of its ingredients but did not envision the success the film eventually encountered. "I thought it was the riskiest project I ever did as far as its boxoffice potential," reveals Zemeckis in his interview with Tierney and Byrge in the *Hollywood Reporter.* "When I read it, I said,

'This is just a wonderful movie that I really have to make economically, and I hope that it finds its audience.' That was my feeling. The screenplay was so compelling that there was nothing I could do but make it." Spielberg commends his long-time friend and contemporary for going ahead and making *Forrest Gump,* which he considers to be Zemeckis' most personal and serious film. Moviegoers appreciated the film too, making *Forrest Gump* the fifth-highest-grossing film in motion-picture history.

■ Works Cited

Ansen, David, "Revenge of the Living Dead," *Newsweek,* August 3, 1992, p. 56.

Byrge, Duane, "By the Seat of Their Pants," *Hollywood Reporter Robert Zemeckis Tribute Issue,* March 9, 1995, pp. Z14-Z15, Z18.

Corliss, Richard, "Beverly Hills Corpse," *Time,* August 3, 1992, p. 72.

Denby, David, "The Numbers Game," *New York,* June 11, 1990, p. 75.

Galloway, Stephen, "Bob," *Hollywood Reporter Robert Zemeckis Tribute Issue,* March 9, 1995, pp. Z21-Z22.

Galloway, Stephen, "Driven to Direct," *Hollywood Reporter Robert Zemeckis Tribute Issue,* March 9, 1995, pp. Z4-Z11.

Horowitz, Mark, "Back with a Future," *American Film,* July-August, 1988, pp. 32-35.

Schickel, Richard, "More Travels with Marty," *Time,* December 4, 1989, p. 101.

Shapiro, Marc, "Lord of the Future," *Starlog,* January, 1990, pp. 37-40, 73.

Spielberg, Steven, "The Maze Master," *Hollywood Reporter Robert Zemeckis Tribute Issue,* March 9, 1995, p. Z13.

Tierney, Randall, and Duane Byrge, "Zemeckis on Zemeckis," *Hollywood Reporter Robert Zemeckis Tribute Issue,* March 9, 1995, pp. Z36-Z38, Z42, Z44, Z48.

Travers, Peter, review of *Who Framed Roger Rabbit?, People Weekly,* June 27, 1988, p. 11.

■ For More Information See

PERIODICALS

New Statesman & Society, December 2, 1992, p. 33.

Newsweek, December 4, 1989, p. 78.

New York, July 18, 1994, pp. 50-51.

New Yorker, June 18, 1990, pp. 91-92; August 24, 1992, p. 80.

People Weekly, January 11, 1993, pp. 17-18; June 28, 1993, pp. 10-11.

Rolling Stone, June 28, 1990, p. 31; August 20, 1992, p. 57; February 4, 1993, p. 37.

Time, June 27, 1988, p. 72.*

—Sketch by Susan M. Reicha

Acknowledgments

Acknowledgements

Grateful acknowledgement is made to the following publishers, authors, and artists for their kind permission to reproduce copyrighted material.

RICHARD ADAMS. Cover of *The Girl In A Swing*, by Richard Adams. Copyright © 1981 by The New American Library. Reprinted by permission of Dutton Signet, a division of Penguin Books USA Inc./ Cover of *The Plague Dogs*, by Richard Adams. Copyright © 1977 by Richard Adams. Reprinted by permission of Ballantine Books./ Cover of *Watership Down*, by Richard Adams. Copyright © 1972 by Rex Collings, Ltd. Reprinted by permission of Avon Books./ Still from the movie, *Watership Down*, by Avco-Embassy, 1978. Reprinted by permission of Avco-Embassy./ Photograph by Peter Hirst-Smith.

JEFFREY ARCHER. Cover of *Not A Penny More, Not A Penny Less*, by Jeffrey Archer. Copyright © 1976 by Jeffrey Archer. Cover illustration by George Angelini. Reprinted by permission of Jeffrey Archer./ Cover of *Kane & Abel*, by Jeffrey Archer. Copyright © 1979 by Jeffrey Archer. Cover illustration by George Angelini. Reprinted by permission of Jeffrey Archer./ Cover of *Honor Among Thieves*, by Jeffrey Archer. Copyright © 1993 by Jeffrey Archer. Cover illustration by Kirk Reinert. Reprinted by permission of Jeffrey Archer./ Cover of *A Twist in the Tale*, by Jeffrey Archer. Copyright © 1988 by Jeffrey Archer. Cover illustration by George Angelini. Reprinted by permission of Jeffrey Archer./ Cover of *A Matter of Honor*, by Jeffrey Archer. Copyright © 1986 by Jeffrey Archer. Cover illustration by Rick McCollum. Reprinted by permission of Jeffrey Archer./ Photograph courtesy of Jeffrey Archer.

PATRICIA BEATTY. Jacket of *Who Comes With Cannons?*, by Patricia Beatty. Copyright © 1992 by the Estate of Patricia Beatty. Jacket illustration copyright © 1992 by Stephen Marchesi. Reprinted by permission of Morrow Junior Books, a division of William Morrow and Company, Inc./ Cover of *Sarah and Me and the Lady by the Sea*, by Patricia Beatty. Copyright © 1989 by Patricia Beatty. Reprinted by permission of Morrow Junior Books, a division of William Morrow and Company, Inc./ Cover of *Lupita Manana*, by Patricia Beatty. Copyright © 1981 by Patricia Beatty. Afterword copyright © 1992 by Lucas Guttentag. Reprinted by permission of Morrow Junior Books, a division of William Morrow and Company, Inc./ Photographs courtesy of The Estate of Patricia Beatty.

MALCOLM BOSSE. Cover of *Deep Dream of the Rain Forest*, by Malcolm Bosse. Copyright © 1993 by Laura Mack. Reprinted by permission of Farrar, Straus and Giroux, Inc./ Cover of *Ordinary Magic*, by Malcolm Bosse. Copyright © 1981 by Laura Mack. Cover photograph by Sharon Stephens, courtesy of The Filmworks, Ltd. Reprinted by permission of Farrar, Straus and Giroux, Inc.

BEN BOVA. Cover of *The Exile Trilogies*, by Ben Bova. Copyright © 1971,1972,1975 by Ben Bova. Cover art by Doug Chaffee. Reprinted by permission of Baen Publishing Enterprises./ Cover of *Mars*, by Ben Bova. Jacket illustration copyright © 1992 by Pamela Lee. Jacket design by Jamie S. Warren Youll. Reprinted by permission of Bantam Books, a division of Bantam Doubleday Dell Publishing Group, Inc./ Jacket of *Orion and the Conqueror*, by Ben Bova. Copyright © 1994 by Ben Bova. Jacket art by Boris Vallejo. Jacket design by Carol Russo. Reprinted by permission of Tom Doherty Associates, Inc./ Jacket of *Millennium*, by Ben Bova. Copyright © 1976 by Ben Bova. Reprinted by permission of Random House, Inc./ Photograph by Carl J. Thome.

PATRICIA D. CORNWELL. Cover of *Cruel & Unusual*, by Patricia D. Cornwell. Copyright © 1993 by Patricia D. Cornwell. Reprinted by permission of Avon Books./ Cover of *All That Remains*, by Patricia D. Cornwell. Copyright © 1992 by Patricia D. Cornwell. Reprinted by permission of Avon Books./ Cover of *Body of Evidence*, by Patricia D. Cornwell. Copyright © 1991 by Patricia D. Cornwell. Reprinted by permission of Avon Books./ Cover of *Postmortem*, by Patricia D. Cornwell. Copyright © 1990 by Patricia Daniels Cornwell. Reprinted by permission of Avon Books./ Photograph © Tom Grimes.

BRIAN DOYLE. Cover of *Covered Bridge*, by Brian Doyle. Copyright © 1990 by Brian Doyle. Cover illustration by Paul Zwolak. Reprinted by permission of Groundwood Books/Douglas & McIntyre./ Cover of *Easy Avenue*, by Brian Doyle. Copyright © 1988 by Brian Doyle. Cover illustration by Ludmilla Temertey. Reprinted by permission of Groundwood Books/Douglas & McIntyre Ltd./ Cover of *Up to Low*, by Brian Doyle. Copyright © 1982 by Brian Doyle. Cover illustration by Paul Zwolak. Reprinted by permission of Groundwood Books/Douglas & McIntyre Ltd./ Cover of *Hey Dad!*, by Brian Doyle. Copyright © 1978 by Brian Doyle. Cover illustration by Paul Zwolak. Reprinted by permission of Groundwood Books/Douglas & McIntyre Ltd./ Photograph courtesy of Megan Doyle./ Photograph of author as young man, courtesy of Brian Doyle.

M.C. ESCHER. All illustrations © 1994 M.C. Escher/Cordon Art-Baarn-Holland. All rights reserved.

McKeating. Reprinted by permission of Houghton Mifflin Company./ Jacket from *When the Road Ends*, by Jean Thesman. Copyright © 1992 by Jean Thesman. Jacket art copyright © 1992 by Robert Wisnewski. Reprinted by permission of Houghton Mifflin Company./ Jacket from *The Rain Catchers*, by Jean Thesman. Copyright © 1991 by Jean Thesman. Jacket design/illustration copyright © 1991 by Vincent X. Kirsch. Reprinted by permission of Houghton Mifflin Company./ Author photograph of Jean Thesman. Courtesy of Houghton Mifflin Company. All rights reserved.

YOSHIKO UCHIDA. Illustration from *The Dancing Kettle and Other Japanese Folk Tales*, retold by Yoshiko Uchida. Copyright © 1949 by Yoshiko Uchida. Illustration by Richard C. Jones. Reprinted by permission of The Bancroft Library, University of California, Berkeley./ Jacket from *The Magic Purse*, retold by Yoshiko Uchida. Text copyright © 1993 by the estate of Yoshiko Uchida. Jacket illustration copyright © 1993 by Keiko Narahashi. Reprinted by permission of Margaret K. McElderry Books, an imprint of Simon & Schuster Children's Publishing Division./ Cover of *Journey to Topaz*, by Yoshiko Uchida. Text copyright © 1971 by Yoshiko Uchida. Prologue copyright © 1984 by Yoshiko Uchida. Illustrated by Donald Carrick. Reprinted by permission of CreativeArts Book Company./ Cover of *The Magic Listening Cap, More Folk Tales From Japan*, retold and illustrated by Yoshiko Uchida. Copyright © 1955 by Yoshiko Uchida. Copyright © renewed 1983 by Yoshiko Uchida. Illustrations copyright © 1987 by Yoshiko Uchida. Reprinted by permission of Creative Arts Book Company./ Photographs reprinted by permission of University of California, The Bancroft Library.

JULES VERNE. Jacket from *The Mysterious Island*, by Jules Verne. Copyright © 1918 Charles Scribner's Sons. Renewal copyright © 1946 Charles Scribner's Sons. Jacket illustration by N.C. Wyeth. Reprinted by permission of Atheneum Books for Young Readers, an imprint of Simon & Schuster Children's Publishing Division./ Jacket from *Michael Strogoff*, by Jules Verne. Copyright © 1927 Charles Scribner's Sons. Renewal copyright © 1955 Charles Scribner's Sons. Jacket illustration by N.C. Wyeth. Reprinted by permission of Atheneum Books for Young Readers, an imprint of Simon & Schuster Children's Publishing Division./ Jacket from *Around the World in Eighty Days*, by Jules Verne. Afterword copyright © 1988 by Peter Glassman. Jacket illustration copyright © 1988 by Barry Moser. Reprinted by permission of Morrow Junior Books, a division of William Morrow and Company, Inc./ Illustration from *Twenty Thousand Leagues Under the Sea*, by Jules Verne. Reprinted by permission of J.M. Dent & Sons, Ltd./ Jacket from *20,000 Leagues Under the Sea*, by Jules Verne. Copyright © 1966, Jacket design: J.M. Dent & Sons, Ltd. Reprinted by permission of J.M. Dent & Sons, Ltd.

JOHN WATERS. Movie still from *"Hairspray"*, New Line Cinema Productions, Inc./ Movie still from *"Crybaby"*, Universal Pictures./ Movie still from *"Pink Flamingo"*, Saliva Films./ Movie still from *"Polyester"*, New Line Cinema Productions, Inc./ Photograph by Lynn Goldsmith/LGI Photo Agency.

AUGUST WILSON. Cover of *Two Trains Running*, by August Wilson. Copyright © August Wilson, 1992. Cover art by Constanza Romero. Cover art copyright © Serino Coyne, Inc. Reprinted by permissions./ Cover of *The Piano Lesson*, by August Wilson. Copyright © August Wilson, 1990. Details from works by painter Romare Bearden. Courtesy of The Nanette Bearden Contemporary Dance Theatre and Nanette Bearden. Cover art copyright © Serino Coyne, Inc. Reprinted by permission./ Cover of *Ma Rainey's Black Bottom, A Play in Two Acts*, by August Wilson. Copyright © 1985 by August Wilson. Reprinted by permission of Dutton Signet, a division of Penguin Books USA Inc./ Cover of *Joe Turner's Come and Gone, A Play in Two Acts*, by August Wilson. Copyright © 1988 by August Wilson. Reprinted by permission of Dutton Signet, a division of Penguin Books USA Inc./ Photograph from AP/Wide World Photos.

TOBIAS WOLFF. Cover of *Back in the World*, stories by Tobias Wolff. Copyright © 1985 by Tobias Wolff. Cover art copyright © 1989 by Tom Hallman. Reprinted by permission of Bantam Books, a division of Bantam Doubleday Dell Publishing Group, Inc./ Cover of *The Barracks Thief and Selected Stories*, by Tobias Wolff. Copyright © 1976,1980,1984 by Tobias Wolff. Reprinted by permission of Bantam Books, a division of Bantam Doubleday Dell Publishing Group, Inc./ Photograph © Jerry Bauer.

ROBERT ZEMECKIS. Still from the film, *"Who Framed Roger Rabbit"*, directed by Robert Zemeckis. Buena Vista, 1988. The Hollywood Reporter, Robert Zemeckis Tribute Issue, March 9, 1995. Copyright © 1995 by HR Industries, Inc., a subsidiary of BPI Communications./ Still from the film, *"Death Becomes Her"*, directed by Robert Zemeckis. Universal, 1992. The Hollywood Reporter, Robert Zemeckis Tribute Issue, March 9, 1995. Copyright © 1995 by HR Industries, Inc., a subsidiary of BPI Communications./ Photograph from the filming of *"Forrest Gump"*, directed by Robert Zemeckis. Paramount, 1994. The Hollywood Reporter, Robert Zemeckis Tribute Issue, March 9, 1995. Copyright © 1995 by HR Industries, Inc., a subsidiary of BPI Communications./ Still from the film, *"I Wanna Hold Your Hand"*, directed by Robert Zemeckis. Universal, 1978. The Hollywood Reporter, Robert Zemeckis Tribute Issue, March 9, 1995. Copyright © 1995 by HR Industries, Inc., a subsidiary of BPI Communications./ Still from the film, *"Back to the Future, Part III"*, directed by Robert Zemeckis. Universal, 1990. The Hollywood Reporter, Robert Zemeckis Tribute Issue, March 9, 1995. Copyright © 1995 by HR Industries, Inc., a subsidiary of BPI Communications./ Photograph by Aldo Mauro.

Cumulative Index

Author/Artist Index

The following index gives the number of the volume in which an author/artist's biographical sketch appears.